Microsoft®
Exchange
Server 5.5
Resource Guide

Microsoft®Press

PUBLISHED BY
Microsoft Press
A Division of Microsoft Corporation
One Microsoft Way
Redmond, Washington 98052-6399

Library of Congress Cataloging-in-Publication Data
Microsoft BackOffice 4.5 Resource Kit / Microsoft Corporation.
     p. cm.
   ISBN 0-7356-0583-1
    1. Microsoft BackOffice.   2. Client/server computing.
  I. Microsoft Corporation.
  QA76.9.C55M525   1999
  005.7'1376--dc21   99-13771
                                         CIP

Printed and bound in the United States of America.

1 2 3 4 5 6 7 8 9 WCWC   4 3 2 1 0 9

Distributed in Canada by ITP Nelson, a division of Thomson Canada Limited.

A CIP catalogue record for this book is available from the British Library.

Microsoft Press books are available through booksellers and distributors worldwide. For further information about international editions, contact your local Microsoft Corporation office or contact Microsoft Press International directly at fax (425) 936-7329. Visit our Web site at mspress.microsoft.com.

Acquisitions Editor: Juliana Aldous
Project Editor: Maureen Williams Zimmerman

Part No. 097-0002190

This book is dedicated to all the hard working writers, editors, reviewers, and production staff at Microsoft who make books like this possible. Thank you!

Contributors to this book include the following:

Group Manager User Education
Stefan Sierakowski

User Education Manager
Allan Risk

Group Lead Writers
Steve Holland, William Harding

Contributing Writers
Thomas Allan, Michael Armijo, Joe Baltimore, Greg Berg, Monique Donaldson, Sylvia French, Allen Gay, Brian Mahoney, Kristina Marx, Joe Orzech, Gabriel Reedy, Dean Simpson, Mark Voss

Group Lead Editor
Mary Harris

Technical Editors
Aimee Davison, Sharon Farrar, Jennifer Linn, Amy Stockett, Valerie Wright

Technical Consultants
Dan Aalberg, Todd Abel, Lucretia Albulet, Erik Ashby, Bruce Baker, Harald Bardenhagen, Derrick Baxter, Scott Bee, William Bellamy, Edward Berry, Nitin Bhatia, Greg Bott, Gordon Brown, Rodney Bryan, Frank Bucci, Kali Buhariwalla, Laurion Burchall, Kevin Bushnell, Behrooz Chitsaz, Seth Cousins, Greg Cox, James Doyle, Nick Duane, Charles Eliot, Alan Erickson, Ken Ewert, Brandon Faloona, Deb Ferrell, George Gianopoulos, John Gilbert, Chris Hallum, Rochelle Hannon, Rick Hantz, Steve Hiskey, Martin Holladay, Joseph Hughes, Brent Jensen, Thomas Laciano, Chris Lester, James McDaniel, Patrick McFarland, Jeff Miller, Mahesh Nasta, Susan Nellis, Jason Nelson, Lawrence Norman, Edwin Pabustan, Joseph Pagano, Steven Parker, Kalpesh Patel, Laura Payne, Vanitha Prabhakaran, Jim Reitz, Joe Richardson, George Ringer, Roger Roark, Rob Sanfilippo, Paul Schafer, Raja Seera, Marc Seinfeld, Neil Shipp, Paul Smietan, Audrey Sniezek, Roger Stanev, Derik Stenerson, Martin Thall, Michael Thomassy, Andrzej Turski, Henry Voight, Andrew Wallace, Henry Webb III, Kristie Westbrook, Zev Yanovic, Steven Yetter, William Zentmayer

Production Lead
Jessica Vu

Production
Mike Birch, Griffin Cole, Michael Heavener, Egan Orion, Mark Anable

Graphic Designer
Blaine Carpenter

Print Production Specialist
Kat Liekhus

Indexers
Lee Ross, Tony Ross

Contents

Part 3   Deployment

Part 4   Administering and Maintaining

Part 6   Integration and Interaction

Part 7   Tools and Utilities

Part 8   Troubleshooting

Part 9   Disaster Recovery

Part 11   Security

Part 12   Public Folders

PART 1

Introduction

Welcome to the *Microsoft Exchange Server 5.5 Resource Guide*. This guide is designed for people who are or want to become expert users of Microsoft Exchange Server. For example:

- Computer professionals can use this guide to help understand the design and architecture of messaging systems based on Exchange.

- Information Technology (IT) and Information Systems (IS) staff can use this guide to plan for, deploy, and maintain Exchange computers.

- Administrators can use this guide to help troubleshoot problems, optimize performance, and keep Exchange running smoothly.

- Developers can use this guide to help design and program collaborative applications that use Exchange to facilitate communication between members of the organization.

The *Microsoft Exchange Server 5.5 Resource Guide* is a technical supplement to the documentation that is included as part of the Exchange 5.5 product. It does not replace that documentation as the source for learning how to use Exchange. The discussions in this publication generally assume you are using Microsoft Outlook™ client software. However, some information about the Microsoft Exchange Client has been included for the benefit of organizations that also have clients running the Exchange Client, which was shipped with earlier versions of Exchange. This guide also includes a glossary for terms that might be unfamiliar to some readers.

Highlights of the Resource Guide

The *Microsoft Exchange Server 5.5 Resource Guide* provides useful information about Exchange Server 5.5, including the following:

Integration with Site Server and IIS   The combination of Exchange, Microsoft Site Server, and Microsoft Internet Information Server (IIS) give you the tools you need to build a knowledge management solution for your organization. Exchange collects and organizes information in public folders while the powerful indexing and searching capabilities of Site Server make that knowledge accessible to the individuals who need it. IIS delivers the query pages that individuals use to request the information they need. For information about integrating these tools to build a knowledge management solution for your organization, see Part 6, "Integration and Interaction."

Setup   Exchange Setup can perform a fault-tolerant upgrade from a previous version of Exchange to version 5.5. For information about how Exchange performs this safer upgrade process, and how to handle a failure during a fault-tolerant upgrade, see Part 2, "Planning."

Clustering   Exchange 5.5 fully supports Microsoft Cluster Server. For information about configuring and administering your Exchange computers in a clustered environment, see Part 2, "Planning."

New and updated performance tools   Performance Optimizer supports new options with Exchange 5.5 that give you a fine degree of control over performance settings. For information on customizing these options and using them to tune Exchange, see Part 5, "Performance Tuning and Optimization."

The Load Simulator tool has been updated and redesigned to run with Outlook as well as the Exchange Client. For information on using Load Simulator to set realistic performance expectations for your environment (without actually setting up a large number of client computers), see Part 5, "Performance Tuning and Optimization."

Collaboration applications   You can combine Exchange with other Microsoft BackOffice® products (such as Microsoft Internet Information Server and Microsoft SQL Server) to create collaboration applications that can help members of your organization work together more effectively and efficiently. For examples and ideas about how you can create your own collaboration solutions using Microsoft products and technologies, see Part 13, "Collaboration."

Exchange 5.5 provides the Active Directory Services Interface (ADSI), which is a Component Object Model (COM) interface to multiple directory services. For information on how to use ADSI with the Exchange directory, see Part 13, "Collaboration."

Updated troubleshooting and disaster recovery information Exchange 5.5 includes a new ESEUTIL utility that can defragment, repair, and check the integrity of the Exchange information store and directory. For information on how to use the ESEUTIL utility as well as updated information about troubleshooting and disaster recovery for Exchange 5.5, see Part 8, "Troubleshooting," and Part 4, "Administering and Maintaining."

Connector for Lotus cc:Mail Exchange includes a Connector for Lotus cc:Mail that allows you to migrate from or coexist with Lotus cc:Mail. For suggestions on how to configure and use the Connector for Lotus cc:Mail, see Part 14, "Exchange Connector for Lotus cc:Mail."

Directory replication The Exchange directory can be replicated within a single site and between multiple sites. For details about the architecture and infrastructure of directory replication, see Part 3, "Deployment."

Successful messaging operations Deploying a successful Exchange messaging system and keeping it running smoothly is important to your organization. For information and recommendations that are based on Microsoft's internal messaging system, see Part 15, "Setting Up a Successful Messaging Operations System."

Public folder re-homing Exchange allows you to re-home public folders so that you can control the home server for a public folder replica. For information on how to accomplish this and how to ensure that public folders cannot be relocated to other sites without the proper permissions, see Part 12, "Public Folders."

Exchange Server 5.5 Features

In addition to the features that are discussed in this guide, other important enhancements and features are included in Exchange 5.5. You can find additional information about these features in your Exchange documentation.

Updated database structure for the information store and directory

Exchange 5.5 uses an updated database that provides significantly larger data storage capabilities than earlier versions of Exchange. Because of this database structure, the information store is limited only by your system's hardware capacity. This allows Exchange to take full advantage of advanced hardware (today and in the future) and to scale up as the needs of your organization grow.

Ability to retrieve deleted items from mailboxes and public folders

After the administrator sets the deleted item retention period for an information store, mailbox, or public folder, users can retrieve deleted items by using the **Recover Deleted Items** command available in Microsoft Outlook version 8.03 or later. This much-requested feature can be run by users themselves, with no need for administrator action or intervention.

Internet enhancements Exchange includes many features and enhancements designed to support Internet standards, including:

- **IMAP4**. Exchange 5.5 supports Internet Message Access Protocol version 4 rev1 (IMAP4rev1).
- **Writeable LDAP**. Exchange 5.5 enables users to make changes to the directory by using Lightweight Directory Access Protocol (LDAP).
- **Enhanced protocol support for Internet Mail Service**. Internet Mail Service supports the following protocols: ETRN, Secure Multipurpose Internet Mail Extensions (S/MIME), Secure Sockets Layer (SSL), and Simple Authentication and Security Layer (SASL).
- **Support for MHTML**. Exchange 5.5 supports MIME Hypertext Markup Language (MHTML), which is the MIME encapsulation of aggregate documents, such as an HTML document with in-line pictures.

Microsoft Cluster Server Exchange 5.5 supports Microsoft Cluster Server, which is included with Microsoft Windows® NT® Server. Cluster Server provides fault tolerance in the event of hardware and software malfunctions. It ensures that mail delivery is never interrupted if an Exchange computer fails. Cluster Server must be installed on the Exchange computer to enable support for clustering.

Microsoft Exchange Scripting You can install Microsoft Exchange Event Service to support the customized public-folder workflow applications you develop. For example, you can develop an application that performs an action when a specified event occurs in a public folder.

Connectivity to Lotus Notes and host systems Exchange now includes the Microsoft Exchange Connector for Lotus Notes, the Microsoft Exchange Connector for IBM OfficeVision/VM, and the Microsoft Exchange Connector for SNADS. By enabling users from other systems to exchange messages with Exchange users, these connectors allow Exchange to coexist in a heterogeneous messaging environment. In addition, the Lotus cc:Mail source extractor supports Lotus cc:Mail version 5.x (DB6), version 6.0, and version 8.0 (DB8), allowing you to migrate from Lotus cc:Mail to Exchange.

Container level search control You can restrict users' access to Address Book views. For example, if you are hosting multiple companies on a single Exchange computer, you can prevent one company from viewing the Address Book views of another company.

Support for multiple and differential offline Address Books Users can download differential entries in offline Address Books so that only the changes made since the last download are downloaded. This feature can significantly reduce overall download time for most large Address Books because they go through relatively small changes over a short period of time.

Advanced security You can set multiple password policies to prevent administrators from making changes to the Key Management (KM) server without authorization from one or more other administrators. Exchange 5.5 also supports trusted messages between organizations, allowing users to verify the source of messages sent from another organization. For example, users in different Exchange organizations can send and receive digitally signed messages, even across the Internet.

Microsoft Exchange Chat Service Exchange now includes chat services that enable users to interact with each other online in real time.

SNMP Madman MIB Exchange supports the Mail and Directory Management Information Base (MADMAN MIB) for use with Simple Network Management Protocol (SNMP) monitoring agents.

Address space and routing enhancements Exchange 5.5 gives you more control over message routing. The **Address Space** property page on connectors has been enhanced to enable scoping restrictions feach address space you specify. Each address space can be configured so that the connector routes messages that originate:

- From anyone in the organization
- Only from within the home site
- Only from within the home server location

In addition, each MTA can be configured to use only the least-cost routes to deliver mail. This means that if the least-cost route is not accessible, messages are returned with a non-delivery report (NDR). These features can help you optimize message delivery, perform load balancing, and control costs.

About the Resource Guide

This guide includes the following parts:

Part 1, "Introduction,"

outlines the highlights of this volume and some of the features in Exchange 5.5 that are not discussed in this book.

Part 2, "Planning,"

describes the Exchange setup process, including unattended setup using custom batch files. It also describes how to customize server installations to accommodate various languages and character sets.

Part 3, "Deployment," describes how to use Exchange Server in a cluster environment and customize client languages. It also explains how to use permissions for directory objects and public folders to restrict or grant access, and it describes how changes to directory objects are replicated within and between sites.

Part 4, "Administering and Maintaining," describes how to plan maintenance to minimize down time, how to back up servers, and how to plan disaster recovery strategies. Discussions include information on monitoring performance, defragmenting and compacting databases, managing log files, procedures for moving and recovering single mailboxes, and procedures for moving Exchange to another computer.

Part 5, "Performance Tuning and Optimization," discusses how to avoid bottlenecks and optimize performance with good topology design and how to improve the performance of Exchange by load balancing and adjusting software settings. It also describes how to monitor servers and disk space for optimal performance and to configure the system to warn of potential problems.

Part 6, "Integration and Interaction," describes how to use Exchange, Microsoft Site Server, and Internet Information Server (IIS) to build a knowledge management solution for your organization that makes it easy for your users to access information in public folders.

Part 7, "Tools and Utilities," briefly describes the tools that are included on the BackOffice Resources Kit compact disc and how to install them.

Part 8, "Troubleshooting," provides symptoms of and solutions to many problems encountered with Exchange. It also includes a detailed discussion of the ISINTEG tool.

Part 9, "Disaster Recovery," describes disaster prevention and recovery plans, recovery procedures, backups, and fire drills. It also includes a section on frequently asked questions and their solutions.

Part 10, "Exchange Architecture," explains the architecture of Exchange, including the information store, directory services, the message transfer agent (MTA), and the system attendant. It also describes how Exchange messages are addressed and routed.

Part 11, "Security," describes how advanced security works, how to change permissions on shared directories, how to choose any method of encryption, how to use encrypted remote procedure calls (RPCs) and fire walls, and how to back up a Key Management server (KM server).

Part 12, "Public Folders," describes how to plan, set up, and replicate public folders. It includes information on developing a public folder strategy, access control, replication strategies, backfilling, and re-homing folders.

Part 13, "Collaboration," provides an overview of collaboration applications and the supporting platform. Examples of various collaboration are provided. It also describes Microsoft Outlook development tools, Microsoft Active Server and Microsoft Active Desktop™ components.

Part 14, "Microsoft Exchange Connector for Lotus cc:Mail," discusses guidelines and recommendations for deploying the Microsoft Exchange Connector for Lotus cc:Mail in you organization.

Part 15, "Setting Up a Successful Messaging Operations System," presents guidelines for establishing a messaging operations group within an organization that is based on experiences with Microsoft's own internal messaging operations group.

Appendix A, "Creating an .Ini File for Microsoft Exchange Server Batch Setup," describes the format of an .ini file that you can run with Exchange Setup in batch mode (Setup /q).

Appendix B, "System Management Checklist," provides checklists for daily, weekly, monthly, and periodic maintenance tasks to ensure that your Exchange computers are operating efficiently.

Appendix C, "Performance Monitor Chart Views," describes the preconfigured Windows NT Performance Monitor chart views that are included with Exchange.

Appendix D, "Microsoft Exchange Client," provides information about the Microsoft Exchange Client, which was shipped with earlier versions of Exchange. This appendix provides information about the Microsoft Exchange Client that might not be available elsewhere.

Appendix E, "Exchange Forms Designer," describes the development of custom forms for use with Exchange Client. These can range from modifying existing sample applications to using high-end development tools to create more complex groupware applications.

Appendix F, "Technical Papers," briefly summarizes the technical whitepapers that are included on the *BackOffice 4.5 Resource Kit* compact disc.

Glossary describes terms used in this manual that might be unfamiliar to some readers.

Additional Information

Many resources are available that provide additional information about Exchange.

Microsoft BackOffice 4.5 Resource Kit, Compact Disc

The *Microsoft BackOffice 4.5 Resource Kit,* compact disc contains Exchange tools and related online documentation.

Web Sites

Visit the following sites on the World Wide Web for up-to-date information about Exchange:

http://www.microsoft.com/exchange The Exchange Web site contains up-to-date information about Exchange and links to other Microsoft BackOffice® products.

http://www.microsoft.com/syspro/technet/boes/bo/mailexch/exch/tools/appfarm/ default.htm The Exchange Application Farm Web site includes sample applications and other development tools that enable you to develop your own applications for Exchange.

http://www.microsoft.com/support The Microsoft Technical Support Web site gives you access to the Exchange Knowledge Base, support information, and answers to frequently asked questions.

http://www.microsoft.com/technet The Microsoft TechNet Web site contains information about subscribing to Microsoft TechNet, which provides in-depth technical information about Microsoft business products, including Exchange and other BackOffice products.

http://www.microsoft.com/train_cert The Microsoft Training and Certification Web site provides information about training options and the Microsoft Certified Professional Program.

All Internet addresses (URLs) in this volume were correct at the time of publication. For more information about Microsoft products, see http://www.microsoft.com.

Conventions in This Book

The following table summarizes the typographic conventions used in the *Microsoft Exchange Server 5.5 Resource Guide*.

Convention	Description
bold	Menus and menu commands, command buttons, property page and dialog box titles, command-line commands, options, and portions of syntax that must be typed exactly as shown.
Initial Capitals	The names of applications, programs, and named windows.
italic	Terminology that is being introduced, book titles, and information that you must provide in a code line, directory name, or address.
KEY+KEY	Key combinations in which you press and hold down one key and then press another key.
`monospace`	Examples, sample command lines, program code, and program output.
SMALL CAPITALS	The names of keys on the keyboard.

PART 2

Planning

This chapter describes methods for planning and setting up Microsoft Exchange Server. It is helpful to understand how Setup works, so that you can troubleshoot problems or customize your server configuration to suit your organization's needs. For example, you can run Setup unattended using customized settings, or you can set up clustered servers to ensure fault tolerance if one of your Exchange computers fails.

Server Setup

How you set up Exchange depends on whether you are installing it for the first time or adding and removing components such as connectors.

The following table is a list of important files that are used during setup.

Caution Do not modify the files used during Setup. Doing so can result in unpredictable results.

File type	Description
.ins files	Setup reads installation (.ins) files to create core services, directories, and processes; share directories; and modify the registry. These files are also used to perform a number of maintenance tasks such as adding Microsoft Windows NT Performance Monitor counters. Most components have an associated .ins file. The most important installation file is the Server.ins file.
.uns files	Setup reads uninstallation (.uns) files to remove previously installed components. Each .ins file has a corresponding .uns file that runs when you select **Remove All** or **Add/Remove** during setup. (To remove a component, the component's corresponding .uns file must be available.)
.scr files	Script (.scr) files are similar to installation files. Setup reads the .scr files and follows the instructions contained in the file. For example, if something goes wrong during Setup and services must be stopped, Setup runs the Stop.scr file.

(continued)

File type	Description
Server.inf	Setup reads this file when it copies files to the server's disk. Server.inf contains a list of all files to be installed and where to install them.
Setup.log	Setup creates this log file when it is initialized. Setup.log is used to record all events that occur on the server during setup. You can refer to Setup.log if you encounter problems during setup.
	Your server might have two Setup.log files. One log file is created in the system partition the first time Exchange is installed, and a second log file is created in the Exchsrvr directory the next time Setup is run. If there are two log files on the server when Setup is run, Setup appends the Setup.log file to the Exchsrvr directory.

Installing New Servers

When you install Exchange for the first time, Setup gathers information, including your organization name and site name, the service account name and password, and whether the server is creating a new Exchange site or joining an existing site. Then Setup does the following:

- Installs core components
- Installs optional components
- Performs directory replication with other servers in the site

Installing Core Components

In the initial installation phase, Setup installs the Exchange core components, including the system attendant, the directory, the information store, and the message transfer agent (MTA). The process involves validating the user account and service account, copying files and installing the core components, building the directory and initiating directory replication, and then starting the remaining core services and updating the system.

Validating the user account and service account. First setup verifies that the account of the user who is currently logged on is valid in the Microsoft Windows NT Server domain and has Administrator permissions for the site and configuration objects. Setup also verifies that the service account and password you are using to install Exchange are valid in the domain. This verification step prevents an unauthorized server from being installed in a site.

The way Setup determines the service account varies according to whether the server is creating a new site or joining an existing site. When you are installing a server in a new site, the account of the user who is currently logged on is used as the default service account. When you are installing a server in an existing site, Setup checks the registry of the remote server and uses that same service account for the new server. If this service account does not already have the following rights on this computer, Setup grants them.

Right	Description
Logon as a service	Enables use of this service account by Exchange services for authentication in the domain.
Restore files and directories	Enables restoration of the information store and the directory from backup if necessary.
Act as part of the operating system	Enables Exchange to act as a secure, trusted part of the operating system.

Copying files and installing the core components.   After the user and service accounts have been validated and the appropriate rights have been assigned, Setup reads the Server.inf file and copies files to directories on the local disk according to the components you have selected. Setup then reads the Server.ins file in the directory where Setup is run. This file instructs Setup to create shared file directories. It also installs core services and updates the server's registry by adding permissions for registry items. Setup then starts the system attendant and directory service.

Building the directory and initiating directory replication.   Setup now installs the directory. Setup provides the directory with the server's computer name and the names of the organization and site that the new server is creating or joining. After the names for the organization and site objects have been added to the directory, they cannot be changed; however, you can change their display names after Exchange is installed.

The process for updating the directory with the name of the organization and the site name is different depending on whether the server is in a new site or joining an existing site. If the server is being installed in a new site, the specified organization and site names are added to the directory. If the server is joining an existing site, the server connects to another server in the existing site and reads the organization and site names from the remote server's directory.

To complete the process of building the directory, Setup performs the following tasks:

- Sets permissions for directory objects.

- Initiates directory replication if the server is joining an existing site. However, Setup prevents directory replication with other directories in the site until the new directory is completely built. This ensures that the objects in the new directory are the correct version.

- Adds objects to the directory for additional components (such as the information store and the MTA) and modifies existing objects.

- Installs templates into the directory.

Few directory operations occur on a server that is joining an existing site. Setup modifies the directory on the remote server that you specified in the existing site. The modified directory is then replicated to the new server. If Setup fails while the directory is being installed, the directory information about the new server continues to exist on the remote computer until it is deleted from the remote server's directory. The following illustration shows how the directory is built and how replication is initiated.

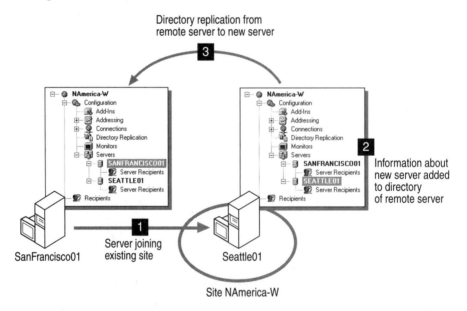

Starting the remaining core services and updating the system. Setup now starts any remaining core services, such as the information store and the MTA. It also adds program items to the Exchange program group and updates the registry.

Installing Optional Components

After the core components are installed and started, Setup installs any optional components that you selected, such as connectors and the Administrator program. Optional components are installed in the same way as core components. However, the services for these components must be started manually. Setup performs the following tasks to install optional components:

- Reads the installation (.ins) file for each component. (The .ins files instruct Setup to perform tasks such as installing services and modifying the registry.)
- Updates the directory with information about the component.
- Adds program items to the program group and updates the registry.

Directory Replication

As Setup completes, the directory is completely replicated in the background. Information that was not replicated during Setup, such as user account information, is replicated from the remote server to the new server at this time.

Updating or Upgrading Exchange

You must run Setup again to add or remove components (such as connectors) after you have already installed Exchange. You must also run Setup again if you want to upgrade to a later version of Exchange or if you need to restore the registry because it has been corrupted. When you Setup again, it detects the existing Exchange installation on the computer and starts a maintenance installation. Maintenance installation includes the options **Add/Remove**, **Remove All**, and **Reinstall**. If you are upgrading from a previous version of Exchange to Exchange 5.5 or are installing a service pack (SP) on an Exchange 5.5 server, maintenance installation includes an **Upgrade** option instead of a **Reinstall** option.

Adding or Removing Components

When you add components by selecting the **Add/Remove** option, Setup runs the installation (.ins) file for each selected component.

When you remove components by selecting the **Add/Remove** option or the **Remove All** option, Setup does the following:

- Deletes the components you have specified from the system by running the uninstallation (.uns) file for each component. If you have selected the **Remove All** option, all Exchange components are deleted.
- Removes the service for each component and then deletes references to the component in the registry and directory.

Reinstalling Exchange

When you select the **Reinstall** option to restore the registry or to upgrade a computer running Exchange 4.0 to Exchange 5.0, Setup does the following:

- Checks the version of the existing installation.
- Overwrites the appropriate files.
- Modifies the registry entries.
- Sets values in the directory.

Setup does not overwrite templates because they can be customized by users. Setup also does not modify the database files for the information store or directory service.

Upgrading Exchange to Version 5.5

If you run setup for Microsoft Exchange Server version 5.5 on a server that is running Microsoft Exchange Server version 4.0 or Microsoft Exchange Server version 5.0, you have the option of upgrading rather than reinstalling your server. Upgrading is a more extensive process than reinstalling, because upgrading reformats the information store and directory databases for Exchange 5.5.

Setup upgrades the databases sequentially before files are copied from the compact disc. For example, if you are upgrading an Exchange computer from Exchange 4.0 to Exchange 5.5, Setup performs the following steps:

1. Upgrades the private information store from Exchange 4.0 to Exchange 5.0.
2. Upgrades the public information store from Exchange 4.0 to Exchange 5.0.
3. Upgrades the directory from Exchange 5.0 to Exchange 5.5.
4. Upgrades the private information store from Exchange 5.0 to Exchange 5.5.
5. Upgrades the public information store from Exchange 5.0 to Exchange 5.5.

When you upgrade your server from Exchange 5.0 to Exchange 5.5, Setup performs only steps 3, 4, and 5.

Upgrade Types

When you run Setup, you can choose to perform a standard upgrade or a fault-tolerant upgrade.

Standard upgrade If you are performing a standard upgrade, Setup copies the new databases over the old databases in their current location. This option requires less disk space than a fault-tolerant upgrade, but it is more risky. If Setup fails while the databases are being upgraded, all data is lost and you must restore the server from a tape backup.

Fault tolerant upgrade If you are performing a fault-tolerant upgrade, Setup copies the existing databases to a new, temporary location on the server's local disk. When all database files have been upgraded they are copied back to the original location. This option is safer than a standard upgrade because data is not lost if Setup fails while the databases are being upgraded. However, the fault-tolerant upgrade requires more available disk space on the Exchange computer than a standard upgrade.

Note The fault-tolerant upgrade option is available only when you upgrade from Exchange 5.0 to Exchange 5.5.

Upgrade Disk Space Requirements

Disk space requirements vary depending on the type of upgrade you are performing. Neither option performs a complete backup of your existing databases. You should perform a full backup of your information store before running Setup.

Note You should also backup your server before upgrading. For more information about backing up your server, see Part 4, "Administering and Maintaining."

Standard upgrade A standard upgrade requires available disk space approximately equal to 17 percent of the largest database you are upgrading.

Fault-tolerant upgrade A fault-tolerant upgrade requires enough available disk space for all of the databases combined. For example, if you are upgrading a 10 megabyte (MB) private information store, a 20-MB public information store, and a 10-MB directory, you must have at least 40 MB of available disk space on the disk you specify as the temporary upgrade location.

What to Do If Setup Fails While Upgrading

If Setup fails while upgrading your Exchange computer, take one of the following courses of action, depending on what upgrade option you have chosen.

Standard upgrade If you are performing a standard upgrade and Setup fails while the databases are being upgraded, you must restore Exchange from a tape backup.

If Setup fails while files are being copied from the Exchange compact disc to the local disk on the Exchange computer, rerun Setup. Setup usually finishes copying the required files and completes the setup process successfully.

Fault-tolerant upgrade If you are performing a fault-tolerant upgrade and Setup fails while the databases are being upgraded, you can restart the server using the previous installation of Exchange.

If Setup fails while the databases are being copied from the temporary location to the location of the previous installation, Setup again.

If Setup fails while files are being copied from the Exchange compact disc to the local disk on the Exchange computer, you should Setup again. Setup usually finishes copying the required files and completes the setup process successfully.

Running Setup Unattended

You can customize your server installation by running Setup unattended using customized default settings that you specify in a Setup.ini file. If you are installing Exchange for the first time on multiple computers and want to use the same configuration on all servers, you can run the Setup program in unattended batch mode.

Running batch mode Setup is useful if you have to install Exchange quickly and do not want Setup to prompt you for additional information. Batch mode Setup (Setup /q) can be used with an .ini file that contains configuration settings that enable you to install Exchange without user input. For example, you can use batch mode Setup to install Exchange in offices that do not have full-time administrators to set up the servers.

Creating an .Ini File for Batch Setup

Before running batch mode Setup, you must create an .ini file that contains the default installation settings. In this .ini file, specify your preferences, such as the installation directory, the organization name, and the components that will be installed. Using an .ini file is equivalent to selecting options in dialog boxes during Setup. However, the .ini file provides additional options to give you more control over your installation.

Use any text editor to create an .ini file with any name. Several .ini file examples are included on the Exchange compact disc in the Support\Samples\Setup directory. The following example shows the format of the .ini file:

```
[Paths]
;Where the server will be installed if selected.
ServerDest= C:\Exchsrvr

;Where Admin will be installed if selected. This entry is optional.
AdminDest= C:\Exchsrvr
```

For more information about .ini file settings, see Appendix A, "Creating an .Ini File for Exchange Batch Setup."

Running Batch Mode Setup

To run batch mode Setup after you have created an .ini file, type the following at the command prompt:

Setup /q*filepath*

where *filepath* is the path and file name of the .ini file.

Clustering with Exchange

The Exchange version 5.5 Enterprise Edition includes many enhancements that provide support for Microsoft Cluster Server version 1.0. Clustering your Exchange computers ensures that messaging services remain uninterrupted even if one of the clustered servers fails. For example, if the processor in a clustered Exchange computer fails, another server in the cluster is available in its place. Users on the failed server do not see a change in their e-mail service. They can continue to send and receive mail, and browse public folders as usual.

Note Clustering is supported only in the Microsoft Exchange Server Enterprise Edition.

Clustering is also convenient if you need to update a server or add new hardware without interrupting service to users. Services can *fail over* to another server in the cluster so the other server takes over the functions of the server you are upgrading.

This section describes procedures for planning, installing, and administering Exchange in a cluster environment. It briefly describes clustering but assumes that you are already familiar with Microsoft Cluster Server operations and concepts. For more information about clustering, see your Microsoft Cluster Server documentation.

The following Exchange components are not supported in a cluster environment.

- Dial-up connection services including.
    - Dynamic RAS Connector
    - Dial-up Internet Mail Service
    - Dial-up Internet News Service
- Microsoft Outlook Web Access
- Microsoft Mail for AppleTalk Networks (now known as Quarterdeck Mail)
- Microsoft Exchange Connector for Lotus Notes
- Microsoft Exchange Connector for SNADS
- X.400 Connector using X.25

- X.400 Connector using TCP/IP
- Microsoft Exchange Connector for IBM OfficeVision OV/VM (PROFS)
- Third-party connectors and gateways

Note For more information about using the Exchange X.400 Connector using TCP/IP in a cluster environment, see the Microsoft Knowledge Base article Q169113, "Using an X.400 Connector with the Transmission Control Protocol/Internet Protocol (TCP/IP) in a Cluster Environment," at the Microsoft Technical Support Web site (http://www.microsoft.com/support).

System Requirements

When planning the hardware and system requirements for your clustered Exchange computers, see *Microsoft Exchange Server Getting Started* and your Microsoft Cluster Server documentation.

If you are using Exchange in a clustering environment, you must install the hot fixes available from ftp://ftp.microsoft.com/bussys/winnt/winnt-public/fixes/usa/nt40/hotfixes-postsp3/roll-up/ before you install Exchange.

Note The Hardware Compatibility List for Microsoft Cluster Server is available on the Web at http://www.microsoft.com/hwtest/hcl/.

Understanding Clustering

The following terminology is used throughout this section:

Primary node The cluster server on which Exchange is initially installed.

Secondary node The other server in a cluster server. The secondary node copies information from the primary node during installation and supplemental updates.

Network name resource The network name of the cluster virtual server. This is the network name accessed by clients connecting to the cluster. This name must be unique within the network.

IP address resource A static Internet Protocol (IP) address associated with the virtual server's network name. This is the IP address accessed by clients connecting to the cluster. The IP address must be unique within the network.

Virtual server   The network interface presented to the network on behalf of the Exchange cluster group. A virtual server is a combination of the network name and the IP address resources. All requests to the Exchange cluster are directed to the virtual server.

Active node   The cluster server that currently owns cluster group resources and responds to network requests made to those services. In an Exchange cluster environment, only one of the clustered nodes can be active at a given time.

Inactive node   The cluster server that does not currently own cluster group resources but is available if the active node fails over.

***Exchange* cluster resource group**   A logical grouping of Exchange cluster resources for the purpose of administration and fail over. For administration, global actions, such as common properties, can be applied to the group as a whole. The Exchange cluster resource group also provides consistency during fail over because fail over of a cluster group includes all resources of that group.

Dependencies   Many clustered resources are dependent on other resources for operation. Setup creates the dependencies for all resources except the Microsoft Mail Connector. You must create the dependencies for this resource, as described in "Configuring Additional Components" later in this chapter.

Physical disk resource   The disk resource shared between servers in a cluster. The physical disk hosts Exchange-related files and databases, and is a member of the Exchange cluster group.

***Exchange* resources**   Many Exchange resources can exist within the Exchange cluster group. Because Exchange is cluster-aware, these services are automatically created and configured during Setup and configuration of Exchange into the cluster.

How Clusters Work

A cluster consists of two Exchange computers (also called nodes) that share one or more common physical disk drives, an IP address, a network name, and Exchange cluster resources.

Within an Exchange cluster, only one of the nodes in the cluster can service network requests at any one time. The node that owns all clustered resources is called the *active node*. It owns the shared disk(s), IP address, and network name for the cluster, and it runs the Exchange services. If the active node in a cluster experiences a hardware failure, Exchange services fail over to the inactive node, which then becomes the active node.

As the following illustration of an Exchange cluster shows, all network requests to the clustered Exchange computer are directed at the virtual server defined by the cluster, not at an individual node. It is the active node that receives and processes these requests on behalf of the cluster.

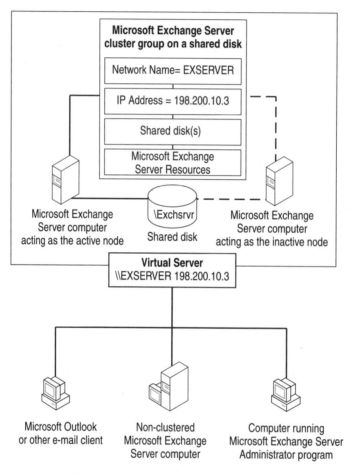

Note When Exchange is installed into a cluster environment, it is configured in a high-availability model, in contrast to a model that provides load balancing. As a result, Exchange assumes the cluster is symmetrical. Both servers in a cluster must be identical in terms of performance and capacity so that each server can host the other's clustered resources.

Implementing Exchange in a Cluster Environment

The following are typical scenarios for implementing Exchange into a cluster environment:

- Installing a new Exchange computer into a cluster.
- Moving users from an existing Exchange computer to a new Exchange computer in a cluster.
- Migrating an existing Exchange computer to a cluster.

The following guidelines apply, regardless of how Exchange is implemented in a cluster environment:

- Exchange must be installed into an operational cluster. It is not possible to install Microsoft Cluster Server onto an existing Exchange installation.
- Nodes in the cluster must have these common attributes:
    - Memory, local hard drive, and processor configurations must be identical because Exchange assumes symmetrical performance of both nodes of the cluster.
    - Before installing Exchange, you must create a cluster resource group for use by Exchange clustered resources.

Installing New Exchange Computers

The procedures in this section describe how to install Exchange into a cluster. They assume that the Exchange cluster is being added to a new or existing site and that Exchange is not installed on the computer.

To install a new Exchange computer into an existing cluster, you must perform the following tasks. Each task is described in detail later in this section.

1. Install Microsoft Cluster Server.
2. Create and name a cluster resource group.
3. Create a new IP address resource.
4. Create a new network name resource.
5. Move the disk to the cluster resource group.
6. Test the cluster.

7. Install Exchange on the primary node.

8. Install Exchange on the secondary node.

Note To upgrade an existing Exchange installation and install it into an existing cluster, move all users from the existing Exchange computer to a new clustered Exchange computer. For more information, see "Migrating an Existing Exchange Computer into a Cluster" later in this section.

Installing Microsoft Cluster Server

For information about installing Microsoft Cluster Server on a computer running Microsoft Windows NT Server Enterprise Edition, see your Microsoft Cluster Server documentation.

Creating and Naming a Cluster Resource Group

Before installing Exchange, you must perform several steps to prepare the cluster. Use the Cluster Administrator program on the computer that owns the shared disk resource. This will be the active node.

▶ **To create a cluster group for Exchange cluster resources and name the group**

1. On the **Start** menu, click **Programs**, click **Administrative Tools**, and then click **Cluster Administrator**.

2. On the **File** menu, click **New**, and then click **Group**.

3. In the **Name** box, type the name of the new cluster resource group; for example, **Ex_cluster**.

4. In the **Description** box, type an optional description of the new cluster resource group; for example, **Exchange Cluster Group**.

5. Click **Next**.

6. Click **Finish**, and then click **OK**.

Creating a New IP Address Resource for the Cluster

Using the Cluster Administrator program on the active node, complete the following procedure.

▶ **To create a new IP address resource for the cluster**

1. Select the newly created cluster resource group.

2. On the **File** menu, click **New**, and then click **Resource**.

3. In the **Name** box, type the name of the new IP address resource; for example, Exchange Server IP Address.

4. In the **Description** box, type an optional description of the new IP address.

5. On the **Resource Type** menu, click **IP Address**.

6. Verify that the **Group** box contains the name of the newly created cluster resource group.

7. Click **Next** twice to accept the default settings.

8. In the **IP Address** box, type the static IP address for the Exchange computer.

9. In the **Subnet Mask** box, type the subnet mask, and then click **Finish**.

Creating a New Network Name Resource for the Cluster

Using the Cluster Administrator program on the active node, complete the following procedure.

▶ **To create a new network name resource**

1. Select the newly created cluster resource.

2. On the **File** menu, click **New**, and then click **Resource**.

3. In the **Name** box, type the display name of the new network name resource; for example, Exchange Network Name.

4. In the **Description** box, type an optional description of the new network name.

5. On the **Resource Type** menu, click **Network Name**.

6. Verify that the **Group** box contains the name of the newly created cluster resource group, and then click **Next**.

7. Click **Next** again to accept the default settings.

8. In the **Available Resources** list, select the IP address resource created in the previous procedure. Click **Add** to move the IP address to the **Resource Dependencies** list, and then click **Next**.

9. In the **Name** box, type the network name of the Exchange computer, and then click **Finish**.

   The name you choose must be unique within your network.

   If you are performing this procedure as part of the disaster recovery procedure, this should be the name of the computer you are upgrading or replacing.

Note   The network name resource becomes the cluster equivalent of your Exchange name. When you administer Exchange, connect to the network name resource for your Exchange computer instead of the network name for the cluster.

Moving the Physical Disk Resources to the Cluster Group

Move the desired physical disk resources to the Exchange cluster resource group by using the Cluster Administrator program on the active node to complete the following drag-and-drop procedure.

▶ **To move the physical disk resources**

1. In the **Disk** group, select the disk you want to move into the Exchange cluster resource group by pressing and holding down the left mouse button.

2. Move the pointer to the Exchange cluster resource group, and then verify that the display name of the cluster is selected.

3. Release the left mouse button. This procedure moves the drive to the selected cluster.

4. Click **Yes** twice.

If you have more than one disk to add to the cluster, perform this procedure for each disk.

Testing the Cluster

When you have finished configuring Microsoft Cluster Server for Exchange, test the cluster by completing the following procedure.

▶ **To test the cluster**

1. On the active node, create a generic application resource for Notepad within the newly created cluster group resource. From the **File** menu, click **New**, and then click **Resource**.

2. In the **Name** box, type the name of the resource.

3. In the **Description** box, type an optional description of the resource; for example, **Notepad resource**.

4. On the **Resource Type** menu, click **Generic Application**, and then click **Next**.

5. Click **Next** to confirm the default settings, and then click **Next** again.

6. In the **Command Line** box, type **Notepad.exe**.

7. In the **Current Directory** box, type the path of your temporary directory.

8. Click **Allow application to interact with desktop**, and then click **Next**.

9. You do not need to add any registry entries. Click **Finish** to accept the default settings, and then click **OK**.

10. Select the newly created cluster resource group.

11. On the **File** menu, click **Bring Online**. The Notepad application starts automatically on this active node. Return to the Cluster Administrator program and make it the active window.

12. Select the cluster resource group again. On the **File** menu, click **Move Group**. This manually fails the resource group to the inactive node. Notepad shuts down on the active node and starts on the inactive node.

13. Manually fail the group back over to the other node by clicking **Move Group** on the **File** menu.

14. Select the cluster resource group and then, on the **File** menu, click **Take Offline**.

15. Select the Notepad resource. On the **File** menu, click **Delete**. This deletes the Notepad resource that you created for this test.

16. Select the newly created cluster resource group again. On the **File** menu, click **Bring Online**.

Installing Exchange on the Primary Node

The following procedure describes how to install Exchange on the primary node.

Note All of the resources in your newly created cluster resource group, including the physical disk resource, the network name resource, and the IP address resource, must be brought online before you run Exchange Setup. To bring a resource online, select the resource, and from the **File** menu, click **Bring Online**.

▶ **To install Exchange on the primary node**

1. On the active node, run Exchange Setup.

2. Select the Exchange cluster resource group you created when you configured Microsoft Cluster Server.

3. Continue with Setup.

   You can install Exchange files only on clustered drives. Setup copies files to the primary node's Windows NT System32 directory, copies files to the clustered drive, and creates resources in the Exchange cluster resource group.

4. After Setup is complete, run Exchange Performance Optimizer.

   After installation is completed, Performance Optimizer runs only on the currently active Exchange cluster node and limits drive analysis to shared SCSI drives.

Installing Exchange on the Secondary Node

After you have installed Exchange on the primary node, install it on the secondary node. Because most files have already been installed on shared cluster drives, it is much easier to install Exchange on the secondary node. When you install Exchange on the secondary node, installation consists primarily of installing files on local disk drives and creating the appropriate services.

Note Performance Optimizer is disabled on the secondary node.

▶   **To install Exchange on the secondary node**

1. On the secondary node, run Exchange Setup.
2. Click **Update Node**.

Setup copies files to the secondary node's Windows NT System32 directory, and creates and registers services.

The secondary node must be updated using the above procedure whenever any of the following components are added or removed from the primary node.

- Internet Mail Service
- Internet News Service
- Microsoft Mail Connector
- Microsoft Exchange Connector for Lotus cc:Mail
- Microsoft Exchange Scripting Service
- Key Management server (KM server)

Migrating an Existing Exchange Computer into a Cluster

If Exchange is already installed and you want to install it into a cluster, you can either move users or perform a variation of the standard disaster recovery procedure. The option you choose depends primarily on the availability and capacity of other Exchange computers in your site, and on your level of familiarity with the disaster recovery process.

Moving Users

Moving users from a non-clustered Exchange computer to a clustered one allows you to take your time implementing your clustered environment because you can gradually migrate your users to the new system without interrupting e-mail services. However, to move users from a non-clustered Exchange computer to a clustered Exchange computer requires that you have sufficient hardware resources available to run two servers simultaneously.

Note You can move users only between Exchange computers that are located in the same site.

Before you move users, you must perform the following tasks:

1. Install Microsoft Cluster Server.
2. Configure the Exchange cluster resource group for Exchange.
3. Install Exchange on the primary node.
4. Install Exchange on the secondary node.

For more information, see "New Exchange Computer Installation" earlier in this chapter.

The following procedure describes how to move users from the old Exchange computer to the new clustered Exchange computer. Before you move users, verify that the new clustered server has been added to the existing site and directory replication is complete.

Note Do not shut down or remove the old server from the site until you are sure that all users have logged on to their mailboxes on the new server. This ensures that all messaging profiles are automatically updated.

▶ **To move users from a non-clustered to a clustered Exchange computer**

1. On the **Tools** menu in the Administrator program, click **Move User** to move all users from the existing Exchange computer to the new, clustered Exchange computer.

2. If the server you are moving users from was the first server in the site, on the **Advanced** property page for each public folder, change the home server to move all public folders from the existing Exchange computer to the new, clustered Exchange computer. For more information, see the Microsoft Knowledge Base article Q152959 "How to Remove the First Exchange Server in a Site" at the Microsoft Technical Support Web site (http://www.microsoft.com/support).

3. After public folder and directory replication is complete and all users have logged on once, you can shut down the old server.

4. In Windows NT Server Manager, remove the old server from the Exchange site, and delete it from the domain.

Using Disaster Recovery

If you are limited by the amount of hardware resources that are available, you can perform a variation of the standard disaster recovery procedure to add an existing Exchange to a cluster. For example, if you don't have an extra server and you plan to use the computer that is currently running Exchange as a node, you can remove Exchange from the computer and reinstall it in the cluster. This option requires no additional hardware, other than the two servers to be clustered.

For more information about disaster recovery, see Exchange *Maintenance and Troubleshooting* or the troubleshooting resources available on the Web at http://www.microsoft.com/exchange.

Note Make sure you log on using the same Windows NT account used to back up the Exchange computer. If the account you are using is not the same as the Windows NT service account used for the Exchange services, ensure that the account has administrator permissions. This will allow your current account to start and stop Exchange services when necessary.

▶ **To add an existing Exchange computer to a cluster**

1. Log on to the Exchange computer as an administrator.

2. As a precaution, back up the information store and directory using Windows NT Backup.

3. Run Exchange Setup, and upgrade to Exchange 5.5.

4. Back up the information store and directory using Windows NT Backup.

   You will use this backup after you have created your new cluster.

5. Shut down the server.

6. Perform a clean installation of Windows NT Server Enterprise Edition on both servers you are clustering.

7. Install Microsoft Cluster Server. For information about installing Microsoft Cluster Server, see your Microsoft Cluster Server documentation.

   Make sure you use the same Windows NT service account for both the Cluster services and the Exchange services.

8. Configure Microsoft Cluster Server for Exchange as described in "Installing New Exchange Computers" earlier in this section.

Note The network name resource must be the same as the computer name of the old Exchange computer.

---

9. Run Exchange Setup on the primary node using the **/r** option. On the **Start** menu, click **Programs**, and then click **Command Prompt**. Change directories to the installation directory of the Exchange compact disc and type **setup.exe /r**. For example, if the installation compact disc is located in the E:\ drive, type **E:\Server\Setup\I386\setup.exe /r**.

Note All of the resources in your newly created cluster resource group, including the physical disk resource, network name resource, and IP address resource, must be brought online before you run Exchange Setup. To bring a resource online, select the resource and, on the **File** menu, click **Bring Online**.

The Exchange computer should use the same configuration as the old Exchange computer. For example, you should use the same service account, install the same components, and specify the same organization and site names.

Note If the server you are removing was originally the first server in the site, verify that the system folders (Eforms Registry and Schedule+ Free & Busy folders) are replicated to other servers in the site. If these folders are not replicated, problems can occur. For more information, see the Microsoft Knowledge Base article Q152959: "How to Remove the First Exchange Server in a Site," at the Microsoft Technical Support Web site (http://www.microsoft.com/support).

---

10. Select the Exchange resource group you created when you configured Microsoft Cluster Server.

    Setup copies files to the primary node's Windows NT System32 directory, copies files to the clustered drive, and creates resources in the resource group.

11. When Setup is completed, run Performance Optimizer.

12. In the Cluster Administrator program, bring the Exchange system attendant resource online. Select the resource and, on the **File** menu, click **Bring Online**.

13. Start Windows NT Backup and restore the information store and directory to the active node. Select the **Do not start services after restore** option.

14. In the Cluster Administrator program, bring the Microsoft Exchange directory service resource online. Select **Microsoft Exchange Directory** and, on the **File** menu, click **Bring Online**.

15. In the Cluster Administrator program, select the Exchange information store resource, click **Properties**, and then click the **Registry Replication** tab.

16. Click **Remove** to remove the old registry checkpoint.

17. Click **Add**, and then type the following registry path to create a new registry checkpoint:

    SYSTEM\CurrentControlSet\Services\MSExchangeIS

18. Click **OK** twice.

19. Bring the Exchange information store resource online. Select the Microsoft Exchange information store resource and, on the **File** menu, click **Bring Online**. This operation can take some time to complete, depending on how large your databases are.

Note The Cluster service normally allows 600 seconds (10 minutes) for the Exchange information store service to start. However, using Setup with the **/r** option to recover an information store running under the Cluster service, startup can take longer than 600 seconds. If this happens, the Cluster Administrator program indicates that the information store service failed to start. In fact, the startup of the information store service can still be waiting for the recovery process to be completed. In this case, you should disregard the status indicator and allow the recovery process to complete without stopping the information store service.

---

20. After the information store has successfully started, select the name of the resource group. Then on the **File** menu, click **Bring Online**.

21. Run Exchange Setup on the inactive node, and then click **Update Node**.

Configuring Additional Components

You can configure or add components in the Exchange cluster environment.

Microsoft Mail Connector Services

When the Microsoft Mail Connector is installed, four new resources are added to the Exchange cluster group:

- MS Mail Connector Interchange
- MS Schedule+ Free/Busy Connector
- Microsoft Exchange Directory Synchronization service
- The maildat$ file share resource

All the new resources except the maildat$ file share remain offline after the initial configuration. While in this state, use the following procedures to ensure proper operation of the Mail Connector in an Exchange cluster. Be sure to note the service name that you are using.

▶ **To configure the Microsoft Mail Connector on a clustered server**

1. In the Cluster Administrator program, bring the Microsoft Mail Interchange (MSMI) resource online.

2. In the Administrator program, configure the Mail Connector as usual.

3. In the Cluster Administrator program, create a new generic service cluster resource for Microsoft Mail (PC) message transfer agent (PCMTA):

   ▪ Name the new resource after the PCMTA service created during connector configuration in the Administrator program.

   ▪ On the **Resource Dependencies** tab, make the service dependent on the MSMI resource and network name.

   ▪ On the PCMTA **Resource Parameters** tab, type the service name of the Windows NT PCMTA service, and click **Use Network Name** for the computer name.

   ▪ On the **Registry Replication** tab, click **Add** and type the following path:

   SYSTEM\CurrentControlSet\Services*service name*

4. In the Cluster Administrator program, start the PCMTA.

5. Update the second Exchange cluster node by running Exchange Setup and clicking **Update Node**.

▶ **To remove an instance of a PCMTA**

1. In the Cluster Administrator program, shut down the PCMTA service.

2. In the Exchange Administrator program, remove the PCMTA service.

3. In the Cluster Administrator program, remove the resource.

After the Mail Connector is configured, you can configure the Microsoft Schedule+ Free/Busy Connector and the Directory Synchronization service.

▶ **To configure Microsoft Schedule+ Free/Busy Connector**

1. In the Cluster Administrator program, select the Microsoft Schedule+ Free/Busy Connector.

2. Click **Properties**, and then click the **Advanced** tab.

3. Click **Restart**, and then click **Affect the Group**.

Repeat this procedure for the Directory Synchronization service.

Now you can bring the resources online. This ensures that the services restart as expected when the node fails over to the other computer.

Microsoft Exchange Connector for Lotus cc:Mail

After installing the Connector for cc:Mail, you must perform the following procedure on the primary node.

▶ **To configure the Connector for Lotus cc:Mail on a clustered server**

1. Copy the required Import.exe and Export.exe files to a location in the search path on the local hard drives of both nodes. If connecting to a cc:Mail version 6 database, also include Ie.ri from the cc:Mail post office.

2. In the Exchange Administrator program, configure the Connector for cc:Mail.

3. In the Cluster Administrator program, bring the new cc:Mail resource online.

4. In Setup, click **Update Node** to update the second node.

KM Server

Important For security reasons, it is not recommended that you install KM server as part of a cluster.

KM server is a special instance of a clustered Exchange resource. When installed, KM server is added to the Exchange cluster group, but the resource is configured not to restart on fail over. For security reasons, you must manually start the KM server service if there is a fail over. You should use the Services application in Control Panel to start the service. After you have started the KM server service, you must bring it online using the Cluster Administrator program. For more information about KM server security requirements, see Exchange *Operations*.

Note KM server is the only service you should start or stop using the Services application in Control Panel.

Administering Exchange in a Cluster Environment

This section describes additional information you should keep in mind when you administer your Exchange clusters.

Exchange Administrator Program

The Administrator program is fully cluster-aware. However, Microsoft recommends that running the Administrator program on the local console of either clustered node. Whenever possible, the Administrator program should be run from a non-clustered server or workstation. This is because the Administrator program can crash if a fail over occurs while it is active on a clustered node.

Starting and Stopping Exchange Services in a Cluster

On both nodes, service entries for clustered Exchange resources are set to manual. This prevents the automatic startup of services. All services are started in order of dependency by the cluster's resource manager.

Managing services in a clustered Exchange environment should be performed using only the Cluster Administrator program. Never stop the clustered resources using the Services application in Control Panel, and never stop the services from a command prompt using the **net stop** *service name* command. Doing so can cause unpredictable results, because the cluster resource manager sees the resource as failed, and either restarts the service or fails over the group.

If services must be taken down for maintenance, use the Cluster Administrator program to stop them. It is recommended that you fail over the entire Exchange cluster group prior to service maintenance.

Windows NT Performance Monitor

Do not run Performance Monitor on either node of a cluster. However, you can monitor the cluster with Performance Monitor from any other remote Windows NT computer. When you add Performance Monitor counters, use the Exchange network name, not the individual cluster names, to gather data.

Windows NT Event Log

Event logging details are generated only against the active node of a cluster. Direct remote event log queries against the Exchange network name cluster resource.

Registry Checkpointing

Registry checkpointing provides consistency between the registry settings for both nodes. For example, if a registry change is made to a service on the active node, that change is replicated to the inactive node. When registry modifications are made to a resource service that is offline, the cluster server will not be aware of the modifications. Therefore, changes made to a cluster service when offline are rolled back when the service is brought back online. The key point to remember is that registry modifications relating to a service that is not started are lost when the service is brought back online.

Customizing for Client Languages

The code pages for Microsoft Outlook languages are installed with Exchange. You also can install language-specific indexes and details templates. Indexes provide users with sort and search orders common for the specified language. Details templates provide users with an Address Book in the language being used by Outlook.

Installing Indexes for Languages

An index for a language contains information on sorting and searching orders for folder hierarchies and the directory. The index is based on the language's conventions.

Installing a language index can minimize the confusion caused by differences in sorting and searching orders between languages; however, using multiple indexes can decrease server performance. To minimize the impact of multiple indexes, you can dedicate a single server to each index. You can also choose not to install languages that are not often needed, or those that have sorting and searching rules similar to languages you have already installed on the server.

If an index for an Outlook language is not installed on the server, the server uses an existing index that is similar to either the language you are installing or to the Windows NT Server language.

▶ **To install a language index**

1. In the Administrator program, click **Servers**, and then click the server on which you want to install the language index.

2. On the **File** menu, click **Properties**, and then click the **Locales** tab.

3. Select the language to be installed on the server.

4. Click **Add**, and then click **OK**.

5. Ensure that Windows NT code pages for the appropriate language are installed, and then restart the server.

Installing Address Book Details Templates for Languages

You can customize the directory details template to change the language of the Address Book. The language details templates show text provided by Exchange (such as user properties in the Address Book) in the Outlook language. Details templates for English, French, German, and Japanese are installed automatically. Installing language details templates does not affect server performance.

Note Templates are not replicated across site boundaries.

You also can customize the text shown in the **Display** dialog box of the Address Book, such as the type of information stored in the directory and the format in which the information is displayed.

For more information about customizing details templates, see *Microsoft Exchange Server Operations*.

Using Russian, Eastern European, Greek, and Turkish Language Character Sets

This section contains information about how to use Internet Mail Service with Russian, Eastern European, Greek, and Turkish language character sets.

Note To ensure that your character set changes take effect, you must restart Internet Mail Service after you make changes to Exchange or to the Windows NT registry.

Russian and Eastern European Character Sets

If you want to use Russian or Eastern European language character sets, follow the procedures presented in the sections below before you try to view one of these languages.

Before making any changes to Internet Mail Service, make sure that either C_1251.nls (Russian) or C_1250.nls (Eastern European Latin2) is in your Windows NT System32 directory and that the values in the following table are added to the registry key **HKEY_LOCAL_MACHINE\System \CurrentControlSet\Control\NLS\Codepage**.

Value	Codepage
1251 : REG_SZ : c_1251.nls	Russian
1250 : REG_SZ : c_1250.nls	Latin2

Installing Russian and Eastern European Character Sets

Use the following procedures to install Russian or Eastern European character sets.

▶ **To install Russian and Eastern European character sets as a global option**

- If you want to install the Russian character set, copy the KOI8-R.trn file from the localized client software to the Exchsrvr\Connect\Trn directory on your Exchange computer. To add the Russian character set as a global option, in the Administrator program, on the **Internet Mail** property page of the Internet Mail Service, set the character sets for multi-purpose Internet Mail Extensions (MIME) and non-MIME to Russian (KOI8-R).

- If you want to install the Polish, Czech, or Hungarian character set, copy the ISO88592.trn file from the localized client software to the Exchsrvr\Connect\Trn directory on your Exchange computer. To add the Polish, Czech, or Hungarian character sets as global options, in the Administrator program, on the **Internet Mail** property page of the Internet Mail Service, set the character sets for MIME and non-MIME to Central European International Standards Organization (ISO) #8859-2.

If you do not want to set Russian or Eastern European character sets as global options, you can specify the message content by e-mail domain.

▶ **To specify message content by e-mail domain**

1. In the Exchange Administrator program, select a server, and then click **Configuration**.
2. Click **Connections**, and then click **Internet Mail Service**.
3. Click the **Internet Mail** tab, and then click **E-Mail Domain**.
4. Add or edit the domain entry.
5. Select the character set you want to use.

Changing the Windows NT Registry to Use Russian or Eastern European Character Sets

To use the Russian character set, add the following values to the registry key **HKEY_CLASSES_ROOT\MIME\Database\Charset\Koi8-r**:

Codepage : REG_DWORD 0x04E3 (1251)

BodyCharset : REG_SZ : koi8-r

To use the Polish, Czech, or Hungarian character set, add the following values to the registry key **HKEY_CLASSES_ROOT\MIME\Database\Charset \iso-8859-2**:

Codepage : REG_DWORD 0x04e2 (1250)

BodyCharset : REG_SZ : iso-8859-2

Greek and Turkish Character Sets

To use Greek or Turkish language character sets, follow the procedures presented in the sections below before you try to view one of these languages.

Before making any changes to Internet Mail Service, make sure that either C_1253.nls (Greek) or C_1254.nls (Turkish) is in your Windows NT\System32 directory and that the values shown in the following table are added to the registry key HKEY_LOCAL_MACHINE\System\CurrentControlSet\Control \NLS\Codepage.

Value	Codepage
1250 : REG_SZ : c_1253.nls	Greek
1251 : REG_SZ : c_1254.nls	Turkish

Installing Greek and Turkish Character Sets

Use the following procedures to install Greek and Turkish character sets.

▶ **To install Greek and Turkish character sets as a global option**

- To install Greek character sets, from your Windows NT Service Pack 3 compact disc, copy the ISO88597.trn file to the Exchsrvr\Connect\Trn directory on your Exchange computer. To add the Greek character set as a global option, in the Administrator program, on the **Internet Mail** property page of the Internet Mail Service, set the character sets for MIME and non-MIME to ISO 8859.

- To install Turkish character sets, from your Windows NT Service Pack 3 compact disc, copy the ISO88599.trn file to the Exchsrvr\Connect\Trn directory on your Exchange computer. To add the Turkish character set as a global option, in the Administrator program, on the **Internet Mail** property page of the Internet Mail Service, set the character sets for MIME and non-MIME to ISO 8859.

If you do not want to set Greek or Turkish character sets as global options, you can specify the message content by e-mail domain.

▶ **To specify message content by e-mail domain**

1. In the Exchange Administrator program, select a server, and then click **Configuration**.

2. Click **Connections**, and then click **Internet Mail Service**.

3. Click the **Internet Mail** tab, and then click **E-Mail Domain**.

4. Add or edit the domain entry.

5. Select the character set you want to use.

Changing the Windows NT Registry to Use the Greek or Turkish Character Sets

To use the Greek character set, add the following values to the registry key **HKEY_CLASSES_ROOT\MIME\Database\Charset\iso-8859-7**:

Codepage : REG_DWORD 0x04E5 (1253)

BodyCharset : REG_SZ : iso-8859-7

To use the Turkish character set, add the following values to the registry key **HKEY_CLASSES_ROOT\MIME\Database\Charset\iso-8859-9**:

Codepage : REG_DWORD 0x04e6 (1254)

BodyCharset : REG_SZ : iso-8859-9

PART 3

Deployment

This chapter describes methods for deploying Microsoft Exchange Server. For example, you can set up clustered servers to ensure fault-tolerance if one of your Exchange computers fails.

Setting Permissions

Organizations that make information available to a diverse audience have to manage access that information. Some individuals and groups need more access to information and resources than others. You can control who can use Exchange resources by granting and restricting access to directory objects, public folders, and mailboxes. For example, you can set permissions for directory objects and public folders, or delegate access to mailboxes so that users can send e-mail on behalf of other users. You can use these features to enhance the security in your organization and to enhance convenience for your users.

Setting Permissions on Resources

You can use Exchange permissions to control the amount of access people have to resources such as directory objects and public folders. The permissions you choose to set depend on your organization's security requirements. For example, if you are the only person administering Exchange, set permissions for only the most critical resources so that no one else can have access to them. If your organization has a large Management Information Services (MIS) department, assign administrators different levels of permissions to control who has access to various resources. You can grant administrators with the most authority access permission for the entire directory, while granting other administrators only the authority to create mailboxes. For additional information about setting permissions, see your Exchange documentation.

Directory Permissions

You can control access to objects in the directory by using the Administrator program to assign *roles* to Microsoft Windows NT Server user accounts and groups. Roles are sets of permissions that are provided in Exchange for the purpose of administrative convenience. They define how much and what type of access a user or group has to an object. For example, the Administrator role gives administrators a number of permissions that help them perform their daily tasks. You can define custom roles, or you can use the following default roles provided with Exchange:

- Admin
- Permissions Admin
- Service Account Admin
- View Only Admin
- User
- Send As
- Search

Each role is defined by a set of permissions that define the specific actions that a particular user account or group can perform on an object. For example, the Delete permission grants the ability to delete an object. The permissions associated with each role are shown in the following table.

Permission	Admin Role	Permissions Admin Role	Service Account Admin Role	View Only Admin Role	User Role	Send As Role	Search Role
Add Child	X	X	X				
Modify User Attributes	X	X	X		X		X
Modify Admin Attributes	X	X	X				
Delete	X	X	X				
Logon	X	X	X	X			
Modify Permission		X	X				
Replication			X				
Mailbox Owner			X		X		
Send As			X		X	X	
Search							X

You can grant permissions to groups of users as well as to individual user accounts. Permissions are also granted to Exchange services. Most permissions apply only to the Exchange Administrator program; however, some permissions, such as Modify User Attribute, can apply to Outlook. The following table provides descriptions of the Exchange permissions.

Permission	Description
Add Child	Creates objects below the selected object in the directory hierarchy. For example, if a user has this permission for the Recipients container, they can create mailboxes in that container.
Modify User Attributes	Modifies user-level attributes associated with an object. For example, a user with this permission can modify the members of a distribution list.
Modify Admin Attributes	Modifies administrator-level attributes associated with an object. For example, a user with this permission can modify the job title and display name fields in a mailbox.
Modify Permission	Modifies permissions for existing objects. For example, without this permission, a user can grant permissions for new mailboxes but cannot modify permissions for existing ones.
Delete	Deletes objects.
Send As	Sends messages with the recipient's return address. For example, all users have this permission for their own mailboxes so that they can send messages with that mailbox's return address. This permission is also granted for server objects in the directory to the service account so that directory service processes can send messages to each other.
Mailbox Owner	Reads and deletes messages in this mailbox. This permission is also granted to the service account for server objects in the directory, so that directory processes can send messages to each other.
Logon Rights	Grants access to the directory. Users need this permission to use the Administrator program. Services also need this permission.
Replication	Replicates directory information with other servers. This permission is required by the Exchange service account to replicate with other servers.
Search	Enables the selected user account to view the contents of the container. This permission is useful for restricting access to Address Book View containers. For more information about using the Search permission with Address Book views, see *Microsoft Exchange Server Operations*.

Setting Permissions for Servers

Administrators need special permissions so they can administer Exchange. For example, certain permissions are required to perform typical tasks on an Exchange computer, including installing Exchange and backing up or restoring data.

Installing Exchange

You must have special permissions to perform the following tasks when you install Exchange:

- Run server Setup. The user account you are using to log on must be a member of the Windows NT Server Administrators local group.

- Join an existing site during setup. The user account you are using to log on must be assigned the Permissions Administrator role for the site's Organization, Site, and Configuration objects.

Performing Administrative Tasks

You must have special permissions to perform the following tasks using the Exchange Administrator program:

- Create a new recipient. Your user account must be assigned the Permissions Admin role for the Site object. No additional permissions are necessary. When you create a new Windows NT user account for a new recipient, your user account must be a member of the Windows NT Server Administrators global group in the domain to which you are adding the account.

- Modify properties for objects other than permissions. Your user account must be assigned the Admin role for the object, or it must inherit this role from another object.

- Modify permissions for objects. Your user account must be assigned the Permissions Admin role for the object, or it must inherit this role from another object.

- View properties for objects without modifying them. Your user account must be assigned the View Only Admin role for the object, or it must inherit this role from another object.

Backing Up and Restoring Data

You must have special permissions to back up and restore data. These permissions are set in Windows NT Server User Manager.

- To back up data, you must be a member of the Windows NT Server Backup Operators group on each server that is backed up. Only users with administrator permissions can add users to this group.

- To restore data from a tape backup, you must be a member of the Windows NT Server Administrators group on each server being restored. Only users with administrator permissions can add users to this group.

Exchange Directory and Directory Replication

This section provides detailed information about deploying directory replication, as well as information about the directory. It discusses what objects in the directory schema are used to determine when, where, and how data is replicated.

The following illustration describes the site topology of the example organization (Ferguson and Bardell) used throughout this chapter.

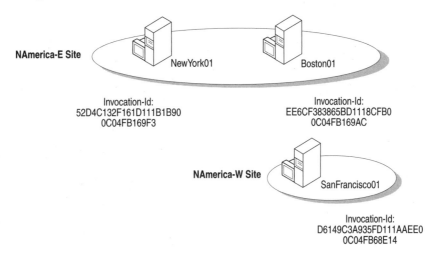

Directory Basics

The directory consists of two main components: the directory database and directory service. The directory database is responsible for storing all information about an organization's resources and users, such as mailboxes, servers, and connectors. It stores this data in the directory tree. The directory service manages information in the directory database and handles requests from users, services, and applications. In addition, the directory service is responsible for providing the Address Book, enforcing the rules governing the structure and content of the directory, and sending directory replication notifications to other servers.

The directory is based on a hierarchical tree with the organization at the root of the tree. The Exchange Administrator program in raw mode allows the directory hierarchy tree to be viewed without any virtual directories or containers generated by other Exchange services (such as the Global Address List and Public Folder containers).

To access the raw properties of directory objects in the Administrator program, you can run the Administrator program in raw mode. Note that you can also view the Schema container in raw mode, even though that container view is not available in the normal Administrator program view.

Caution Making changes to the directory in raw mode can result in loss of functionality and data loss. Extreme caution should be taken when running the Administrator program in raw mode. You should not make changes to the directory unless directed to do so by a Knowledge Base article or a Microsoft Support Engineer.

▶ **To run the Administrator program in raw mode**

1. At the command prompt, type **admin /r**.

2. In the Administrator program, on the **View** menu, click **Raw directory**.

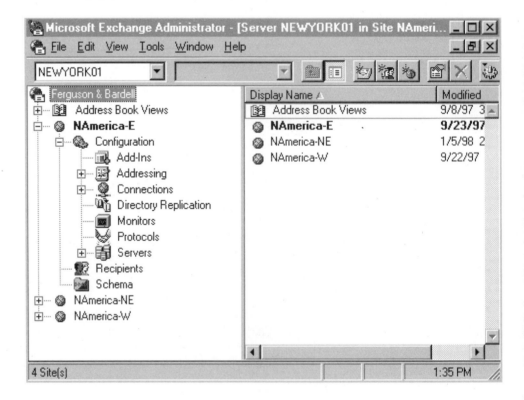

Directory Replication Infrastructure

The directory uses the directory structure and various values stored in the directory database to complete the replication process. These values can be broken down into three basic areas:

- Naming contexts
- Naming context replication attributes
- Object replication attributes

Naming Contexts

The directory hierarchy is composed of various naming contexts. Naming contexts can contain one or more containers. Individual naming contexts are replicated separately, and in some cases differently than other naming contexts. There are five naming contexts in a single site-organization (there can be multiple site naming contexts in a multisite environment).

Naming context	Address
Organization	/o=Organization
Address Book Views	/o=Organization/ou=A_BViews
Site	/o=Organization/ou=Site
Configuration	/o=Organization/ou=Site/cn=Configuration
Schema	/o=Organization/ou=Site/cn=Microsoft DMD

For information about how permissions for naming contexts are inherited, see *Microsoft Exchange Server Concepts and Planning*.

Naming Context Replication Attributes

The following naming context replication attributes determine when, where, and how the objects of a naming context are replicated.

Replication attribute	Description
Reps-From	A replica link attribute that determines how and where directory information will be replicated. Lists the servers from which Exchange will accept changes for a particular naming context.
Reps-To	A replica link attribute that determines how and where directory information will be replicated. Lists the servers to which Exchange will send changes for a particular naming context.

(continued)

Replication attribute	Description
Reps-To-Ext	A replica link attribute that determines how and where directory information will be replicated. Lists the servers to which Exchange will respond to requests for changes for a particular naming context.
Period-Rep-Sync-Times	Used to determine when the directory service will make a REQUEST for changes from servers on the Reps-From attribute list.
Replicator notify pause after modify (secs)	A registry entry used to determine how often the directory service will NOTIFY servers on the Reps-To attributes that changes have occurred. By default, this is 5 minutes. This registry setting can be set in seconds under the following registry key: HKEY_LOCAL_MACHINE\System\CurrentControlSet\Services\MSExchangeDS\Parameters

Object Replication Attributes

Several object replication attributes are also used to determine the replication state of individual objects in the directory, including the following. You can view these object attributes in the Administrator program in raw mode by viewing the raw properties of the object.

- Obj-Dist-Name
- Object-Version
- DSA-Signature
- USN-Changed
- USN-Created
- USN-Source

For example, the following illustration shows the USN-changed value for Bill
Lee's mailbox on Boston01.

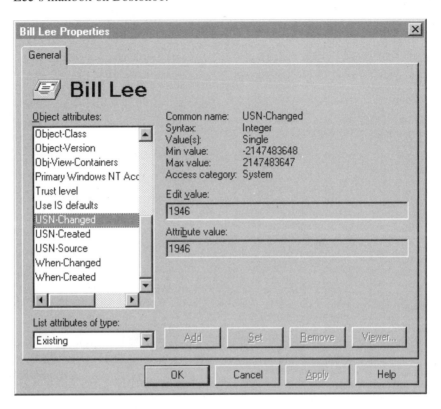

Every object in the directory is uniquely identified by its *Obj-Dist-Name* (Object Distinguished Name). The Obj-Dist-Name is an X.500-type address composed of the containers it is a member of and its directory name (RDN). For example, in the NAmerica-E site in the Ferguson and Bardell organization, the Recipients Container Obj-Dist-Name would be /o=Fab/ou=NAmerica-E/cn=Recipients. A mailbox called Bill Lee would have an Obj-Dist-Name of /o=Ferguson&Bardell/ou=NAmerica-E/cn=Recipients/cn=Bill Lee.

Every object in the organization has an *Object-Version*. The Object-Version is the version of the object or the number of changes it has had, including creation. The Object-Version should be the same on all servers in the organization if replication has completed.

The *DSA-Signature* of an object is the *Invocation-ID* of the last directory to modify the object. The Invocation-ID is used to uniquely identify each directory in an organization, and can be determined by viewing the raw attributes of the server's directory service.

Every directory keeps track of changes to its own database through *Unique Sequence Numbers (USNs)*. Each directory increments its USNs separately from other Exchange directories and applies these values to the objects in its directory database. Every time there is a change to the directory, the USN value is used to track the change, and the USN counter is incremented.

These changes are tracked through the *USN-Changed* attribute. The USN-Changed attribute is the USN value assigned by the local directory for the latest change, including creation.

The *USN-Created* attribute is the USN-Changed value assigned during object creation.

The *USN-Source* is the value of the objects USN-Changed attribute on the remote directory that replicated the change to this server, except on the originating directory at creation.

Site Replication

There are two primary differences between replication between sites and within a site. Replication between sites is mail-based, while replication within a site occurs with direct Remote Procedure Calls (RPC) communication between directory servers. Whether replication is RPC or mail-based also determines who is responsible for initiating replication. Whether a particular naming context is RPC-based or mail-based, and when replication occurs is determined by the Reps-From, Reps-To, and Reps-To-Ext properties of the naming context.

Replication Within a Site

When replication is RPC-based (within a site), the server that makes changes to its directory is responsible for initiating replication by notifying the servers specified in its Reps-To list for that particular naming context. Below is the Reps-From attribute details for the Site container. You can view this information by bringing up the raw properties of the Site object, selecting the Reps-To or Reps-From attribute, clicking **Viewer**, and selecting the Replica link viewer type. The following illustration shows the Reps-To value for the Boston01 Site container in the NAmerica-E site.

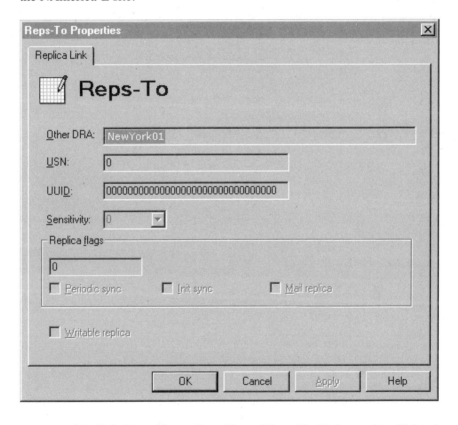

Every replica link (Reps-From, Reps-To and Reps-To-Ext) contains all the above values. The **Other DRA** value is the name of the server to be replicated. Note that this may be an X.500-type value in the case of a server in a different site. The Reps-To attribute does not use many values because you notify the Other DRA of the USN value based on the **Replicator notify pause after modify** (secs) registry setting. The Reps-From attribute has significantly more information, including the remote servers UUID and the USN of the last change committed to the directory for this naming context.

Note the check boxes for Periodic sync, Init sync and Mail replica.

Option	Description
Periodic sync	Defines whether request changes for this naming context are based on the Period-Rep-Sync-Times attribute.
Init Sync	Specifies whether or not the directory will request an update for this naming context at directory service startup.
Mail replica	Defines whether the directory uses mail-based replication or RPC-based replication.
Writeable replica	Defines whether clients can make changes to this naming context and is not used for replication.

In the example, this is a replica within a site because the Mail replica option is not selected. The directory is replicated as follows.

1. The local directory service notifies other directories in the site when naming context has changed.

2. The remote directory service requests changes from the originating directory service.

3. The originating directory service responds with the changes.

4. The remote directory service writes the changes to its directory.

5. The directory sends Notify, Request, Response, and Write messages.

Example: Replicating Within a Site

You can now use your understanding of the directory replication infrastructure and replication within a site to track the replication of an object between two servers in a site. Server NewYork01 and server Boston01 are the only two servers in site NAmerica-E.

In the following example, mailbox Bill Lee (/o=Ferguson&Bardell/ou=NAmerica-E/cn=Recipients/cn=Bill Lee) on server Boston01 will be modified to let it replicate to server NewYork01.

First, determine the replication state of the object on both servers before the modification, starting with server Boston01. Determine the replication state of an object by looking at the Object Replication attributes in raw mode. By viewing these attributes, note that the DSA-Signature is EE6CF383865BD1118CFB00C04FB169AC, and that the USN-Changed, USN-Created and USN-Source are all 1946. The DSA-Signature states that the last directory service to modify the object was Boston01. In this case, all the USN values are the same. When the USN-Changed, USN-Created and USN-Source are the same, you can determine that the object was created on the local directory and that it has not been modified since creation.

Now examine the object replication state on server NewYork01. The DSA-Signature of the Bill Lee mailbox object on server NewYork01 is EE6CF383865BD1118CFB00C04FB169AC. The USN-Created and USN-Changed values are 1157. The USN-Source value is 1946. These values state that the object was last modified by Server Boston01 (based on the DSA-Signature). USN-Created and USN-Changed are unique to this server and happen to be 1157. USN-Source is the USN-Changed value from the server that replicated the object. In this case, go back and see that 1946 is indeed the USN-Changed value from server Boston01.

Your next step is to modify this object on Server NewYork01 and see what changes when it is replicated to server Boston01. In the Administrator program, change the City attribute of the mailbox to London, and review the new state on server NewYork01.

As a result of the modification, DSA-Signature on server NewYork01 is changed to 52D4C132F161D111B1B900C04FB169F3. USN-Changed attribute has been modified to 1220. USN-Created remains at 1157 and the USN-Source remains at 1946. DSA-Signature has changed, because by definition it is the Invocation-ID of the last directory to modify it, in this case server NewYork01. USN-Changed is changed because the object has been modified. Whenever an object is modified, the USN counter on the directory is incremented and the value is assigned to the USN-Changed attribute of the object. USN-Created should not change anymore because it should only be set when an object is created on a particular Exchange directory. USN-Source can change, however, in this case it will not. Remember that by definition USN-Source is the USN-Changed value from the directory service that last replicated the change. Because the object was changed on this server, the last server to replicate a change was Boston01, and therefore USN-Source does not change.

At this point, you have a new change on the Site naming context (/o=Ferguson&Bardell/ou=NAmerica-E) for server NewYork01. The directory is replicated as follows.

1. Server NewYork01 notifies all the servers in its Reps-To list. Server Boston01 is the only server on the Reps-To list and will be notified based on **Replicator notify pause after modify (secs)**. The default is 5 minutes.

2. Server Boston01 requests the changes from server NewYork01.

3. Server NewYork01 responds with the changes for the naming context.

4. Server Boston01 writes those changes to its local directory database.

5. The directory sends Notify, Request, Response, and Write messages.

At this point, look at the state of the object on server Boston01. The object Bill Lee on server Boston01 now has a new set of object attributes as a result of the replication. DSA-Signature is 52D4C132F161D111B1B900C04FB169F3 (Server NewYork01s DSA-Signature). USN-Changed value is 1966, a unique value to this server. USN-Created stays at 1946, the original USN number assigned to this object. Finally, the USN-Source value is 1220, the USN-Changed value from the remote directory that replicated the change (server NewYork01).

Important Notes about Replication Within a Site

The following are important points to keep in mind about directory replication and replication within a site.

- USN-Created does not change after creation even when the object is modified.
- USN-Source does not change when the object is locally modified. By definition, USN-Source is the USN-Changed value of the object on the last remote directory that replicated the change to the local directory.
- You can always determine the last directory that modified the object based on the DSA-Signature of the object. This value changes even if the object is modified locally.

The most important point to remember about replication within a site is that all RPC-based replication uses Notify, Request, Response, and Write messages.

Replicating Between Sites

This section discusses the methods of replication between sites. It also tracks the changes to the object replication attributes. Every step discussed here can be tested in your own environment, and object replication states can be tracked using the Administrator program in raw mode.

In the following example, an object is created in the NAmerica-W site and replicated to the NAmerica-E bridgehead server. Eventually it will replicate to the downstream servers in the NAmerica-E site. This section will discuss the method used by replication in both instances and how that method is determined based on the naming context replication attributes.

A mailbox on server SanFrancisco01 is created with the directory name of Maria Black in site NAmerica-W. This new mailbox object has the following object replication attributes on server SanFrancisco01.

Object replication attribute	Value
Obj-Dist-Name	/o=Ferguson&Bardell/ou=NAmerica-W/cn=Recipients/cn=Maria Black
DSA-Signature	D6149C3A935FD111AAEE00C04FB68E14

(continued)

Object replication attribute	Value
USN-Changed	1489
USN-Created	1489
USN-Source	1489

This object was created in the /o=Ferguson&Bardell/ou=NAmerica-W naming context. The SanFrancisco01 server has only one replica link attribute in its /o=Ferguson&Bardell/ou=NAmerica-W naming context. SanFrancisco01 has a Reps-To-Ext attribute with server Boston01 listed in the following format: EX:/o=Ferguson&Bardell/ou=NAmerica-E/cn=Configuration/cn=Servers/cn=Boston01/cn=Microsoft DSA

This means that for this naming context, changes are sent to the Boston01 servers directory on request. Now, look at this naming context on the Boston01 server.

The Boston01 server has a value on the Reps-From field listing server SanFrancisco01. This value says changes are requested from the directory service on SanFrancisco01. It also provides other important information. For example, the Periodic Sync option is selected, which says changed information is requested based on the Period-Rep-Sync-Times attribute value. The Init Sync option is selected, which states that change requests are made on this naming context at directory startup. The Mail replica option is selected, which states that this naming context is replicated using a mail transport rather than RPC.

The USN value presented here is the last USN that was successfully replicated to this server for this naming context. What that means is that changes are requested from server SanFrancisco01 will have a higher USN number than 1485. The DSA-Signature is important because it uniquely identifies the replicating server in the organization.

Before continuing with the replication process note that the value of Period-Rep-Sync-Time is the same as the schedule specified for the Directory Replication object.

It is important to understand how the values that each Directory Replication Connector in the two sites placed in this field affects replication. For example, the schedule for the Directory Replication Connector in site NAmerica-E is set to replicate every two hours. The Directory Replication Connector in site NAmerica-W is set to **Always** (replication every 15 minutes). Therefore, site NAmerica-E will only request changes from the NAmerica-W site at the scheduled times.

Note You should not set replication to **Always** in a production environment unless near real-time replication is required and there is sufficient bandwidth and CPU available to handle the overhead.

It is important to remember that the NAmerica-W naming context is read-only within the NAmerica-E site. That means if site NAmerica-E changes the replication schedule, that change needs to be replicated to site NAmerica-W and replicated back to site NAmerica-E for the change to take effect for the /o=Ferguson&Bardell/ou=NAmerica-W naming context. In other words, there can be some latency between the schedule being changed and the schedule taking effect.

The Maria Black mailbox object it has been created on server SanFrancisco01 in the /o=Ferguson&Bardell/ou=NAmerica-W naming context. There is an entry on the Reps-From attribute for this naming context on server Boston01. Therefore, the requested changes for this naming context, based on the Period-Rep-Sync-Times schedule from server SanFrancisco01, are as follows:

1. Boston01 asks for changes for this naming context with a USN value higher than 1485 (from the Reps-From attribute).
2. SanFrancisco01 responds with the changes for the naming context.
3. Boston01 writes those changes into its local directory.
4. The directory sends Notify, Request, Response, and Write messages.

At this point, the replicated Maria Black mailbox object on server Boston01 in site NAmerica-E has the following object replication attributes on server Boston01.

Object replication attributes	Value
Obj-Dist-Name	/o=Ferguson&Bardell/ou=NAmerica-W/cn=Recipients/cn=Maria Black
DSA-Signature	D6149C3A935FD111AAEE00C04FB68E14
USN-Changed	2037
USN-Created	2037
USN-Source	1489

DSA-Signature is provided by server SanFrancisco01 because it was the last directory to modify the object. USN-Changed and USN-Created are 2037, new values unique to server Boston01. Finally, USN-Source is 1489, the USN-Changed value from server SanFrancisco01. Replication is complete between the two servers in different sites. Also of interest is the new USN value on the Reps-From attribute. Note that it has been updated to reflect that server Boston01 has received changes up to USN 1489.

Now that the object has been successfully replicated to the NAmerica-E site, it must be replicated to other servers within the site. A look at the naming context replication attributes of the /o=Ferguson&Bardell/ou=NAmerica-W shows that server Boston01 is responsible for replicating the content of this naming context to server NewYork01.

Based on the fact that server NewYork01 is listed in the Reps-To field, we know that we will replicate this object using intrasite replication methods.

1. Server Boston01 notifies server NewYork01 that there are changes to naming context /o=Ferguson&Bardell/ou=NAmerica-W(default notify every 5 minutes based on **Replicator notify pause after modify (secs)**.

2. Server NewYork01 requests the changes from server Boston01.

3. Server Boston01 responds with the changes.

4. Server NewYork01 writes the changes to its directory.

5. The directory sends Notify, Request, Response, Write messages.

At this point, the mailbox object Maria Black now exists on the NewYork01 server with the following replication attributes.

Object replication attributes	Value
Obj-Dist-Name	/o=Ferguson&Bardell/ou=NAmerica-W/cn=Recipients/cn=Maria Black
DSA-Signature	D6149C3A935FD111AAEE00C04FB68E14
USN-Changed	1360
USN-Created	1360
USN-Source	2037

Note that the DSA-Signature is that of server SanFrancisco01. This is because that was the last directory to modify the object. Also note that the USN-Source is the USN-Changed number from Boston01. That is because server Boston01 was the last remote directory to replicate the change to us. It does not matter that it was not the directory that made the change, only that it was the last directory to replicate the object to us.

Replication of the object throughout the organization is complete.

Resolving Conflicts

Directory replication conflicts can occur when an object is modified on two servers in the same site before the change has a chance to be replicated. Exchange uses the following method for handling conflicts during directory replication. When a change is received by the directory, it checks the Object-Version of the object. Usually the Object-Version is higher than the existing Object-Version of the object in the local directory, and the change is committed to the directory. If the Object-Version is lower, the change is ignored. If the Object-Version is the same, the directory compares the existing DSA-Signature of the object to the incoming DSA-Signature of the object. If the DSA-Signatures match, the change is committed to the directory again. If the DSA-Signatures are different, the directory uses the more recent change based on the When-Changed attribute of the object and applies that version of the object to the directory.

Replication Message Details

There are basically three types of directory replication messages:

- Notification
- Request
- Response

Note For the purpose of this document we are not differentiating between RPC and mail-based messages unless specifically stated in the text.

Notification Used by directory replication to notify servers on the Reps-To list that there are changes to a particular naming context. For example, if the Site naming context had changed, you would notify other servers on the Reps-To list about the change. The only information in the Notification message is:

- Notification of a change
- The name of the naming context and server that has changed

Request Can be triggered by the receipt of a Notification message or on a schedule based on the Period-Rep-Sync-Time. It can also be triggered through the Administrator program. The Request message includes:

- The name of the server from which the directory is requesting changes
- The naming context for which the directory is requesting a change
- The USN value of the last change received for that naming context

Responses Includes all the information that needs to be replicated, including object details. The Response message includes:

- The name of the server sending the changes
- The name of the naming context for which these changes are being sent
- The replicated objects including all object attributes (not just changed attributes)

When Response information is sent between servers, it is packaged based on the number of changes and not the size of the objects or the changes. During replication within a site, the maximum number of changes that can be sent in one RPC communication is 100. During replication between sites, the maximum number of changes that can be sent in one mail-based replication message is 512.

This means that if many changes have occurred to a particular naming context, it may take multiple messages to complete replication. The directory can commit changes from one Response message before it receives all changes, as long as the changes are in order.

Replication Attributes

The following are organization attributes.

Attribute name	Attribute type	Scope	Definition
Reps-From	Naming context replication attribute	Different on each naming context	Lists the servers the directory will accept changes from for the defined naming context.
Reps-To	Naming context replication attribute	Different on each naming context	Lists the servers who the directory will notify of changes and servers to whom the directory will send changes on Request for the defined naming context.
Reps-To-Ext	Naming context replication attribute	Different on each naming context	Lists the servers to whom changes will be sent on request for the defined naming context.
Period-Rep-Sync-Times	Naming context replication attribute	Different on each naming context	When the directory service will make a request for changes from servers on the Reps-From attribute list.

(continued)

Attribute name	Attribute type	Scope	Definition
Replicator notify pause after modify (secs)	Registry entry under HKEYLM\System\ CurrentControlSet\ Services\MSExchange DS\Parameters	Same for each naming context on a server	How long the directory service will wait to notify the other servers on the Reps-To list after a change has been made on a particular naming context.
Obj-Dist-Name	Object replication attribute	Unique per object, static throughout Organization	Object Distinguished Name (dn). X.500-type address used to uniquely identify an object throughout the organization.
Object-Version	Object replication attribute	Same across Organization, minus replication latency	Version of the object in the organization. Number of changes the object has had, including creation.
DSA-Signature	Object replication attribute	Same across Organization, minus replication latency	Invocation-ID of the last directory to modify the object.
USN-Changed	Object replication attribute	Unique to directory	USN value assigned by the local directory for the latest change, including creation.
USN-Created	Object replication attribute	Unique to directory	USN-Changed value assigned at object creation.
USN-Source	Object replication attribute	Unique to directory	Value of the USN-Changed attribute of the object from the remote directory that replicated the change to the local server.
Invocation-Id	Server attribute	Unique to directory	Used to uniquely identify each Exchange directory in the organization.
When-Changed	Object replication attribute	Unique to directory	Used during conflict resolution to determine the most recent change.

Object Replication State for Replication Examples

This section describes object replication states for replication between and within sites.

Note The server name that is represented by its DSA-Signature is used in these tables instead of the actual DSA-Signature.

Replication Within a Site

The following tables shows the state of the mailbox object Bill Lee before modification.

Server	DSA-Signature	USN-Changed	USN-Created	USN-Source
NewYork01	Boston01	1157	1157	1946
Boston01	Boston01	1946	1946	1946

The following table shows the state of the mailbox object Bill Lee after being modified on server NewYork01, and before it is replicated to server Boston01.

Server	DSA-Signature	USN-Changed	USN-Created	USN-Source
NewYork01	NewYork01	1220	1157	1946
Boston01	Boston01	1946	1946	1946

The following table shows the state of the mailbox object Bill Lee after being modified on server NewYork01 and after it has been replicated to server Boston01.

Server	DSA-Signature	USN-Changed	USN-Created	USN-Source
NewYork01	NewYork01	1220	1157	1946
Boston01	NewYork01	1966	1946	1220

Replication Between Sites

The following table shows the state of the mailbox object Maria Black when it is created on server SanFrancisco01, before it has been replicated.

Server	DSA-Signature	USN-Changed	USN-Created	USN-Source
NewYork01	N/A	N/A	N/A	N/A
Boston01	N/A	N/A	N/A	N/A
SanFrancisco01	SanFrancisco01	1489	1489	1489

The following table shows the state of the mailbox object Maria Black after replication from server SanFrancisco01 to server Boston01.

Server	DSA-Signature	USN-Changed	USN-Created	USN-Source
NewYork01	N/A	N/A	N/A	N/A
Boston01	SanFrancisco01	2037	2037	1489
SanFrancisco01	SanFrancisco01	1489	1489	1489

The following table shows the state of the mailbox object Maria Black after replication from server Boston01 to server NewYork01.

Server	DSA-Signature	USN-Changed	USN-Created	USN-Source
NewYork01	SanFrancisco01	1360	1360	2037
Boston01	SanFrancisco01	2037	2037	1489
SanFrancisco01	SanFrancisco01	1489	1489	1489

PART 4

Administering and Maintaining

Maintenance is essential to the high-quality performance of your messaging system. Perform regular maintenance on your server and make sure you understand how to back up and restore servers. Failure to perform system maintenance can cause performance degradation and increase the risk of disasters, such as server failures and the loss of critical data.

System Maintenance Overview

The best way to ensure optimal performance of your system is to develop a maintenance plan, a backup plan, and a disaster recovery plan.

The process of maintaining a high-quality system includes:

- Planning maintenance
- Performing maintenance
- Reviewing event logs
- Monitoring performance
- Performing trend analysis
- Diagnosing and correcting problems
- Evaluating the organization's changing needs

Planning Maintenance

Putting together an effective maintenance plan includes:

- Developing maintenance guidelines and procedures
- Scheduling and tracking maintenance to ensure all requirements are met
- Documenting completed maintenance to create a historical record
- Developing topology maps to identify all the major components in your messaging environment

- Designing and configuring the system so that duplicate components can continue to operate during maintenance downtime
- Training administrators on maintenance guidelines and procedures
- For more information on planning maintenance, see the Microsoft Exchange Maintenance and Troubleshooting documentation.

Performing Maintenance Tasks

Tasks that should be done routinely to ensure reliability of your Microsoft Exchange Server installation include:

- Monitoring the information store
- Verifying replicated directory information
- Performing backups
- Moving mailboxes and public folders
- Creating, modifying, and removing old mailboxes
- Cleaning mailboxes
- Creating, modifying, and removing old e-mail addresses
- Making batch changes to mailboxes, distribution lists, and custom recipients
- For more information on performing maintenance tasks, see the Microsoft Exchange Maintenance and Troubleshooting documentation.

Reviewing Event Logs

Exchange writes messages to the Microsoft Windows NT Server application log. These messages contain important information about the completion of normal tasks such as directory replication, as well as error messages about problems that occur.

You should review the messages in the application log on a regular basis. If you have problems with your Exchange Server, be sure to save the application log in case it is needed by Microsoft Product Support.

The *Microsoft BackOffice Server* compact disc contains a complete database of messages written by Exchange. The database is provided as a Help file. To install the database on your computer, copy the files Exmsgref.hlp and Exmsgref.cnt from the \Exchange\Docs directory of the compact disc to a working directory.

For quick reference, the following table lists the source identifier for a message displayed by the Windows NT Event Viewer, and the Exchange component that generates that message. The message database contains the complete details about each message.

Source	Component Name
CCMailProxy	Microsoft Exchange Server Administrator Program
EDB	Exchange Dababase Engine
ESE97	Microsoft Extensible Store Engine
InternetProxy	Microsoft Exchange Server Administrator Program
Loadsim	Microsoft Exchange Server Load Simulator
MAPI	Messaging API (MAPI)
MSExchange IMAP4 Interface	Microsoft Exchange Server Information Store
MSExchange NNTP Interface	Microsoft Exchange Server Information Store
MSExchange Pop3 Interface	Microsoft Exchange Server Information Store
MSExchangeAdmin	Microsoft Exchange Server Administrator Program
MSExchangeATMTA	Microsoft Mail Connector
MSExchangeCCMC	Microsoft Exchange Connector for Lotus cc:Mail
MSExchangeChat	Microsoft Exchange Chat Service
MSExchangeDS	Microsoft Exchange Directory Service
MSExchangeDSExp	Microsoft Exchange Server Administrator Program
MSExchangeDSImp	Microsoft Exchange Server Administrator Program
MSExchangeDX	Microsoft Mail Directory Synchronization
MSExchangeES	Microsoft Exchange Event Service
MSExchangeFB	Microsoft Schedule+ Free/Busy Connector
MSExchangeIMC	Internet Mail Service
MSExchangeIS	Microsoft Exchange Server Information Store
MSExchangeIS Private	Microsoft Exchange Server Information Store
MSExchangeIS Public	Microsoft Exchange Server Information Store
MSExchangeKMS	Microsoft Exchange Advanced Security
MSExchangeMig	Microsoft Exchange Migration Wizard
MSExchangeMigDS	Microsoft Exchange Server Administrator Program
MSExchangeMSMI	Microsoft Mail Connector
MSExchangeMTA	Microsoft Exchange Server Message Transfer Agent

(continued)

Source	Component Name
MSExchangeNTExt	Microsoft Exchange Server Administrator Program
MSExchangeNWExt	Microsoft Exchange Server Administrator Program
MSExchangeSA	Microsoft Exchange Server Administrator Program
MSExchangeSetup	Microsoft Exchange Server Administrator Program
MSExchangeWEB	Microsoft Outlook Web Access
MSProxy	Microsoft Exchange Server Administrator Program
NT Backup	Microsoft Extensible Store Engine
X400Proxy	Microsoft Exchange Server Administrator Program
<name of MS Mail (PC) MTA service>	Microsoft Mail Connector

Monitoring Performance

Monitor the following to ensure that Exchange continues to perform reliably:

- Server performance, to make sure it is optimized
- Message transfers by the message transfer agent (MTA), connectors, and gateways, to ensure messages are routed appropriately and to eliminate bottlenecks
- Statistics for Exchange components, to ensure that server resources are being used appropriately
- Directory and public folder replication, to ensure that directories and public folders are replicated and synchronized correctly

Performing Trend Analysis

Trend analysis is the evaluation of historical trends in system performance data to identify and diagnose problems as they develop. Trend analysis can help you identify the changing needs of your organization.

Configure and use Windows NT Performance Monitor to identify trends. On the basis of these trends, you can add system resources or reconfigure the system to meet the changing needs of your organization.

For information about Performance Monitor, see "Monitoring" later in this section, and in your Windows NT documentation.

Diagnosing and Correcting Problems

Exchange and Windows NT provide the following tools and resources to help you diagnose and correct common problems:

- Performance Monitor and event logs, to view system data
- Diagnostics logging in the Windows NT event log, to gather information about problem areas
- Message tracking, to help gather information about message transfer problems
- Message queue property pages, to view queues, change message priorities, and delete messages

For information about diagnosing and correcting problems, see Part 8, "Troubleshooting."

Evaluating the Organization's Changing Needs

As the needs of your organization change, a maintenance plan ensures that the system is reconfigured periodically and resources are added appropriately. For example, if many new users join your system each week and message traffic increases rapidly, you can use trend analysis to anticipate load imbalances and message bottlenecks. You can then adjust routing costs and add more servers, information stores, or connectors as necessary.

Developing Disaster Recovery Strategies

Proper routine maintenance can greatly reduce the need for disaster recovery except in the case of natural disasters. However, disasters can occur to your messaging system and cause you to lose key components or critical data. Disasters range from losing the information store when your hard disk fails to losing an entire data center during an earthquake.

The following tasks can help you recover from disasters and minimize downtime and loss of productivity:

- Performing and verifying timely backups
- Implementing and practicing a disaster recovery plan
- Using dedicated recovery systems and recovery toolkits
- Training administrators to implement the disaster recovery plan
- Considering server design and configuration when developing your plan

For more information on disaster recovery planning, see Part 9, "Disaster Recovery."

Recording Server Configuration

The following tables illustrate examples of server configuration sheets that you can use when setting up your hardware and software specifications.

Hardware Configuration

You can use the following hardware table to record hardware specifications for your organization.

Hardware Item	Description
Computer model	
Display model	
Serial number	
BackPlane	
CPU	
Hard disk(s)	
Floppy disk	
RAM	
Network adapter	
SCSI card	
CD-ROM	
Tape backup	
Network type	

Windows NT Installation Configuration

You can use the following Windows NT installation table to record specifications for your organization.

Item	Description
Windows NT Server Version	
Windows NT Server Role	
Domain Name	
Computer Name	
Install Director	
Swap File	
Protocols	
Disk Configuration	

(continued)

Item	Description
Licensing	
Printer	
Special Groups	
This computer's IP Address	
Subnet Mask	
Default Gateway	

Microsoft Exchange Server Installation

You can use the following table to record Microsoft Exchange Server specifications for your organization.

Item	Description
Organization name	
Site name	
Computer name	
Service account	
Service account password	
Connectors	

Microsoft Exchange Performance Optimizer

Running Microsoft Exchange Performance Optimizer is important during recovery to ensure that the recovery server is tuned properly. Hardware being equal, similar performance can be experienced following a full restore when Exchange is reinstalled to a recovery server. Note that the Performance Optimizer log stored in the Winnt\System32\perfopt.log directory does not display the specific settings that were chosen during optimization.

Server Name: _____

Estimated Number of Users	X	Type of Server	X	Number in Organization	X	Limit Memory Usage (MB)
Less than 500		Private store		Less than 1,000		
500 - 999		Public store		1,000 - 9,999		

(continued)

Estimated Number of Users	X	Type of Server	X	Number in Organization	X	Limit Memory Usage (MB)
1,000 - 4,999		Connector/directory import		10,000 - 99,999		
5,000 - 24,999		Multiserver		100,000 - 499,999		
25,000 - 49,999		POP3/IMAP4/ NNTP only		500,000 or more		
50,000 or more						

Component Locations

The following table lists the names of Exchange components and their locations.

Component	Location
Private information store	Exchsrvr\Mdbdata
Public information store	Exchsrvr\Mdbdata
Information store logs	Exchsrvr\Mdbdata
Directory service	Exchsrvr\Dsadata
Directory service logs	Exchsrvr\Dsadata
Message transfer agent	Exchsrvr\Mtadata
Internet Mail Service	Exchsrvr\Imcdata

Server Backups

Always back up your Exchange computers so that you can restore servers with minimum downtime in the event of a disaster.

Use Windows NT Backup to back up the information store and directory. In addition, keep records of critical Windows NT settings, such as the production server Internet Protocol (IP) address information and computer name. Note that some optional components, such as the Key Management server (KM server), have their own backup procedures.

You only need to back up and restore the directory and information store, because other components (such as the MTA and Microsoft Mail Connector) contain highly transient data. For example, backing up the MTA records messages that are delivered seconds after the backup and then restoring this information might result in duplicate messages.

Note Any values you have manually configured in the Windows NT Registry should be reconfigured after reinstalling Exchange.

For information about backing up servers, restoring the information store, and restoring the directory, see Part 9, "Disaster Recovery," and *Microsoft Exchange Server Maintenance and Troubleshooting*.

Services Required for Backup

In order to back up Exchange, the directory and the information store services must both be running on the server. If one of the services is not running or is unresponsive, the backup will fail.

Permissions Required for Backup

Only Backup Operator permissions are required for a backup. However, to log on to the console, Server Operator permissions or higher are needed. Windows NT Backup uses the permissions of the current logon to do the backup. Third-party backup utilities run as Windows NT Server services that use permissions from their service startup parameters, which are typically the permissions set to the Exchange service account.

Defining Data to Back Up

You must back up two types of data — user data and configuration data. Exchange user data is stored in the public information store (Pub.edb) and the private information store (Priv.edb), personal folder (.pst) files, offline folder (.ost) files, personal address (.pab) books (PABs), and transaction logs. Exchange configuration data is stored in the Exchange directory (Dir.edb), the Windows NT registry, and in various subdirectories in the Exchange installation path (and potentially in paths created after you run Performance Optimizer). Depending on the type of backup and restoration required, these data points must be considered in your procedures.

The Exchange database files are located in the directories shown in the table below. Although the default path of the Exchsrvr directory is used in this table, you can change the location of the database files. To place the transaction logs on a separate physical disk from the information store and directory files, run Performance Optimizer. You can also reconfigure the paths for all database files by using the **Database Paths** property page for the server object.

Data	Path Name
Private information store	Exchsrvr\Mdbdata\Priv.edb
Public information store	Exchsrvr\Mdbdata\Pub.edb
Directory	Exchsrvr\Dsadata\Dir.edb
Information store transaction logs	Exchsrvr\Mdbdata*.log

Creating and Verifying Daily Backups

Creating and verifying daily backups is a critical step in successful disaster recovery. Failure to verify backups is one of the most common mistakes administrators make because they often assume that backup tapes are being swapped and that data is being properly backed up. Make it part of your daily routine to review all backup logs, and then follow up on any errors or inconsistencies.

Full (normal) backups reset transaction logs and then remove them, which creates free disk space. Free disk space is less of an issue if circular logging is enabled. If circular logging is not enabled and daily full backups fail, transaction logs are not purged, and they can fill up the entire transaction log disk drive.

Backing up Manually

A dynamic-link library (DLL) (Edbbcli.dll) that extends the Windows NT Ntbackup.exe program is available on the Exchange compact disc. One of the benefits of Exchange and the Ntbackup.exe program is that they provide live backup of the information store and directory without interrupting the messaging system. Ntbackup.exe also provides file-based backup services that back up the Windows NT registry.

Exchange does not have to be taken offline to perform backups. The entire information store, directory, MTA, and system attendant remain in service during an online backup. Although the information store and directory can be backed up online, files in directories that are being accessed by other Exchange for Windows NT services, such as the Directory Synchronization Component or Microsoft Mail Connector (Appletalk) MTA, should be backed up when the respective service is not running. You can automate and schedule backups by using the Winat.exe command.

When you want to back up your files manually, you can use command-line switches with Ntbackup.exe.

Caution   In a batch file, limit the command line to 256 characters. Exceeding this limit can result in files not being backed up and can stop the process without warning.

The syntax for this command is as follows:

Ntbackup operation path [**/a**][**/v**][**/r**][**/d**"*text*"][**/b**][**/hc**:{**on** | **off**}] [**/t**{option}][**/l**"*file name*"][**/e**][**/tape**:{n}]

Ntbackup switches are listed in the following table.

Switch	Description
Path	If backing up a drive, specifies one or more paths of the directories to be backed up. If backing up Exchange components, specifies the component and the server as <*DS server /IS server*>. Server is the name of the server you are backing up, preceded by two backslashes. "DS" indicates that you are backing up the directory, and "IS" indicates that you are backing up the information store.
/a	Adds backup sets after the last backup set on the tape. When **/a** is not specified, the program reuses the tape and replaces previous data. When more than one drive is specified but **/a** is not, the program overwrites the contents of the tape with the information from the first drive selected and then appends the backup sets for the remaining drives.
/v	Verifies the operation.
/r	Restricts access.
/d "text"	Specifies a description of the backup contents.
/b	Specifies that the local registry is to be backed up.
/hc:on or **/hc:off**	Specifies that hardware compression is on or off.
/t <*option*>	Specifies the backup type. The option can be one of the following: normal, copy, incremental, differential, or daily.
Normal	All selected files or Exchange components are backed up and marked as such on the disk.
Copy	All selected files or Exchange components are backed up, but they are not marked as such on the disk.

(continued)

Switch	Description
Incremental	Among the selected files or Exchange components, only those that have been modified are backed up and marked as such on the disk.
Differential	The selected files or Exchange components that have been modified are backed up, but they are not marked as such on the disk.
Daily	Among the selected files, only those that have been modified the same day are backed up, but they are not marked as such on the disk. This can be useful if you want to take work home and need a quick way to select the files that you worked on that day. This option is not available when you are backing up Exchange components.
/l "file name"	Specifies the file name for the backup log.
/e	Specifies that the backup log includes exceptions only.
/tape:<n>	Specifies the tape drive to which the files should be backed up, where n is a number from zero through nine that corresponds to the tape drive number listed in the registry.

Automating Online Backup

Use the following procedure to automate online backups of the information store and directory service.

1. From the *Microsoft Windows NT Resource Kit* compact disc, install the Winat.exe program on the local Windows NT directory of your local computer.

2. Create a Windows NT common group called Microsoft Exchange Server Backup.

3. Create an icon for the Backup.log file. This provides quick access to review the backup log for review.

4. Copy the Ntbackup.exe icon from the Administrative Tools group to the Exchange Backup group.

5. Create an icon for Winat.exe in the Exchange Backup group.

6. In Windows NT Control Panel, double-click **Services**.

7. Select the Schedule service, and then choose **Startup**. Configure for automatic startup and assign an ID that is a member of the Windows NT Backup Operators group. Make sure you enter the correct password. If the administrator ID password changes, you must change the password for the Schedule service. This account must also have "Admin Role" rights within the Microsoft Exchange Organization Site and Configuration containers you are backing up.

8. Start the Schedule service.

9. Create the backup batch file. Name this file Back.bat, and save it in the Winnt subdirectory.

10. Run the Winat.exe program, and then schedule the Back.bat file. You do not need to have a logon session on the computer on which Winat.exe is running, because the Schedule service logs on to perform the operation under the defined security context.

11. Set the batch job for interactive mode.

Windows AT Command Scheduler

When you use Windows AT Command Scheduler, the Windows NT Schedule service runs all jobs that have been scheduled. Because batch jobs are run in the context of the Schedule service, Windows NT security must be considered. When configuring the Schedule service, configure the account as a member of the Windows NT Backup Operators group. This enables a full backup of the information store and directory.

Make sure the Back.bat jobs are set for interactive. This is required by the Ntbackup.exe program.

Sample Batch File for Online Backup

The following is a sample batch file you can use for backing up your files while the server remains online.

```
rem ** 3/7/96 Backup Written by <name>
rem ** This will back up the information store and directory service on
<server_name 1> and <server_name 2>.
ntbackup backup DS \\Server_name1 IS \\Server_name1 /v /d "Server-name1
IS-DS" /b /t Normal /l c:\winnt\backup.log /e
ntbackup backup DS \\Server_name2 IS \\Server_name2 /a /v /d
"Server_name2 IS-DS" /b /t Normal /l c:\winnt\backup.log /e
exit
```

Sample Batch Files for Offline Backup

The following are sample batch files you can use for backing up your files when the server is offline. You may need to experiment with the order in which you stop the services, so that you are not prompted when a service is dependent upon the one you are stopping.

Example 1

```
rem ** Stop Microsoft Exchange services.
rem ** You can stop Microsoft Exchange services and restart them
automatically to backup.
rem ** Files that a particular service may hold open
REM // stop all services
echo Stopping Services...
net stop MSExchangeMSMI
net stop MSExchangePCMTA
net stop MSExchangeFB
net stop MSExchangeDX
net stop MSExchangeIMC
net stop MSExchangeMTA
net stop MSExchangeIS
net stop MSExchangeDS
net stop MSExchangeSA
ntbackup backup c:\ d:\ /a /v /d "Full File Based Backup" /b /l
c:\winnt\backup.log /e
REM edbutil OPTIONS
net start MSExchangeSA
net start MSExchangeDS
net start MSExchangeIS
net start MSExchangeMTA
net start MSExchangeIMC
net start MSExchangeDX
net start MSExchangeFB
net start MSExchangePCMTA
net start MSExchangeMSMI
```

Example 2

You can start and stop Microsoft Mail (PC) MTA (PCMTA) services by enclosing the service name in quotation marks. You can determine the service names from the Exchange Administrator program or Windows NT Control Panel, or by viewing the Windows NT registry.

If you are viewing the Windows NT Registry, open the following registry key:

HKEY_LOCAL_MACHINE\SYSTEM\CurrentControlSet\Services

All services are listed in alphabetical order.

```
rem Batch File To Stop and Restart Microsoft Exchange Services
rem For File Based Backup
echo Stopping Services ...
net stop MSExchangeMSMI
net stop MSExchangePCMTA
net stop MSExchangeFB
net stop MSExchangeDX
net stop MSExchangeMTA
net stop MSExchangeIMC
net stop MSExchangeIS
net stop MSExchangeDS

net stop "PC MTA - HUB"
net stop MSExchangeSA

ntbackup BACKUP d:\exchsrvr\mdbdata /v /d "File Based Backup" /b /l
c:\winnt\backup.log /e
net start MSExchangeSA
net start MSExchangeDS
net start MSExchangeIS
net start MSExchangeMTA
net start MSExchangeIMC
net start MSExchangeDX
net start MSExchangeFB
net start MSExchangePCMTA
net start MSExchangeMSMI
net start "PC MTA - HUB"
```

Restoring Data After a Catastrophe

If a server is catastrophically destroyed, the data must be restored from a backup. For procedures, see Part 9, "Disaster Recovery." In addition, note the following:

- You cannot restore the directory to a computer in a different Windows NT domain. Make sure you add the restored machine to the original Windows NT domain.

- If the Microsoft Exchange Server you are restoring is a primary domain controller, as can be the case in small remote sites, the security ID on the restored server must match the security ID of the original server. If the security IDs do not match, you cannot access the information store until you restore only the information store and then manually rebuild the Windows NT accounts.

Log Files and Circular Logging

To optimize recoverability, log files can be used to recover message transaction data if a hardware failure corrupts the information store or the directory database files, provided you have backed up the logs or the logs are intact. Log files are usually maintained on a physical disk drive separate from the information store and directory database files.

If database files are damaged, a backup can be restored and any data that has not been backed up but has been recorded in the transaction logs can be played back. These transactions are entered into the restored database file to bring the database up-to-date to the point in time where the database files were damaged.

Using Log Files

The directory and information store services use the following logs and files:

- Transaction logs
- Previous logs
- Checkpoint files
- Reserved logs
- Patch files

Exchange maintains several database files. The information store consists of two databases — the private information store (Priv.edb) and public information store (Pub.edb). The Exchange directory is stored in the Dir.edb file.

Exchange services use transaction log files for each database. Exchange implements the log files to accept, track, and maintain data. To optimize performance and recoverability, all message transactions are written immediately to log files and to memory, and then to their respective database files. Transaction records are written to the log files sequentially and are always appended to the end of the file. However, transaction records are distributed across the database files rather than written sequentially.

Transaction Logs

Transaction logs can be kept on a physical drive that is separate from their respective .edb files. However, by default, information store logs are maintained in the Exchsrvr\Mdbdata directory and directory service logs are maintained in Exchsrvr\Dsadata directory.

Each subdirectory contains an Edb.log file, which is the current transaction log file for the respective service. Both the information store subdirectory and the directory service subdirectories maintain separate Edb.log files. Log files should always be 5,242,880 bytes in size; if they are not this size, they are probably damaged.

Because transactions are first written to the Edb.log files and then written to the database, the current actual or effective database is a combination of the uncommitted transactions in the transaction log file, which also reside in memory, and the actual .edb database file.

Previous Logs

Each Exchange database transaction is written to the transaction log before being written to the database. At any given time there will be an "inactive" part of the transaction log consisting of transactions that have already been committed to the database, and an "active" part consisting of transactions still to be committed. During an online, full backup or an online, incremental backup, the "inactive" part of the transaction log is deleted.

The transaction log comprises a set of files, each of which is exactly 5 megabytes (MB) in size. New transactions are written to the file Edb.log. As the Edb.log file becomes full (that is, after 5 MB of transactions have been written to it), it is renamed and a new Edb.log file is created. The renamed log file is stored in the same subdirectory as the Edb.log file but is not committed to the database. Log files are named in a sequential order using hexadecimal numbers (for example, Edb00009.log, Edb0000A.log, and so on).

Note When circular logging is enabled, previous .log files are not maintained and therefore are not purged by backup operations. Incremental and differential online backups are not permitted when circular logging is enabled.

When the service is shut down normally (that is, with no errors), transactions in log files are committed to the respective .edb file. For example, when the information store service is shut down normally, transactions that existed in log files and not in Priv.edb or Pub.edb files are committed to the .edb files. Note that .log files should not be manually purged while services are running. In general, it is best to purge logs using the backup process.

Checkpoint Files

Checkpoint files are used to recover data from transaction logs into .edb files. The checkpoint is the place marker within the Edb.chk file that indicates which transactions have been committed. Separate Edb.chk files are maintained by the information store and the directory service. Whenever data is written to an .edb file from the transaction log, the Edb.chk file is updated with information that indicates the transaction was successfully committed to its .edb file.

During the data recovery process, Exchange determines which transactions have not yet been committed to the respective .edb file by reading the Edb.chk file or by reading the transaction log files directly. Note that the Edb.chk file is not required.

The information store and the directory service each read their Edb.chk file during startup. Any transactions that have not been committed are restored into the .edb files from the transaction logs. For example, if an outage occurs on an Exchange computer, and transactions have been recorded into the transaction log but have not yet been installed to the actual database file, Exchange attempts to recover this data upon startup, by transferring transactions from the logs to the respective database files automatically.

Reserved Logs

The directory and information store services each independently maintain two reserve files — Res1.log and Res2.log. These files are stored in the Mdbdata and Dsadata directories. Reserve log files are used when the directory or information store service renames its Edb.log file and attempts to create a new Edb.log file without enough disk space available. This is a fail-safe mechanism that is only used in the event of an emergency. When this situation occurs, an error message is sent to the respective service. The service flushes any transactions in memory that have not yet been written to a transaction log into the Res1.log file and, if necessary, the Res2.log file. When this process is complete, the service shuts down and records an event in the Windows NT Event Log. Note that like other transaction log files, RES (reserve) transaction log files are always 5 MB.

Patch Files

The patch file mechanism was designed for situations where transactions are written to a database during a backup. A convenient feature of Exchange is the ability to back up databases without interrupting service to end users.

During the backup operation, data is read from the .edb files. If a transaction is made to a section of the .edb file that has already been backed up, it is recorded in a patch (.pat) file. If a transaction is made to a section of the .edb file that has not yet been backed up, it is processed and does not need to be written to the patch file. A separate .pat file is used for each database — Priv.pat, Pub.pat, and Dir.pat. Note that these .pat files are exposed only during the backup process. The online backup operation process is as follows:

1. A .pat file is created for the current database.
2. The backup operation for the current .edb file begins.
3. Transactions that must be written to sections of the .edb file that have already been backed up are recorded to both the .edb file and the .pat file.

4. The .pat file is written to the backup tape.

5. The .pat file is deleted from the Mdbdata or Dsadata directory.

Temp.edb File

The Temp.edb file is used to store transactions that are in progress. Temp.edb also is used for some transient storage during online compaction.

Purging Log Files

When circular logging is disabled, log files accumulate on the transaction log disk drive until an online normal (full) or incremental backup is performed. The online backup operation process is as follows:

1. The backup process copies the specified database files.

2. Patch files are created as required. During a backup operation, patch files maintain transactions written to the portion of an .edb file that has already been backed up.

3. Log files created during the backup process are copied to tape.

4. Patch files are written to tape.

5. Log files older than the checkpoint at the start of the backup operation are purged. These files are not required because the transactions have already been committed to the .edb files and the .edb files have been written to tape.

Using Database Circular Logging

Circular logging is enabled by default. Database circular logging uses transaction log technology but does not maintain all previous transaction log files. Instead, a few log files are maintained and eventually purged as new log files are created. Although circular logging helps manage disk space and prevents the buildup of transaction log files, you cannot perform differential and incremental backups because these backups rely on past transaction log files.

When database circular logging is enabled, you may see several Edbxxxxx.log files in the Mdbdata or Dsadata directories because Exchange maintains a window of four log files for circular logging. However, if the server input/output (I/O) load is large, more than four log files will be used.

▶ **To verify whether database circular logging settings are enabled**

1. In the Administrator program, choose a server, and then select **Configuration**.

2. Select the server object within the Servers container.

3. From the **File** menu, click **Properties**.

4. Click the **Advanced** tab.

Circular logging can be set separately for the information store and directory, and you can change these settings at any time by using the Administrator program. However, Exchange will stop the corresponding service and restart it after making changes.

Maintaining Address Book Views

Address Book views is a feature that allows administrators to control which entries users are allowed to see in the global address book. This feature also allows users to sort their views of the Address Book by mailbox attribute, depending on the permissions they have been granted by the administrator. Address Book views are grouped into containers comprised of recipients with common attributes.

When you create an Address Book view, you can group mailboxes by any four of eight standard attributes and ten custom defined attributes. Subcontainers are created that correspond to the four groupings. In addition, you, as an administrator, can assign search roles to the view. The search role limits who has access to an address book view. Thus, you can limit users' search capabilities to only those containers for which they have permissions.

Clients not on a local area network (LAN) or wide area network (WAN) who are working offline will see a different view. They will view the offline Address Book. If Address Book views for the offline Address Book are put in place before the first synchronization of the offline Address Book, the offline user is presented with a choice of address book views to download, depending on their permissions. However, if the client who is working offline has downloaded a full copy of the offline Address Book before the address views have been implemented, that client will always be able to see the full membership of the offline Address Book. If you subsequently limit that client's access by using address book views, the client will still be able to view all the members of the Address Book that were replicated to the offline Address Book.

Lightweight Directory Access Protocol (LDAP) clients can access Exchange Address Books, and the same permissions and views apply as for Messaging Application Programming Interface (MAPI) clients.

For more information, see *Microsoft Exchange Server Operations.*

Moving Users

You can move mailboxes from one server to another server in a site by choosing **Move Mailbox** from the **Tools** menu in the Administrator program. However, you can only move the mailboxes to the Recipients container. If this is acceptable, using the **Move Mailbox** command is the easiest way to move mailboxes. If it is not acceptable, see the following section, "Moving Exchange to Another Computer."

Moving Exchange to Another Computer

You might need to move Exchange from one computer to another computer. This section outlines the procedure required to move Exchange from one computer to another.

The steps you perform to move a server to another computer vary depending on whether the computer names and hardware platforms are the same.

- If the servers have different, unique computer names, use procedure A (Enterprise edition or Standard edition). When you perform procedure A, it doesn't matter whether the hardware platforms are the same or different. For example, you can move Exchange from an Intel computer to an Alpha computer, or from an Intel computer to another Intel computer.

- If the servers have the same computer names and hardware platforms, use procedure B.

- If the servers have the same computer names, but different hardware platforms, use procedure C.

Be sure to read the following introduction before you proceed with any of the procedures described in the following sections.

You can move Exchange from one computer (Server A) to another computer (Server B), if Server B is either in the same Windows NT domain as Server A or is in a Windows NT domain that has a trust relationship with the domain that contains Server A.

Before moving Exchange to another computer, take these precautions:

- Verify that a domain controller is available. Before moving Exchange to the new computer, verify that the computer to be replaced is not the only Windows NT domain controller in the domain. After this computer is brought down as part of the procedure to move Exchange, there must be another domain controller that can validate Windows NT logon requests.

- If Exchange is being moved from a primary domain controller computer, make sure there is at least one other backup domain controller in the Windows NT domain. After bringing down the computer to be moved, upgrade the backup domain controller to a primary domain controller.

- If the computer to be moved is a backup domain controller, make sure that the domain's primary domain controller is running and operational, or at a minimum, that there is another backup domain controller computer that can be upgraded to the primary domain controller.

Procedure A

The steps for moving a server differ depending on whether the server is running the Enterprise edition of Exchange or the Standard edition. Perform the steps in the following sections if you're moving a server running the Enterprise edition of Exchange to a computer with a different computer name. Note that the two computers do not need to have the same hardware platform. These steps are describe in more detail in the following sections.

Procedure A for the Enterprise Edition

Perform the following steps if you are moving a server running the Enterprise edition of Exchange to a computer with a different name. These steps are described in more detail in the following sections.

1. Back up the original server.
2. Export mailboxes from the original server.
3. Install Exchange on the new server computer.
4. Move public folders, mailboxes, and user messages.
5. Move the services.
6. Recreate the distribution lists.
7. Move the connectors.
8. Remove the original server from the site.

▶ **To back up the original server (Server A)**

1. Stop all services on Server A.

2. Back up the entire Exchsrvr directory.

   If the logs and database files are on different drives, make sure you back these up as well, or run Performance Optimizer and move all logs and databases to the Exchsrvr directory where Exchange was installed. Make sure there is enough free disk space to move these files back.

   If you have the KM server installed, make sure to back up the Security directory that was created by default on drive C: by KM server. Note, however, that the Security directory might not be under the Exchsrvr directory. You also need to back up the KM server startup disk.

▶ **To export mailboxes**

1. From the Support\Sample\Csvs\Mailbox directory on the Microsoft Exchange Server compact disc, copy Mailbox.csv to the Server A hard drive.

2. Clear the **Read-Only** check box for this file.

3. From the Support\Samples\csvs\Dl directory on the Microsoft Exchange Server compact disc, copy Dl.csv to the hard drive.

4. Clear the **Read-Only** check box for this file.

5. In the Microsoft Exchange Server Administrator window, click **Directory Export** from the **Tools** menu.

6. In the **Directory Export** dialog box, under **Export objects**, select only the **Mailboxes** check box.

7. In the **Home Server** list, click **Server A**.

8. Select the **Include subcontainers** check box, and then select Mailbox.csv as the export file.

9. Edit Mailbox.csv to change all occurrences of Server A to Server B. Save the file as Mailbox-Server B.csv. If there is more than one top-level container, you must perform steps 7 through 9 for each one. Be sure to use unique file names.

10. In the Administrator window, on the **Tools** menu, click **Directory Export**.

11. Select only the **Distribution list** check box.

12. Under the **Home Server** list, click **All**.

13. Click the **Include subcontainers** check box, and then select Dl.csv as the output file. If there is more than one top-level container, you must perform steps 10 through 13 for each one. Be sure to use unique file names.

▶ **To install Microsoft Exchange on the New Server (Server B)**

1. If Server A is a primary domain controller and you do not plan to leave it running after moving Exchange, install Windows NT on Server B and make it a backup domain controller in the Windows NT domain where Server A is located.

2. Install Exchange on Server B, joining the Exchange site of Server A.

3. Install the same connectors on Server B that were installed on Server A.

4. Upgrade Server B to the same Exchange service pack as Server A.

5. Check to see that all users on Server A appear in the global address list for Server B. It might take some time for the list to become populated.

If Server A was the first server to be installed in the site, add instances of the Organization Forms, Microsoft Schedule+ Free/Busy Information, and offline Address Book folders to the public information store on Server B.

By default, the first server in a site contains and is responsible for the site folders, which consist of the offline Address Book folder, the Microsoft Schedule+ Free/Busy Information folder, and the Organizational Forms folder, if one exists. Other servers installed in the site rely, by default, on the first server for this information.

The following procedure ensures that all folders in the site are replicated to Server B. After all steps for moving Server A to Server B are completed, individual public folders can be removed from the public information store on Server B if there are replicas of these folders on other servers in the same Exchange site.

▶ **To move public folders to Server B**

1. In the Administrator window, double-click Server B, and then click **Public Information Store**.

2. On the **File** menu choose **Properties**, and then click the **Instances** tab. All of the public folders on Server A should appear.

3. In the **Public folders** list, select all folders, and then click **Add** to move all the public folders to the local information store on Server B.

4. In the Administrator window, choose a server, and then choose a site.

5. Click **Public Information Store**, and then click **Public Folder Resources**.

6. Change the **Public Folder Server** setting to Server B.

7. In the Administrator window, click **Configuration**.

8. Double-click **DS Site Configuration**.

9. Click the **Offline Address Book** tab.

10. In the **Offline Address Book server** list, select Server B.

▶ **To reassign routing calculation**

1. In the Administrator window, click **Configuration**.

2. Double-click **Site Addressing**.

3. Click the **General** tab.

4. In the **Routing calculation server** list, select Server B.

5. Note that **Apply** is not enabled when you select Server B from the **Routing calculation server** list. To enable this option and ensure that the change to the routing calculation server setting is recorded, in the **Display Name** box, add and then remove any character.

6. In the Administrator window, choose **Recipients**, and then for each distribution list, verify on the **Distribution List** property sheet that the expansion server is not set to Server A.

Move all the mailboxes on Server A to Server B, keeping the mailboxes in the same containers or subcontainers they were in on Server A.

▶ **To move mailboxes to Server B**

1. Select all mailboxes in the Server Recipients container on Server A.

2. On the **Tools** menu in the Administrator program, click **Move Mailbox**.

3. Select Server B as the destination server.

▶ **To move the KM server**

Note   Server B must be set up as a Cert Server client to the same Cert Server to which Server A was a client.

---

1. Stop the KM server service on Server A. This is very important because it closes all transactions with the KM server database, making everything consistent.

2. Back up the Kmsdata directory on Server A by copying all .edb files in the directory to a safe place, such as tape or a network drive.

3. Uninstall the KM server from Server A by running Microsoft Exchange Server Setup, choosing **Add/Remove** at the prompt, and then deselecting the KM server component.

4. Install the KM server on Server B by running Microsoft Exchange Server Setup.exe, choosing **Add/Remove**, and then selecting KM server. Choose the same location for the KM server password that was used on Server A. Make sure that you do not write over your original password.

5. Delete all files in the Kms directory on Server B. The .log and .chk files will be recreated after you start the KM server service.

6. Copy all the .edb files you backed up in step 2 to the Kmsdata directory on Server B.

7. On Server B, start the KM server service with the original password from Server A. Complete the next steps, if either version 2 or version 3 was installed on Server A.

8. Install Microsoft Exchange Server version 5.5 Service Pack 1.

9. Open the Certificate Administrator object and select Enrollment property page.

10. Change to the option that was set on Server A (version 2 or version 3).

11. Enter the name of the same Microsoft Certificate Server that was used on Server A, and then follow any prompts.

▶ **To move the Microsoft Mail Connector**

Note The following steps are applicable only if you have the Microsoft (MS) Mail Connector installed on Server A.

1. Run the Administrator program for Server A, noting the settings for Microsoft Mail Connector.

2. On Server A, stop MS Mail Connector Interchange, PCMTA services, and the Microsoft Exchange Directory Synchronization service.

3. Check whether Microsoft Mail Connector is installed on Server B. If it is not installed, install it.

4. On Server B, configure Microsoft Mail Connector exactly as it was configured on Server A.

▶ **To move the directory synchronization server**

Note The following steps are applicable only if you have the Microsoft Mail Connector installed on Server A.

1. In the Administrator window for Server B, click **Connections** for the server B site. On the right side of the window, double-click the directory synchronization object.

2. In the **Directory Synchronization Server Properties** property page, change the **Server** setting to Server B. When you do so, the following warning message appears:

   "Changing the server in Responsible DXA can cause the loss of Directory Synchronization information. A full export of Directory Synchronization information will occur in the next scheduled cycle."

3. Click **OK** to dismiss the warning, and then click **OK** again.

4. Run the Microsoft Mail Administrator program for each Microsoft Mail requester postoffice. Select **Config**, and then **DirSync**, **Requestor**, **Export**, and **Import**.

5. On Server B, start the MS Mail Connector Interchange service, PCMTA services, and the Directory Synchronization service.

At the next scheduled time, Microsoft Mail and Exchange will be resynchronized. You may also use the InterOrg Synchronization tool that is available on the *Microsoft BackOffice Resource Kit, Second Edition* compact disc to synchronize two servers that are in different sites. For more information, see the online documentation.

▶ **To move the Directory Synchronization Requester**

Note   The following steps are applicable only if your Exchange computer is acting as a directory synchronization requestor.

---

1. In the Administrator window for Server B, right-click **Directory Synchronization Requester** to display its properties.

2. Change the **Server** setting to Server B. When you do so, the following warning message appears:

   "Changing the server in Responsible DXA can cause the loss of Directory Synchronization information. A full export of Directory Synchronization information will occur on the new Responsible DXA in the next scheduled cycle."

3. Click **OK** to dismiss the warning, and then click **OK** again.

4. Click the **Requester** tab, and then click **Full Export** and **Import on the Next Cycle**.

▶ **To move X.400 connectors**

1. On Server B, install the required MTA transport stacks.

2. On Server B, display the properties for each X.400 Connector.

3. Change the MTA transport stack so that it is a stack installed on Server B.

4. On Server A, delete the MTA transport stacks.

5. On Server B, request a full directory update.

6. In the Administrator window, select Server B, and then from the **File** menu, click **Properties**.

7. Click the **General** tab. Click **Update Now**, and then click **Refresh all items in the directory**.

▶ **To move directory replication connectors**

1. On Server B, display the properties of each directory replication connector.

2. Change the local bridgehead server to Server B, if it is currently Server A. You might have to change the remote bridgehead settings on the remote directory replication connector if the remote server is not available on the network.

▶ **To move Internet Mail Service**

- Reconfigure each instance of Internet Mail Service on Server B.

▶ **To move third-party gateways**

- Reinstall all third-party gateways installed on Server A.

▶ **To remove Server A**

Note Make sure that both Server A and Server B are running. Server A should be kept running until every client has logged on at least once. This ensures that the Outlook client profiles are automatically redirected to Server B instead of Server A, which eliminates the need to manually modify client profiles.

After all clients have logged on to Exchange at least once, use the following procedure to remove Server A from the organization. If Server A is removed before all clients have logged on, you must modify the profile on the clients to point to Server B.

---

1. In the Administrator window for Server A, click **Public Information Store**.

2. From the **File** menu, click **Properties**.

3. Click the **Instances** tab.

4. Remove all public folder instances from this store.

5. On Server A, run the Microsoft Exchange Server Setup program, and then remove the installed connectors.

6. Run the Administrator program in raw mode by typing **Exchsrvr\bin\admin/r**.

7. On the **View** menu, click **All**.

8. Select the Recipients container. In the right side of the window, click **Microsoft Schedule+ Free/Busy Connector**.

9. On the **File** menu, click **Raw Properties**.

10. Change every occurrence of Server A to Server B and include the Computer Name, Display Name, Home-MDB, and Home-MTA. Choose **Set**.

11. In the Administrator window for Server B, click Server A, and then press DELETE. When you do so, a warning message appears stating that there is still one mailbox and gateway on Server A. This warning refers to the system attendant mailbox on Server A, which you can safely delete.

12. Click **Yes**. The following warning appears:

"The contents of all public folder instances on this server will be deleted. Are you sure you want to delete server 'Server A'?"

13. Click **Yes**.

All data has now been moved from Server A to Server B. Server A will be deleted from the Exchange directory on Server B.

Procedure A for the Standard Edition

Perform the following steps if you are moving a server running the Standard edition of Exchange (version 4.0 or version 5.0) to a computer with a different computer name.

Because the Standard edition of Exchange (version 4.0 or version 5.0) supports only a single server in a single site, you must install the Microsoft Exchange Connector on Server A before moving it to Server B. The Exchange Connector is a separate software package that must be purchased separately.

After you've installed the Exchange Connector on Server A, perform the steps described above in "Procedure A for the Enterprise Edition."

Procedure B

The following procedures describe how to move Exchange to a new computer that has the same hardware platform and same name as the original computer. For this example, the two computers are referred to as Server A and Server B, even though both computers have the same network basic input/output system (NetBIOS) computer name.

▶ **To back up information from Server A**

1. Start the Administrator program on Server A. Make note of the organization and site names. (These names are case-sensitive.)

2. On Server A, stop all Microsoft Exchange Server services.

3. Copy the entire Exchsrvr directory to another computer on the network, or to a tape drive. If the Exchange log and database directories are on different drives, use Performance Optimizer or the Administrator program to move all of the directories to their corresponding locations under the Exchsrvr directory where Exchange was installed. This should be done before you back up the Exchsrvr directory.

4. If the KM server is installed, stop the KM server service and back up the Security directory. Back up the KM server service Startup disk as well.

5. Make sure that there is an operational domain controller in the Windows NT domain, and then shut down Server A.

Use the following procedure to install Windows NT and Exchange on Server B.

▶ **To install Windows NT and Exchange on Server B**

1. Turn off Server A.

2. Install Windows NT and service packs on Server B with the same computer name as Server A. If necessary, make it a backup domain controller.

3. On Server B, at the command prompt, type **Setup** to install Exchange.

4. Create a new site using the same organization and site names that were used on Server A. Install all of the connectors that were installed on Server A. To do so, select the **Custom** installation option. Install Exchange service packs as necessary.

5. During setup, when you are prompted for the Exchange service account, select the same service account that you used for Server A because if a new service account is selected, it will not have permissions on the directory.

Important Do not run Performance Optimizer at the end of the Setup program.

---

6. Make sure that no Microsoft Exchange Server services are running.

7. If the MS Mail Connector was installed on the original server, configure the MS Mail Connector exactly as it was on the original server. You must do this before the directory is restored onto the new server in order to recreate directory and registry entries required by the connector.

8. If you were using the KM Server on the original server, install the KM Server on the new server. Select the option to create a startup disk. After the installation has completed successfully, stop the KM Server Service on the new server.

▶ **To restore data on Server B**

1. From the backup copy of the Exchsrvr directory on Server A, copy all of the files to the Exchsrvr directory on Server B.

Caution If Server A and Server B have the same name, but do not have the same hardware platform, do *not* copy the contents of the entire Exchsrvr directory to Server B. Doing so destroys the executable files. For more information on how to re-create data on a new server that does not have the same hardware platform, see "Procedure A" earlier in this section.

---

2. Start the Exchange system attendant and directory services.

3. At the Windows NT command prompt, type the following to run the ISINTEG troubleshooting utility:

   ISINTEG -patch

   See Part 8, "Troubleshooting," and Part 9, "Disaster Recovery," for discussions of the ISINTEG tool.

4. Start the information store service.

5. In the Administrator window, click **Server B**.

6. On the **File** menu, click **Properties**.

7. Click the **Advanced** tab. Click **Consistency Adjuster**, and then click **All Inconsistencies**.

▶ **To move the KM server (where applicable)**

Note The following steps are applicable only if you already have the KM server running on Server A and security is enabled for the Exchange mailboxes on Server A.

Server B must be set up as a Cert Server client to the same Cert Server to which Server A was a client.

1. Stop the KM server service on Server A. This is very important because it closes all transactions with the KM server database, making everything consistent.

2. Back up the Kmsdata directory on Server A by copying all .edb files in the directory to a safe place, such as tape or a network drive.

3. Uninstall the KM server from Server A by running Microsoft Exchange Server Setup.exe, choosing **Add/Remove** at the prompt, and then deselecting KM server.

4. Install the KM server on Server B by running Microsoft Exchange Server Setup.exe, choosing **Add/Remove**, and then selecting KM server. Choose the same location for the KM server password that was used on Server A. Make sure that you do not write over your original password.

5. Delete all files in the Kms directory on Server B. The .log and .chk files will be recreated after you start the KM server service.

6. Copy all the .edb files you backed up in step 2 to the Kmsdata directory on Server B.

7. On Server B, start the KM server service with the original password from Server A. Complete the next steps, if either version 2 or version 3 was installed on Server A.

8. Install Microsoft Exchange Server version 5.5 Service Pack 1.

9. Open the Certificate Administrator object and select Enrollment property page.

10. Change to the option that was set on Server A (version 2 or version 3).

11. Enter the name of the same Microsoft Certificate Server that was used on Server A, and then follow any prompts.

Restore Site Connector and X.400 Connector Information

Restore all Site Connector and X.400 Connector information on Server B. Any Microsoft Mail, Internet Mail Service, or Dynamic RAS Connectors must be reconfigured. If you use third-party connectors, they also need to be reconfigured.

Microsoft Exchange Client Profiles

Exchange should now be running on Server B as it ran on Server A. Exchange clients should be able to connect to Server B in the same way they connected to Server A.

Monitoring

Monitoring your server is an important part of keeping Exchange up and running.

Monitoring Servers

You can use the following tools to monitor Exchange:

- Performance Monitor counters
- Server and link monitors
- Alerter service
- Log files

For information about scheduling server maintenance, see Appendix B, "System Management Checklist."

Using Performance Monitor Counters

Use Windows NT Performance Monitor to obtain information about the server status. You can keep Performance Monitor running on each computer that is monitoring Exchange. Exchange includes several preconfigured Performance Monitor chart view (.pmw) files. These files are described in Appendix C, "Performance Monitor Chart Views."

Using Server and Link Monitors

The Exchange Server Administrator program includes server and link monitors.

- Use server monitors to monitor Exchange services, such as the message transfer agent (MTA) or any other Windows NT Server services that are running on an Exchange computer. Configure server monitors to send a notification if the services go down and to automatically restart the service.

- Use link monitors to verify the connections between servers and foreign systems.

For more information, see *Microsoft Exchange Server Maintenance and Troubleshooting*.

Setting the Alerter Service

You can configure Exchange to notify a computer or user with system alerts (for example, when disk space is low).

▶ **To configure system alerts**

1. In Control Panel, double-click the **Server** icon.

2. Click **Alerts**.

3. Type the computer or user names to which you want to send alerts in the **New Computer or Username** box.

4. Click **Add** to add computers or user names, or click **Remove** to remove them.

Maintaining Log Files

To keep log files from building up and consuming disk space, set up your server to maintain the log files or perform routine backups automatically. It is important to monitor the transaction log files and message tracking log files. The transaction log files track all information store and directory transactions. The message tracking log files track message deliveries and receipts.

Automatically Deleting Log Files

By default, message tracking log files are deleted automatically after seven days. If you want a shorter or longer time interval, you can change it. Also, if you do not want your server to delete files automatically, you can configure your server to not delete them. However, you must then manually delete the files on a regular basis.

▶ **To change the time interval for deleting message tracking log files**

1. In the Administrator window, choose the site, the Configuration container, the Servers container, and the server name.

2. Double-click **System Attendant**, and then click the **General** tab.

3. Click **Remove log files older than __ days**, and then type the number of days the log files should be retained.

Tracking Download Logging Information

The Exchange download logging feature writes events to the Windows NT Event Log when users download attachments, messages, and folders from public or private folders. You can use this information for billing or tracking download costs.

A download event is logged when the user moves or copies an item from the private or public information store to a different store, such as a personal folder file (.pst). The item can be a message, attachment, or folder, depending on the configuration you have selected.

The following information is logged:

- User name
- Mailbox name
- Size of item downloaded
- Document type
- Document identifier

For example, if Log Downloads is set to 1 in the **ParametersPublic** registry subkey, an event is logged every time a user moves or copies a message with an attachment to the user's personal folder file.

The following example is an event generated by the download feature:

```
Ann Devon (ADEVON) downloaded 1456 bytes from attachment 6A
```

You establish download logging by editing the registry of Exchange with RegEdit, a Windows NT administrative tool. The values you add apply to all public and private folders on the server.

Caution   You should not change any of the Exchange registry key values unless you are aware of the full effect of the change.

▶ **To start download logging**

1. Start Regedt32.

2. Select the following registry key:

   HKEY_LOCAL_MACHINE\SYSTEM\CurrentControlSet \Services\MSExchangeIS

1. Select **ParametersPublic** to log downloads from public folders. Select **ParametersPrivate** to log downloads from private mailboxes.

2. From the **Edit** menu, click **Add Value**.

3. In the **Value** box, type **Log Downloads**.

4. In the **Data Type** box, click **REG_DWORD**.

5. In the D_WORD **Editor** dialog box, type a decimal or binary value from the following table.

To log downloads from	Enter this registry value	
	(Decimal)	(Binary)
Attachments only	1	001
Messages only	2	010
Attachments and messages	3	011
Folders only	4	100
Attachments and folders	5	101
Messages and folders	6	110
All	7	111

Use Windows NT Event Viewer to review events recorded by the download logging feature.

▶ **To view logged downloads**

1. In the Windows NT Administrative Tools program group, click **Event Viewer**.

2. On the **View** menu, click **Filter Events**.

3. In the **Source** box, select **MSExchangeISPub** or **MSExchangeISPriv**.

4. In the **Category** box, click **Download**.

5. Double-click an event to see its details.

Monitoring Disk Space

You can use Windows NT Performance Monitor to observe disk space use on the drive that contains the information store. The LogicalDisk object, along with the % Free Space and Free Megabytes counters, are used to monitor and trigger alerts when disk space is low.

If circular logging is turned off, the information store or the directory can run out of operating space as log files accumulate on the drive. To prevent this, do any one of the following:

- Write the log files to a different drive. Change the location where the information store or directory store transaction logs are written. To do so, select the server object. On the **File** menu, click **Properties**, and then click the **Database Paths** tab. Change the path names for the information store and directory transaction logs, and then click **OK**.

- Back up the Exchange computer. Use Windows NT Backup to perform a normal (full) or incremental online backup of the server. This utility automatically deletes transaction logs that are no longer needed (that is, they have been committed to disk). If you do not run Windows NT Backup, the log files continues to grow.

- If possible, delete any sample applications to free additional disk space.

PART 5

Performance Tuning and Optimization

Your system's performance is affected by the system's topology and the server's software and hardware configurations. In this chapter are suggestions for ways to maximize the number of users you can support and at the same time keep response times low. These suggestions for optimizing the performance of Microsoft Exchange Server are grouped into four categories:

Optimizing your topology Plan your system setup, and make sure the system has adequate network bandwidth to handle the traffic between clients and servers.

Optimizing your server Take advantage of the hardware and software resources on your Exchange computer to provide the fastest, most reliable service possible for your users. Use Microsoft Windows NT Performance Monitor and the Exchange Performance Optimizer to help you optimize server performance.

Balancing users per server Determine the number of users your server can support so that you can achieve the required level of performance. You can use Exchange Load Simulator (Loadsim.exe) to estimate usage levels and measure the expected load on the server.

Note If you are running Exchange in a production environment, be very cautious about making changes to your system.

For information about troubleshooting performance, see Part 8, "Troubleshooting." For more information about optimizing performance, see *Microsoft Exchange Server Concepts and Planning*.

Optimizing Your Topology

Several aspects of your organization's topology, including how your sites and servers are laid out, the amount of traffic your system supports, and the network bandwidth, can have a significant effect on overall system performance. Optimizing the topology of your system includes planning server locations, site boundaries, and replication settings to increase the speed of directory and public folder replication as well as message delivery.

These are some strategies for optimizing system topology:

- Control the amount of traffic your system supports. For example, you can restrict the number of messages users can send or limit the size of the messages. Factors that can affect traffic are the type and number of messages, the frequency of public folder replication, the size of replicated public folders, the frequency of directory replication, and the size of the directory changes.

- Make sufficient network bandwidth available to handle the amount of traffic your system has to support. The more traffic you have, the higher the bandwidth connections must be.

- Balance public folder replication traffic with network traffic. If many users need access to a public folder in another site, minimize traffic to the other site by replicating the public folder to the local site. However, if only a few users need access to a public folder in another site, configure the system so that these users connect to the public folder in the other site.

- Arrange your sites in a hub-and-spoke configuration, with one central site and multiple satellite sites. Servers in the hub site can be dedicated to message-switching functions and act as the messaging transfer agent (MTA) backbone of the system.

The bandwidth between servers in different sites is not as critical as the bandwidth between clients and servers. Network connections between clients and servers should have a high bandwidth to ensure the fastest client/server response times possible. Tests performed by the Exchange Performance Team have shown that 56K per second throughput is the threshold for communication within a site; however, this threshold can vary depending on the traffic in your organization.

If you have a connection that is slow, consider placing it between two sites because communication between sites does not have to be as fast as communication within sites. However, if you don't want to administer two sites, connect clients to a central site over the slow connection; this configuration is most effective when you have only a small number of clients. The two connection options are shown in the following illustration.

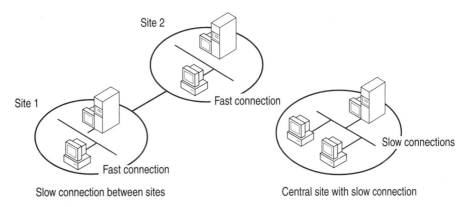

Optimizing Your Server

Your system's performance is also affected by the server's software and hardware configurations. You can minimize performance bottlenecks by adjusting software settings and by balancing server hardware resources to support the expected load. You can use the Performance Optimizer to tune your server's software and Performance Monitor to help you balance your server's hardware resources.

Before you install Exchange and run Performance Optimizer, you should optimize your disk subsystem. The following is the recommended disk configuration for an Exchange computer:

- A physical disk that contains the operating system and the pagefile.

- A physical disk dedicated to the transaction log files so that information can be written to them sequentially. To increase fault tolerance, you can mirror the disk that contains the transaction log files.

- A stripe set that consists of multiple physical disks for all other Exchange components so that access to Exchange databases is the most efficient.

Performance Tuning for Different Server Roles

Servers can function in one or more of several roles in your messaging topology. The recommendations presented in this section for server performance tuning are based on the assumption that you want your server to function at full capacity. If you don't need to push the server to the limit of its capacity, you might not need to implement some of these recommendations.

Mailbox Servers

Adjustments to the following components of your server can improve performance on servers whose primary role is to support user mailboxes:

- The disk subsystem
- Memory and network capacity
- CPU subsystem

Disk subsystem

In most customer configurations, the disk subsystem and memory are the first resources to become overloaded in an Exchange computer. One way to improve disk performance is to put the information store log files onto their own physical disks, apart from other files in the system. Because the logs are always written sequentially, having dedicated disks means that the disk heads won't be used for other activities and will always be in the right place for writing the next file. This improves performance because seeking is the slowest thing a disk does.

In the case of the information store database files, which are randomly accessed, the best thing you can do is put the disks in a RAID array for maximum random access performance.

You also can improve performance by using good disk controllers. Caching controllers increases your disk's performance for reading and, if the controller has battery backups, improves write performance as well. If the controller has a write cache, it must have a battery backup. Problems with cache writes (for example, in the event of a power outage) cause the computer to lose data. The batteries are on the card to keep data on the card backed up. If the data is cached and there is a power outage, the data is saved. Make sure you don't create a bottleneck by putting too many disks on one controller.

It is important to look carefully at the reliability of your disks because users depend on them. It might be wise to mirror the log files and to use RAID 5 on the database.

Summary of Recommendations

- Use the fastest possible disks for the information store log and database.
- Use dedicated disks for information store logs.
- Stripe the information store database.
- Use a sufficient number of high-performance controllers.

Memory and network capacity

Two other resources that can become overloaded are memory and network capacity. Insufficient memory in the system causes the system to *thrash*, that is, to page excessively. Normally, you do not notice paging at all; so if the system is paging excessively, it is obvious. Fortunately, it is easy to add memory, which corrects the problem. You can also fix thrashing by removing the load on the server.

If there is not enough *network capacity* (bandwidth) between the users and the server, your efforts to provide a responsive server will be unsuccessful. The network becomes your bottleneck.

When you are using a local area network (LAN), you have the option of replacing a 10-megabyte (MB) Ethernet with a 100-MB Ethernet network.

When you are using a wide area network (WAN), it is important to remember two things:

- WAN traffic is characterized by large bursts of activity.
- Bandwidth demand varies widely from company to company and from site to site. You might see wide range characteristics of per-usage bandwidth utilization, depending on the usage patterns. It is typical for server-to-client traffic to be three to four times greater than the client-to-server traffic because there are more server responses to client requests.

Summary of Recommendations

- Make sure you have adequate memory.
- Make sure you have adequate network bandwidth.

CPU subsystem

After the disks and memory, the resource most likely to become overloaded is the CPU.

If the server supports only users and does not run connectors and other processes, there are limits to how much work you can offload by adding CPUs. Therefore, use the fastest possible CPU. However, if the server performs other processing functions, there is a definite benefit in adding more processors. For example, it might be useful to add processors if your server supports connectors or if it doubles as a messaging hub, a domain controller, or a Microsoft SQL Server database

To make the best use of your processors, use a large L2 cache. This keeps the processor from waiting while data is retrieved from main memory. Also, in a multiprocessor server, the cache keeps the load off the system bus, which improves your overall throughput.

Summary of Recommendations

- Use the fastest available CPUs.
- Use multiprocessor-ready computers.
- Use the largest available caches.

Servers That Support Connectors

When a server must support connectors, it affects server performance. The following tasks create additional work for a server:

- Connecting sites using the Site Connector, X.400 Connector, or Internet Mail Service.
- Connecting to other types of messaging systems, for example, using the Internet Mail Service, X.400 Connector, or Microsoft Exchange Connector for Lotus cc:Mail.
- Supporting protocols that require content conversion, for example, Post Office Protocol version 3 (POP3), Network News Transfer Protocol (NNTP), or Hypertext Transfer Protocol (HTTP).

The message transfer agent (MTA), for example, is involved when connectors are used. The MTA secures all messages to disk, so if there is a lot of traffic, disk input and output can become important. One option for improving performance when you are using connectors is to provide a separate disk for MTA files; another option is to maintain the MTA files in the stripe set with the information store database. The same is true for the Internet Mail Service because it also secures messages to disk.

Make sure that you have adequate network bandwidth to carry the traffic. Connector traffic is often carried over WAN links and, as mentioned earlier, the traffic patterns can vary widely from company to company. Use Network Monitor to verify that you have capacity available on the links.

Most connectors require the system to send and receive messages in a format that is different from the storage format. Mapping content from the storage format into another format or protocol is a CPU-intensive task; in this case, performance could benefit from the addition of more processors.

Summary of Recommendations

- Use a separate disk for MTA queues, or place them in a stripe set with the information store database.

- Use a separate disk for Internet Mail Service queues, or place them in a stripe set with the information store database.

- Make sure you have adequate bandwidth between sites.

- Consider adding more processors.

Public Folder Servers

The usage patterns for public folders vary from company to company. Some companies don't use public folders, some support discussion groups and news in public folders, and some deploy intensive workflow applications. If your organization supports large-scale public folder activity, this affects your system performance. But keep in mind that the public information store is separate from the private information store. It has its own database file. This means that you can maintain the public information store database files on a logical drive that is separate from the private information database for maximum random I/O performance. Likewise, you can maintain the public store database on a separate drive, although this is less likely to increase performance if you already have a stripe set for the database.

Many site administrators might want to provide Internet newsgroups and store this data in public folders for uniform user access. In such a case, the incoming news feeds can generate a large amount of write activity in the public store, so be sure to optimize the log drives.

Although the public and private stores are separate databases, a single instance of the database engine runs both. They also share the same memory buffers. If your organization experiences heavy use of public folders you can improve performance by splitting the public folders onto separate servers. This reduces competition for computer resources, including buffers. A pool of public folder servers can also provide flexibility in load balancing.

Summary of Recommendations

- Define your company's usage pattern.

- If there is a large amount of read activity, focus your attention on the information store public database disks.

- If there is a large amount of write activity, focus your attention on the information store public log disks.
- Consider using a pool of public folder servers.

Servers That Support Other Loads

If your organization supports other applications (such as SQL Server) in addition to Exchange, or if you use file and print services or domain controllers, you must benchmark the workload and the configuration you expect to run. This is the only reliable way of determining system performance under the expected load. To emulate the Exchange part of the workload, you can use the Load Simulator utility (Loadsim.exe).

Other Factors That Affect Server Load

Server load can be affected not only by the roles the server performs, but also by the following factors:

- Whether messages are delivered to a personal folder (.pst) file or the server's private information store
- How public folders are used and replicated
- How often rules and views are used
- The frequency of directory replication
- How much activity the MTA is experiencing
- The type of network you are using

Message Delivery

You can minimize server load by having users designate .pst files as the default delivery location for messages instead of server-based storage. This offloads server processing and frees it to perform other tasks. Whenever a user requests data from a personal folder, the server does not read the attributes and data into the buffer cache. Instead, all of the processing occurs on the client because that is where the data is located. The server does not have to be involved at all. If a user saves a copy of everything in the Sent Mail folder, the process is performed locally. Also, when a user deletes a message, a copy is saved in the local Deleted Items folder, and, again, the server is not involved.

Public Folder Use and Replication

Using public folders on an Exchange computer can have a dramatic effect on the server's performance. Size, frequency of user access, various views on that folder, the number of replicas, the replication schedule, and how often its content changes are all factors that affect server performance. If many users frequently use a public folder, the server is going to be kept busy satisfying those requests. The public folder also keeps track of the expansion state of each folder and the read/unread state of each message on a per-user basis.

Although public folder replication is a rapid process, changes to a public folder are replicated according to a schedule set up by the administrator. Even if the replication schedule is set to **Always**, replication occurs only every 15 minutes. If replication starts when a user is accessing a public folder or the public folder hierarchy, the user will notice a sudden slowdown that improves only after the replication process is completed. If there are a number of public folder replicas to update, this places even more stress on the server and extends the replication process.

Public folders can contain messages and free-standing documents. Messages are like any other mail message in terms of the resources they consume on a server. Free-standing documents, however, are another performance issue because they are frequently large documents. For example, whenever a user opens a 1 MB file in a public folder, 1 MB of data must travel across the network. This affects the performance of the server for every user.

Rules and Views

Rules are user-defined actions that require a server to perform on behalf of the user. Typical examples of rules are: displaying a notification when a message is received from a specific person, and automatically moving messages into a specific folder according to the content of the message. Typically, rules have very little effect on overall server performance until most users have more than 10 rules set up.

For views, the server must store and keep track of the indexes that make up a view. Although a cache is used to store the most recently used indexes, a user might notice a small decrease in performance when opening a seldom-used view.

Directory Replication

Because the amount of directory replication is proportional to the number of directory changes that occur, it is difficult to predict how it is going to affect the overall performance of a bridgehead server. During a migration to Exchange, when the directory is changing often, or in an organization where hundreds of directory updates occur every day, the directory replication process can have a negative impact on performance.

Message Transfer Agent

The primary function of the MTA is to route messages between multiple servers. But even in a single-server scenario, the MTA has other tasks to perform, including the expansion of distribution lists and the routing of outgoing gateway or connector messages. The MTA has the greatest impact on performance when the system has multiple Exchange computers.

Network Type

If you place an Exchange computer on a Fiber Distributed Data Interface (FDDI) ring with a 100-MB capacity, it provides better connectivity and performance than a server attached to a token-ring network. An overloaded Ethernet segment with many collisions occurring can also reduce the performance of a server. WAN connectivity and quality should also be considered, especially if you are trying to determine site boundaries or whether to give clients access to a server across the WAN.

Adjusting Software Settings

Using Performance Optimizer is an essential step in maximizing your server's performance. This utility selects the software settings that are appropriate for your configuration and places Exchange files in the best locations. It configures your server on the basis of the following factors:

- The number of users that the server supports and the number of users in your organization.
- The types of activities the server is to perform.
- The server's hardware resources, including the amount of random access memory (RAM) and the number and type of disks and processors. It is recommended that the amount of RAM remain at zero, which means that Exchange will use all available memory. Note that this ultimately depends on the organization, as an organization might run another process on the same server.

For example, Performance Optimizer uses the number of clients that the server supports to determine the number of MAPI/RPC threads to allocate for the information store.

Run Performance Optimizer after you run Setup and when you change your server's hardware configuration. In particular, you should run Performance Optimizer after you do any of the following:

- Make changes to your server's disk.
- Add a caching controller.

- Change the amount of RAM.

- Add a processor.

- Change the number of users that the server is to support.

- Add or remove a component on the server.

You can customize Performance Optimizer settings by typing **perfwiz -v** at the command prompt in the Exchsrvr\Bin directory. When you run perfwiz -v, Performance Optimizer displays six additional screens that provide the options shown in the following table.

Option	Description
# of information store buffers	The maximum number of 4-Kilobyte (KB) buffers allocated to the information store database.
# of directory buffers	The maximum number of 4-KB buffers allocated to the directory store database.
Minimum # of information store threads	The minimum number of threads that the information store will use to service Messaging Application Programming Interface (MAPI) clients, such as Microsoft Outlook.
Maximum # of information store threads	The maximum number of threads that the information store will use to service MAPI clients, such as Microsoft Outlook.
# of directory threads	The maximum number of threads used by the directory.
Maximum # of concurrent read threads	The maximum number of directory threads available to service replication requests.
# of background threads	The number of threads available for background tasks and to the Gateway In/Out, Send, and Delivery thread pool.
# of heaps	The number of areas of memory used for dynamic memory allocation.
# of private information store send threads	The number of threads that process messages submitted by MAPI clients, such as Microsoft Outlook.
# of private information store delivery threads	The number of threads that the private information store can use to deliver messages to mailboxes.

(continued)

Option	Description
# of public information store send threads	The number of threads that process public folder replication messages and messages generated by public folder rules.
# of public information store delivery threads	The number of threads that the public information store can use to deliver messages to public folders.
# of information store gateway in threads	The number of information store threads that deliver mail from the message transfer agent (MTA) to the information store for routing elsewhere. For optimal performance, the number of threads should be increased only if the server has multiple processors.
# of information store gateway out threads	The number of information store threads delivering mail from the information store to local mailboxes, or to the MTA. For optimal performance, the number of threads should be increased only if the server has multiple processors.
Buffer Threshold Low Percent	The percentage of available buffers remaining before buffers are flushed to disk. Lower values limit the number of writes to disk; however, low values can degrade performance.
Buffer Threshold High Percent	The percentage of available buffers that must be reached before flushing of buffers to disk stops. For optimal performance, set the percentage value equal to, or slightly greater than, the Buffer Threshold Low Percent.
Maximum # of pool threads	The maximum number of threads servicing Internet connections such as Internet Message Access Protocol, Version 4rev1 (IMAP4), Post Office Protocol version 3 (POP3), and Network News Transfer Protocol (NNTP) into the information store. This value is per processor.
# of information store users	The number of users for which this server routes mail.
# of concurrent connections to LAN-MTAs	The number of concurrent network associations to MTAs.
# of concurrent connections to RAS LAN-MTAs	The minimum number of concurrent network associations to Remote Access Service (RAS) MTAs.
# of LAN-MTAs	The minimum number of network MTAs supported by the MTA.
# of X.400 gateways	The maximum number of remote MTAs connecting through X.400 using X.25, Transport Control Protocol/Internet Protocol (TCP/IP), or Transport Class 4 (TP4).

(continued)

Option	Description
ds_read cache latency (secs)	The number of seconds before the directory service read cache expires. Performance improves when items are loaded in the cache by limiting the number of directory service reads.
# of dispatcher threads	The total number of threads used to route messages.
# of transfer threads	The total number of threads used to transfer messages.
# of kernel threads	The total number of threads allocated to process the Open Systems Interconnection (OSI) protocol stack.
# of submit/deliver threads	The total number of MTA submit and deliver threads. For example, if this value is set to 3 the total number of threads is 6. Submit threads receive messages from the information store and deliver threads deliver messages to the information store.
# of RAS LAN-MTAs	The maximum supported number of concurrent network associations to other RAS MTAs.
# of database data buffers per object	The number of 4 KB buffers configured per cached MTA database file. The MTA saves a copy of each message until the message has been accepted by the information store, or another MTA.
# of RTS threads	The total number of threads available to the Reliable Transfer Service (RTS) level of the OSI protocol stack.
# of concurrent MDB/delivery queue clients	The maximum number of information store and XAPI MA delivery queue clients supported. Each client can have more than one session. For optimal performance, the value should be at least 2, to support both the public and private databases.
# of concurrent XAPI sessions	The maximum number of sessions to information store and XAPI MA delivery queue clients, XAPI MA retrieval queue clients, and XAPI MT gateway clients.
Max # of RPC calls outstanding	The maximum number of concurrent remote procedure call (RPC) threads. This limits the maximum number of RPCs that will be processed at one time.
Min # of RPC threads	The minimum number of concurrent RPC threads. This sets the minimum number of RPCs that will be processed at one time.
# of MT gateway clients	The maximum number of XAPI MT gateway clients supported, which is the maximum number of gateways the MTA can support.
# of retrieval queue clients	The maximum number of XAPI MA retrieval queue clients supported.

(continued)

Option	Description
# of TCP/IP control blocks	The maximum number of TCP/IP connections supported.
# of TCP/IP threads	The maximum number of MTA DMOD threads processing TCP/IP connections.
# of TP4 control blocks	Maximum number of supported concurrent TP4 connections.
# of TP4 threads	Maximum number of MTA DMOD threads processingTP4 connections, including multiple thread connections.

If Internet Mail Service is already installed, the following options will also appear.

Option	Description
# of inbound threads	The number of threads available to perform content conversion and move inbound mail from the Internet Mail Service to the information store.
# of outbound threads	The number of threads available to perform content conversion and move outbound mail to the Internet Mail Service from the information store.
# of InOut threads	The number of threads available to perform content conversion and move both inbound and outbound mail between the Internet Mail Service and the information store.
# of threads per processor	The number of threads available for traffic between the Internet Mail Service and the Internet.

Balancing Hardware Resources

After you have installed Exchange, balancing your server's hardware resources is an essential step in optimizing your system's performance. Because a server's hardware resources work together to accomplish tasks, it's not always easy to determine what resource is the performance bottleneck. Even if your server appears to be using one hardware resource inefficiently, another resource can actually be at fault. For example, if your server's disk is thrashing due to excessive paging, the server needs more memory, not a larger disk. For information about using Performance Monitor to help detect bottlenecks, see Part 8, "Troubleshooting."

The four main hardware resources to consider when you are balancing hardware resources to optimize server performance are:

- CPU
- Disk
- Memory
- Network

Guidelines for minimizing bottlenecks in these resources are described in the following sections.

Balancing CPU Usage

There is not a lot you can do to optimize your CPU. However, it is important to note that more CPUs does not necessarily mean greater performance. For example, an Exchange computer with more than four CPUs does not provide a significant boost in performance. The extra three CPUs could be put to better use elsewhere in the system. As far as the type of CPU is concerned, the faster the better. Therefore, using a Pentium 133 chip provides much better performance than a 486/66 and more performance than a Pentium 100.

If your server's CPU is a performance bottleneck, you can do one or any combination of the following:

- Restrict the amount or type of mail users can send.
- Move Exchange components or other applications to another server.
- Move some or all mailboxes and public folder replicas to another server.
- Add a faster processor.
- If your server is a symmetric multiprocessor (SMP), add additional processors.
- Optimize the way that the system responds to foreground and background applications. In Control Panel, click System and then click the **Performance** tab. Under **Application Performance**, move the slider bar to halfway between **None** and **Maximum**.
- Upgrade to a CPU that has more Level 2 (L2) caching, particularly if the server has less than 256 KB of L2 cache. Some systems allow up to 2 MB or more of L2 memory. L2 cache is faster than RAM.

Balancing Disk Usage

If your server's disk is a performance bottleneck, you can do one or more of the following:

- Move Exchange transaction logs to another physical disk or another physical disk that is using a disk controller, other than the one used by the databases.
- Restrict the amount or type of mail users can send.
- Add more RAM and run Performance Optimizer to increase the database buffers.
- Add more disks to the stripe set.
- Use multiple disk controllers.
- Add one or more caching disk controllers that cache read and write operations.

Balancing Memory Usage

If Exchange uses all of the memory you can give it, up to the total size of your information store, your entire database is in memory. The minimum amount of RAM recommended for Exchange is 24 MB, but testing has shown that 64 to 128 MB of RAM provides much better performance than an upgraded CPU.

If memory is a performance bottleneck, you can do one or more of the following:

- Add more RAM.
- Increase the size of your pagefile. In Control Panel, click System, and then click the Performance tab. Under **Virtual Memory**, set a large pagefile for **Paging File Size For Selected Drive**. You can approximate the pagefile size by adding 125 MB to the amount of physical RAM available on your server. For example, if your server has 64 MB of RAM, you should set your pagefile size to 189 MB.
- Move the pagefile to a separate physical disk.
- Ensure that Windows NT Server is optimized for network applications. In Control Panel, click Network, and then click the **Services** tab. Select **Server** in the list of installed network services. Click **Properties**, and then click **Maximize Throughput for Network Applications**.
- Restrict the amount or type of mail users can send.
- Move Exchange components or other applications to another server.

- If your server is paging excessively, adjust the size of the database buffer caches by typing **perfwiz -v** at the command prompt. You should reduce the size of the buffer cache by 10 to 30 percent. Use caution when changing this setting. Make small adjustments and monitor the results until you are satisfied with the changes.

- Move some or all mailboxes and public folder replicas to another server.

Balancing Network Usage

If your server's network adapter or the network is a performance bottleneck, you can do one or more of the following:

- Use a higher speed network type, such as 100-MB/sec Fast Ethernet or fiber.

- Use a high-performance network adapter and multithreaded driver.

- Segment your network by using multiple network adapters in a single server.

- Reduce the amount of network traffic by:

    - Optimizing your public folder replication topology

    - Optimizing your directory replication topology

    - Restricting the times users can log on to minimize user traffic

    - Limiting the size of messages users can send

Balancing the Number of Users Per Server

You can develop an understanding of what the workload is that is being placed on the system by asking this question: What are your users doing? Definitions of users and acceptable performance vary from organization to organization. For example, a person who sends and receives a lot of e-mail might need a faster system than a user who sends e-mail infrequently. Two tools are available to help you assess your system's workload: Mailbox Statistics and Load Simulator.

Mailbox Statistics

Use the Mailbox Statistics tool (StorStat.exe) to gather data about mail use patterns, which provides you with sizing information. The tool is available in the Exchange directory on the *Microsoft BackOffice 4.5 Resource Kit* compact disc. See the online Help for information on installing and using the tool.

Load Simulator

Use the Exchange Load Simulator (Loadsim.exe) to help you determine the acceptable level of performance for your organization. The tool is designed to provide you with a load level that is realistic by simulating the user behavior on one or more client computers. It provides a user interface for defining test topologies, user behavior, and controlling simulations. Load Simulator is a multiclient emulator program that allows you to carry out large-scale user load experiments without actually configuring a large group of client computers. The tool sends user messages to the server on which you are running Load Simulator by simulating an actual client. With Load Simulator, you can test how your messaging server will perform under different message loads. It allows accurate observations of server behavior under controlled conditions. You can then use this information to determine the optimum number of users per server, pinpoint performance bottlenecks, and evaluate server hardware performance.

Load Simulator can be used in the following ways:

- To test the capacity and to compare performance of server hardware
- To determine network bandwidth requirements for different user behaviors
- To test tuning adjustments, such as making configuration changes, without affecting actual users

Load Simulator takes advantage of multithreading, multiprocessing, and shared-memory features in Windows NT Server to create and manage up to several hundred simulated users on a single client computer. This makes it possible to run large server load simulations with a relatively small amount of hardware.

The number of users that can be emulated on a single client machine varies with the protocol module and the client hardware being used. A Pentium 200 with 256 MB of memory can emulate 400 Exchange users.

Installing Load Simulator

Load Simulator is not included on the *Microsoft BackOffice 4.5 Resource Kit* compact disc. You can download Load Simulator and complete documentation for the tool from the Microsoft Download and Trial Center area of the Microsoft BackOffice Web site at http://backoffice.microsoft.com/downtrial/default.asp?product=5.

Load Simulator should not be run on the same computer where you have installed Exchange. You can run Load Simulator on Microsoft Windows NT Server version 4.0 or later or Microsoft Windows NT Workstation version 4.0 or later. The client computers must have either Outlook or the Exchange Client installed on them.

Using Load Simulator

Load Simulator comes with two client modules: a Microsoft Outlook module and a Microsoft Exchange Client module. Each module emulates the behavior of the specific type of client. The Outlook module simulates the load placed on the server by the Outlook client. The Exchange Client module has been developed to mimic as closely as possible the calls made by Exchange Client versions 5.0.

Client modules share certain core tasks, such as sending mail, but differ in their RPC semantics to the server. In addition, modules implement different tasks according to the functionality of the simulated client. For example, the journaling task is only found in the Outlook module.

Load Simulator allows you to construct models of user behavior and server topology. You can specify the following attributes:

- The number of times per day a user sends a message
- How many times a day the user reads messages
- The percentage of messages that are deleted, saved in folders, or forwarded to others
- The number of servers
- The number of users assigned to each server
- The protocols that are to be used

As Load Simulator runs a scenario, it generates a users load according to the model you provide. For example, if the model says that users send 22 messages in an 8-hour day, Load Simulator generates messages for each user at an average rate of 2.75 messages per hour, although the intervals between messages are not uniform. The intervals are random because real users' activities vary considerably.

▶ **To run a Load Simulator test**

1. Install Load Simulator.
2. Set up your Load Simulator topology.
3. Set the type of test you want to run.
4. Create and initialize your mailboxes.
5. Run the test.
6. Use Lslog.exe to generate a score.
7. Analyze the data.
8. Repeat the test.

Concepts and Terminology

Understanding the key concepts of Load Simulator will help you to get the most out of this tool.

Score

A *score* is a numerical value. It is measured in milliseconds and represents a server's responsiveness under a given load. Each client module has its own score because each protocol has its own specific user and server interactions. For example, an Outlook client and an Exchange client might both have a task that sends mail, but they have different scores because they talk to the server in different ways.

Percentile Score

Users tend to notice long response times from a server, not more typical response times. Therefore, by default, Load Simulator Log reports 95th percentile response times, not average (arithmetic mean) times. This sets Load Simulator apart from other comparable tools, which generally report average server response times. If you prefer to work with averages or wish to use a different percentile, you can select them using the Load Simulator Log command-line options.

As Load Simulator runs a scenario, it collects the response times in the Lsperf.log file. The Load Simulator Log then sorts and orders the response times and reports the 50th percentile score, the 95th percentile score, the mean score, and the standard deviation.

Load Simulator Log computes percentile scores by picking the time that is higher than 95 percent and 50 percent of the times and reporting them as the 95th percentile and 50th percentile scores. Another way of looking at this is to say that if the 95th percentile response time is X, then 95 times out of 100 the response time is going to be less than X when the server is under the same load.

Canonical User Profile

Some user behaviors are consistent regardless of the messaging client they use. For example, the number of messages a user sends each day can vary from person to person according to their business needs; however, the business needs are the same regardless of client type.

Load Simulator provides three generic (*canonical*) user profiles with typical sets of loads that you can use for comparison with your own system's loads: Light User, Medium User, and Heavy User.

Note These generic user profiles are provided for comparison purposes only. They are designed only to provide you with a way of comparing data in common scenarios.

These profiles and their corresponding loads are shown in the following table.

Load	Light User	Medium User	Heavy User
Send Mail	2	4	6
Process Inbox	12	12	12
Browse Mail	5	15	20
Calendaring	1	5	10
Number of messages in Inbox	1	4	9
Number of messages in Deleted Items folder	1	1	1
Number of new folders (five messages per new folder)	20	40	60

A medium user is defined as one who sends 14 messages per day regardless of the type of client. This message load is a combination of new messages, replies to messages, and messages that are being forwarded to other recipients. However, the frequency of tasks performed and the number of messages and folders created during initialization vary according to the profile.

Message File

Load Simulator reads in a predetermined set of message files and uses those messages according to a specified distribution. You can tailor the messages by using message files of your own, defining the distributions, and saving the message files in the Load Simulator directory.

.sim file Settings specified in Load Simulator are saved in a .sim file. You can create and save files that contain different scenario configurations. When you run Load Simulator it automatically reads the last file used.

.log file Individual action timings collected by Load Simulator are saved in the Lsperf.log file. After you run Load Simulator, use the Load Simulator Log (Lslog.exe) tool to generate scores that are based on the contents of one or more log files.

.out file The Loadsim.out file contains a history of all actions, including errors generated when Load Simulator is running. The messages here are exactly the messages that are displayed when Load Simulator is run. Each error line begins with the word "Error" for easy searches.

Topology

Your experimental topology should designate the servers that are to be used, and the number and types of users involved with each server. The number and size of distribution lists, the Windows NT authentication account, and the public folder hierarchy are also part of the Load Simulator topology.

There are many aspects of your experiment's topology that you should understand and take into account, even though you do not specify them in Load Simulator. They include the configuration of your server hardware and software, the types of networks that connect clients to servers and servers to other servers, the use of connectors between sites, and the use of backbone, hub, or bridgehead servers in the network.

User Groups For each Load Simulator client computer, user groups define how many users are to be connected to each server and what client module is to be used. Each user group is also given a user profile, which can be one of the profiles provided by Load Simulator or a custom profile.

Mailbox and Distribution List Naming Mailboxes are created automatically. During initialization, names are created for emulated users in the Load Simulator scenario. First names consist of four alphabetic characters. Last names consist of a single alphabetic character, followed by the server name, a hyphen, the Load Simulator client module that is to control the user, and the user number for that module on that server. Thus, the name Nbaa Zserver2-exch39 indicates that the mailbox is hosted on server2 using the Exchange module. This mailbox has the alias of server2-exch39. Mailbox numbers start at zero, so if there are 2000 Exchange mailboxes on this server, they have the aliases server2-exch0 through server2-exch1999.

Because of this naming scheme and the fact that alias names are limited in length, there is a trade-off between the length of a server name and the number of mailboxes that can be created. For best results, use short server names.

The naming convention for distribution lists consists of three alphabetic characters followed by the letters *DL*, the site name, a hyphen, and a number (for example, LaaDLmysite-11). The alias for this distribution list is mysite-DL11.

The purpose of the third alphabetic character is to create randomness for both mailboxes and distribution lists. Directory entries are evenly distributed within the alphabet, making directory lookups more realistic.

Planning Your Simulation

When you are planning your simulation, use the following questions to develop a scenario that will produce reliable results.

- **What is the goal?** Is it to find an adequate server sizing? To determine your network bandwidth needs? To determine what tuning adjustments can squeeze the most performance out of a given server?

- **What is your network topology?** Make sure your experiment uses a network that is similar to the one you use in real life. Consider using line speed simulators to reproduce the bandwidth of your connections. Bandwidths between clients and servers are often different than bandwidths between servers.

- **Is your topology meaningful?** Single-server tests are interesting, but they are usually not the most realistic. Servers usually communicate with other servers as well as with clients. Are your servers also domain controllers? Do your servers run other services in addition to Exchange? Check your hardware and software configurations carefully. For example, if you forgot to set parity on the RAID disk array, this changes the performance.

- **What are the server roles?** Some servers support end-user mailboxes directly. Some servers run connectors, and others support public folders.

- **What are the server hardware configurations?** In addition to the obvious things, like CPU type and speed, memory size, disk type and speed, network interface type and speed take into account the system buses, processor cache sizes (L2 cache), and disk controller caches. All of these elements affect server performance.

- **How do your users behave?** Few people behave in a manner that is identical to the behaviors of the canonical users defined in the Load Simulator profiles. If your company uses a lot of e-mail and few public folders, you would set up the experiment differently than if your company uses more public-folder-based forms. If you already have some users running on Exchange, you can study the Exchange performance counters using Performance Monitor to learn more about your existing (real world) load. There are many aspects of user behavior in addition to messages users send and receive, such as deleting mail, moving mail to other folders, rereading, forwarding, and replying to messages. Each client module has a somewhat different set of tasks. Review them to see what information you will need.

Introduction to Bottlenecks

A system *bottleneck* is the service center with the highest demand in your organization. *Demand* is the number of visits to a service center multiplied by the average time each visit takes. For example, if a workload is causing 100 disk accesses per second and the disk accesses takes 1 millisecond, then the demand for the disk is 100 milliseconds per second, or 10 percent. Keep the following concepts in mind when analyzing bottlenecks:

- A *service center* is a resource in the system that requires tasks to wait when the resource is servicing another task. The CPU, disks, controllers, and network are all examples of service centers. Other examples are logical resources such as locks or critical sections in software. Memory is not such a resource. Even though the system starts paging when there is not enough memory, memory itself is not the bottleneck. Rather, insufficient memory causes the disk subsystem to become a bottleneck.

- All bottlenecks are observed in the context of a workload. When a server is fulfilling a file-server role, its disks can be the source of the bottleneck. When the same server is acting as a domain controller, its CPU can be the bottleneck.

- For any server and workload combination, there is a bottleneck. The bottleneck resource usually is not overloaded during normal operation. When it is, a queue builds up in front of that resource, and service times climb. Then you must eliminate the source of the bottleneck.

The following illustration shows a characteristic response-time curve that all multiuser servers share. As the load on the server increases, usage of the bottleneck resource comes closer to saturation (100 percent utilization) more of the time. As it does so, queuing in front of the resource increases, which causes response times to slow down. As the resource nears 100 percent utilization, the response time slows rapidly.

A server that hosts satisfied users is not operating with its resources very close to saturation. There is "elbow room" for the bottleneck resource, and the system operates in the part of the response rate curve that is below the acceptable response time limit. When the system is operating above that line, it's time to relieve the bottleneck.

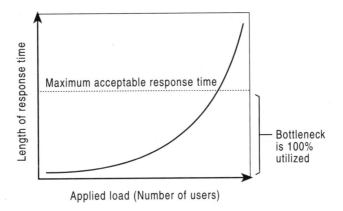

Applied load (Number of users)

Eliminating Bottlenecks?

There are two ways to eliminate a bottleneck:

- Decrease the visit rate to the resource (for example, by adding disks and spreading the load over them, which decreases the visit rate on each disk). Keep in mind that one way to reduce the visit rate is to decrease the workload on the system (for example, by moving some users to another server).

- Decrease the visit time (for example, by installing faster disk drives on your computer).

When the server appears to have slow response times, you might try to install a faster processor without realizing that the disk subsystem is the actual bottleneck. By doing this, you can improve response times somewhat because the disk is faster. However, the capacity of the system does not change; the bottleneck remains.

The following illustration shows what happens if you fail to identify the bottleneck correctly or improve the wrong resource. The capacity of the system does not change at all. At load levels approaching saturation, response times do not improve.

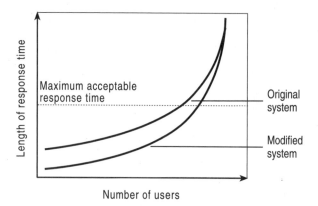

The following illustration shows what happens when a bottleneck is correctly identified and relieved. Not only are response times improved at light loads, but the saturation point moves further out. Users experience acceptable response times except at higher load levels. You can see that there is still a bottleneck in the system, but the capacity might be high enough to provide acceptable performance. If not, the new bottleneck must be identified and resolved.

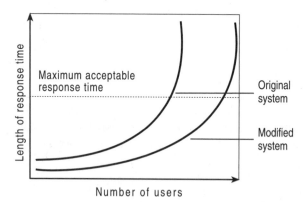

Impact of Memory and Cache

The server's memory and L2 cache (processor cache) usually do not become bottlenecks because they are not service centers; that is, processes don't wait for these resources. If there is insufficient memory in the system, the system starts paging. This increases the visit rate on the disk, and the disk becomes the bottleneck. This situation is commonly known as *disk thrashing*. When you investigate a disk bottleneck, you must also examine the paging rate. If the paging rate is more than 20 pages per second, consider adding memory. Although memory isn't technically the bottleneck, adding memory can solve the problem by relieving the disk.

An inadequate L2 cache can cause the processors to stall while waiting for data from main memory. Excessive cache misses can cause the system bus to become a bottleneck. This is commonly known as *bus thrashing*, and is an element to watch for, especially in multiprocessor systems. If you believe this is happening in your server, you can install the Pentium counters available in the *Microsoft Windows NT Resource Kit* compact disc and monitor bus utilization by using Performance Monitor.

Monitoring a Server

The most effective way to optimize your server is to examine the behavior of the system while it is in operation. You can do so by using Performance Monitor. One of the most important elements of performance tuning is to maintain Performance Monitor logs. If you don't record this information, you will have no data for evaluating performance. You can set these logs to record only every two or five minutes; but this is sufficient for most performance tuning work and doesn't require a lot of storage space.

There are three major areas to watch when you are monitoring a server that has online users:

Trends in submitted loads Observe whether users are sending more messages now than they did a few months ago and whether the average message size is increasing. These factors change the load on the server, and if you are not aware of them, the load can slowly increase until you have a response-time problem. Exchange provides counters that indicate the overall workload.

Service times If you monitor only the server, it is nearly impossible to calculate the actual response times that users experience. However, if you observe the server components of the response time, you can get a general idea of whether slow server response times are becoming an issue. Exchange provides Performance Monitor counters that indicate server response times.

Resource use By observing the utilization of various resources, you can see where the bottleneck in a system is and even get an idea of where the next bottleneck might occur after you resolve the current bottleneck.

The following sections describe the counters of most interest to an administrator, performance analyst, or capacity planner.

Watching for Trends in the Load

The counters described in the table that follows do not provide a complete picture of the load on your Exchange computer, but they do indicate trends over time if you track them.

Object	Counter	Description
MSExchangeIS	User Count	The number of connected client sessions.
	Active User Count	The number of users who have been active in the last 10 minutes.
MSExchangeIS Private	Messages Submitted/min	The rate of messages being submitted to the private information store.
	Message Recipients Delivered/min	The rate of messages being delivered by the private information store. This will be higher than the submission rate because many messages have multiple recipients.
MSExchangeIS Public	Messages Submitted/min	The rate of messages being submitted to the public information store.
	Message Recipients Delivered/min	The rate of messages being delivered by the public information store. This will be higher than the submission rate because many messages have multiple recipients.
MSExchange MTA	Messages/sec	The rate at which the MTA is processing messages.
	Messages Bytes/sec	The number of bytes in the messages being processed by the MTA. Divide this by the Messages/sec counter, and you can determine the average message size.

Watching Service Times

The counters described here do not provide a complete picture of the responsiveness of your Exchange computer, but they do indicate trends over time if you track them.

Object	Counter	Description
MSExchangeIS Private	Send Queue Size	Indicates whether the private information store is keeping up with the submitted load. The queue can be non-zero at peak traffic times, but it shouldn't stay there long after the peak has passed.
	Average Time for Delivery	Indicates how long it takes the private information store to deliver messages.
MSExchangeIS Public	Send Queue Size	Indicates whether the public information store is keeping up with the submitted load. The queue can be non-zero at peak traffic times, but it shouldn't stay there long after the peak has passed.
	Average Time for Delivery	Indicates how long it takes the public information store to deliver messages.
MSExchange MTA	Work Queue Length	Indicates whether the MTA is keeping up with the submitted load. The queue can be non-zero at peak traffic times, but it shouldn't stay there long after the peak has passed.

Processor Utilization

Windows NT also provides counters that can help you analyze processor usage, but many of these counters are more useful to a developer than to an administrator. The counters described here are relevant to bottleneck analysis.

Object	Counter
System	% Total Processor Time
Process	% Processor Time

If you observe processor utilization at a fine granularity (for example every one or five seconds), note that the counters fluctuate rapidly and frequently hit 100 percent for short periods of time. For this reason, monitoring processor use is more useful when the saturation points are averaged over a longer period of time. If you find that the processor usage reaches 100 percent and remains at that level for minutes or hours, your users are probably becoming impatient with response times. You might want to size your system for around 60 percent or 70 percent processor utilization during peak times, so that there is extra room for unexpected demands and for growth.

When you are running other services in addition to Exchange on the server computer, it is recommended that you analyze per-process processor usage. This enables you to determine what services are using most of the CPU time and how to appropriately balance the load.

If the processor is your bottleneck, consider taking the following actions.

- Use a faster processor or multiple processors.
- Use a larger L2 cache. This can improve processor efficiency.

Disk Counters

There are two sets of disk counters: LogicalDisk and PhysicalDisk. LogicalDisk is the most useful counter because it simplifies tracking drive usage. You must enable the disk counters. By default, they are turned off because they have a small impact on performance.

▶ **To enable Performance Monitor disk counters**

- At the command prompt, type **diskperf -y**. The counters begin functioning when the server is next rebooted.

The following are the important disk counters for Exchange.

Object	Counter
LogicalDisk	Disk Bytes Written/sec
	Disk Bytes Read/sec
	Disk Reads/sec
	Disk Writes/sec
	Avg. Disk Queue Length
	% Disk Time (general indicator only; not a reliable indicator of disk saturation).

Compare the disk operations per second that are recorded with the specifications for sustained operations provided by your vendor. If your disk operations per second are getting close to the vendor's specifications, you are nearing capacity. Note that the % Disk Time counter is not a fair indication of disk saturation. A disk that is busy 100 percent of the time might actually be capable of doing much more work as a result of using smart disk controllers and scheduling methods, such as elevator algorithms.

If the disk subsystem is your bottleneck, consider taking the following actions:

- Use the fastest possible disks for the information store log and database.
- Use dedicated disks for the information store log.

- Use stripe sets on the information store database disks.
- Mirror the information store log; use RAID 5 on the information store database.
- Use high-performance controllers, and make sure that there are enough of them for your disks.
- Use a separate disk for MTA queues, or place MTA queues in the stripe set with the information store database.
- Use a separate disk for Internet Mail Service queues, or place Internet Mail Service queues in the stripe set with the information store database.

Information Store Disk Demands

The following are the important information store database counters for Exchange.

Object	Counter
Database: Information Store	File Bytes Read/sec
	File Bytes Written/sec
	Cache % Hit

Check the amount of disk activity that is generated by the information store. If you add up the read/write counters shown above, you can determine how much of the disk's activity on your information store database drive is due to the information store, and how much is generated by other services that might share the information store drive.

Memory

The following are the important memory counters for Exchange.

Object	Counter
Memory	Pages/sec
	Page Faults/sec
	Available Bytes
	Committed Bytes
Process	Page Faults/sec
	Working Set

The Pages/sec counter indicates the rate at which pages are physically read or written on the paging drive. This indicates the contribution that paging makes to the demand for the disk.

The Page Faults/sec counter indicates the rate at which pages are faulted into the working sets of processes. A page fault occurs when a process refers to a virtual memory page that is not in its working set in main memory. The number of pages actually being read and written to disk is much less than the number of page faults because of the page pool in the virtual memory system. The page faults are of interest if you are running other services in addition to Exchange. In this situation, you can examine the rate of page faults on a per-process basis and determine where they are occurring. Then, with this information, you can make application-tuning changes. For example, you might consider carefully adjusting the trade-off between the information store buffer pool and the system memory pool. Also, by checking the per-process working sets, you can identify the major memory allocations. If your paging rate is over a small amount (for example 20 pages/sec), consider adding memory.

The Available Bytes counter indicates how much physical memory is available at any given time. The system adjusts working sets of processes to keep this above a certain threshold, generally 4 MB. If this level is approached, you should see higher paging and page fault rates. The Committed Bytes counter indicates the amount of virtual address space that the system has committed to applications. This must be backed by the paging file on the disk, so make sure that there is space in the paging file. Anticipate memory issues by tracking trends in available and committed memory.

Buffers

The following are the important buffer counters for Exchange.

Object	Counter
Database: Information Store	File Bytes Read/sec
	File Bytes Written/sec
	Cache % Hit
Database: Directory	File Bytes Read/sec
	File Bytes Written/sec
	Cache % Hit

Depending on your usage patterns, you might be able to optimize the use of server memory by adjusting the number of information store buffers. Monitor the % Buffer Cache % Hit counter. If it is consistently very close to 100 percent, try decreasing the number of buffers. You should also monitor the information store disk activity. If the activity doesn't increase, your setting is correct. However, if you notice that the cache hit rate is less than 95 percent, try increasing the number of buffers. As long as the paging activity does not increase, the setting is correct. You should use caution when changing these settings. Make only small adjustments, and monitor the results until you are confident the changes you have made work appropriately.

Recommendations

- Consider using **perfwiz -v** to adjust your information store buffer usage if the cache hit rate is very high or very low.

- If you cannot find a happy medium for this setting, you probably need to add more memory.

The Network Interface object can be obtained by installing the *Microsoft Windows NT Resource Kit*. If your network connection is a point-to-point link, the counters described below show all traffic on the link. If the connection is a LAN, these counters will show the traffic to and from the server you are monitoring.

Object	Counter
Network Interface	Bytes Received/sec
	Bytes Sent/sec
	Packets Received/sec
	Packets Sent/sec

If you know the capacity ratings of your network and network interface card (NIC), you can compare these ratings to the values for the Network Interface counters shown above and determine how close to capacity you are operating. For a more complete overview of network traffic, you can also use the Network Monitor tool available with Microsoft Systems Management Server (SMS). Note that Network Monitor is a stand-alone tool. You do not have to have other SMS components installed to run Network Monitor.

If you discover that the server is operating at or near network capacity, you can upgrade the network speed (for example, by moving from a 10-MB Ethernet to a 100-MB Ethernet network, or moving from a 64-KB line to a T1 line). You might also want to consider using multiple Ethernet connections for the server or multiple 64-KB lines, rather than one faster connection or line. Consider faster links, multiple interfaces, and multiple links.

System Bus

If you suspect that bus saturation is affecting your server, you can monitor its activity on Pentium and Pentium Pro servers and then change your server's configuration as necessary. To view Pentium counters, run the **Pperf** utility in the P5ctrs directory that is available on the *Microsoft Windows NT Resource Kit* compact disc.

The following are important bus counters for Exchange.

Object	Counter
Pentium	Bus Utilization (clks)/sec
	% Code Cache Misses
	% Data Cache Misses

If your system bus is near saturation, you have two options:

- Use larger CPU caches if there are many cache misses
- Split the load onto multiple servers. Start by offloading any non-Exchange services, if they are being used.

P A R T 6

Integration and Interaction

Microsoft Exchange Server is one component of the Microsoft BackOffice family of integrated products. By combining two or more BackOffice products, you can create powerful solutions to business problems.

Knowledge Management

Knowledge management involves collecting knowledge in your organization, refining that knowledge, and making it available to individuals who need it. There is not a single best way to implement knowledge management for all organizations. Rather, you need to build a solution that fits the needs of your particular organization.

The combination of Microsoft Exchange Server, Microsoft Site Server, and Internet Information Services (IIS) give you the tools you need to build a knowledge management solution for your organization. Exchange collects and organizes information in public folders while the powerful indexing and searching capabilities of Site Server make that knowledge accessible to the individuals who need it. IIS delivers the query pages that individuals use to request the information they need.

Hardware Requirements

- Either an Intel® Pentium 100 MHz or faster processor (Intel Pentium 166 MHz recommended), or a Digital Equipment Corporation (DEC) Alpha processor*
- 64 megabytes (MB) of RAM, 96 MB if Microsoft SQL Server is installed on the same computer (128 MB recommended)*
- 200 MB of virtual memory
- 1 gigabyte (GB) of available hard disk space (2 GB recommended)*

- CD-ROM drive
- Network adapter card
- VGA or Super VGA monitor compatible with Microsoft Windows NT Server 4.0 set to 1024 x 768

*In a production environment, the actual requirements will vary based on the volume of traffic at your Web site.

Software Requirements

- Microsoft Exchange Server version 5.0 or higher if Exchange and Site Server are on *different* computers
- Microsoft Exchange Server version 5.5 with Service Pack 1 if Exchange and Site Server are on the *same* computer
- Microsoft Site Server version 3.0 with Service Pack 1

Process Overview

There are four basic processes in a typical knowledge management solution:

1. Determine the data structure, or how you are going to allow information to be searched or grouped.
2. Collect information, or identify existing information you already have stored.
3. Index or catalog the information so that it can be searched efficiently.
4. Provide a means for users to search and retrieve the specific information they need.

Information is located in many different places throughout a company, such as on file systems, Web servers, databases, e-mail discussion servers, and document management systems. These files, database records, and e-mail messages are generally referred to as *documents*. The integration of Exchange and the Search component of Site Server make those types of documents more accessible from one application.

You can use Search to build a catalog from these documents. Search finds and gathers the documents and then indexes them in a catalog. When you set up a Web site that allows site visitors access to that cataloged information. The visitors easily search and find documents that they need. The site visitor enters a query on a search page, and any documents in the catalog that match the search query are listed on a results page. The site visitor clicks a link, and the original document is displayed.

Determining the Data Structure

Before you can set up your servers to extract information, you must first determine the type of information you want to make available for searching. Do you want to limit the available information to Exchange public folders, or do you want to provide information from a variety of sources such as information on file systems, Web servers, databases, or e-mail discussion server? For the purposes of this chapter, the focus is on how to integrate Exchange and Site Server to provide information stored in public folders, which can include information from replicated news groups.

Collecting Knowledge

The knowledge management solution we are describing uses Exchange public folders to collect and store knowledge. Public folders store e-mail messages, forms, task items, attachments, graphics, sound bites, and many other types of information in one location. You can use one or more of the following methods to get information into a public folder:

- Add the public folder to distribution lists. The public folder acts as an archive of the messages sent to the distribution lists.

- Create a Microsoft Outlook or Web form that adds structured messages to the public folder. The advantage of this method is that you can add custom attributes to the message. Later, users can limit their searches based on those custom attributes.

- Replicate Network News Transfer Protocol (NNTP) newsgroups, including USENET newsgroups, into the folder. This enables you to create an archive of information posted to a newsgroup.

Users can also simply store information in the public folder using Outlook, and you can also use knowledge management to improve access to existing public folders in your organization.

You must create one or more Search catalogs that contain information about all the content site visitors can search and browse in Knowledge Manager.

Configuring Exchange

In order for Search to access and retrieve (also known as *crawling*), information stored on an Exchange server, you must correctly configure Exchange so that it can be accessed by Search. Without the permissions being set correctly, Search will not be able to access information on the Exchange server.

Search is configured to work with one Exchange server in an Exchange installation for cataloging and searching messages. This Exchange server must be version 5.0 or higher. If you install Site Server on the same computer as Exchange, Exchange must be version 5.5 with Service Pack 1 installed.

Note It is recommended that you run Search and Exchange on different computers.

All public folders that you want to catalog and search must be hosted (*homed*) on this server or another server in the same site. With some additional limitations, you can search public folders that are homed in other sites, either by creating replicas in the local site or by accessing the other site over the network by means of site affinity settings.

Replicated Folders

Exchange public folders can be replicated to multiple servers within an Exchange site or to servers in other Exchange sites within your organization, thereby allowing users to have fast access to a replica of the folder through a local server. Replicated public folders can affect Search in several ways. By default, Search can crawl public folders homed on any server within the same Exchange site as the primary Exchange server that you configured. Once you specify the initial folder for the start address, if any of the subfolders are located on different servers within the site, automatic connections will be made to those servers as needed. No special configuration is necessary in this case.

Your Exchange site may contain local replicas of public folders that are homed in other sites. In this case, the administrator for the other site may have chosen to make this folder a secure public folder. Search needs administrative access to the folder to successfully crawl it. The administrator of the other Exchange site will need to either disable this setting or grant Owner permissions to the Windows NT account under which Search is running.

Note To disable this setting in the Administrator program, click the Folder object, then on the **File** menu, click **Properties**. On the **General** tab, clear the **Limit administrative access to home site**.

Finally, the Exchange site administrators may have configured public folder *affinity* settings between their sites. These settings are used to indicate that folders in one site are *directly accessible* over the network from another site. (Such connectivity is not a requirement. In general, Exchange sites are only required to have *e-mail* connectivity between them.) Again, Search needs administrative access to all folders being crawled.

Permissions

Search requires administrative access on the Configuration Object for each site that hosts public folders to be cataloged, including the sites that host any affinity or replicated folders.

▶ **To add the Search Administrator to Exchange**

1. In the Administrator program, under the **Site** object for your site, click **Configuration**.

2. On the **File** menu, click **Properties**, and then click the **Permissions** tab.

3. Add the Microsoft Windows NT account under which the Search service will run.

4. Do one of the following:

   ▪ Set the account's role to Administrator.

   ▪ Add an administrative account to the Site Configuration object, and Search can use this account.

Setting up the Exchange Public Folders

Exchange public folders must also be set up to allow site visitors to access messages in them. Your site visitors will only be able to see search results for those public folders where they have at least (Reviewer) access. The administrator or folder owner must modify the permissions on each public folder to include users who are allowed to search it by granting Reviewer rights. For information about setting permissions on public folders, see your Exchange documentation.

In addition to assigning permissions to individual Exchange mailboxes or distribution lists, you can assign public folder permissions to Default (authenticated users—those who have logged into a mailbox with a user name and password) and Anonymous (unauthenticated users—those who have not). Granting access to Anonymous has no effect on authenticated users; to grant access to all users, grant permission to both Default and Anonymous.

Setting the Anonymous and Default user permission has implications for how to set up public folder permissions, for example, when using Outlook Web Access to search for information. When site visitors click on a search results link that points to an Outlook Web Access server and the public folder message in the search results specifies authenticated access only, then the site visitor must log on to Outlook Web Access before viewing the message. If the message can be viewed by unauthenticated users, Outlook Web Access displays the message without prompting the site visitor to log on. For this reason, if you set up a Search site for public folder content that can be viewed by anyone, you might want to grant read privileges (for example Reviewer rights) to Anonymous. Then, users will not have to log on to read the messages.

By default, new public folders will inherit the permissions of their parent folders. Changing permissions on a parent folder does not automatically propagate the changes to the subfolders. Administrators can manually propagate a parent folder's permissions through an entire folder tree by using the Administrator program.

Configuring Site Server

Just as Exchange requires correct configuration for communication with Site Server, Site Server must be configured to work correctly with Exchange. You must set up your Search host for cataloging and searching Microsoft Exchange messages. If you are using more than one Search host, you must set up the following items *on each host*.

Security

Search security accounts must be set up to enforce rights present on Exchange public folders, so that when site visitors search a catalog, the results display on those messages for which they have access privileges.

- When Search accesses messages in a public folder, it uses a site-specific content access account defined in a site rule for the Exchange site. Or if that does not exist, it uses the default content access account defined on the catalog build server.

- A content access account must be configured with a domain account that has administrative rights on the Configuration Object for each site that hosts public folders to be cataloged (including the sites that host any affinity folders or replicated folders) or the domain account must have explicit owner rights on any Replicated Secure folders from another site. For more information, see your Site Server documentation.

- There are two accounts – the content access account and administrative access account. The administrative access account must be an administrator on both the catalog build machine and search machine. For more information, see your Site Server documentation.

- The Search service account must have administrative rights on the Site Configuration object for each Exchange site to be cataloged and searched, or must have explicit Owner rights on any Replicated Secure folders from another site (see). This account must also have administrator privileges on the catalog build server host and be a member of a privileged administrator group. For more information, see your Site Server documentation.

- Granting administrative privileges to the Site Configuration object of the Exchange site means that the Search service account will have administrator access to much of your Exchange site. For security reasons, you should limit access to this account only to trusted individuals. For further information on the security implications of allowing administrative access on the Site Configuration object, see your *Exchange* documentation.

Timeout Periods

Set the timeout periods for each catalog build server higher than the default. We recommend a setting of 60 seconds.

▶ **To set timeout periods for crawling from MMC**

1. On the **Start** menu, point to **Programs**, point to **Microsoft Site Server**, point to **Administration**, and then click **Site Server Service Admin (mmc)**.

2. In the console tree of the **Microsoft Management Console**, under **Search**, double-click the host to expand it, and then select **Catalog Build Server**.

3. On the **Action** menu, click **Properties**.

4. The **Search - Host - Catalog Build Server Properties** dialog box appears.

5. Click the **Timing** tab.

6. In the **Wait for a connection** box, enter the timeout period to wait when trying to establish a connection with a site or server.

7. In the **Wait for request acknowledgement** box, enter the timeout period to wait for requesting a page or file.

8. Click **OK**.

▶ **To set timeout periods for crawling from WebAdmin**

1. On the **Start** menu point to **Programs**, point to **Microsoft Site Server,** point to **Administration**, and then click **Site Server Service Admin (HTML)**.

2. In the menu frame, click **Server Properties**.

3. On the **Server Properties for Host** page, click **Site Hit Frequency**.

4. On the **Edit Site Hit Frequency Rules** page, in the **Wait for a connection** box, type the number of seconds to wait for a connection with the site or server.

5. In the **Wait for request acknowledgment** box, type the number of seconds to wait for a document or file.

6. Click **Submit**.

▶ **To set an account for Search**

1. On the **Start** menu, point to **Settings**, and then click **Control Panel**.

2. Double-click the **Services** icon.

3. From the **Service** list, click **Site Server Search**, and then click **Startup**.

4. Under **Log On As**, click **This Account**.

5. In the **This Account** box, type the domain and user name for the account, separated by a backward slash (\). For example, type *Domain\Username*.

6. In the **Password** box, type your password, and then type it again in the **Confirm Password** box.

7. Click **OK**.

8. With **Site Server Search** selected, click **Stop** to stop the service.

9. Click **Yes** to confirm.

10. The Site Server Search service will restart itself eventually, but to restart it immediately, click **Site Server Search**, and then click **Start**.

11. Click **Close**.

Setting Exchange Properties on the Search Host

Set the following Exchange properties on each Search host:

- **Outlook Web Access Server**. Provide the name of the Outlook Web Access server. This server is used if you write links from a search query that require Outlook Web Access. If you are not using Outlook Web Access for search results, you do not have to provide this information.

- **Exchange Server**. Provide the name of the Exchange server that Search will use to access public folders. Public folder replication lets you use any Exchange server in your site.

- **Exchange Site**. Provide the name of the site that contains the Exchange server.

- **Exchange Organization**. Provide the name of the organization that contains the site.

When configuring the Search hosts with Exchange properties, it is essential to correctly configure the name of the site that contains the Exchange server and the name of the organization that contains the site. If this information is not correctly set, Search will not be able to catalog or search Exchange messages. The Exchange administrator can find this information by running the Exchange Administrator program.

Setting Exchange Properties in Site Server

You can configure the Exchange properties from Microsoft Management Console (MMC) or from Web-based Administration (WebAdmin).

▶ **To set Exchange properties from MMC**

1. In the console tree of Microsoft Management Console, under **Search**, select the host for which to set properties.

2. On the **Action** menu, click **Properties**.

3. Specify the following properties:

- In the **Outlook Web Access server name** box, type the name of the Exchange server with Outlook Web Access enabled. If you are not using Outlook Web Access for search results, leave this field empty.

- In the **Exchange server name** box, type the name of an Exchange server from which public folders are to be cataloged.

- In the **Exchange server site name** box, type the name of the site that contains the Exchange server. Contact your Exchange administrator for this site name.

- In the **Exchange server organization name** box, type the name of the organization that contains the site. Contact your Exchange administrator for this organization name.

> **Note** If this information is not set correctly, Search will not be able to catalog or search Exchange messages.

4. Click OK.

▶ **To Set Exchange Properties from WebAdmin**

1. In the menu frame, click **Microsoft Exchange Properties**.

2. On the **Edit Exchange Properties** page, specify the following properties:

3. In the **Outlook Web Access** box, type the name of the Exchange server with Outlook Web Access enabled. If you are not using Outlook Web Access for search results, leave this field empty.

4. In the **Microsoft Exchange Server** box, type the name of one Exchange server from which public folders are to be cataloged.

5. In the **Site Name** box, type the name of the site that contains Exchange. Contact your Exchange administrator for this site name.

6. In the **Organization name** box, type the name of the organization that contains the site. Contact your Exchange administrator for this organization name.

> **Note** If this information is not set correctly, Search will not be able to catalog or search Exchange messages.

7. Click **Submit**.

Search utilizing catalogs to extract information from the Exchange server.

Crawling Files

Crawling is the process through which Search gathers content by following links contained in documents or by following directory trees in a file system. When integrating Exchange and Search, crawling to extract information in public folders.

There are several different ways that you can crawl information:

Web Link Crawl. Using HTTP, you can crawl documents by following links, for example, when crawling Web documents on an intranet site or external Internet site. Search gathers a page on the Web site or file system you set as the start address. Search takes the links found on that page and follows them to other pages, gathers those documents, and so on. Search can crawl documents on any type of Web server.

For crawling Web links, Search supports HTML version 3.2 and above, Microsoft Internet Explorer 4.0 HTML, HTTP version 1.0 and above. Search does nothing special for HTTP version 1.1.

File Crawl. Using the File protocol, you can crawl documents that are located in one directory, for example, documents on a file system, such as in shared folders in Windows NT or Windows 95. Search starts crawling from a file directory you set as the start address, then gathers all the documents found in that directory and in all of its subdirectories. File crawling also allows you to preserve the security access control lists (ACLs) on files in the Windows NT file system.

Search can crawl any file system that can be mounted remotely in Microsoft® Windows, such as NetWare.

Note If Site Server indexes a file from another machine, and the file's permissions are based on that machine's local groups, Site Server will not display that file as a search result even to people who are in that local group. This is because Site Server will not know about that machine's local groups. To prevent this, be sure to use domain groups for file permissions.

Microsoft Exchange Crawl. If you are crawling messages on an Exchange server, your start address will be an Exchange public folder. Using the Exch protocol, Search gathers all messages and associated attachments in the folder. Search also enforces rights present on Exchange public folders.

Transaction Log

For each crawl, Search creates an internal transaction log to keep track of all the documents to gather:

- When performing a *Web crawl*, Search marks all the links it finds in each document as *pending* in the transaction log.

- When performing a *File crawl*, Search creates links for all the files in the starting directory and its sub-directories, and marks them as *pending* in the transaction log.

- When performing an *Exchange crawl*, Search creates links for all the messages in the public folder, and marks them as *pending* in the transaction log.

After Search has finished gathering one document, it follows the next pending link in the transaction log to another document. Search gathers that document, and so on. After Search successfully gathers a document, the link in the transaction log is marked as *done*.

Crawl History

The crawl history is an internal record of all links that have been crawled. Whenever Search encounters a new link, it is added to the crawl history. When Search finds a new link, Search compares it to the crawl history before adding it to the transaction log, thereby ensuring that links are not crawled twice.

Note If anything disrupts a crawl, such as a power failure, Search uses the transaction log and crawl history to resume the crawl from where it left off. The crawl does not have to start over from the beginning.

How Far Search Crawls

A crawl is finished when all links in the transaction log have been followed. However, the following choices you make determine which links will go into the transaction log:

- When crawling a file system, Search crawls all the documents in the specified directory and its subdirectories. Or, you can set the directory depth, which specifies how many levels of subdirectories to crawl.

- When following links, you can specify how many page hops and site hops Search can make when crawling. The number of page hops is the number of jumps Search can make in any direction from the start address. Similarly, site hops is the number of site boundaries Search can cross when making jumps from the start address.

- When following links, you can limit Search to crawling only the sites for which you have defined site rules. Similarly, you can limit Search to crawling certain paths on these sites.

- When crawling an Exchange public folder, Search crawls all the documents in the folder and their attachments.

Full and Incremental Crawls

The first time you crawl, Search performs a *full crawl*—starting with an empty catalog, Search follows every link in the transaction log and gathers every document. However, an important consideration when crawling is the time it takes to complete a crawl, and the bandwidth it uses. Therefore, Search provides you with the option of performing an *incremental crawl* to update your catalogs after the first full crawl. An incremental crawl starts with the previous catalog, and gathers only those documents that have changed since the last crawl, which substantially reduces both crawling time and bandwidth use. For example, you can perform frequent incremental crawls, such as every night, and full crawls on a less frequent schedule, such as once a week.

When Search builds a catalog, it keeps a crawl history, which is a record of every document that was crawled in the previous build.

Search compares the last-modified date for each document link in the crawl history to the date on the current version of the document. If the dates are different, Search gathers and catalogs the document.

Changes to a document's access control lists (ACLs) do not affect a document's date; therefore, Search will not recrawl these documents during an incremental build unless the content has changed.

Search compares each document link in the crawl history to the rules and restrictions in the catalog definition. Any new restrictions are applied to the document.

For example, you add a rule to a catalog definition to avoid a site, and then start an incremental build. The previous build contained documents from this site, so there are links from this site in the crawl history. These links are compared to the rules and restrictions in the current catalog definition, and the new rule causes Search to delete the corresponding documents from the catalog.

However, not all changes you make to the catalog definition affect the resulting catalog when you start an incremental build, especially if you remove restrictions. For example, your catalog definition contains a rule to avoid a certain site; you remove this rule, then start an incremental build. Even though the rule has been removed, the site will not be crawled unless a new or modified document has an explicit link to that site. The site was excluded from the previous build, and therefore does not exist in the crawl history. Changes to page hops and site hops are also not reflected in an incremental build.

Note The first crawl for a catalog is always a full crawl because there is no crawl history with which to make file comparisons.

We recommend starting a full build periodically, especially after changing the catalog definition.

Indexing (Cataloging) the Knowledge

Site Server provides the indexing and cataloging functionality that enables users to quickly and easily locate the information they need. By default, Site Server creates indexes of properties including the message subject, author, and date sent. You can also add indexes for custom properties.

Once the text and properties have been extracted from a document, Search indexes the information. Indexing consists of keeping track of which words are used and where they are located in each document. For example, the index might indicate that the word *Microsoft* is found at word number 423 in Default.htm, and at words 638 and 982 in Products.doc. This index allows a quick and efficient search for all documents containing certain words, as well as advanced search operations, such as phrase searches (searching for *white elephant* means looking for documents with *white* followed by *elephant*) and proximity searches (searching for all documents where *big* occurs within fifty words of *house*).

To prevent the index from becoming bloated with words that do not help site visitors find documents, Search ignores *noise words*, such as *a*, *and*, *the*, and so on. Search provides noise word lists for nine languages. These noise word lists should be sufficient for most normal operations, but can be modified for specific environments. For example, high-tech companies might want to add the word *computer* to their noise word list.

Each of these indexes (catalogs) can support up to 5 million documents, and Search can support up to 32 catalogs per server.

Creating and Managing Catalog Definitions

A catalog definition contains the instructions and parameters for building a catalog. Catalog definitions are stored in the catalog build server on the host used for building catalogs.

You can set up catalog definitions for the following types of catalogs:

Crawl. A crawl catalog is built by crawling documents on the Internet, on intranets, file systems, and public folders.

Notification. A notification catalog is built by receiving information from a notification source.

Database. A database catalog is built by crawling a table in an ODBC database. A database catalog and its definition can be managed using WebAdmin only.

After you identify the catalog type, you must choose between two build options:

Full Build. A full build starts with an empty catalog and uses only your start addresses as the starting points for the crawl.

Incremental Build. An incremental build starts with the start addresses, and the catalog and list of URLs from the previous build and updates any changes made to the content since the last crawl. After one full build, incremental builds are typically much faster than full builds.

Defining a crawl catalog can be done using an MMC or WebAdmin wizard.

▶ **To Create a Definition for a Crawl Catalog using an MMC Wizard**

1. In the console tree of the Microsoft Management Console under **Search**, double-click a host to expand it, and then select **Catalog Build Server**.

2. On the **Action** menu, point to **New**, and then click **Catalog Definition with a Wizard**.

3. The New Catalog Definition Wizard appears.

4. Read the information, and then click **Next**.

5. In the **Catalog Name** box, type a name for the catalog.

6. Catalog names may contain up to 39 characters, must be alphanumeric, cannot contain spaces, and must be unique on the catalog build server.

7. Click **Next**.

8. The **Specify the Crawl Type** page appears, where you can specify information for one start address.

9. Specify how you want Search to crawl from the start address you will specify.

   - **Web link crawl**. Search will crawl documents by following links from each document to other documents.

   - **File crawl**. Search will crawl all the documents in a directory and its sub-directories.

   - **Exchange crawl**. Search will crawl all the messages in a folder and its sub-folders.

10. Click **Next**.

11. If you selected **Exchange crawl** but you have not yet specified the Exchange properties for your host, you are prompted to do so. If this information is not correctly set, Search will not be able to catalog or search Exchange messages.

12. In the **Exchange server name** box, type the name of an Exchange server from which public folders are to be cataloged.

13. In the **Outlook Web Access server name** box, type the name of the Exchange Server with Outlook Web Access enabled. If you are not using Outlook Web Access for search results, leave this field empty.

14. Click **Next**.

15. In the **Exchange server site name** box, type the name of the site that contains the Exchange server. Contact your Exchange administrator for this site name.

16. In the **Exchange server organization name** box, type the name of the organization that contains the site. Contact your Exchange administrator for this organization name.

17. Click **Next**.

18. In the **Start address** box, type the location where you want the crawl to start.

    A start address can be a URL, a UNC path, a file path, or a path to an Exchange folder, and should be spelled out fully. For example,

    http://example.microsoft.com/default.htm

    C:\Microsoft Site Server\SiteServer\Docs

\\host\share\directory

exch://Public Folders/All Public Folders/FolderName

Note If the name of a public folder contains a slash (/) or a percent sign (%), you must replace these characters in the start address as follows: replace "/"with "%2F" and replace % with "%25".

For example, to crawl a public folder such as "100% Solution" requires the following start address: exch://*ExchangeServer*/public folders/All public folders/FolderName/100%25 Solution.

---

6. Specify the crawling policy.

   ▪ If you selected **Web link crawl**, you can limit the number of page hops and site hops, or crawl only the sites for which you will define site rules. For more information, see your Site Server documentation.

   ▪ If you selected **File crawl**, you can either crawl documents in all sub-directories, or limit the depth of sub-directories to crawl.

   ▪ If you selected **Exchange crawl**, you can either crawl documents in all sub-folders, or limit the depth of sub-folders to crawl.

7. Click **Next**.

8. In the **Hosts** box, select the hosts to which to propagate the catalog (by default, the local host is already selected), and then click **Next**.

9. To build the catalog immediately, select **Start build now**. Or, you can build the catalog later.

10. Click **Finish**.

11. The catalog definition is added under the host's **Catalog Build Server** in the console tree of the Microsoft Management Console. To set additional properties for this catalog definition, select the catalog definition, and then on the **Action** menu, click **Properties**.

▶ **To Create a Definition for a Crawl Catalog with the WebAdmin Wizard**

1. In the menu frame, click **Catalog Build Definitions**.

2. On the **Catalog Build Definitions** page, click **Create**.

3. The **Create New Catalog Definition Wizard** appears.

4. Click **Web sites, file systems, and Microsoft Exchange folders**, and then click **Next**.

5. In the **Catalog Name** box, type a name for the catalog.

6. Catalog names may contain up to 39 characters, must be alphanumeric, cannot contain spaces, and must be unique on the catalog build server.

7. If you want to add a start address, click **Next**. Otherwise click **Finish**, and use the catalog definition property pages to complete the catalog definition.

8. Specify how you want Search to crawl documents.

   - **Web link crawl**. Search will crawl documents by following links from each document to other documents.

   - **File crawl**. Search will crawl all the documents in a directory and its sub-directories.

   - **Exchange crawl**. Search will crawl all the messages in a folder and its sub-folders.

9. Click **Next**.

10. In the **Start address** box, type the location where you want the crawl to start.

    A start address can be a URL, a UNC path, a file path, or a path to an Exchange folder, and should be spelled out fully. For example,

    http://example.microsoft.com/default.htm

    C:\Microsoft Site Server\SiteServer\Docs

    \\host\share\directory

    exch://*ExchangeServer*/public folders/All public folders/FolderName

    ---

    Note If the name of a public folder contains a slash (/) or a percent sign (%), you must replace these characters in the start address as follows: replace "/"with "%2F" and replace % with "%25".

    For example, to crawl a public folder such as "100% Solution" requires the following start address: exch://*ExchangeServer*/public folders/All public folders/FolderName/100%25 Solution.

    ---

11. Specify the crawling policy.

12. If you selected Web link crawl, you can limit the number hops and site hops, or crawl only the sites for which you will define site rules. For more information, see your Site Server documentation.

13. If you selected **File crawl**, you can either crawl documents in all sub-directories, or limit the depth of sub-directories to crawl.

14. Click **Next**.

15. To build the catalog immediately, click **Start build now**. Or, you can build the catalog later.

16. Click **Finish**.

17. If you selected to build the catalog immediately, click **OK** when the catalog is finished.

8. To set additional properties for this catalog definition, select the catalog definition, and then click **Properties**.

Retrieving the Knowledge

Once you have determined the type of data that you are going to permit users to retrieve and configured the servers correctly to permit access, you now must determine the type of client application you want for the front-end. There are two types of client software that are supported with this integration, Microsoft Outlook Web Access and Microsoft Outlook.

Outlook Web Access

You can configure Search to allow site visitors to access public folder messages using a Web browser through Outlook Web Access. In this case, Outlook Web Access server must be version 5.5 or later. The Exchange server connected to the Outlook Web Access server must be version 5.0 or later.

Outlook Web Access does not have to be on the same computer as Exchange; it can be a stand-alone Web server, or it can be the same Web server on which Search is installed. If you install Outlook Web Access with Site Server, you must first install a patch to Windows NT. For more information, see the Exchange Server 5.5 release notes.

The Exchange server used for crawling, the Outlook Web Access server, and the Exchange Server that is connected to the Outlook Web Access server do not have to be the same computer. However, both Exchange servers must be in the same organization, and must share the public folders. Specifying different computers for the Exchange server in the Exchange configuration properties and the Exchange server connected to the OWA server allows you to access messages from one location and display them from another.

Outlook

You can configure Search to allow site visitors to access public folder messages using Outlook. In this case, the site visitor must be running Microsoft Outlook 97 version 8.03 or later and Internet Explorer version 3.0 or later, on Windows 95 or Windows NT 4.0 or later.

Designing the Web Search Page

Search comes with a default Web page that you can make available to your site visitors. This page presents users with a field to enter a word or phrase to search for and a list of all the catalogs on your search server to choose from. It includes a tips page to provide site visitors with information on the search query syntax and advanced search options. The page is set up to handle catalogs that include NNTP messages and public folders, as well as HTML and Microsoft Office documents. It requires NTLM or Basic authentication in order to preserve security of any secure indexed documents.

The default search page is available to your site visitors from the following URL:

http://Your_server_name/Siteserver/Knowledge/Search

To make this search page available to your users, create a link from your Web site to this URL.

Before making this page available to your site visitors, check the following:

- Are the right catalogs available? If you do not want to use all the catalogs on your search server, you will need to modify the Searchleft.htm page to use a specific list of catalogs.

- If your catalogs include public folder messages, check the value of the ExchangeViewer variable in the Searchright.asp page. By default, it is set to **both**. This setting is used when your site visitors can either view messages using the Outlook client on their computers or use Outlook Web Access (OWA) to view messages. If either of these options is not available at your site, you need to change the ExchangeViewer variable to either **OWA** or **Outlook**.

If you want to modify the source for the default search page, the files can be found by default in C:\Microsoft Site Server\SiteServer\Knowledge\Search.

Note If you have installed Knowledge Manager, two sample catalogs are installed, KMCatalog1 and KMSampleCatalog2. You should delete these catalogs before making the default search page available on your site.

Sample Web Search Pages

Search comes with 12 sample pages. Each sample page emphasizes different features of Search; therefore, you can start from a sample page that matches your search needs.

To view the sample pages, go to
http://*Installation_server*/Siteserver/Samples/Knowledge/Search, where
Installation_server is the server where Site Server is installed using the default
directory structure. This list includes a sample page created specifically for
searching Exchange, permitting site visitors to search public folders by author.

You must have at least one catalog to use any of the sample pages. For sample
content, see the list of sample content which can be used to create sample catalogs
to use with the sample pages.

The first step is to create the sample catalogs. Then you can find or edit the
sample pages. If a sample page matches your search needs, you can use a sample
page on your site.

All the sample pages are commented to make them easy to understand and extend.
They include a detailed readme file that describes any required setup, suggests
terms to use to explore the sample page, and provides information on modifying
the sample page for use at your site. At the top of each page, a View Source Code
link displays the source code for the sample.

All the sample pages are set up to require Basic or NTLM authentication in order
to ensure that security of searched documents is maintained.

Server Performance

Creating catalogs and searching catalogs are both resource-intensive processes,
which use memory, processor, and network resources. If you are using one server
as your catalog build server, and a separate server as your search server, you can
optimize each server separately. If you are using one host for both, you need to
balance your configuration to maximize performance for both applications.

The following options provide you with several ways to enhance the performance
of your servers.

- **Stop Index Server**. Index Server does not need to be running if you are not
  using it. Closing Index Server reduces system resource use. Since Content
  Management uses Index Server, do not stop Index Server if you use Content
  Management.
- **Minimize the Number of Columns in the Catalog**. Select only the properties
  that you need to search and display because extra data in the catalog slows the
  crawl. You can also reduce the size of the catalog by adding words to the noise
  words list. These changes will also help search performance.

- **Use Incremental Crawls when Building a Catalog**. After you do a full catalog build, use incremental catalog builds for subsequent crawls if your catalog definition remains stable. Incremental catalog builds only pick up new or changed files so fewer files will need to be processed. You should schedule a full crawl after several incremental catalog builds in order to pick up changes such as ACL changes that are not picked up in incremental builds.

- **Schedule Catalog Builds**. Build your catalogs during periods of low network usage, such as evenings, early mornings, or weekends.

  1. Make sure you schedule your builds during so that they do not interfere with scheduled network backups.

- **Set the Site Hit Frequency for Crawling**. You can control how much delay there is between gathering each document.

- **Set Time Out Periods for Crawling**. If you are crawling over a fast network such as a corporate intranet, you can reduce the timeout values for waiting for a connection and waiting to request acknowledgement. This will prevent you from adding time to the catalog creation process if one of the servers you are crawling is non-operational.

- **Set the Resource Use**. You can control what percentage of system resources are available for creating catalogs. Use the Performance Monitor to monitor CPU usage while creating catalogs. If you have one computer that is solely a catalog build server, if CPU usage is less than 100%, move the slider toward **Dedicated**.

- **Modify the Indexing Limit for a Catalog in the Windows NT Registry**. After a file has been filtered, Search does not index the content after a 300,000 byte limit. This improves performance by limiting the amount one file can contribute to the catalog and also protects your Search system against malicious files.

PART 7

Tools and Utilities

This section describes the tools, utilities, and documentation included on the *Microsoft BackOffice 4.5 Resource Kit* compact disc. For updates about the contents of the compact disc, see the file Readme.doc in the root directory of the compact disc.

Exchange Tools

The *Microsoft BackOffice 4.5 Resource Kit* compact disc includes almost 100 tools to help you plan, install, and manage Exchange. Many of the tools are command-line utilities that you can call from automation scripts that you write. Online documentation is provided for all of the tools.

New and Updated Tools

The following tools are new or updated for the third edition of the *Microsoft BackOffice 4.5 Resource Kit.*

- The new Mailbox Agent is a collection of components that allow you to monitor and process mail in a mailbox.

- The new IMS Extension allows you to pre- and post-process e-mail messages that travel through the Internet Mail Service. It also allows you to add text to the body of a message. Your company can use this feature to add disclaimer text to Internet mail.

- The updated Mailbox Cleanup Agent enables you to delete and move outdated messages from users' mailboxes. This version fixes a problem in the previous version that deleted users' contacts.

- The documentation for the EXLIST List Server sample application is updated.

Tool Descriptions

The Exchange tools are grouped into the following categories. When you run the main setup program, you can choose to install all of the tools in one or more of these categories.

For complete information about any tool, see the online documentation file Exchange\Docs\Exchtool.chm on the compact disc.

Administration Tools The administration tools help you with administration tasks such as viewing and managing event logs and distribution lists. There are tools to delete old messages from user mailboxes, move mail between mailboxes, and to collect data on mailbox usage. Other tools monitor services or generate reports.

Client Tools The client tools enhance Exchange client programs and help manage local data such as personal address books and personal folder files. Other tools make it easier to use more than one client program or synchronize data between the client and Exchange.

Developer Tools The developer tools help developers of applications that work with Exchange create and test code. A sample application demonstrates how to process mail with an event script and Web interface.

Microsoft Mail Resource Kit Tools The Microsoft Mail resource kit tools help you connect Microsoft Mail with Exchange. Also included are tools that are designed to repair and maintain the database for Microsoft Mail for PC Networks.

Migration Tools The migration tools help administrators migrate users from other e-mail systems to Exchange. There are tools to move and convert messages and tools to create accounts.

Public Folder Tools The public folder tools help you manage permissions, verify replication, and collect data about public folders.

Security Tools The security tools enable users to encrypt and decrypt all messages in a file, and to manage passwords when connecting to Exchange from other platforms.

Web Tools The Web tools enable you to create a Web site that automatically displays the current status of critical Exchange services, and enable users to update their personal information in the global address list from a Web browser. A sample Collaboration Data Objects (CDO) application demonstrates how to extract and display organization information from the Exchange global address list.

Exchange Tools Installation

There are three ways to install the Exchange tools, depending on which tools you select. Most of the tools are installed using the main setup program on the compact disc. Other tools have their own setup programs or must be installed manually.

Running the Main Setup Program

The main setup program installs most of the Exchange tools. The following sections explain how to install the tools that are not installed by the main setup program. Those tools either have individual setup programs or must be installed manually.

A complete installation of all of the Exchange tools installed by the main setup program requires approximately 60 megabytes (MB) of disk space.

▶ **To install Exchange tools using the main setup program**

1. Insert the *Microsoft BackOffice 4.5 Resource Kit* compact disc in the CD-ROM drive.
2. Click **Install BackOffice Resource Kit** from the Microsoft BackOffice Resource Kit Setup page.
3. Follow the instructions on the screen. When prompted, click **Custom/Complete**.
4. Select **Exchange Tools**, and then click **Change Option**.
5. Select the categories of Exchange tools you want to install, and then follow the instructions on the screen to complete the installation.

Running Individual Setup Programs

The following tools are installed by individual setup programs:

- Crystal Reports 4.5 for Microsoft Exchange Server
- EFD Hand Code Agent
- Mailbox Cleanup Agent
- Microsoft Exchange Administrative Mailbox Agent
- Windows Domain Planner
- Microsoft Exchange Server Modeling Tool
- Microsoft Mail Export/Import Tool
- Natural Language Support Configuration Tool
- Exchange Monitor Report Generator

- GW Client
- Microsoft Exchange Forms Designer
- InterOrg Synchronization Tool
- NetAdmin Web Status Tool
- Migration Wizard for AT&T Mail
- Mailbox Replication Service

▶ **To run individual setup programs**

1. Insert the *Microsoft BackOffice 4.5 Resource Kit* compact disc in the CD-ROM drive.
2. Click **More MS Exchange Tools** from the Microsoft BackOffice Resource Kit Setup page, and then select the tool you want to install.

Installing Manually

The following tools are not installed by the BackOffice Resource Kit main setup program. To install these tools manually, follow the installation instructions for each tool located in the online documentation file Exchange\Docs\Exchtools.chm on the compact disc.

- Address Book Lookup
- Address Book Export
- Archive Client Extension
- AutoFill
- CleanSweep
- GAL Modify
- Global Send Options
- IMS Extensions
- Internet Idioms
- Microsoft Exchange Server Preview Pane Extension
- Microsoft Schedule+ Address Book Assistant
- PAB-GAL Synchronization
- Server Space Client Extension
- Simple Mail Handler
- SwitchForms
- IMS Extension
- Mailbox Agent

Tools Documentation

Documentation for all of the Exchange tools is provided in Help files. You can choose to install the documentation when you run the main setup program. The documentation is located in the specified directory on the compact disc.

File	Description
Readme.doc	Current information and updates about the contents of the compact disc
Exchange\Docs\Exchtool.chm	Documentation for Exchange tools
Exchange\Docs\Eperfmon.hlp	Descriptions of performance monitor counters for Exchange
Exchange\Docs\Exmsgref.hlp	Exchange message reference
Exchange\Docs\Excrk.chm	This book in online form
Exchange\Docs\Splusdk.hlp	*Microsoft Schedule Plus Programmer's Reference*

Exchange Message Reference

The Exchange message reference lists all Exchange error and event log messages with descriptions and recommended actions. The message reference is included in Help format that you can search and read (Exchange\Docs\Exmsgref.hlp) and in a comma-separated value file (Exchange\Docs\Exmsgref.csv) that you can import into a database or spreadsheet.

Sample Code

The *Microsoft BackOffice 4.5 Resource Kit* compact disc contains sample code that demonstrates how to program with Exchange. The samples are located in \Exchange\Samples directory on the compact disc. For complete information about these samples, see the online documentation file Exchange\Docs\Exchtool.chm.

PART 8

Troubleshooting

Exchange provides a variety of tools and diagnostics that can be used to troubleshoot problems in your organization. This chapter includes some problems you might encounter while using Exchange. It is organized into the following sections:

- Setup Problems
- Database Problems
- Directory Problems
- Internet Mail Problems
- NNTP Support Problems
- Performance Problems
- General Mail Delivery Problems
- Registry Access Problems
- Troubleshooting Tools

Setup Problems

The following section describes problems that can occur during setup and installation of Exchange.

Setup Fails While Installing Exchange

If Setup fails while installing Exchange, in most cases you should reinstall the product.

Setup failures can also be caused by network problems. In these cases, first verify that the network connection is working correctly, and then complete the following steps to ensure that Exchange is properly installed.

1. Turn off all Exchange services.
2. Restart the server.
3. Run the Setup program, and reinstall any components that Setup did not install successfully during the initial installation.

Setup Fails While Adding a New Server to a Site

In general, you have to reinstall the server or the components that failed to install Exchange correctly.

Caution Information about the new server might have been replicated to other servers in the site. To prevent the site's directory from becoming corrupted, remove the new server from the site's directory before you reinstall the server.

▶ **To ensure that Exchange is installed correctly in the site**

1. In the Administrator program on the remote server that you specified during Setup, delete the server object for the new server.
2. Run Setup again on the new server, and select **Remove All**.
3. Run Setup again on the new server, and reinstall Exchange.

Public Folders Fail to Replicate

Public folder replication cannot occur until the directory has been replicated. If the interval between directory replications is long, the information store might try to replicate public folders before the new site has been added to the directory.

You can wait for the directory to replicate the new site information or force directory replication to occur.

▶ **To ensure that public folders replicate successfully**

1. Click the **General** property page for the server directory.

2. Click **Update Now**.

Note If you force directory replication to occur, choose a time when the server's performance is not critical and connection costs are low.

Database Problems

The following section describes problems that can occur with the database.

Information Store on Microsoft Exchange Does Not Start

If the information store on your server does not start, review the Windows NT application event log for the following event log identifiers (ID).

Event log ID	Message text
1087	The information store was restored from an offline backup. Run ISINTEG -patch before starting the information store.
1089	The information store was not started because the system distinguished name of *<a distinguished name representing the mailbox root>* in the mailboxes table could not be found.
	The database might have been restored to a computer that does not contain the original database.
	Run ISINTEG -patch before attempting to start the information store again.
2083	The information store was restored from an offline backup. Run ISINTEG -patch before starting the information store.
7202	The database has been copied from the server*<server1>* to the server *<server2>*.
	The database cannot function until ISINTEG -patch has been run.

The appearance of any of these event log IDs indicates that a restore patch is missing. Running the ISINTEG utility with the Patch option fixes these problems. For more information see Part 9, "Disaster Recovery."

Note When running in Patch mode, ISINTEG does not perform database integrity tests. For this you need to run ISINTEG in Test mode. Patch mode and Test mode cannot run concurrently.

Database Inconsistency, Background Thread, and Failure-to-Move-Mailbox Error Messages

The following table maps various event IDs and messages to specific ISINTEG options that you can use to correct the problem. The first column contains the event IDs found in the Windows NT application event log. The second column contains the event log message. The last column contains the ISINTEG command-line option that you use to test and fix the problem.

Note The events shown in the following table might be, but are not necessarily, a result of a corrupted information store. As a result, there are some cases where the suggested option does not repair the problem associated with the event log ID and description. If the suggested test does not resolve the problem, Microsoft Technical Support can direct you to other diagnostic methods.

Event log ID	Description	Correction option
1025	An error occurred. Function name or description of problem: EcGetRestriction. Error: 0x57a	-test search
1186	A database inconsistency (EcSetSpecialRights/ACLID) was encountered while performing an upgrade.	-test acllistref
1186	A database inconsistency (2.1A/AMIDRefCt) was encountered while performing an upgrade.	-test aclitemref
	A database inconsistency (2.1A/AMIDRef) was encountered while performing an upgrade.	
	A database inconsistency (2.1B/AMID) was encountered while performing an upgrade.	
	A database inconsistency (2.2D/AMID) was encountered while performing an upgrade.	
1186	A database inconsistency (2.1A/ACLID) was encountered while performing an upgrade.	-test acllistref
	A database inconsistency (2.1B/ACLID) was encountered while performing an upgrade.	
	A database inconsistency (2.2D/ACLID) was encountered while performing an upgrade.	
	A database inconsistency (2.1A/ACLRef) was encountered while performing an upgrade.	
1186	A database inconsistency (2.1B/cnset) was encountered while performing an upgrade.	-test aclitemref

(continued)

Event log ID	Description	Correction option
1198	A database inconsistency was encountered while performing an upgrade to version 2.19.	-test folder
	FID: *<value>*	
	MID: *<value>*	
	INID: *<value>*	
	A database inconsistency was encountered while performing an upgrade to version 2.2a.	
	FID: *<value>*	
	MID: *<value>*	
	INID: *<value>*	
7200	Background thread FDsWaitTask halted due to error code *<value>*.	-test mailbox
7200	Background thread EcFlushInTransitUserMail halted due to error code *<value>*.	-test folder
7201	Background thread FDoMaintenance encountered a problem. Error code *<value>*.	-test folder, artidx
7201	Background thread FDoPeriodic encountered a problem. Error code *<value>*.	-test rowcounts, dumpsterref
8500	Unable to move mailbox *<mailbox name>*.	-test message
	A problem occurred while opening an attachment.	
	Internal parent folder ID: *<value>*, parent message ID: *<value>*; Error code: *<value>*.	
8501	Unable to move mailbox *<mailbox name>*.	-test message
	A problem occurred while opening an attachment.	
	Parent folder name: *<name>*, parent message subject: *<subject>*; Error code: *<value>*.	
8502	Unable to move mailbox *<mailbox name>*.	-test message
	A problem occurred while opening an attached message.	
	Internal parent folder ID: *<value>*, parent message ID: *<value>*; Error code: *<value>*.	

(continued)

Event log ID	Description	Correction option
8503	Unable to move mailbox *<mailbox name>*.	-test message*
	A problem occurred while opening an attached message.	
	Parent folder name: *<value>*, parent message subject: *<value>*; Error code: *<value>*.	
8504	Unable to move mailbox *<mailbox name>*.	-test folder*
	A problem occurred while getting the properties for a folder.	
	Internal folder ID: *<value>*; Error code: *<value>*.	
8505	Unable to move mailbox *<mailbox name>*.	-test folder*
	A problem occurred while getting the properties for a folder.	
	Folder name: *<value>*; Error code: *<value>*.	
8506	Unable to move mailbox *<mailbox name>*.	-test folder, message*
	A problem occurred while getting the properties for a message.	
	Internal parent folder ID: *<value>*; Message ID: *<value>*; Error code: *<value>*.	
8507	Unable to move mailbox *<mailbox name>*.	-test folder, message*
	A problem occurred while getting the properties for a message.	
	Parent folder name: *<value>*; Message subject: *<value>* Error code: *<value>*.	
8508	Unable to move mailbox *<mailbox name>*.	-test attach
	A problem occurred while getting the properties for an attachment.	
	Internal parent folder ID: *<value>*, parent message ID: *<value>*; Error code: *<value>*.	
8509	Unable to move mailbox *<mailbox name>*.	-test attach
	A problem occurred while getting the properties for an attachment.	
	Parent folder name: *<value>*, parent message subject: *<value>*; Error code: *<value>*.	

* The problems causing this message to appear might not be related to the integrity of the information store.

Diagnosing Other Problems Using ISINTEG Tests

You can use the ISINTEG utility dumpsterref test if the Performance Monitor information for Total Count of Recoverable Items or Total Size of Recoverable Items is incorrect for the MSExchangeIS Private object or the MsExchangeIS Public objects. These counts can become incorrect if the information store crashes before the current data is copied to disk. The dumpsterref test is fairly lengthy.

Note Stop the information store service before running ISINTEG.

In the following example, ISINTEG performs the folder and message tests on the private information store database and writes the results to the log file named c:\Systest\Private.log.

```
isinteg -pri -test folder,message -l c:\systest\private.log
```

In the following example, ISINTEG performs the aclitemref test on the public information store, fixes errors, and then writes the results to the default log file named Isinteg.pub.

```
isinteg -pub -fix -test aclitemref
```

Directory Problems

The following section describes problems that can occur with the directory. These problems include addresses that do not display in the correct language and objects that cannot be modified.

Language Display for Addresses Is Incorrect

If the global address list doesn't display addresses in the correct language, you might not have installed the correct language display template in the directory. For information about installing language display templates, see Part 3, "Deployment."

Directory Objects Cannot Be Modified

You might not be able to modify directory objects in a site for the following reasons:

- The objects are read-only.
- You are logged on under an account that does not have permission to modify objects.

To change an object's properties on an object, verify that you have permission to modify it. Keep in mind that some objects can reference objects in another site, so you might also need permission to modify those objects.

Internet Mail Problems

The following section describes problems that can occur with Internet mail.

Exchange Server Does Not Send or Receive Internet Mail

This section describes troubleshooting tips for the following problems:

- Outbound Internet mail sits in the queue or is returned to the sender as Host Unknown.
- Inbound Internet mail arrives at the domain name server and sits in the queue.
- Mail sent from the Internet addressed to users in the organization is returned as Host Unknown or Recipient not Recognized.

The following paragraphs describe these troubleshooting steps:

- Verify the Exchange site address.
- Verify the Windows NT TCP/IP DNS settings.
- Verify that Domain Name System (DNS) is configured correctly.
- Verify that the Internet Mail Service address space is valid.
- Perform the DNS Resolver test to verify your configuration.
- Verify that the computer appears in the Host list.

Verify the Site Address

The default Exchange Simple Mail Transport Protocol (SMTP) domain name is based on the organization and site name you specified during installation. For example, Ferguson and Bardell's organization name (FAB) and site name (NAmerica-SW) are used to generate the following domain name:

```
namerica-sw.fab.com
```

The domain name is appended to the mailbox name to generate an SMTP address for messages sent through the Internet Mail Service. For example, a user named Fran Wilson sending an SMTP message from this site has the following SMTP address:

```
franwilson@namerica-sw.fab.com
```

It is important to verify that the SMTP address for the site matches the address specified in DNS or the hosts file.

▶ **To check the SMTP site address**

1. In the **Administrator** window, choose **Configuration**.

2. Double-click **Site Addressing**.

3. Select the **Site Addressing** property page.

4. If the SMTP site address is incorrect, edit it. Make a note of the site address for later use.

For more information about site addresses, see *Microsoft Exchange Server Concepts and Planning* and *Microsoft Exchange Server Operations.*

Verify the Windows NT TCP/IP DNS Settings

Whenever possible, the TCP/IP DNS host and domain names should match the Exchange organization and site names.

▶ **To check the Windows NT TCP/IP configuration**

• In Control Panel, choose **Network** to open the **Network** dialog box.

If you do not maintain a DNS server in your organization, you should work with your Internet service provider to ensure that the correct DNS records are specified for your organization.

It is important to understand how address (A) records and MX records are used to verify their accuracy. The A record should match the domain name in the Windows TCP/IP configuration. If the site name does not equal the host name specified in DNS, you need an MX record. For more information, see *Microsoft Exchange Server Operations.*

For example, suppose the TCP/IP host name is tucson03 and the domain name is fab.com. The SMTP site address is @NAmerica-SW.fab.com. It is likely that a message will be sent to user@fab.com rather than user@NAmerica-SW.fab.com, so an MX record is needed to correlate NAmerica-SW with fab.com. The A record and MX record for this example are shown below:

```
Tucson03.fab.com.   IN A 10.31.67.198

NAmericaSW.fab.com IN MX 10 Tucson03.fab.com.
```

For more information about DNS, see *Microsoft Exchange Server Concepts and Planning, Microsoft Exchange Server Operations*, and your DNS server documentation.

Verify the Address Space

The address space of a connector creates a path for messages. It identifies the recipient type and the addresses that the message passes through. If the address space is not defined, messages cannot pass through it. If the address space is incorrect, some messages might not pass through it. Verify the address space for the Internet Mail Service by completing the following steps:

1. In the Administrator window, click **Connections**.

2. Double-click **Internet Mail Service**.

3. Click the **Address Space** property page.

4. In the example shown in the figure above, the address space is configured to process all SMTP type addresses (*.*). If the address space is not defined, create a new one. If it is not defined correctly, edit it.

For more information about address spaces, see *Microsoft Exchange Server Operations*.

Perform the DNS Resolver Test

The Internet Mail Service DNS Resolver Test performs a DNS query for MX records that match the specified domain. The test creates a list of one or more IP addresses in the same order of preference Internet Mail Service uses when delivering mail for that domain.

If the MX query returns no results, the test performs a query for the A record that matches the domain. The result is a single IP address. If the A record search returns no results, the test checks the host file on the local computer. If a match is found, the result is a single IP address.

The DNS Resolver Test is useful for checking DNS or host file configurations and for troubleshooting delivery problems.

Run the Internet Mail Service DNS Resolver Test from the Support\Utils directory on the Exchange compact disc. Run the test from the same computer that runs the Internet Mail Service after TCP/IP and DNS are configured.

To run the IMC DNS Resolver Test with options, type the following at the command prompt:

```
restest [-debug] domain
```

Using *-debug* causes additional information to be displayed at each step of the search.

Verify That the Exchange Computer Is Listed in the Hosts File

The Hosts file is read every time a Microsoft Windows Sockets (Winsock) application attempts to resolve a host name. There are no #PRE options to preload entries (LMHOSTS). You can add the Exchange entry to the Hosts file and then try again without having to restart Windows. The Hosts file on Microsoft Windows 95 is located in the Windows directory. On Microsoft Windows NT, it is located in the Windows\System32\Drivers\Etc directory.

Internet Mail Service Does Not Start

When the Internet Mail Service does not start, ensure the host name and domain name have been specified in the Windows NT TCP/IP configuration.

NNTP Support Problems

If you are having problems with NNTP support, you should understand where information about NNTP is stored. Exchange maintains essential information for NNTP support in two main locations: the Ics.dat file and NNTP system folders

Ics.dat File

The Internet News Service creates a file called the Ics.dat file that is located in the Insdata directory. If the Ics.dat file is corrupted or lost, the Internet News Service creates a new Ics.dat file. During the next NNTP connection, the Internet News Service attempts to replicate all the messages in the newsgroup public folders included in the newsfeed. To prevent this from occurring, choose **Mark All as Delivered** in the **Advanced** property page for that newsfeed.

NNTP System Folders

The public information store maintains information in the following system folders in the public folder hierarchy in the Administrator window. These folders are used by the system only. Therefore, you should not attempt to modify them.

Article Index   Contains a list of all messages in newsgroup public folders that are maintained in the public information store.

NNTP Control Folder   Contains all the NEWGROUP and RMGROUP control messages that the Internet News Service has received. Use the **Control Messages** property page on the NNTP object for the site or server to access these control messages.

Internet Newsgroups Public Folder   The default location for Internet newsgroup hierarchies. Exchange creates an instance of this public folder on each server. The Internet Newsgroups public folder cannot be deleted. However, it can be configured as a hidden public folder. The folder's display name can also be changed, and you can move the folder within the public folder hierarchy.

Performance Problems

The following section describes common performance problems. For many performance problems, you can use Windows NT Performance Monitor to help troubleshoot problems that affect Exchange. For others, such as slow client startup, you should follow a logical troubleshooting process is best.

Windows NT Performance Monitor provides information about performance statistics such as processor use, memory use, server throughput, queue size, and number of write/read operations per second. You can use the preconfigured Performance Monitor chart views that are included with Exchange to help you improve your system's performance and identify bottlenecks. For information about the Performance Monitor chart views for Exchange, see Appendix C, "Performance Monitor Chart Views."

The following are the most typical indications of performance bottlenecks:

- Microsoft Outlook Client is slow.
- Exchange is slow.
- Mail delivery is slow.

Microsoft Outlook Startup Is Slow

A common reason for a slow startup is the failure to resolve the TCP/IP host name. Another possible cause is remote procedure call (RPC) binding order. If the host name resolves normally but the client starts up slowly, the RPC binding order might need to be modified. For more information, see Knowledge Base article Q136516: "Improving Windows Client Startup Times."

This section outlines a procedure for identifying and eliminating host name resolution problems on client computers running TCP/IP.

Note Before troubleshooting TCP/IP, make sure Microsoft Outlook is not running.

General Function Check for TCP/IP Host Name Resolution

The following procedure not only tests name resolution, but also initiates a basic ping to the Exchange computer. The ping utility determines whether a TCP/IP network connection can be made between two computers.

A slow response to the **Check Name** function can be the result of a slow connection or slow name resolution. It should not take more than 30 to 40 seconds to resolve the name. If it does, you need to determine whether the problem is related to host name resolution or network connection problems.

▶ **To test TCP/IP host name resolution**

1. In Control Panel, double-click the Mail icon.

2. In the **Services** property page, click **Exchange**.

3. Click **Properties**.

4. In the **General** property page, ensure that the correct **Exchange** name and the mailbox name appear in the text boxes.

5. Click **Check Name**. (If the **Check Name** button is deactivated, add a character to the name in the Mailbox text box and then delete it again. Then click **Check Name**.)

If DNS does not respond immediately to the request, additional attempts are made at 5–, 10–, 15–, and 20–second intervals. This is the design of DNS and is usually the cause of slow client startup.

Testing for TCP/IP Network Connection

If the host name resolution fails, the next step is to determine whether the problem is caused by the DNS server or a faulty network connection. If the name eventually resolves, you can assume that a network connection exists. If the host name does not resolve, at the command prompt, ping the Exchange computer by IP address.

Ping Succeeds If pinging the Exchange IP address works in a timely manner, you have established that a network connection to the server exists.

If pinging the IP address is successful but a profile checkname fails to resolve the IP address, the RPC binding order might be incorrect. Verify that the RPC binding order includes **ncacn_ip_tcp** first in the list.

If the ping is excessivley slow to respond, you might want to look for other causes such as an overloaded router or other network bottlenecks.

Ping Fails If pinging the IP address fails, there might be a networking issue or a TCP/IP configuration problem that is preventing connection to the Exchange computer. This problem must be resolved before the client can connect to the server over TCP/IP.

Testing Host Name Resolution

At this point, you have established that the Exchange computer is responding to the network. The next step is to verify the host name resolution.

At the command prompt, ping the Exchange by computer name.

Ping Succeeds If pinging the Exchange name works in a timely manner, but the client starts up slowly, the RPC binding order might need modification. For more information, see Knowledge Base article Q136516: "Improving Windows Client Startup Times."

Ping Fails If pinging the name fails, run **IPCONFIG** /all or **WINIPCFG** on Windows 95, and check for an address in the DNS field or DNS Servers entry box respectively. The DNS can be set for all TCP clients through the dynamic host configuration protocol (DCHP) or by using the TCP configuration in Control Panel for the individual computers.

Verifying That the DNS Server Is Available

If **IPCONFIG** or **WINIPCFG** displays an IP address in the **DNS Servers** box (as shown in the illustration below), the client computer is configured to resolve host names through the DNS.

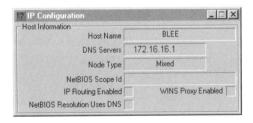

The next step is to verify that the DNS server is available. At the command prompt, ping the DNS IP address.

Ping Fails If pinging the IP address fails, the client computer is configured for a DNS server that is down or otherwise not available. DNS must be either disabled or configured for a DNS server that is available at all times.

Ping Succeeds If pinging the IP address succeeds the DNS server is available but does not resolve the host name in question. Provided that the DNS server is configured properly, the Exchange computer name and IP address must be added to the DNS database. After this is done, pinging the Exchange computer name should resolve to an IP address by the DNS server, enabling faster startup times for Microsoft Outlook.

Exchange Is Slow

If the Exchange computer appears to be slower than normal, one or more of the following conditions probably exist:

- CPU activity is high.
- Disk activity is high.
- Memory (RAM) usage is high.

To isolate the problem to one of these areas, ask the following questions:

- Is the server supporting other applications?
- Is the server handling too many users?
- Has user activity changed? (Are users sending more mail than usual, sending mail with large attachments, or sending to large distribution lists?)

The following sections describe how to isolate the problem further.

High CPU Activity

To determine whether the CPU is overworked, run the Performance Monitor Server Health chart view. If the CPU is the problem, your chart will look similar to the following illustration.

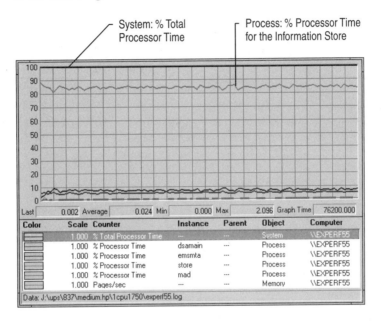

You can isolated the problem further by running the Performance Monitor Users chart view. If the Users Count counter is high, the server might be supporting more users than it is capable of supporting.

To improve CPU use, do any of the following:

- Restrict the amount or type of mail users can send.
- Move Exchange components or other applications to another server computer.
- Move some or all mailboxes and public folder replicas to another server computer.
- Add a faster processor.
- If your server is a symmetric multiprocessor (SMP), add additional processors.
- Optimize the way that the system responds to foreground and background applications. In Control Panel, click **System** and then click the **Performance** tab. Under **Performance**, move the slider bar to a position halfway between **None** and **Maximum**.
- Upgrade to a CPU that has more Level 2 (L2) caching, particularly if the server computer has less than 256K of L2 cache. Some systems allow up to 2 megabytes (MB) or more of L2 memory. L2 cache is faster than RAM.

High Disk Activity

Run the Performance Monitor Server Health chart view to determine whether the disk is overworked. If the disk is causing the problem, the chart will look similar to one in the following illustration.

Note If you haven't done so already, you should start the disk performance counters by typing **diskperf -y** at the command prompt. Then, add the LogicalDisk: Disk Bytes/sec and LogicalDisk: % Disk Time counters to the **Exchange** Health chart view. These counters indicate the amount of data that is transferred to or from the disk during write or read operations. For more information about adding counters to charts, see your Windows NT Server documentation.

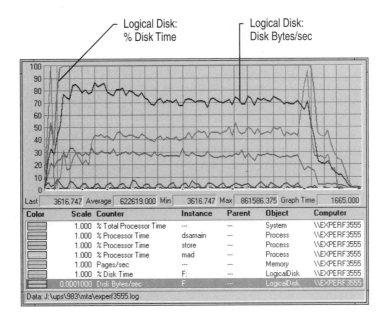

Look at the disk and pages/sec counters to determine which disk is causing the problem. If paging is high, the disk containing the pagefile is causing the problem.

To improve disk use, do any of the following:

- Move Exchange transaction logs to either another physical disk or another physical disk that is using a disk controller other than the one the disk containing the databases is using.

- Restrict the amount or type of mail users can send.

- Add more RAM, and run Performance Optimizer to increase the database buffers.

- Use multiple disk controllers.

High Memory Usage

Run the Performance Monitor Server Health chart view to determine whether the server is running out of memory. If RAM is causing the bottleneck, the pages/sec counter will be high (typically greater than 100 pages per second), and the chart will look similar to the one in the following illustration.

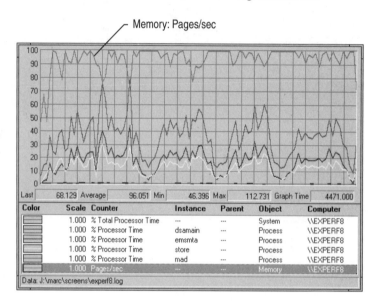

To improve memory use, do any of the following:

- Add more RAM.

- Increase the size of your pagefile. In Control Panel, click **System**, and then click the **Performance** tab. Click **Change**. Under **Paging File Size For Selected Drive**, set a large pagefile. You can approximate the pagefile size by adding 125 MB to the amount of physical RAM available on your server. For example, if your server has 64 MB of RAM, you should set your pagefile size to 189 MB.

- Move the pagefile to a separate physical disk.
- Make sure Windows NT Server is optimized for network applications. In Control Panel, click **Network**, and then click the **Services** tab. Under **Network Services**, click **Server**, and then click **Properties**. Click **Maximize Throughput for Network Applications**. Click **OK**.
- Restrict the amount or type of mail users can send.
- Move Exchange components or other applications to another server computer.
- If your server computer is paging excessively, adjust the size of the database buffer caches by typing **perfwiz -v** at the command prompt. You should reduce the size of the buffer cache by 10 to 30 percent.
- Move some or all mailboxes and public folder replicas to another server computer.

Slow Mail Delivery

If the Exchange computer appears to be delivering mail more slowly than normal, you can backlog one or more of the following avenues:

- The message transfer agent (MTA) queue
- The information store (public or private) queue
- The Internet Mail Service queue

Ask the following questions to isolate the problem:

- Is the server handling too many users?
- Has the user activity changed? (Are users sending more mail than usual, sending mail with large attachments, or sending to large distribution lists?)

The following sections describe how to isolate the problem further.

Backlogged MTA Queue

Run the Performance Monitor Server Queues chart view to determine whether the MTA queue is the bottleneck. This chart view shows how much traffic the MTA is transmitting to and from other servers, sites, or organizations. If the MTA is causing the mail to be delayed, the Work Queue Length counter will be high and the chart will look similar to the one in the following illustration.

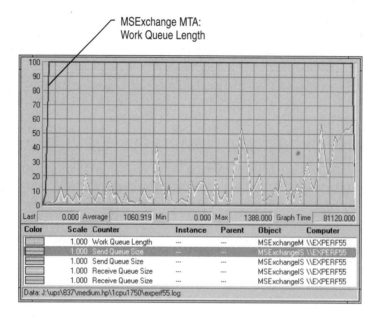

If the MTA queue is backlogged and there is high disk activity, the disk containing the databases is causing the problem. The queue can be backlogged because the MTA cannot write to the disk quickly enough.

To improve the speed of message processing in the MTA queue, do any of the following:

- Restrict the amount or type of mail users can send.
- Add more disks to the stripe set.
- Use multiple disk controllers.
- Add one or more caching disk controllers that cache read and write operations.

Backlogged Private Information Store Queue

Run the Performance Monitor Server Queues chart view to determine whether the private information store queue is the bottleneck. This chart view shows how many messages the private information store is delivering to mailboxes. If the private information store is causing the mail to be delayed, your chart will look similar to the one in the following illustration.

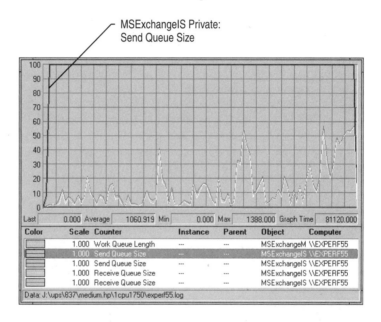

To improve the speed of message processing in the private information store queue, do any of the following:

- Restrict the amount or type of mail users can send. For example, require users to send mail to public folders instead of distribution lists.

- Move some or all mailboxes to another server.

- Add more disks to the stripe set.

- Use multiple disk controllers.

- Add one or more caching disk controllers that cache read and write operations.

Backlogged Public Information Store Queue

Run the Performance Monitor chart view Server Queues to determine whether the public information store queue is the bottleneck. This chart view shows how many messages the public information store is delivering to public folders. For example, if it is taking longer than usual for public folder changes to be replicated throughout your system, the following counters will show increased activity:

- MSExchangeIS Public: Send Queue Size
- MSExchangeIS Public: Receive Queue Size

To improve the speed of message processing in the public information store queue, do any of the following:

- Configure public folder replication to occur at a less busy time or less frequently.
- Move some or all public folders to another server computer.
- Add more disks to the stripe set.
- Use multiple disk controllers.
- Add one or more caching disk controllers that cache read and write operations.

Backlogged Internet Mail Service Queue

Run the following Performance Monitor chart views: —Server IMC Traffic, Server IMC Statistics, and Server IMC Queues— to determine whether the public information store queue is causing the problem. These chart views show how much traffic the Internet Mail Service is transmitting to and from the Internet.

To improve Internet Mail Service processing speed, do any of the following:

- Restrict the amount or type of mail users can send to the Internet.
- Move the Internet Mail Service to another server.
- Add more disks to the stripe set.
- Use multiple disk controllers.
- Add one or more caching disk controllers that cache read and write operations.

For more information about troubleshooting the Internet Mail Service, see "Internet Mail Service" in this chapter.

General Mail Delivery Problems

The following problems occur when the X.400 address is deleted on an object, such as a mailbox, connector, or distribution list:

- Event ID 2168 occurs when you start the Internet Mail Service.
- The Microsoft Mail Connector stops delivering mail.
- Messages delivered to a distribution list fail and users get a Recipient Not Recognized message.

To solve these problems, try re-creating the X400 address.

The Exchange MTA is a native X.400 MTA. Therefore, X.400 addresses exist for every object. In a native X.400 system, it is important to have the X.400 address available for each object at all times. The Exchange MTA can route and deliver on the distinguished name (DN) but requires that an X.400 address exist if there are problems with the DN. Exchange also uses the X.400 address information to make routing decisions to foreign systems. In this case, the X.400 address and the foreign address information is used to route the message within the Exchange topology.

Registry Access Problems

If you encounter an error message that indicates Exchange cannot access the registry, an incorrect value probably has been detected in this single instance and the registry could not be updated.

To resolve this problem, delete the instance and then add it back. Deleting the instance removes the old instance and enables you to start over.

Note If you are concerned that you might be deleting a critical element from your program, call Microsoft Technical Support before making any changes.

However, sometimes deleting an instance that has a corrupt registry entry might not be successful. You can follow up by performing the following steps:

1. Stop the external instance in the **Control Panel\Services** dialog box.
2. Remove the instance name from the following registry value:

    CurrentControlSet\NT External\Linkage\Export" MULTI_SZ

3. Delete the following instance key from the registry:

    CurrentControlSet\<_Instance Name_>

This removes the external instance completely.

Troubleshooting Tools

The following is a list of tools available for troubleshooting Exchange:

- Performance Monitor (perfmon)
- Server Monitor
- Link Monitor
- Windows Event Log file
- MTAcheck
- ISINTEG
- SNMP Agents
  - MADMANMIB
  - Exchange.MIB
  - SNMPutil
- Winnt Diagnostics
- Pview
- RPC Ping
- Ping-1
- Netstat

The discussion in this section is limited to the ISINTEG and ESEUTIL utilities. The remaining tools are discussed in *Microsoft Exchange Server Maintenance and Troubleshooting*.

ISINTEG Utility

The Information Store Integrity Checker (ISINTEG) utility finds and eliminates errors from the Exchange public and private information store databases. These errors can prevent the information store from starting or prevent users from logging on and receiving, opening, or deleting mail. ISINTEG is not intended for use as a part of normal information store maintenance. Its purpose is to assist you in situations where the database has become damaged.

Installing ISINTEG

ISINTEG is located in the Exchsrvr\Bin directory of the Exchange compact disc. You can run it from the Windows NT Server command line.

Using ISINTEG

ISINTEG has two main functions:

- It can test, and optionally, fix errors in the information store. When run in Patch mode, ISINTEG repairs information stores that will not start after being restored from an offline backup. See Part 9, "Disaster Recovery," for a discussion of this function.

- It can patch the information store after a restore from an offline backup.

In Test mode, ISINTEG searches the information store databases for table errors, incorrect reference counts, and unreferenced objects. During this operation, ISINTEG displays the results and also writes them to a log file.

The Fix option in the Test mode should be used only with the advice of Microsoft Technical Support. In Test and Fix modes, ISINTEG tests the information store database and corrects any errors it finds. It is recommended that you back up the information store before you run this utility to fix errors in the database.

Testing and Fixing Information Store Integrity

ISINTEG validates the referential integrity of the information store database by scanning it and examining all references. The utility creates a temporary database to store the reference counts. At the end of the process, the reference counts collected in the temporary database are compared with those in the information store database. If errors exist, and if you have selected the **-fix** option, ISINTEG corrects the problem. By default, the temporary database is created in the same directory as the existing database. But you can specify a different directory for the location of the temporary database. In either case, the temporary database is removed upon completion of the test. When run in Test mode, ISINTEG must be run separately on the public and private information stores.

By default, ISINTEG errors are displayed on your screen and saved in a log file. It is recommended that you save the log file created by ISINTEG in case you require the assistance of Microsoft Technical Support to solve any of the problems.

The **-fix** option instructs ISINTEG to repair any errors it finds. Details of all repairs are recorded in a log file. If a log file name is not specified, the results are written to either Isinteg.pri or Isinteg.pub, depending on whether you choose the private or public information store for testing.

Note The **-fix** option should be used only on the advice of Microsoft Technical Support.

Running ISINITEG in Test Mode

To run ISINTEG in Test mode, you must first stop the information store service (if it is running) and then run the ISINTEG utility.

1. In the Services application in Control Panel, click the Microsoft Exchange Information Store service, and then click **Stop**.

2. At the command prompt, switch to the Exchsrvr\Bin directory, and type:

   isinteg -test *\<options\>*

   where *\<options\>* is one or more of the command-line options listed in the following table.

Option	Description
-?	Displays the list of options. Does not run the utility.
-pri	Tests the private information store.
-pub	Tests the public information store.
-fix	Tests and corrects errors in the specified information store. This option should be used only with the advice of Microsoft Technical Support.
-detailed	Performs additional tests beyond what is normally covered in the default Test mode.
-verbose	Reports the details of all testing activity.
-l *filename*	Specifies the name of the log file. The default name is Isinteg.pri or Isinteg.pub.
-t *RefDbLocation*	Specifies the location of the temporary reference database that ISINTEG constructs while it is running. If you specify the location for the temporary database on a disk different from the one on which the information store database is stored you can improve the tool's performance.
-test *testname1, testname2...*	Specifies the specific test(s) to perform.

ISINTEG can take a long time to run on large information stores because of the intensive nature of the referential integrity-checking operation. Rather than running the entire set of tests, it is strongly recommended that you select tests based upon the specific problem you encounter (as recommended by Microsoft Technical Support). This reduces the amount of time ISINTEG takes to run.

Tip If more than one test is required, each can be combined in a single ISINTEG run, which takes less time than running each test in a separate ISINTEG run. For example,

```
isinteg -pri -test folder,message
```
is faster than running them separately as shown below:

```
isinteg -pri -test folder
isinteg -pri -test message
```

Each test and its parameters are described in the following table.

Test name	Description	Test length depends on
aclitemref	Verifies reference counts for access control list items.	Number of folders in the information store and the number of members of each access control list.
acllist	Examines folders and validates access control lists.	Number of folders in the information store.
acllistref	Verifies the access control list reference counts.	Number of folders in the information store.
allacltests	Combines the acllist, acllistref, and aclitemref tests.	(See description for each subtest.)
allfoldertests	Combines the folder, fldsub, and search tests.	(See description for each subtest.)
artidx (public store only)	Tests the consistency of the NNTP article index.	Number of NNTP messages and folders.
attach	Validates properties for all attachments.	Number of attachments in the information store.
attachref	Validates attachment reference counts.	Number of messages and attachments in the information store.
deleteextracolumns	Deletes all cached indexes and some "extra" columns.	Number of folders in the information store.

(continued)

Test name	Description	Test length depends on
delfld	Examines deleted folders, validates properties, and accumulates reference counts.	Number of deleted folders and number of messages in each folder.
dumpsterref	Combines the msgref and msgsoftref tests. Also checks the item count of recoverable items and the size of the recoverable items available for Deleted Item Recovery.	(See description for msgref and msgsoftref.)
dumpsterprops	Runs the dumpsterref test and validates the presence of some required columns in the folder table.	(See description for dumpsterref.)
fldrcv (private store only)	Validates counts of special system folders, including Restrictions, Categorization, Inbox, Outbox, SentMail, Deleted Items, Finder, Views, Common Views, Schedule, and ShortCuts.	Number of mailboxes and folders in the information store.
fldsub	Validates the number of child folders and number of recoverable child folders available for Deleted Item Recovery.	Number of folders in the information store.
folder	Examines folder tables and validates properties. Also examines message tables, validates properties, and accumulates reference counts.	Number of folders and messages in the information store.
mailbox (private store only)	For each mailbox, examines folders, deleted folders, and tables. Also validates properties, special folders (for example, Inbox, Outbox, Sent Items, Deleted Items, and others) in the folder table, and checks the respective sizes.	Number of mailboxes, folders, deleted folders, and messages in the information store.

(continued)

Test name	Description	Test length depends on
message	Examines message tables and validates message table properties.	Number of messages in the information store.
morefld	Checks the search links (subset of the search test). In Fix mode, deletes all of the cached categorization and restriction tables.	Total number of cached categorization and total number of restriction tables.
msgref	Validates message reference counts in the messages.	Number of folders, messages, and attachments in the information store.
msgsoftref	Validates message reference counts for messages marked for Deleted Item Recovery in the message table.	Number of folders and messages in the information store.
namedprop	Examines the folder, message, and attachment tables, and also validates the named properties.	Number of folders, messages, and attachments in the information store.
newsfeed (public store only)	Validates newsfeed table properties, including permissions.	Number of folders in the information store.
newsfeedref (public store only)	Validates newsfeed reference counts.	Number of folders in the information store.
oofhist (private store only)	Validates out-of-office history information for all users.	Number of out-of-office rules set.
peruser	Validates per user read/unread information.	Number of folders per user in the information store
rcvfld (private store only)	Cross-checks receive folders with the folder table.	Number of receive folders in the information store.
rowcounts	Validates the number of rows for all tables.	Number of folders, messages, and attachments in the information store.
search	Validates the search links.	Number of folders in the information store.
timedev	Counts the number of timed events (maintenance, periodic tasks, and so forth).	Number of timed events.

ESEUTIL Utility

The ESEUTIL utility defragments, repairs, and checks the integrity of the **Exchange** information store and directory. Unlike ISINTEG (see the Disaster Recovery part in this volume), which is sensitive to the use and content of data in the information store, ESEUTIL examines the structure of the database tables and records.

Installing ESEUTIL

ESEUTIL is located in the Windows NT System32 directory. You can run it on one database at time from the Windows NT Server command line.

Caution You should use ESEUTIL only in consultation with Microsoft Technical Support. It is an optional component provided solely for troubleshooting purposes. It should not be used as a regular maintenance tool.

Using ESEUTIL

You can use ESEUTIL to perform the following operations:

- Defragment a database
- Check database integrity
- Repair a corrupt database

Defragmenting a Database

The defragmentation option makes used storage contiguous, eliminates unused storage, and reduces the database size.

ESEUTIL copies database records to a new database. When defragmention is complete, the original database is deleted or saved to a user-specified location, and the new version is renamed as the original. If the utility encounters a bad record, it stops and displays an error.

Note Defragmenting a database requires disk space equal to twice the size of the database being processed.

▶ **To defragment a database**

1. Stop the directory using the Services application in Control Panel.
2. At the command prompt, type **eseutil /d**, a database switch, and any desired options.

For example, the following command runs the standard defragmentation utility on the directory and saves the copy in the user-defined file.

```
C:\EXCHSRVR\BIN> eseutil /d /ds /t c:\dbback /p
```

Use one of the following database switches to run ESEUTIL on a specific database.

Database switch	Description
/ds	Directory
/ispriv	Private information store
/ispub	Public information store

Select one or more of the following options to specify the operations to be performed on the database.

Option	Description
/b *path*	Makes a backup copy of the original uncompacted database at the specified location.
/p	Retains the old, uncompacted database in its original location and stores the new compacted database in the default file, \Exchsrvr\Bin\Tempdfrg.edb.
/t *filename*	Renames the new compacted database.
/o	Does not display the **Exchange** banner.

Checking Database Integrity

The integrity option searches the database for damaged or unreadable records and displays the results. It verifies the integrity of the database but does not repair any errors it finds.

▶ **To check database integrity**

1. Stop the directory using the Services application in Control Panel.

2. At the command prompt, type **eseutil /g** followed by a database switch.

   For example, the following command runs a consistency check on the server's public information store:

   ```
   C:\EXCHSRVR\BIN> eseutil/g /ispub
   ```

Database switch	Description
/ds	Directory
/ispriv	Private information store
/ispub	Public information store

Repairing a Corrupted Database

The repair option evaluates the information in the database and then reassembles the database tables using only the uncorrupted information. If you repair the database, you must also run the ISINTEG utility.

▶ **To repair a corrupted database**

1. Stop the directory using the Services application in Control Panel.

2. At the command prompt, type **eseutil /p** followed by a database switch.

   For example, the following command repairs the server's directory:

   ```
   C:\EXCHSRVR\BIN> eseutil /p /ds
   ```

Database switch	Description
/ds	Directory
/ispriv	Private information store
/ispub	Public information store

For more information on using ESEUTIL to recover databases, see Part 9, "Disaster Recovery."

PART 9

Disaster Recovery

This chapter describes techniques that can be used for Microsoft Exchange Server disaster recovery and disaster recovery planning. For quick answers to many frequently asked questions, see the "Frequently Asked Questions" section later in the chapter.

Because Exchange uses Microsoft Windows NT security for authentication, you must include Windows NT operating system backup and restoration procedures in your planning, as well as procedures for Exchange backup and restoration. Because of this relationship, Exchange disaster recovery cannot be considered independently from Windows NT disaster recovery.

For complete information about Windows NT disaster recovery, see your Windows NT documentation. This chapter describes the aspects of recovery that are unique to Exchange.

Disaster Recovery Planning

Although Exchange is a robust and stable messaging platform, it is essential that you have a working plan to restore Exchange computers and data in a timely way if a system crash or another disaster occurs. Recovery planning includes not only planning what to do after the disaster occurs but also what steps to take during the initial setup of a system to minimize the possibility of disaster later.

Developing a Recovery Plan

By developing a recovery plan, you can minimize downtime for your organization and provide the quickest possible data recovery. However, it is important that you do not take this information for granted. Instead, you should test, formulate, and verify your disaster recovery plans.

Determining Downtime Cost

Determining the cost of downtime is useful when you must justify the purchase of recovery equipment. There are different models for calculating the per-hour downtime cost, which varies for each business. These calculations include lost orders per hour, delayed financial transactions, and the cost of delayed time-sensitive market decisions. For more information on justifying disaster recovery expenditures, see the *National Computer Security Association News* (July 1996).

Analyzing Server Computer Roles

When deploying equipment, avoid making your Exchange computer a primary domain controller. If the primary domain controller becomes unavailable, an alternate domain controller must be promoted to the role of primary domain controller. If the Exchange computer is not the primary domain controller, you do not have to worry about promotions and demotions of domain controllers in a recovery situation.

Some companies prefer to place the Exchange server on a backup domain controller in the Accounts domain so that a second computer is not required for Windows NT authentication in remote offices. This can save the cost of purchasing another computer. However, make sure you take into account the additional RAM overhead required for the Windows NT security accounts manager as well as the Exchange memory requirements. Windows NT domain controllers require RAM equal to two and a half times the size of the security accounts manager.

If the Exchange computer is a member server and not a primary domain controller or backup domain controller, additional memory overhead for the domain security accounts manager is not required. However, for remote offices, companies can save money by using the local Exchange server to provide authentication, serve as a backup domain controller, and provide messaging services.

Important For a proper directory service restore, access to the original security accounts manager is required. Do not install a Exchange computer in a domain that does not have a backup domain controller.

An alternative is to place the Exchange computer in a large resource domain that trusts each account's domain. In this case, Exchange can be placed on a backup domain controller without incurring significant memory overhead because the security accounts manager for the Exchange resource domain will be relatively small.

Dedicating Recovery Equipment

It is important to dedicate recovery hardware. If you have a dedicated recovery server at each location, you can install Exchange before a recovery is necessary, greatly reducing recovery time.

Dedicating recovery hardware might be less expensive. Using the ESEUTIL troubleshooting utility to recover and defragment a database requires up to twice the disk space of the information store database on the largest production server. Thus, it might be more cost effective for an organization to maintain a single recovery server that has sufficient disk space rather than equipping all production servers with sufficient disk space to perform a recovery.

If you decide to dedicate recovery equipment, do not allow that equipment to become production equipment without replacing it. Make sure recovery equipment is always in working order and is available at a moment's notice. Some companies purchase recovery equipment, but then install test-only software. They become dependent on this equipment for production use. In short, keep recovery equipment in dedicated recovery mode.

If the recovery server will be shared among sites, maintain a copy of the Windows NT installation code and service pack on the hard drive of the recovery computer. By doing so you can install Exchange based on the required site and organization without having the paths for this Exchange installation match the paths of the production Exchange being recovered. For information on settings for protocol addresses, partitioning information, protocols, options, tuning, and other options, see your production Windows NT Server configuration data.

Creating a Disaster Recovery Kit

Planning ahead reduces recovery time. It is critical to build a kit that includes the following:

- An operating system configuration sheet
- A hard drive partition configuration sheet
- A hardware configuration sheet
- An Extended Industry Standard Architecture/Micro Channel Architecture (EISA/MCA) configuration disk
- A Exchange configuration sheet that includes the following:
    - Windows NT tuning settings
    - Path information
    - Protocol addresses
    - Exchange connector configurations

- Windows NT emergency repair disk
- Microsoft Exchange Performance Optimizer settings sheet
- Any other items you might need for your site configuration

Maintaining Off-Site Tapes and Equipment

Store backup tapes at an off-site location. For legal or security reasons, some companies choose not to send backup tapes to a third-party, off-site location. One alternative is to send tapes to an off-site location within the same company.

Devising an Archiving Plan

Implement an archiving plan that enables your users to move server-based messages either to their local store files or to a disk or server that is separate from the information store. This reduces the size of the server-based information store. Otherwise, data is reduced in the information store but added to another area of the same disk or logical drive.

The impact of storing .pst files on the server disk is considerable because .pst storage maintains messages in both rich text format (RTF) and ASCII format. Because you cannot set disk space limits on .pst files, you might want to dedicate a file server for archiving them. Include all sensitive data in backup strategies, including users' .pst files. Use encryption when creating .ost files and .pst files.

Keeping Accurate Records of All Configurations

Keeping accurate records is necessary when you configure the recovery server. Records should include:

- Windows NT tuning settings
- Path information
- Protocol addresses
- Exchange connector configurations

These records should be part of your disaster recovery kit.

Additional Information Sources

The following references are sources of additional information for planning or maintaining a disaster recovery plan in your organization:

- Microsoft TechNet: (800) 344-2121; technet@microsoft.com
- Microsoft Knowledge Base: http://www.microsoft.com/kb

- - Microsoft Knowledge Base Article Q154792: "Exchange and Schedule+ White Papers and Their Locations"

  - Microsoft Knowledge Base Article Q155269: "Microsoft Exchange Administrators' FAQ"

- *Microsoft Exchange Server Maintenance and Troubleshooting*

- *Microsoft Exchange Server Concepts and Planning*

- Microsoft Exchange home page: http://www.microsoft.com/Exchange

- Public Listserver (not maintained by Microsoft): E-mail msexchange-request@insite.co.uk (use the word SUBSCRIBE in the message body). This list can generate several dozen messages per day.

- Microsoft Press® Books (MSPRESS): In the United States (800) MSPRESS; In Canada (800) 268-2222

- Microsoft Consulting Services (MCS): In the United States (800) 426-9400; In Canada (800) 563-9048

- Microsoft Solution Provider Program: (800) SOLPROV

- National Computer Security Association: http://www.ncsa.com

Configuring and Deploying Resources

How you configure and deploy your equipment can affect your ability to recover quickly from a disaster. Careful planning can not only reduce the time required for recovery but also reduce the risk of a disaster.

Deploying and Testing a UPS

Make sure you are protected by an uninterruptible power supply (UPS). Do not assume that if the Exchange computer did not fail during a power outage, no other servers failed. Although many computer rooms are supposedly UPS protected, it is possible that not all of the outlets are UPS protected. If you do not have a dedicated UPS, talk to the local electricians or operations personnel about how the circuits are configured and test the outlets. Also note that server-class UPS batteries have a life expectancy of approximately three years and might require replacement.

Configuring Disks

For optimal performance and recoverability, the operating system drive should be mirrored, the transaction logs placed on a dedicated physical drive (which can also be mirrored), and the Windows NT swap file and Exchange information store placed on a mirror or RAID 5 disk set. Because off-line maintenance and repair routines require up to twice the disk space of the database file being administered with the ESEUTIL utility, be sure you allow sufficient disk space.

Configuring MTA Frequency

Configure the message transfer agent (MTA) frequency so that queues are cleared quickly. This prevents queued messages from accumulating in the information store. Also, design a redundant MTA path so that messages keep flowing if a link outage occurs. It is important that MTAs be able to keep up with the traffic that flows through them. Because it takes considerably more time to process messages from the information store than it does from memory, it is important to keep messages in the information store to a minimum to ensure timely message delivery.

Placing Transaction Log Files on Dedicated Physical Disks

Placing transaction log files on dedicated physical disks is the single most important key to Exchange performance. There are also recovery implications in maintaining transaction log files on separate dedicated physical disks, because transaction logs provide an additional mechanism for recovery if a disk failure occurs.

Disabling SCSI Controller Write Cache

Recoverability is the only consideration in deciding whether write cache should be disabled. If you have a RAID controller or if the disk controller has a battery back up, it does not matter whether write cache is on or off.

In the absence of either of the above, disable the small computer system interface (SCSI) controller write cache to avoid the possibility of losing data. At a programming level, if the SCSI write-through flag is set, Windows NT does not use buffers but writes directly to disk. When a program receives a write-complete signal from Windows NT, it has a guarantee that the write was completed to disk. This guarantee is critical to the Exchange transaction logging process. If write cache is enabled, Windows NT cannot discriminate between whether the SCSI controller cached the data or wrote it to disk. This causes it to erroneously inform the calling application that a write has been made, which could result in data corruption if your computer crashes before this lazy-write operation makes it to the disk.

Disabling Circular Logging

If you have a solid backup strategy in place, transaction log files will be purged on a regular basis, freeing up disk space and eliminating the need for circular logging. Because the total size of the active transactions are less than the total amount of RAM on a given computer, with circular logging enabled, the system has complete recoverability with respect to hard and soft crashes. However, circular logging sacrifices the protection against media failure.

Circular logging writes log files, but after the checkpoint has been advanced, the inactive portion of the transaction logs is discarded. The discarded portion usually represents the majority of the potential log data. Since transaction log history is cyclical under these conditions, it cannot be restored. In addition, although circular logging can help conserve disk space, incremental and differential backups are not possible when it is enabled.

Placing Limits on Information Store Attributes

Configure mailbox storage limits and the maximum age of server-based messages. Also, limit MTA message sizes and the size of messages that users can send. These precautions limit the amount of data you must back up and restore in case of a disaster.

Evaluating the Environments in Which Server Computers Are Placed

Inspect the area when deploying servers. Be sure there is enough power, and, if possible, dedicate power lines for your equipment. Review existing amperage and new amperage requirements. Make sure that servers are not placed under fire sprinklers. Also, make sure that your servers are in a physically secure location and that the room has adequate cooling capacity for additional equipment.

Disaster Prevention

Modifying your daily operations can reduce your risk of disaster. In addition to planning for recovery, you can implement the risk reduction procedures discussed in this section to minimize the chance of a disaster occurring.

Creating and Verifying Daily Backups

Creating and verifying daily backups is a critical step in successful disaster recovery. However, you can only recover valid data if the backup is valid. Failure to verify backups is one of the most common mistakes administrators make because they often assume that backup tapes are being swapped and that data is being backed up properly. Make it part of your daily routine to review all backup logs, and then follow up on any errors or inconsistencies.

Although the information store and directory can be backed up online, files in directories that are accessed by other services, such as the directory synchronization component or Microsoft Mail Connector (AppleTalk) MTA, should be backed up when the respective service is not running. You can automate and schedule backups using the At.exe utility provided with Windows NT.

For more information about backups, see Part 4, "Administering and Maintaining," and *Microsoft Exchange Server Maintenance and Troubleshooting*.

Standardizing Tape Backup Formats

Recovery equipment must be compatible with production tape equipment. If you deploy a new type of tape drive, make sure that you use a compatible model for your recovery equipment. You should also test reading and restoring production tape backups on the tape drive you are using for recovery.

Performing File-Based Backup

To capture all configuration data, it is best to perform a full file-based backup periodically. Services should be shut down so that open files can be backed up. This ensures that you have backed up all possible Exchange-related files. You might want to perform this backup during scheduled maintenance. File-based backup is not required for backing up the information store and directory databases; online backups are recommended for backing up the information store and directory.

Checking Windows NT Event Logs

Take a proactive approach; review logs daily. This can help you identify problems before they have a serious impact on your system.

Monitoring the Information Store

Take a proactive approach to monitoring server performance and the growth of the information store. Prepare a plan to remedy any issues. Set up Windows NT disk space alerts to monitor remaining disk space. Windows NT Performance Monitor objects exist for the information store and should be used. The LogicalDisk object, along with the % Free Space and Free Megabytes counters, is used to monitor and trigger alerts when disk space is low.

Log files accumulating on the disk can cause the information store or directory to run out of operating space. To prevent this, do one of the following:

- Write the log files to a different drive.

- Change the location where the information store or directory store transaction logs are written. To do so, select the server object. On the **File** menu, click **Properties**. Then click the **Database Paths** tab. Change the path names for the information store and directory transaction logs, and then click **OK**.

- Use Ntbackup.exe to perform a normal (full) or incremental online backup of the server. This utility automatically deletes transaction logs that are no longer needed (they have been committed to disk). If you do not run Ntbackup, the log files continue to accumulate.

Note This method is not supported on servers where circular logging is enabled because the transaction logs are required for incremental and differential backups.

- If possible, delete any sample applications to increase disk space.

Publishing a Maintenance Schedule

It is important to set user expectation levels by publishing the maintenance schedule, especially when users expect service 24 hours a day, 7 days a week. Maintenance is inevitable because the nature of the data processing business includes service pack updates, software upgrades, and hardware upgrades. Although rare, it might be necessary to take down the information store service to reduce the size of store files using the ESEUTIL troubleshooting utility, which is available on the Exchange compact disc in the \Exchsrvr\Bin directory.

Performing Fire Drills

Periodic fire drills are an effective way to measure your ability to recover from a disaster and to validate your disaster recovery plans. This is the most valuable experience you can have in your disaster recovery planning. Conduct the fire drill in a test environment, and attempt a complete recovery. For the maximum effect, provide no notice to your staff that you are performing a drill. Make sure you use data from production backups. Record the time it takes to recover. This information will assist you in estimating the time it would take to recover after a real disaster. Up to one-third of your recovery time can be spent preparing and getting the correct tools in place to complete the job.

Data Recovery Procedures

You can use the procedures for data recovery scenarios discussed in this section to recover the following:

- An information store to a different server
- An information store from an offline backup
- A transaction log file
- A single mailbox
- A full Exchange computer

Notes on Restoring an Information Store to a Different Server

An information store can be restored to a Exchange other than the one from which it was backed up. Use this method as a last resort to recover individual items (messages or folders) from a backup without restoring on a server that is in use. This method requires an additional computer that meets the hardware requirements to run Exchange. The server should not be connected to the organization and should have enough disk space to restore the entire backup. In addition, note the following:

- Do not use this method when a server fails. This method restores only the information store; it does not restore the directory.
- When you are finished restoring the backup, reconfigure permissions on the mailboxes.

Notes on Recovery from Offline Backup

After running an offline information store restore, but before starting the information store service, run the **isinteg -patch** command.

During startup, Exchange validates a globally unique identifier (GUID) in the information store with an entry stored in the Windows NT Registry and the Exchange directory. The information store service cannot be started if the GUIDs do not match in each of the three places. Mismatches can occur if the information store has been restored from an offline backup.

If a copy of the information store (Pub.edb and Priv.edb) is restored from an offline backup and **isinteg -patch** has not been run, it fails and a -1011 error is generated when the service is restarted. The -1011 error produces an entry in the Windows NT Event Viewer Application Log with source ID 2048. The error message reads as follows: "The information store was restored from an offline backup. Run **isinteg -patch** before restarting the information store."

This error occurs because the GUIDs used by the information store that was restored are old and matching GUIDs might already exist. The GUID for this restored information store must be replaced to ensure that it is unique.

An error message, DS_E_COMMUNICATIONS_PROBLEM, will also appear.

When run with the Patch option, ISINTEG resets the entries for the GUIDs in the database, directory, and registry. It also patches information used during replication to prevent incorrect backfilling. After it has been patched, the information store service can be started again.

Patching the Information Store

To replace the GUIDs used by the restored information store, run **isinteg -patch**. This command enables the ISINTEG utility to run in patch mode against the entire information store (Pub.edb and Priv.edb) and generate new GUIDs. Replication information is also patched to prevent incorrect backfilling.

▶ **To run the isinteg -patch command**

1. Ensure that the directory and system attendant services are running. If these services are not running, ISINTEG fails, displaying the following message:

   DS_COMMUNICATIONS_ERROR

2. At the command prompt, switch to the Exchsrvr\Bin directory, and then type **isinteg -patch**. At this point, the GUIDs have been replaced, and the ISINTEG will report that the information store has been updated.

3. Restart the information store service.

Patching the Information Store on a Microsoft Cluster Server

Before you run **isinteg -patch** on a Exchange running on a Microsoft Cluster Server, you must set the environment variable _CLUSTER_NETWORK_NAME_ to the network name of the cluster. If _CLUSTER_NETWORK_NAME_ is not set, the ISINTEG utility displays the following error: "The private store could not be updated Reason: JET_errKeyDuplicate"

For example, to configure a cluster network name as EXCLUSTER, type the following at the command prompt:

```
SET_CLUSTER_NETWORK_NAME_=EXCLUSTER
```

Be sure to use the correct network name or the patch will fail.

Transaction Log Recovery

The following example describes how transaction logs are recovered.

The circumstances are as follows:

- Circular logging is not enabled.
- The transaction logs are stored on a disk separate from the database files.
- The last full (normal) backup took place two days ago.
- Because of a hardware failure (such as a bad hard disk), the information store databases have become damaged, but the transaction log drive remains intact.

Will you lose two days of production data? The answer is no. Because the transaction logs are complete, they contain all transactions from the point of the last full backup.

After you have restored the hardware, you need to perform a full restore. Do not select **Erase All Existing Data.** Not selecting this option will instruct the backup program to keep any existing log files. The full restore writes the database files and the log files that were backed up with the last full backup.

The restored log files include any log file saved up to the first log file on the current transaction log drive. For example, suppose that the full backup copied Edb00012.log through Edb00014.log. The log files on the transaction log drive would be Edb00015.log and up. The full restore will copy Edb00012.log through Edb00014.log and the information store database files that are part of the backup set.

When the information store service is started, it restores transactions from Edb00012.log through the last log file (such as Edb00019.log) and Edb.log, the most recent log file. When the process is complete, the database will be up-to-date. The log files contain signatures, which ensure that they are included in the sequence to be restored.

Single Mailbox Recovery

Data recovery for a single mailbox might be necessary in the event of an accidental mailbox or mailbox data deletion. The procedures in this section enable single mailbox recovery for any server in your organization, regardless of the server name. In a centrally supported organization, affiliate offices can mail tapes to an internal recovery center.

A single mailbox recovery server can be maintained online with production servers because the recovery server name does not need to be the same as the production server running Exchange. This recovery server, however, should not perform directory service replication with the production servers.

To recover individual mailboxes, you must restore the entire information store and then retrieve data from the desired mailbox.

Caution This procedure should not be performed on a server that is in production. As noted below, this procedure requires restoring data to a server that is not part of your production Exchange site. The dedicated recovery server is installed using the same site and organization name as the production site; however, it is installed by selecting **Create New Site**.

The following items are required to recover a single mailbox:

- A dedicated server with enough capacity to restore the entire private information store database
- A backup of the private information store database
- Microsoft Outlook Client and Exchange installation code
- Windows NT and the latest Windows NT Service Pack installation code (Exchange version 5.5 requires Service Pack 3 for Windows NT version 4.0)

The overall process for recovering a single mailbox is as follows:

1. Prepare a server running Windows NT Server, Exchange, and the Microsoft Outlook client on the recovery server.
2. From a backup tape, restore only the information store.
3. Log on with Microsoft Exchange Administrator permissions.
4. Assign the Windows NT Administrator ID access to the desired mailbox.
5. Restore mailbox data to a .pst file.
6. Attach the .pst file to the desired user profile.

Use the following procedures to implement recovery.

Note In these recovery procedures, it is assumed that you are using a tape from an online backup. If you are using an offline tape, do not start the services after the restore.

▶   **To prepare the nonproduction recovery computer**

For the fastest recovery, the nonproduction computer should be running and available for recovery at all times. If you do not already have a dedicated recovery server, prepare one using the following procedure.

1. Run Exchange Setup, and select **Complete Installation**. Use the same site and organization names as those of the mailbox you are restoring. The server name of the restore computer does not matter because for this procedure, you are only restoring the information store, not the directory.

2. Do not join the existing production site. The recovery computer should be a stand-alone computer.

3. Make sure there is enough disk space for restoring the entire information store from your backup tape.

▶   **To restore the information store from tape**

1. Insert the backup tape, and then log on to the recovery domain as an administrator.

2. From the **Administrative Tools** program group, run Ntbackup.exe.

3. On the **Operations** menu, click **Microsoft Exchange**.

4. Select the Tapes icon, and then double-click the tape name.

5. On the right side of the **Tapes** window, select **Org**, select **Site**, select **Server**, and then select **Information Store**.

6. In the **Backup** dialog box, click **Restore**.

7. In the Restore Information window, type the name of the destination server in the **Destination Server** box.

8. Select **Erase All Existing Data**, select **Private**, select **Public**, select **Verify After Restore**, and then select **Start Service After Restore**. Then click **OK**.

   The following message appears:

   You are about to restore Microsoft Exchange components. The Microsoft Exchange services on the destination server will be stopped.

9. Click **OK**.

10. In the **Verify Status** dialog box, click **OK**.

   If you are restoring from a full backup, you can skip step 11 and go directly to step 12.

11. At the command prompt, switch to the Exchsrvr\Bin directory, and then type **isinteg -patch**. This runs the ISINTEG troubleshooting utility in patch mode. After you run ISINTEG, a message appears stating that the databases have been successfully updated. Now you can start the Exchange information store and the other services.

12. In Control Panel, double-click the Services icon, and then verify that the relevant Exchange services are running.

▶ **To recover a user's mailbox**

1. Log on to the recovery server as an Administrator.

2. In the Microsoft Exchange Administrator window, click **Servers**; then select the server on which the user's mailbox is located.

3. On the **File** menu, click **Properties**.

4. Click the **Advanced** tab, and then click **Consistency Adjuster**.

5. Click **All Inconsistencies**.

6. Click **OK**. Click **OK** again for each message that appears. Then click **OK**.

7. In the Microsoft Exchange Administrator window, click **Recipients**. On the right side of the window, double-click the user's mailbox name.

8. Click the **General** tab, and then click **Primary Windows NT Account**.

9. Click **Select an existing Windows NT account**, and then click **OK**.

10. Under **Names** in the **Add User or Group** dialog box, select **Administrators**, and then click **Add**. Click **OK**. Click **OK** again for each message that appears.

11. In the mailbox's **General** properties page, click **OK**.

12. In Microsoft Outlook, start the Exchange services.

13. Configure a profile for the appropriate user.

14. Add a .pst file to the profile.

15. Restart Microsoft Outlook.

16. In the left side of the window, click **Mailbox - Username**.

17. In the right side of the window, select the first folder or item in the list.

18. On the **Edit** menu, click **Select All**.

19. On the **File** menu, click **Copy**.

20. In the **Copy** dialog box, select the appropriate .pst file.

21. Click **OK**. All data will be copied to this .pst file.

22. Copy the .pst file to the destination location.

23. Add this .pst file to the user's profile on the production server or send the .pst file to the user with instructions. If you have network access, you can copy the recovered .pst file to the appropriate server.

Full Server Recovery

You can *restore data* from one Exchange computer to a different computer, as well as *move* Exchange data from one computer to a new computer. This section describes how to restore data from one Exchange computer to a different computer. For more information about moving data to a different computer, see Part 4, "Administering and Maintaining."

Overview

A full server recovery is more complex than a single mailbox recovery. *Full server recovery* is defined as restoring an original production Exchange so that all Windows NT security and configuration information as well as Exchange configuration information and other data is recovered. A full server recovery enables users to use their current passwords to log on to their mailboxes when the recovery server is deployed.

Although single-mailbox recovery requires that only the information store be restored, full server recovery requires that both the information store and directory service be restored. Exchange relies on Windows NT security for providing access to mailbox data. Exchange uses Windows NT account SID information in object properties within the Exchange directory.

A full server recovery is a special case because Windows NT is reinstalled and a new registry is created. In this situation, a new Windows NT security identifier (SID) must be created for the recovery computer in the domain.

Note The Windows NT Registry can be restored to the same physical computer. This can be useful when you are replacing a hard drive on the same computer. In this case, if you restore the Windows NT Registry, the computer maintains its unique security identifier (SID), so you do not need to create a new SID.

In addition to performing a full restore of the Exchange databases (information store and directory), it might also be necessary to restore the Windows NT security accounts manager (SAM) database. Exchange automatically adds two accounts upon initial installation — the Windows NT service account and the Windows NT account. Although both accounts receive special privileges during installation, to restore the Exchange directory service, you need only the Windows NT account SID used during the original installation. The Exchange directory service will not be accessible unless this SID exists in the Windows NT environment. If no domain controllers for the original domain are available, you must restore the Windows NT primary domain controller security accounts manager.

You need the following items to implement a full server recovery:

- A full backup of the information store and directory
- A replacement computer with the same or greater hardware capacity as the production server
- Access to the original Windows NT security accounts manager
- A Windows NT Server production server configuration sheet
- Exchange installation code
- Windows NT Server and the latest Windows NT Service Pack installation code
- An Exchange production server configuration sheet

For a successful directory service recovery, two key conditions must be met:

- The directory service must be restored to a Windows NT Server computer that has the same site, organization, and server name as the production server.
- The recovery server must have access from the domain in which Exchange was originally installed.

A full server recovery usually involves three computers—two computers in production and one nonproduction or non-essential computer (meaning that such a computer is in production performing some other task but is available at any time for recovery). One computer is a primary domain controller. The second computer, usually an Exchange computer, has been configured as a backup domain controller. The third computer is designated as the recovery server.

Note It is not necessary to configure a backup domain controller as long as the primary domain controller is available to authenticate account and password information.

The requirement for a configuration that incorporates a primary domain controller, backup domain controller, and recovery server is because of the way in which Exchange uses the Windows NT security accounts manager database to provide authentication to directory objects. Because full server recovery includes the information store and directory, it requires access to the security accounts manager from the domain in which the Exchange computer was first installed. When the Exchange directory is restored, it expects the security properties of all directory objects to match the Windows NT security accounts manager for the respective accounts.

As an example, suppose there is a dedicated primary domain controller, a production Exchange computer that acts as a backup domain controller, and a recovery server. The production Exchange computer (which is also a backup domain controller) fails. You can build a Windows NT domain controller from the recovery server with the same computer name as the Exchange computer that failed. You can then connect this computer to the domain as a backup domain controller, which provides you with a copy of the security accounts manager from the domain in which the production Exchange computer resided. To do this, use Server Manager. First delete the original computer name, the backup domain controller definition, from the primary domain controller. Then add it again during the backup domain controller installation. This procedure is necessary because each computer name receives a unique SID when it is added to the domain; you also must have a new SID for the recovery computer. After you have done this, install Exchange using the same site and organization name. By default, the same server name is used because Exchange uses the computer name to create the Exchange name. If you are recovering a server and joining an existing site during this reinstallation, see *Microsoft Exchange Server Operations*.

Recovery Procedure

The following procedure describes how to recover a failed Exchange using a backup tape of the production server information store and directory service. It assumes that a normal (full) online backup of the information store and directory was performed.

▶ **To prepare the recovery computer**

1. Install Exchange on the new or repaired server computer. Make sure this computer is equipped with a tape drive that is compatible with the tape drives deployed on production servers. If the production server is a backup domain controller, make sure there is a primary domain controller or backup domain controller available.

2. Run Setup. Do not join an existing site.

   Note Use the Setup command to install Exchange. Do not type **setup /r**. This creates a problem that you will encounter when you attempt to upgrade this recovery server to the latest Exchange Service Pack.

3. Give the server computer its original organization and site name. Site and organization names are case-sensitive.

4. When prompted, select **Create New Site**. Even though you have chosen to create a new site, when you restart the server, it will synchronize automatically with other servers in the site because you have a backup copy of the Exchange directory database.

5. Select the same service account that you used for the production server.

6. Upgrade the recovery server to the same Microsoft Exchange Service Pack as the production server.

7. Run the Microsoft Exchange Performance Optimizer to optimize Exchange for the same configuration that was used on the production server. For more information, see your production server configuration documentation.

8. First delete and then re-add the computer name on the primary domain controller to create a new SID for the recovery computer.

9. Install Microsoft Outlook on the recovery server.

▶ **To perform the restore**

1. Insert the restore tape.

2. In the **Administrative Tools** group, double-click the Backup icon.

3. Double-click the Tapes icon.

4. Double-click **Full Backup Tape**.

5. In the right side of the window, select the directory and information store that you want to restore.

6. Click **Restore**.

7. In the **Restore Information** dialog box, select the following check boxes: **Erase all existing data**, **Verify After Restore**, and **Start Service After Restore**.

Note If the public information store is on a separate computer, do not select the **Erase all existing data** check box. Instead, select these check boxes: **Private**, **Public**, **Verify After Restore**, and **Start Services After Restore**. If you inadvertently erase the public store, contact Microsoft Technical Support.

---

8. Type the name of the destination server in the **Destination Server** box.

9. Click **OK**.

10. If the directory service and information store were backed up using separate backup jobs, do not start these services until both have been restored.

11. When the restore prompt appears, click **OK**. This opens the **Restore Status** dialog box.

12. After the restore is completed, click **OK**.

13. Click **Close** to close the Backup program.

14. After the restore, at the command prompt, type **isinteg -patch** to run the ISINTEG tool. Make sure that the directory service is started before you start the information store service.

▶ **To verify that each user's mailbox has an associated Windows NT account**

1. In the Exchange Administrator program, select a server, and then click
    Recipients.

2. Double-click the first user's name.

3. Review the **Primary Windows NT Account** box to verify that the
    Windows NT account matches the mailbox.

4. Repeat this procedure as needed for each user.

Note If you have a .csv file (from a Directory Export on the server before it
went down), you can use the Directory Import feature to import all the
information for each mailbox, including the primary Windows NT account.
This allows you to update all mailboxes quickly without having to update each
one manually. The **Directory Import** and **Directory Export** options are found
on the **Tools** menu in the Administrator program.

▶ **To test a user's logon password from Microsoft Outlook**

1. Start Microsoft Outlook.

2. Verify that the user's password is accepted.

Authoritative Restore

The Authoritative Restore tool (Authrest.exe) that is available on the Exchange
compact disc enables you to force a restored directory database to replicate to
other servers after restoring from a backup. For assistance in using this tool,
contact Microsoft Technical Support.

A restored database is usually assumed to be less current than the collective
information held on all other directory replicas in the organization. Therefore, a
restored directory normally replaces its information with more recent data held by
other servers. Although this functionality is appropriate when the reason for the
restore is that a database or server was destroyed, it is not always appropriate. For
example, if an administrative error deleted thousands of mailboxes or vital
configuration information, the goal of restoring from backup is not to restore one
server to functionality but to move the entire system back to where it was before
the error was made.

Without the Authoritative Restore tool, you would have to either restore every
server in the organization from a backup that predates the error or restore every
server in the site and then force all bridgeheads in other sites to resynchronize
from scratch. If only one server is restored, or if servers are restored one at a time,
the restored server quickly overwrites its restored data with the more recent
(incorrect) information held by all other servers in the site.

The Authoritative Restore tool enables you to restore one server (presumably the server with the most recent pre-mistake backup) rather than all servers. Normal replication then causes the restored information to spread to all servers throughout the organization. The Authrest.exe file is available from the Support\Utils\<*platform*> directory on the Exchange compact disc.

Frequently Asked Questions (FAQs)

This section provides answers to frequently asked questions regarding disaster recovery and Exchange.

Q: If I have a good backup of the directory and information store and I am restoring a server to an existing site by reinstalling Exchange, should I create a new site or join an existing site during the Exchange installation?

A: Create a new site. Do not select **Join Existing Site**. If you attempt to join the existing site, an error occurs because other servers in the site already have knowledge of the server you are restoring. When the server is restarted after the restoration of the databases, the restored server automatically synchronizes with existing servers in the site, even though you selected **Create a New Site** during server installation.

Q: If I want to keep a spare server online for performing single mailbox recovery, should I select **Join Existing Site** or **Create a New Site** during the installation of Exchange?

A: Select **Create a New Site**. Also, use a unique computer name when installing Windows NT. Do not select **Join Existing Site**. When maintaining a single mailbox recovery server, you must configure the server with the same organization and site name as the site from which you plan to recover single mailbox data. It is important that you do not select **Join Existing Site** during the installation. If you inadvertently join a site and then complete the single mailbox recovery procedures, undesired replication behavior will result after you run the DS/IS consistency adjuster because you have two sets of mailbox data for the same users within the site after restoring a Priv.edb.

Q: I have some users that use .pst files and remain logged on at night. How can I back up their .pst files?

A: The client automatically disconnects from the .pst file after 30 minutes of inactivity. When activity resumes, the client automatically reconnects to the .pst file. Because of this feature, you can back up .pst files during periods of inactivity (usually at night) while the client is logged on to Exchange.

Q: I know that I need to run **isinteg -patch** after restoring an offline information store backup to patch the globally unique identifiers (GUIDs), but what is a GUID?

A: A GUID is a hexadecimal string that uniquely tags an object in time and space. Within the information store, the private and public information stores have base GUIDs that they use to generate GUIDs for all other objects in the information stores, including folders, messages, attachments, and so on. The patch that the ISINTEG tool performs changes the base GUIDs in the information store. The patch must be run because when you restore an information store, you are essentially rolling back time on that server. If you roll back the server and do not change the base GUID, new objects created in that information store could have GUIDs that are identical to other existing objects in the organization. This would cause problems in referencing objects because they could no longer be uniquely identified. If you only have one server in your organization, this is not a problem because when you restore, there are no other objects in the organization that have IDs that might be generated again for new objects.

Q: What is the tradeoff regarding location of log files? I have computers with a total of five disk drives. The first two drives are mirrored and the other three are set up in a RAID 5 stripe set. Should I not mirror the operating system and use one of those drives to dedicate for transaction log files to gain performance?

A: In Microsoft Exchange Server, the best performance is gained through dedicating a physical drive for transaction log files. This is because transaction log files are written sequentially on a dedicated drive and the disk read/write head does not have to respond to calls from other processes. However, it might not be worth sacrificing operating system mirroring in favor of performance. In this case, it is best to maintain the Windows NT swap file and the Exchange database files on the three-disk stripe set (RAID 5) and to maintain the transaction log files on the mirror set. With enough RAM in the system, there should be little disk head contention on the operating system drives and transaction log performance should be high.

Q: How important is transaction log file redundancy?

A: In general, transactions are committed to the databases quickly. However, on a very busy system, transactions written to log files can accumulate before being committed to the database files. If the transaction log drive crashes before transactions are written, this data is lost.

Q: How can I shut down Exchange services without using Control Panel? Sometimes these services take a long time to shut down.

A: You can issue commands from the command line to shut down services, or you can use the batch file example shown below. If you want to shut down the entire system from a batch file, use the shutdown command, which is available on the *Microsoft Windows NT Resource Kit* compact disc. The purpose of this command is to shut down services in reverse dependency order. To shut down a Microsoft Mail (PC) message transfer agent (PCMTA) service that includes spaces in the name, use quotation marks.

```
REM // stop all services
echo Stopping Services...
net stop MSExchangeMSMI
net stop MSExchangePCMTA*
net stop MSExchangeFB
net stop MSExchangeDX
net stop MSExchangeIMC
net stop MSExchangeMTA
net stop MSExchangeIS
net stop MSExchangeDS
net stop MSExchangeSA
REM - call the shutdown command here. (This command requires that
you have the Windows NT Resource Kit compact disc.)
*service name is user defined
```

Q: My tape drive is not working, but I need to back up the databases. How can I do this?

A: If you have enough disk space, shut down services and copy the Priv.edb and Pub.edb files from the Exchsrvr\Mdbdata directory (the default installation point). Also copy the Dir.edb file from Exchsrvr\Dsadata (the default installation point). You do not have to copy the transaction log files because when services are shut down normally, outstanding transactions are committed to the database. If you need to restore from this backup method, remove the log files and Edb.chk from their respective directories, copy the previously copied files back in, and follow the procedure for running **isinteg -patch**. When the services start up, a new Edb.chk file is created, along with new transaction log files. Make sure to back up files before you purge them. If you need additional assistance with these procedures, contact Microsoft Technical Support.

Q: How long does it take to defragment a database?
A: Approximately 10 gigabytes per hour using the ESEUTIL utility.

The databases are defragmented automatically as a background process, so unless the file size of the databases must be reduced, you should not have to run offline compaction (defragmentation with file size reduction).

Q: Do I need a backup of the directory database to recover a server?
A: You need at least one backup of the directory service for each computer. Regardless of how old the backup is, the directory service rebuilds itself on that computer and becomes current from the other directory services in the site after the restore. After installing a new server in a site and ensuring that it is replicated and current, you should make a backup of the directory service.

After a restore, run DS/IS (Directory Services/Information Store) consistency adjuster after the directory service has been synchronized. This ensures that all objects in the information store on that computer are restored back into the directory service.

Note Make sure all directory replication connectors are working properly before running DS/IS consistency adjuster. It is possible to rehome public folders to this server as a result. For more information, see these Knowledge Base articles: Q156705 and Q141342.

If you don't have a backup of the directory service for a server to restore from, your only option is to delete the server from the site and then reinstall it. However, this option is not advisable because you will lose all of your information store data. Instead, make a backup of the directory service as soon as possible after you install a new server, and then lock the backup in a safe place. Replace the backup with more up-to-date backups on a regular basis. This way, you do not have to wait long for the directory service to resynchronize after a restore.

Q: Why do I need to back up the system following the migration of users to the server? Also, why do I need to back up the system after running an offline ESEUTIL operation?
A: If a server crashes after a migration and you have not backed up the system data, you must perform the migration again. This can be time-consuming.
After you run an offline ESEUTIL operation, the database is in a new state. If your system experiences a crash, you must perform the operation again. This can also be time-consuming.

Q: When I shut down services, they keep trying to restart. Why does this happen, and what can I do?

A: This problem is most likely caused by a server monitor session that is configured for the server on which you are trying to shut down services. By running the Administrator program **admin/t** (maintenance mode) command at least one polling interval before stopping services, you ensure that the server monitor is notified that subsequent polls of the server in maintenance mode will not result in alerts or alarms. After running this command, you can stop services and perform maintenance. When maintenance is complete, rerun **admin /t** to re-enable monitoring. For command-line Help on Administrator program command-line switches, change to the Exchsrvr\Bin directory and type **admin /?**.

Q: Is it a good idea to periodically perform a directory export?

A: Yes. It is a quick operation that saves time if you are unable to restore your directory database in the future. You should never have to rely on this procedure, but it is an extra safety measure that enables you to add users quickly if necessary.

Q: Where can I find more information about information store startup problems?

A: Articles in the Microsoft Knowledge Base can be provide additional information about information store startup problems and other issues. For access to the Knowledge Base, visit http://www.microsoft.com/kb. Perform a search on "Microsoft Exchange," and then enter relevant keywords.

Q: What are lazy and non-lazy commits, and how does Exchange use them?

A: After transaction logs are flushed to disk, the transaction is durable. If your system crashes, these logs can be restored and nothing is lost. *Non-lazy commits* retain data on the hard drive; *lazy commits* indicate that the transaction logs have not been saved.

Q: Should I disable the SCSI controller write cache?

A: Yes, unless you have RAID or a disk controller with a battery backup, in which case data loss is not an issue. Disabling write cache enables you to avoid the potential for data loss where you do not have either RAID or battery backup. At a programming level, if the write through flag is set, Windows NT does not use buffers. Therefore, when a program receives a write complete signal from Windows NT, it is guaranteed that the write was completed to disk. This is critical to the Exchange transaction logging process. If write cache is enabled, Windows NT responds as if a write has made it to disk and informs the calling application of this "false" information. This could result in data corruption if the system crashes before this lazy write operation makes it to disk.

Q: When is a transaction committed to the database and how does this work? Is it first cached in memory so that it is virtually available, or is it necessary to read back from log files before writing to the database files?

A: Transactions are on both log files and fast memory pages. Log disk heads are never moved back to read old data, so only sequential writes occur on log files. After transactions are written to a log file, an operation is considered complete. The transaction is immediately available in server memory before it is actually committed to the database files. Remember that an operation is not complete (that is, the client does not receive an acknowledgment) until all transactions are written to the transaction log (on disk).

Q: How can I measure how the transaction logging process is doing?

A: Use Performance Monitor and select the MSExchangeDB object. Configure the following counters:

- **Log Bytes Write/sec**—The rate at which bytes are written to the log.

- **Log Checkpoint Depth**—A number proportional to the time that recovery will take after a system crash, depending on the performance of the individual system. A data page might be cached and not flushed to the .edb file for a long time. The earliest logged operations on the page can date back a significant time. To ensure that your system recovers from a crash, do not restore too many logs, and set the checkpoint depth to determine how many logs you can expect to replay during recovery.

- **Log Sessions Waiting**—The number of sessions waiting on a log commit to complete a transaction.

Q: What is the advantage of disabling circular logging?

A: Disabling circular logging provides for additional recoverability. This is because a history of transaction logs are maintained for all transactions. These log files are purged only when a full or incremental online backup is performed and they are no longer needed. For example, suppose your last good backup occurred on Monday, and on Thursday your database drive crashes. If you disabled circular logging and your transaction log files are configured on a separate physical drive from the drive that crashed, you can restore the Monday backup. In this case, you should *not* erase existing data, and you should verify that the log files created since the Monday backup have been restored back into the database. This process restores your data to the point immediately before the crash.

Q: When I try to run the **isinteg -patch** command, it does not run and I receive the following error message: DS_E_COMMUNICATIONS_PROBLEM. How do I solve this problem?

A: Make sure the directory service is started before running the command.

Q: How can I back up an Exchange computer if the Windows NT Server computer I am using does not have the Administrator program installed?

A: If you are copying files from an existing Exchange computer, find and copy to the backup machine the Edbbcli.dll file found in the Winnt Root\System 32 directory on the existing server. This file is necessary in order for Ntbackup.exe to back up an Exchange. The Edbbcli.dll file is also available on the Exchange installation compact disc.

Q: Do I need to run the DS/IS consistency adjuster after restoring the directory and information store?

A: No. You only have to run the DS/IS consistency adjuster if you restore only the information store. The consistency adjuster scans the information store and ensures that a directory service object exists for each information store object. If the directory service object does not exist, one is created. The consistency adjuster also scans the directory service and ensures that a corresponding information store object exists. If it does not exist, the directory service object is deleted. Finally, the consistency adjuster also verifies the access control list (ACL) for each object and strips any invalid entries from the list. You can also set the DS/MDB Sync diagnostic logging level to maximum and then check the application log.

Q: Should I avoid running the DS/IS consistency adjuster?

A: If you restore only the information store and must run the DS/IS consistency adjuster to re-create the directory service object for the mailboxes in the store, this sets the HOME-MDB attribute on all public folders in the hierarchy (replicas or not) to this server. In addition, it strips the public folder ACLs of any invalid entries (that is, users who do not exist in the current directory).

If you do this and then re-create a replication connector into the organization, there will be a conflict. The new server will probably win because it has newer changes to the public folder property. Accordingly, the public folder will be homed on the new server, and the new server's ACL will most likely be the ACL that is kept. This will result in lost permissions for some users.

Q: I cannot find the backup set on my tape. What might cause this?

A: Make sure that you catalog the tape before restoring any data. This process enables you to gather information on the files available on the tape, and it enables the restore process to take place. After the catalog is complete, you can start the restore process. To load a catalog of the backup sets on a tape, follow this procedure:

- In the Tapes window, select the tape whose catalog you want loaded.

- Choose **Catalog** in one of three ways: double-click the icon for the appropriate tape, click **Catalog**, or click **Catalog** on the **Operations** menu.

After you search the tape, a complete list of backup sets appears in the Tapes window. Question marks are displayed in each icon to indicate that their individual catalogs have not been loaded.

Q: If you delete a computer name from the domain, re-add it to the domain, and then restore the Windows NT Registry from tape, is it true that the local SID from the restored Windows NT Registry will not match the new SID created in the domain?

A: Yes. You should delete and re-add the name of an Exchange computer in the domain only if a new server is required for recovery. The Windows NT Registry should be restored only to the same physical computer because the Windows NT Registry contains computer-specific data. This situation can occur if only the operating system hard disk was replaced and a Windows NT restore is performed.

Another issue to consider is that the Exchange directory database maintains information about Windows NT IDs in the domain, such as ACL information. If you cannot access the security accounts manager from the original domain and you create a new security accounts manager by installing a new domain, and then restore the directory service, you have a disconnect between the object security in the directory service (such as the Exchange service account, user mailboxes, and administrator's account) and the new domain security accounts manager. As a result, you do not have access to any object in the Exchange directory.

Q: What is the impact of configuring Exchange computers as backup domain controllers?

A: Configuring Exchange computers as backup domain controllers can increase recoverability and reduce costs. However, the memory requirements for these computers are also increased. For example, suppose that a Exchange computer configured as a primary domain controller has to be replaced. Although the Windows NT domain controller can be rebuilt and the information store restored, the directory service cannot be restored successfully to a domain that does not have the original security accounts manager.

Q: Does a full server restore to a different physical computer require the recovery server to be configured as a backup domain controller or primary domain controller?

A: No. The important thing is that the computer account is deleted and then re-added to the production domain so that the recovery computer can obtain a new SID that uses the same name as the original production server.

Q: How do you defragment the information store databases?

A: Exchange automatically defragments the information store and directory databases without interruption to messaging. Online defragmentation takes place in the background, marking items for deletion and defragmenting the database files. The resulting empty pages are returned back to the file system.

You can also use the ESEUTIL utility to compact the information store databases. Running the **eseutil /D** command reduces the size of the information store database files and defragments the database. In contrast, online defragmentation defragments the database files but does not decrease their size. If you use the **/D** (defragment) command-line option when running ESEUTIL, you must first stop the information store service.

Q: How do compaction, defragmentation, and information store maintenance differ?

A: By default, *information store maintenance* occurs between 1:00 A.M. and 6:00 A.M. The following tasks are typically completed during information store maintenance: tombstone compression, column aging, index aging, clean per user read, and message expiration. To view these settings from within the Administrator program, select the appropriate server under **Org**, **Site**, and **Configuration**. On the **File** menu, click **Properties** and then click the information store **Maintenance** tab.

Defragmentation is the online process that optimizes the structure of the database.

Compaction is the offline process of reclaiming disk space and defragmenting the database files. The process is accomplished using the **eseutil /D** command and reclaims space, having reduced the size of the database files.

Q: At what point do log files wrap around when database circular logging is used?

A: This is usually limited to four files, but if there is a heavy load on the server, such as during a large import/migration operation or a public folder backfill, the checkpoint and window grow to more than four log files.

Q: What is the Temp.edb file and why does it get created?

A: If long-term transactions are taking place, the Temp.edb file is used to store transactions that are in progress. This file is also used for transient storage during online compaction.

Q: When should the **eseutil /P** command be used?

A: You should use ESEUTIL only in consultation with Microsoft Technical Support. This command can delete data. Before running **eseutil /P**, you should always attempt a restore.

Q: What are the Res1.log and Res2.log files used for?

A: These are reserve log files that are not used unless the transaction log hard disk fills up. They are reserved for transactions that might be required to shut down the information store if the disk fills up. This way, even if the hard disk fills up, there is reserved space to record transactions from memory to disk. These files are 5 MB each, regardless of the number of transactions in the log files.

Q: If an information store is in recovery after a system crash, will Exchange be smart enough not to duplicate pre-existing transactions in the database and only play back uncommitted transactions?

A: Yes. Log files are read and this is a fast operation. If the transaction version number is already in the database, the transaction is not recommitted.

Q: Will Exchange automatically play back uncommitted transactions from logs when the services come up the first time following a crash?

A: Yes. If the database shut down was not clean, Exchange records that and replays all transactions from the checkpoint forward at startup.

Q: If circular logging is enabled, is it true that you cannot play back logs (those that are present in the circular window)?

A: Yes. With circular logging enabled, you cannot restore from a backup and play forward. You can only restore from backup at the point the backup was taken. By default, Exchange is configured with circular logging enabled.

Q: If circular logging is disabled, how can you play back transaction log files if required?

A: With circular logging disabled, you can play back logs from the last full backup. It depends on how you are performing backups. For example, suppose that you perform a full weekly backup on Sunday and incremental backups on Monday through Saturday. If you lose a hard drive or other data on Thursday, you need to restore tapes in the following order:

- Sunday: Full restore. Don't start services.

- Monday: Incremental restore. Don't start services.

- Tuesday: Incremental restore. Don't start services.

- Wednesday: Incremental restore. Don't start services.

After these restore operations are completed, start the information store service. You can restore all of these backup sets in one job and then select **Start Services** after the restore. When you do so, Ntbackup.exe does not start services until the files from all sets are restored. Ntbackup.exe restores the data and log files from Sunday and adds the log files for Monday through Wednesday when the services restart. Finally, Ntbackup.exe replays all log files from after the point of the full backup on Sunday until the present time (that is, Monday through Wednesday, plus any log files created after the Wednesday backup).

Incremental backups delete log files after a backup is completed. Differential backups do not delete log files; instead these files are written to tape. If you were performing differential backups, you would not have to restore the Monday through Wednesday backup because you would still have those log files on the system.

Incremental and differential backups back up all log files since the last backup, as well as the Edb.chk file. The difference between these two backup types is that differential backups do not delete log files from the system.

Q: What is the difference between running the **isinteg - fix** command and the **eseutil /P** command?

A: The **eseutil /P** command should only be run as a last resort in order to repair a database file. You should use the ESEUTIL tool only in consultation with Microsoft Technical Support. The **isinteg - fix** command repairs high-level objects, while **eseutil /P** repairs low-level database corruption. The **isinteg - fix** command repairs any "scheme" and other high-level data or structure problems. If you have to run both commands, run **eseutil /P** first; then run **isinteg - fix**. Only run both commands if you do not have a backup from which to restore and log files to play forward.

Restoring data from a backup and then playing logs forward is the recommended way to restore a corrupted database due to hardware failure. These procedures are recommended because they enable you to recover all your data. If you do not have a backup to restore and run the **eseutil /P** and **isinteg - fix** commands instead, you will lose all of your data.

Q: Can Exchange perform information store compression on the fly? Should administrators perform manual compression on a periodic basis?

A: Exchange can perform online defragmentation, which is different than compression.

Exchange reuses the space before growing the file, so database defragmentation takes place in the background on a running server. The only time you should have to shut down a server for offline compaction is when you want to physically recover the free space on the disk. To reduce .edb file size, stop Exchange services and then run the **eseutil /D** command.

Q: What is the purpose of log files?

A: On an Exchange computer, the public information store, private information store, and directory service each have log files. These files are the transaction logs for all transactions that occur on the database. In the event of a system crash, hard drive failure, power failure, or another disaster, these files can be used for soft and hard recovery and for restore after backup. The Priv.edb file on a running server is always inconsistent because of the database cache that is in RAM on the server. The consistent state of a server is made up of the data in the .edb file and the data in the memory cache on the server. If a server computer crashes and you don't replay the logs, this results in a corrupt database.

The log files permit automatic playback of transactions that have occurred on the database but are not yet committed to the .edb file. There is a check-point file, Edb.chk, that contains the current transaction point in the log files that have been committed to disk.

Log files continue to consume disk space until you do one of the following:

- Back up the server (by performing a full backup or an incremental backup). This writes all logs to the tape up to the check point and then deletes the logs written to tape from the hard drive. If you have to restore the database, the backup copies the database file from the tape, replays the logs on the tape, and then replays all the logs on the disk.

- Run with circular logging enabled.

If you browse the .edb file directories, you also see *.pat files. These files are created when a backup is performed and contain all the changes (patches) since the backup started. You can write the patch file when performing a backup and be completely current. The following table lists files that you see in the Exchsrvr\Mdbdata directory.

File	Description
Priv.edb	Private database file
Pub.edb	Public database file
Edb.log	Current log file being written to
Edbxxxxx.log	Previous log files no longer opened or being used; new .log file every 5 MB
Res1.log	Log file reserved in case the database or log file drive fills up the server
Res2.log	Log file reserved in case the database or log file drive fills up the server
Priv.pat	Backup patch file for Priv.edb
Pub.pat	Backup patch file for Pub.edb
Edb.chk	Checkpoint file

Q: When I am restoring a server in a site, if I do not have a backup of the directory (Dir.edb) for the server, can I backfill the directory from a replica on another server in the site?

A: No. It is critical that you have a backup of the directory for each Exchange computer because the directory is unique for each computer. Even if you have only the original directory backup, you can restore this backup and then backfill changes from another server in the site.

Q: What is the purpose of the Exchange **setup /r** command?

A: The **setup /r** command enables recovery of an existing Exchange computer to new hardware. Restoration of a valid database backup is also required. Run the **setup /r** command when you want to move a server installation to a different computer or if you are restoring data to a new computer.

Q: Is a differential backup required only when both the transaction drive and the .edb drive must be recovered?

A: Yes. If circular logging is disabled and the transaction logs are intact, you can restore the last full backup. When the service is started, logs from the point of the full backup are played through the current Edb.log file to bring the database up-to-date. In this case, do *not* select **Erase all existing data** during the restore, or the transaction logs will be erased and you will have to restore the differential tape.

Q: Why can't I start services between restoring a full tape and a differential or incremental tape, or between sequential tapes being restored?

A: This is because at the end of a restore, Exchange plays back all logs in sequential order. After it does this, the database is set to a new state. For example, if the services are started between a Monday incremental tape restore and a Tuesday incremental tape restore, a new state is set. When you attempt to perform the Tuesday incremental restore, the restore is not possible because the state of the database is expected to be exactly what it was at the point of the Tuesday backup. This behavior prevents overwriting new operations that have occurred on the database after services have been started.

PART 10

Exchange Architecture

Understanding the architecture of Microsoft Exchange Server and how Exchange components communicate can help you maintain and troubleshoot your Exchange organization.

For more information about Exchange architecture, see the *Microsoft Exchange Server Programmer's Reference* or the *Messaging Application Programming Interface (MAPI) Programmer's Reference.*

Organizations and Sites

To simplify administration and provide scalability, Exchange consists of organizations and sites. An *organization* is the larger administrative unit; it contains all of the servers that provide the messaging functionality for a company. Each organization consists of one or more connected sites. A *site* is a group of Exchange computers that share the same directory information and can communicate over high-bandwidth, permanent, and synchronous network connections. If your company has several offices in different cities, the servers for each office can be in different sites.

You can connect sites using a variety of methods, such as wide area networks (WANs), the Internet, or even dial-up lines. Connecting sites enables users in different locations to send messages quickly and efficiently and to share information using public folders. It also allows the administrator to manage servers from remote locations and ensure that directory information in all sites is the same.

You can manage your organization and sites using the Microsoft Exchange Administrator program, which you can run on either a Microsoft Windows NT Server or a Microsoft Windows NT Workstation computer. Use the Administrator program to view and configure all of the objects in your organization, such as sites, servers, connections, and message recipients.

Integration with Windows NT Server

All Exchange components run on Windows NT Server as multithreaded Windows NT services. Exchange takes advantage of important features provided by the operating system, such as security. The resources in sites, such as mailboxes, rely on Windows NT Server domains to perform essential security operations. For example, to prevent unauthorized users and services from gaining access to Exchange resources, domains authenticate users when they log on to their mailboxes.

Exchange components, such as the information store, the directory, and the system attendant, use a type of Windows NT user account called the site's *service account*, which allows components access to the system. For example, the directory service uses the site's service account to read and write to the local directory and to directories on other servers. Each site can have only one service account. Therefore, a message transfer agent (MTA) on one server uses the same service account as the MTA on another server in a site.

Just as users must be authenticated by a domain to log on to the network with a client computer, Exchange services also must be authenticated by a domain to run in a site. A site's service account must be authenticated either by the domain that contains the Exchange computers or by a trusted domain before the Exchange components can interact.

Communication Between the Client and Server

Exchange services communicate with each other as client and server processes by using remote procedure calls (RPCs). An *RPC* is a routine that transfers functions and data between client and server processes; it is an industry standard protocol for client/server communication. With RPC, clients and servers can communicate with one another efficiently on almost any type of network. When the client and the server run on the same computer, RPCs are mapped to local procedure calls, which are much faster than RPCs.

Server Architecture

The Exchange architecture is composed of modular components that provide integrated and reliable messaging, scheduling, and information-sharing functions. The core and optional components maintain address and message databases, log transactions, and allow you to connect with other Exchange computers and foreign systems.

Core Components

The following core components of Exchange are installed during Setup and must be running on the server at all times:

- Information store
- Directory
- Message transfer agent (MTA)
- System attendant

The following illustration shows how the core components interact. The information store, directory, and MTA process requests from the client and from each other. The system attendant maintains server operation and performs key functions, such as generating e-mail addresses for new recipients; it is the background process that makes sure the system runs smoothly and the e-mail is routed correctly.

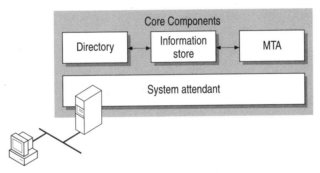

The information store, directory, and MTA function like elements of the postal service. When you send a message, the message is delivered to a central post office called the information store. The information store then determines where the message should be delivered by looking in the directory, which is like an address book. Then, the mail carrier (the MTA) delivers the message.

Information Store

The information store maintains and provides access to the message database. The information store is visible to users as Inboxes and folders in the Microsoft Outlook client. It can store all types of information, including word processing documents, spreadsheets, and messages.

The information store maintains information in two databases — the private information store (which contains user mailboxes) and the public information store (which contains public folders). It uses single-instance storage of messages, which means that a message sent to many recipients is stored only once on the server. This conserves disk space.

A server can have both a private information store and a public information store, or it can be dedicated to providing only one of these services. Dedicating a server to one of these functions can significantly improve performance for users. To make a server a dedicated mailbox server, delete the public information store; to make it a dedicated public folder server, delete the private information store.

When the information store receives a request to access a message, it performs the following tasks:

- Determines whether the message is already in memory (the buffer)
- Searches the message database for the message if the message is not already in memory
- Returns the requested message or a "not found" message to the requesting client

When the information store receives a message that a user on the local server wants to send, it performs the following tasks:

- Resolves individual addresses
- Logs the message in the information store transaction log
- Queries the MTA and directory to expand distribution lists if a message is addressed to users on the same server
- Writes the message to the user's Inbox and notifies the client application
- Applies rules the recipient has set when the message is delivered to the user's Inbox
- Forwards the message to the MTA for routing, if the recipient is on another server

Users, administrators, and applications all have access to the information store.

Users   Users have access to information store objects (such as messages) and to private and public folders.

Administrators   Administrators have access to the information store through the Administrator program, and they have permissions to perform the following tasks:

- Create or delete mailboxes.
- Modify the attribute values of information store objects.
- Create and modify permissions on public and private folders.

Applications   Other applications running on Windows NT Server have access to and are accessible by the information store. The information store must have access to the directory or MTA to complete the following tasks:

- Request address information from the directory to resolve addresses or expand distribution lists.

- Retrieve messages requested by users.

- Forward messages it receives for other Exchange computers to the MTA for routing.

- Forward messages for foreign gateways through the appropriate connector for delivery.

The information store's memory cache increases performance by maintaining the most recently requested messages in memory rather than reading them from the hard disk for every request. This buffer allows quick access to a message that has been read or modified recently in subsequent requests.

When a message is created, modified, or deleted, the information store records the transaction in a log file. The log is written sequentially to increase performance. If the server fails before changes are written to the database, the information store uses this log to restore those changes.

Directory

The directory provides a single, central location where users and applications can look up and configure information about an object. It stores all the information about an Exchange organization (such as addresses, mailboxes, distribution lists, public folders) and configuration information about sites and servers. The directory also generates the Address Book, which users can use to look up information about other users and to address messages. The Address Book contains all of the recipients in the organization. It is organized into lists, such as the global address list.

The directory makes the following tasks possible:

- Find information about Exchange users, custom recipients, and other e-mail recipients of such as distribution lists and public folders.

- Centrally manage all objects in a site by using either the Administrator program or a custom application that calls the Exchange directory functions.

- Write custom applications and add-on services that can store configuration information and make it available through an extension to the Administrator program as a custom property page. (This task is important to developers of third-party applications.)

- Use the directory to look up the information required to provide a specific service. For example, the system attendant looks up connector configuration information to build the routing table. The MTA looks up a user's address and uses it with the routing table to route a message.

All information about an organization is stored as configurable elements or objects in a database. Each object in an organization is represented in a hierarchical structure and has a set of attributes or properties. You can customize your organization by changing the properties for directory objects in the Administrator program. For example, you can set message storage limits for mailboxes by setting properties for the information store object for a server. You can also specify who has permission to make changes to directory objects.

The directory is automatically replicated among servers in a site to ensure that all servers have the same information. Among sites, the directory is replicated by directory bridgehead servers according to a schedule you set in the Administrator program. Each site has one or more directory bridgehead servers that are responsible for keeping the site's directory synchronized with the directories in other sites.

Note Keeping the directory current is important. If directory information is outdated, messages might not reach their destinations. For example, if a new mailbox is added to a server, servers in another site will not have that information until the directory is replicated to that site. Also, users cannot send messages to the new mailbox until the directory on the mailbox's home server has been replicated. For more information about directory replication, see *Microsoft Exchange Server Operations*.

When the directory receives an address request, it performs the following tasks:

- Searches to see whether the address is already in memory (the buffer).

- Searches the directory database for the address if the address is not already in memory.

- Returns the requested address or a "not found" message to the requesting client.

When the directory receives an address change, it performs the following tasks:

- Logs the change in the directory transaction log
- Writes the change to the memory buffer
- Returns a confirmation to the user who requested the change
- Writes the change to the directory database

Users, administrators, and applications all have access to the directory.

Users Users have access to objects in the directory such as mailboxes, distribution lists, custom recipients, and public folders, all of which are addressable objects.

Administrators Administrators have access to the directory through the Administrator program. They have permissions to perform the following tasks:

- Create or delete most types of individual directory objects.
- Modify the attribute values of directory objects.
- Perform certain import and export operations.

- In most cases, you can perform these tasks on one object at a time. After a directory object has been created, you can edit it using property pages, which display the most commonly accessed attributes.

Applications Other applications running on Windows NT Server and custom applications developed for Exchange have access to the directory. They can perform the following tasks:

- Manipulate a large number of directory objects, for example, during administration of custom add-on services.
- Synchronize the Exchange directory with directories of foreign systems.
- Automatically update Windows NT user accounts when their associated directory objects (such as mailboxes) are updated.
- Look up routing tables that are stored in the directory.

The directory uses a memory cache to minimize the time that is required for processing requests and a transaction log buffer to minimize wait time while read and write requests are logged. The directory's memory cache increases performance by maintaining the most recently requested information in memory rather than reading from the disk for every request.

When an address is created or modified, the directory logs the transaction in the transaction log file. The log is written sequentially to increase performance. If the server fails before changes are written to the database, the directory uses this log to restore the changes.

Message Transfer Agent

The Message Transfer Agent (MTA) routes messages among Exchange computers within a site and to MTAs in other sites. It also expands distribution lists. The MTA uses a memory cache for increased performance.

When the MTA receives a message, it performs the following tasks:

- Secures the message in the message transfer database and queues the message until it can be sent
- Queries the directory to determine where the message should be routed
- Routes the message to the MTA of the recipient's server or to the information store for local delivery or delivery through a connector
- Deletes the message after it is routed

The MTA uses the following two types of X.400 interfaces when routing messages:

- The message access (MA) interface is used between X.400 clients and X.400 MTAs. The MTA uses this interface to communicate with the other Exchange components.
- The message transfer (MT) interface is used between X.400 MTAs. The MTA uses this interface to communicate with other Exchange MTAs and X.400 compatible MTAs.

Administrators and applications have access to the MTA.

Administrators Administrators have access to the MTA through the Administrator program, and they have permission to perform the following tasks:

- Set the MTA name or password.
- Set limits on message sizes.
- Recalculate the routing tables.
- Configure distribution list expansion.

Applications Other applications running on Windows NT Server have access to and are accessible by the MTA. The MTA has access to the directory, information store, and system attendant to perform the following tasks:

- Request address information from the directory when it must resolve addresses or expand distribution lists.
- Send log entries to the system attendant for message tracking.
- Deliver messages received from remote MTAs to the local information store.
- Route messages from the local information store to remote MTAs.

System Attendant

The system attendant serves several miscellaneous functions. It rebuilds the routing tables, manages the server and link monitors, and sets up advanced security for Microsoft Outlook users.

Administrators and applications have access to the system attendant.

Administrators   Administrators have access to the system attendant through the Administrator program to set time limits for keeping message tracking logs.

Applications   Other applications running on Windows NT Server have access to and are accessible by the system attendant. The system attendant has access to the directory, MTA, and Key Management component to perform the following tasks:

- Build routing tables for the MTA.

- Generate e-mail directory addresses for new recipients.

- Check the consistency of directory replication.

- Store and manage digital signatures and encryption information for a mailbox during the configuration of advanced security.

- Send and receive e-mail for the link monitor.

- Initiate and maintain link and server monitors.

Optional Components

You can install optional components and benefit from added features, such as connectivity to other messaging systems and advanced security. For example, if your users have to send messages to Internet users, you can install Internet Mail Service. If you have Microsoft Schedule+ users who are on both Microsoft Mail for PC Networks and Exchange, you can install the Schedule+ Free/Busy Connector so that users on each system can view each other's free and busy information.

The following optional components can be installed on an Exchange computer.

Key Management   Manages security information used for digitally signing and encrypting messages sent between users within an organization. For more information, see Chapter 7, "Security."

Internet Mail Service   Enables users on Exchange to send messages to and receive messages from users on the Internet. Internet Mail Service also can be used to connect sites over a Simple Mail Transfer Protocol (SMTP) backbone.

Microsoft Mail Connector Enables users on Exchange to send messages to and receive messages from users on Microsoft Mail for PC Networks and Microsoft Mail for AppleTalk Networks (now known as Quarterdeck Mail). Microsoft Mail Connector includes all components required to connect to Microsoft Mail post offices, including the directory synchronization component and the Schedule+ Free/Busy Connector.

X.400 Connector Can be configured to connect sites or to route messages to foreign X.400 systems. The X.400 Connector conforms to the 1984 and 1988 International Telegraph and Telephone Consultative Committee X.400 standards.

Microsoft Exchange Connector for Lotus Notes Enables Exchange users to exchange messages with Lotus Notes users.

Microsoft Exchange Connector for SNADS Enables Exchange and IBM SNA Distribution System (SNADS) users to exchange messages.

Microsoft Exchange Connector for IBM OfficeVision/VM (PROFS) Enables Exchange and OfficeVision/VM users to exchange messages.

Microsoft Exchange Connector for Lotus cc:Mail Provides message transfer and directory synchronization between Exchange and Lotus cc:Mail systems.

The following illustration shows the relationship between optional components and core components.

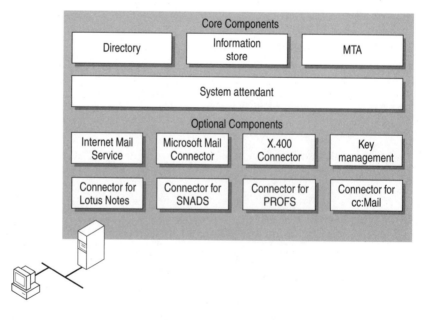

Addressing and Routing

Understanding how addressing works and how e-mail messages are routed through Exchange can help you optimize Exchange performance and reliability. Understanding the process will also help you troubleshoot message routing problems.

Exchange can accommodate e-mail messages sent to recipients that are on the local server, on other Exchange computers, and on foreign systems. Communication between a local server and servers that are in other Exchange sites or foreign systems is accomplished by routing messages through gateways, which are called *connectors*.

Each connector has at least one path, called an *address space,* associated with it. Each address space describes an address format required by the type of system for which it is responsible. The connector's address spaces are used by the message transfer agent (MTA) to select the connectors that are candidates for routing a particular message.

To connect a local server to another Exchange computer in a remote site, Exchange uses one of the following:

- Site Connector
- Dynamic Remote Access Service (RAS) Connector
- Internet Mail Service
- X.400 Connector

To connect a local server to a server in a foreign system, Exchange uses one of the following:

- Internet Mail Service
- Microsoft Mail Connector for PC Networks
- Microsoft Mail Connector for AppleTalk Networks
- X.400 Connector
- Microsoft Exchange Connector for Lotus cc:Mail
- Lotus Notes Connector
- Third-party gateways

Addressing

Exchange stores recipient addresses in a directory. Rather than requiring a user to supply the recipient's address for each message, the user only needs to type the recipient's name, which Exchange then resolves into a complete address. The user must supply addresses for recipients who are not in the Address Book. Although users see only the names or the e-mail aliases in the Address Book, the directory is a database (and a service) that contains additional addressing information for name resolution and routing purposes.

Addresses have two parts:

- A site address for each Exchange computer. Exchange uniquely identifies sites by using the c, a, p, and o components of the originator/recipient O/R address space.
- A recipient address for each mailbox.

Site and recipient addresses are stored in the directory. Custom addresses also can be created for recipients on foreign mail systems. Exchange creates a site address using the organization name and site name that you provided during setup. Because recipient addresses are created using site addresses, confirm that you have valid site addresses before you add mailboxes or connectors.

Exchange defines the following address types that can be present in the gateway routing table (GWART), which the MTA searches when it is routing a message to the appropriate connectors:

EX Denotes a distinguished name on Exchange. This address type is searched only when a distinguished name for the recipient exists in the directory.

MS Denotes Microsoft Mail for PC Networks.

SMTP Denotes the standard Internet mail protocol Simple Mail Transport Protocol.

X400 Denotes the O/R address, which is used for addressing under the X.400 protocol.

The address types MS and SMTP are created automatically during setup. If you install other gateways, Exchange also generates other address types.

Address Components

Addresses are made up of several components, each of which is used for a specific purpose. Not all addresses have all components.

Distinguished Names   The native Exchange address format. Exchange creates a distinguished name for every object in the directory, such as a mailbox, public folder, or distribution list. The MTA uses the distinguished name to route messages within the Exchange organization. A distinguished name can be used to identify a custom recipient.

When Exchange cannot use a distinguished name (for example, when there is no distinguished name to use or the distinguished name is invalid), it uses the X.400 address of the object to route the message. For this reason, you must retain the X.400 address for every object in the directory, even if you are not connecting to another X.400 system.

X.400 O/R Addresses   The native X.400 address type. An originator/recipient address (or O/R name) consists of either the distinguished name or an X.400 O/R address, or both. Users of a message transfer system are identified by an O/R name, which is included in the P1 message header. The message header is used to route and deliver the message. The O/R address consists of required and optional fields that contain both standard O/R attributes and various domain-defined attributes.

A *one-off* routing address is a manually entered O/R address that is not held in the directory and therefore has no distinguished name. A valid X.400 O/R address is required for routing out of the site, even if only a Domain Defined Attribute (DDA) is specified in the one-off routing address.

Domain Defined Attributes (DDAs)   Optional fields within the O/R address that are defined by the recipient's domain. Under X.400 protocols, up to four DDAs are allowed. For example, the SMTP DDA might be John.Doe@isp.com. Other DDAs define other address attributes. DDAs also are used with custom or third-party gateways.

Target Address   A DDA that identifies the address type required by the recipient system.

Custom Recipient Addresses   A recipient on a foreign system that has an address stored in the Exchange directory is called a *custom recipient*. Each custom recipient has only one target address, but can also have multiple proxy addresses of different types. The target address type matches the native e-mail system that delivers e-mail to the particular custom recipient.

When a message is routed to a custom recipient, the distinguished names of the recipient and originator are replaced in the message header with addresses of the type used in the recipient's native system. This ensures the message can be delivered to the foreign system and that a reply can be routed back to the originator with the correct address type. The following diagram illustrates the conversion of a recipient address.

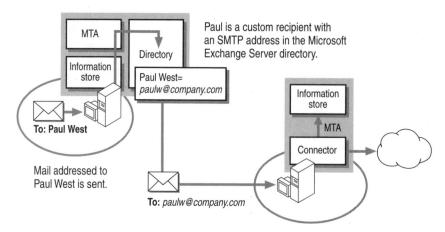

If the recipient is not in the Exchange directory, the originator must write the address in the form required by the foreign system. In this case, only the originator's address is converted to the native format of the foreign system.

For more information about site and recipient addresses, see *Microsoft Exchange Server Concepts and Planning*. For information about how to view and modify site and recipient addresses, see *Microsoft Exchange Server Operations*.

Name Resolution

The name resolution process in Exchange is as follows:

1. Microsoft Exchange searches for a distinguished name in the recipient's address. If it finds a distinguished name, it reads the O/R address for that distinguished name.

2. If it does not find a distinguished name, it checks whether a distinguished name has been saved within the DDA fields. If it finds a distinguished name in the DDA fields (which means an MTA previously constructed this recipient's O/R address), it reads that distinguished name.

3. If the original distinguished name is invalid or no distinguished name exists, it scans the local proxy addresses for a match with the O/R address.

4. If it finds a match, it obtains the distinguished name. If the initial scan of proxy addresses fails but a common name or surname exists, it performs a "fuzzy match" scan for a unique matching distinguished name.

5. If the current O/R address is invalid, it adds the local X.400 proxy fields to make it valid.

6. If it finds new address information for a recipient, it re-encodes the P1 recipient address into the message.

Remote Mailboxes

An Exchange recipient that is not local and also not a distribution list or custom recipient is treated as a remote mailbox. Remote mailboxes must always have a valid O/R address (a distinguished name is optional) so that the X.400 backbones can transmit the message. If a distinguished name is routed successfully through the GWART and no O/R address is available, a new address is constructed from the remote-site-proxy O/R address information in the connected sites. If the new O/R address contains no DDA information, the distinguished name is saved in the DDA of the O/R address with the special "MSXCHNGE" DDA type to mark it as artificially constructed. This mechanism also enables encapsulation of Exchange distinguished names over 1984 X.400 backbones.

Target Addresses

Custom recipients have a distinguished name that is of local significance only; therefore, the distinguished name of a custom recipient is always ignored when searching the GWART for the recipient. Although the custom recipient's distinguished name and primary X.400 proxy O/R address are contained in the P1 recipient address, they are not used in the routing process. Instead, routing is accomplished through the Target Address attribute of the custom recipient.

During routing only, an X.400 target address overrides a standard O/R address and route. A non-X.400 target address overrides the DDA portion of an O/R address and routes the message using the DDA attributes found in the GWART. The target address does not overwrite the O/R address in the P1 header of the message. If the target address is not specified in the message, it is created from the X.400 proxy address found by reading the distinguished name, as for mailboxes.

If no target address is found for the custom recipient, the primary X.400 proxy O/R address (if any) is used for routing.

Routing

E-mail messages are routed to each recipient individually. If the recipient is local to the originating Message Transfer Agent (MTA), local routing takes place. If it is not local, remote routing takes place.

Messages are submitted to the Exchange computer by a local user, by another Exchange computer, or by a foreign e-mail system through a connector or gateway.

Messages can be routed to the following:

- A recipient on the same server computer
- A recipient on a different server computer in the same site
- A recipient in a different site or foreign system

The MTA can route e-mail messages externally to:

- Exchange MTAs in the same site using remote procedure calls (RPCs).
- Exchange MTAs in a different site through the Site Connector or Internet Mail Service.
- Exchange MTAs in a different site through a Dynamic RAS Connector.
- Remote X.400 MTAs through an X.400 Connector, which can be configured for various transport protocols such as X.25, Transport Control Protocol/Internet Protocol (TCP/IP), or Transport Class 4 (TP4).
- Gateways (for example, Microsoft Mail Connector).

Route Selection Process

The MTA compares the recipient address to the addresses in the GWART to determine the group of connectors to which the message can be delivered. The search for a match in the GWART is done in the following order:

1. **Distinguished name.** This address format is searched only if a distinguished name for the recipient has been found. An exact match on the enterprise (organization) and site of the distinguished name is required.

2. **DDA.** An exact, wildcard, or partial match on the domain-defined attribute value (DDAV) is required with an exact or partial match on the domain-defined attribute type (DDAT). Wildcard matches are used in order of the exactness of the match (that is, with the exact match first, followed by the wildcard that has the most matching characters, and so on).

3. **O/R address.** An exact or wildcard match on the address space is required. Each field of the address is compared hierarchically with the contents of the GWART until either a match is found or it is determined that no match is present, at which point this recipient is marked for a non-delivery report (NDR). The order of the search is as follows:

1. Country
2. Administrative management domain (ADMD)
3. Private management domain (PRMD)
4. Organization
5. Organizational unit

The routing process is used for the following tasks:

- Message and probe routing
- Distribution list expansion (routing to Home-MTA and detecting loops in the distribution list expansion tree)
- Rerouting all object types
- Report routing (normal and distribution list-specific)

Local and Same-Site Routing

If the recipient is *local*, that is, on the same server as the originator, the Exchange information store delivers the message directly to the recipient's mailbox. The recipient's distinguished name is used to deliver the message.

As shown in the following illustration, the information store can deliver a message from MarcOl to NelsJ and RoseG on the same server.

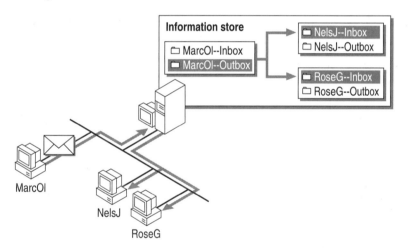

A recipient is considered to be local if a distinguished name for the recipient is available in the directory that matches the local site and this distinguished name does not identify a custom recipient. If the recipient has only an O/R address that matches the local site O/R address space, a distinguished name is found by proxy search if the recipient is a valid local recipient.

Address space filtering is performed in the routing routine to ensure that O/R addresses matching the local site O/R address space are not sent out of the site. If a recipient is to be routed through the GWART but matches the local O/R address space, this recipient is marked for an NDR.

▶ **To avoid NDRs**

1. In the Administrator window, click Configuration.

2. In the right side of the window, double-click **Site Addressing**.

3. In the **General** properties page, click **Share address space with other X.400 systems**.

4. Click **OK**.

If a local recipient originally had a distinguished name and an O/R address is found by a proxy search, the P1 recipient address is not re-encoded because the O/R address is not required when routing locally. The exception to this is when disclosure of recipients is allowed, in which case the O/R address must be included to prevent interoperability problems.

Remote-Site Routing

Using connectors, the Exchange MTA can route messages to the following:

- Another Exchange MTA in a different site using a site connector, Internet Mail Service, or a Dynamic RAS Connector

- A remote X.400 MTA using the X.400 Connector

- Other connectors or gateways that connect to foreign systems, such as Microsoft Mail Connector

Two processes are involved in determining what connector is used to send a message — *routing* (determines what connectors can deliver the message) and s*election* (determines which of these connectors is the fastest or least costly connector to use.) Often, selections are made to balance loads among servers.

Connectors and Address Spaces

Messages to other systems are routed to connectors using the address type appropriate to the receiving system, such as an SMTP address for a message traveling over the Internet.

The path a connector uses to send messages outside the site is represented by an address space. The address space identifies the address types associated with the foreign system as well as some DDAs.

Each connector must have at least one address space. As shown in the following example, the sender is using Internet Mail Service to establish a link to the company's West Coast Internet provider. The Internet Mail Service address space type is SMTP, and the address is *.com. The MTA uses the Internet Mail Service only to process SMTP messages addressed to recipients with the .com domain identifier. Notice that the message with the *.edu address is not processed even though it is an SMTP address.

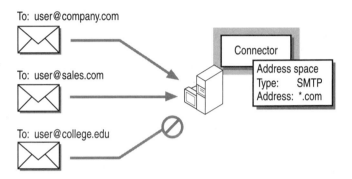

For more information about address spaces, see *Microsoft Exchange Server Concepts*

Gateway Routing Table

Associated with each connector is an address space (or spaces), the cost of using a particular route, and possibly a connected site (or sites). Each connector can have one or more connected sites associated with it. These associations are used to generate the Gateway Routing Table (GWART). The GWART is replicated throughout the organization so that each server computer is aware of all possible routes. An enterprise-wide GWART is created in each site by the Routing Information Daemon (RID), which uses local information and replicated site GWARTs to build a consolidated local GWART. Address space and connected sites information is defined in the **Address Space** and **Connected Sites** property pages in the Exchange Administrator program.

Each line of the GWART indicates an available routing path. You can view the contents of the GWART, including the address type each connector routes, in the **Routing** property page of the Site Addressing object as shown in the following illustration.

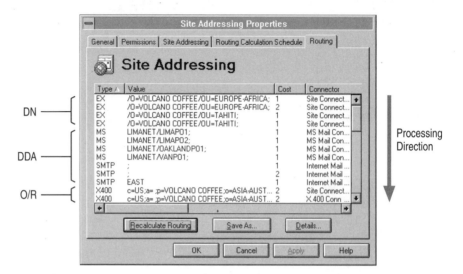

Connector Selection

When a message is sent, the MTA scans the GWART and compares the recipient's address type with the address spaces in the GWART. It chooses connectors with address spaces similar to the recipient's address. If more than one connector can send the message, a connector selection process determines which connector is the most efficient to use. This determination is based on a number of factors. If no connectors can service the address space, the message is returned to the originator with a non-delivery report (NDR).

Each time a connector or group of connectors meets the initial selection criteria, it is passed to the next step in the selection process. Each step applies to MTA-to-MTA connections, which include the X.400 Connector, the Dynamic RAS Connector, and the Site Connector. You can adjust some of the settings that are used in this selection process. Connectors and gateways for foreign systems are chosen only on the basis of the address spaces they process and the cost of the address space.

The following steps outline how the MTA selects a connector.

1. **Check for X.400 1984 Connector.** Eliminate this connector if it is an X.400 1984 protocol connector, and the message has not been downgraded to the X.400 1984 protocol.

2. **Check for looping message.** Eliminate the connector if the message was just received from that connector.

3. **Check message size and destination.** Eliminate connectors according to message size and destination constraints.

4. **Compare open retry count to maximum open retries.** Each connector has a maximum-open-retry counter and an open retry timer that is configured in the Administrator. Connectors that have an open retry count less than the value set for maximum open retries.

The maximum open retries count specifies the number of times the system can attempt to transfer a message through that connector. Site Connectors use a site-wide configurable value. The *open retry count* is the number of times the MTA has attempted to transfer a message using a specific connector. The open retry count for each connector is stored in the message in question and is updated during rerouting.

5. **Choose active connectors.** Site Connectors, Internet Mail Service, and Microsoft Mail Connectors are always active. Other connectors have activation schedules, including the X.400 Connectors and Dynamic RAS Connectors. There are four activation states. They are, in order of preference:

   ▪ Active now

   ▪ Will become active

   ▪ Remote initiated

   ▪ Never active

   The activation states are processed in the following order:

   1. Choose a subgroup of connectors that are *active now*.

   2. If there is no match and there are connectors that *will become active*, find the subgroup of connectors that will become active at the earliest time. (Several could become active in five minutes.)

   3. If there is no match and there are connectors that are *remote initiated*, choose this subgroup of connectors.

   4. If there is no match, use the connectors that are *never active*.

6. **Choose connectors with low retry counts.** The open retry count starts when the connection to the remote MTA fails. The connector attempts to establish the connection again when the Open Retry timer expires. The number of times the connector attempts the connection is based on the configuration of the Max Open Retries counter. The open retry counts are compared to each other, and connectors with the lowest number of open retries are chosen.

If the initial attempt to open an association fails, a timer is started (with a length defined as Open Retry) for the association control block (ASB) handling the original association. After the timer begins, another attempt to open an association is processed for that ASB. The process is repeated for each connector until the maximum open retry count is reached. After the maximum number of retry counts has been used on all available connectors, an NDR is issued for the set of recipients for which that connector was to be used.

7. **Choose connectors that have not failed.** Each MTA maintains an Open Retry timer for each connector that is on the same server. Connectors on other servers skip this step. Any connector that is not in a retry state is chosen. The open interval value determines how long the connector waits before attempting the connection again. This prevents the MTA from routing a message to a connector that failed the last time it tried to establish a connection.

For example, if you are using a Site Connector and Dynamic RAS Connector and the local area network (LAN) is down, a message is routed to the Site Connector because it has a lower cost. The connection fails because the LAN is down, so the message is routed to the Dynamic RAS Connector. The next message to arrive before the open retry timer expires on the Site Connector is routed directly to the Dynamic RAS Connector.

8. **Compare costs.** Connectors with the lowest cost are chosen first. You specify the costs when the address spaces are determined for each connector.

9. **Choose local connectors.** A local connector can send the message directly to the remote site. The MTA selects local connectors first to avoid an extra hop to the remote MTA in the site. Remote connectors require the MTA to pass the message to a messaging bridgehead server before the message can be passed to the remote site. Using local connectors reduces the need for additional processing power and bandwidth to transmit the message.

Site Connectors are counted as local if they are not homed on any particular server; otherwise the Site Connector has an actual location. If a Site Connector is remote (as indicated by the Home-MTA attribute), it means that the connector exists on another MTA within this site (that is, the message is routed to that Exchange MTA). Otherwise, no connectors exist to service this address space, and the message is marked with an NDR for this recipient.

10. **Balance connector load**. After the final group of connectors has been chosen, the MTA randomly chooses one of the connectors in the final group (because they all have equal cost) rather than calculating current queue size, message size, and so on.

After a connector has been routed for a message recipient, it is preferentially routed again when that connector is found in a subsequent recipient's final connector group. This prevents a message for multiple recipients from being routed to the same connector group (because one message has been split into several messages). The first connector chosen from a group is used for later recipients.

If a Site Connector is selected, the Exchange MTA balances the message load among target MTAs through *cost-weighted randomization*. However, cost 0 target MTAs are always tried first and cost 100 target MTAs tried last. Cost-weighted randomization takes place only after routing has been attempted to all of the cost 0 target MTAs. All administrator-designated target MTAs are tried on that Site Connector before the message is rerouted to a different connector.

For more information about target MTAs and connection costs, see *Microsoft Exchange Server Concepts and Planning* and *Microsoft Exchange Server Operations*.

Preemptive Routing

Connectors are chosen from among those that are not currently retrying (waiting on an Open Retry timer). This approach, known as *preemptive rerouting*, is used so that the MTA does not attempt to route a message to a connector that failed the last time it tried to establish a connection.

Suppose that you have a Site Connector and a Dynamic RAS Connector with a higher cost, and the LAN is down. A message is first routed to the Site Connector because it has a lower cost. When the connection fails because the LAN is down, the message is rerouted through the Dynamic RAS Connector. Although the cost is higher, this preemptive rerouting is more likely to achieve timely delivery of the message.

Any new message that comes in before the Open Retry timer has expired on the Site Connector skips the Site Connector and is routed first to the Dynamic RAS Connector.

Rerouting and Retries

When a message is routed to a connector that fails to connect to the other MTA, the retry count is incremented and the MTA attempts to reroute the message. When a message is rerouted, the MTA performs routing and selection again to find the most efficient connector. A retry count is stored on each message for each connector that has been tried. If the message cannot be delivered after all the connectors have been tried, the message is returned with an NDR.

The maximum number of transfer retries and transfer interval are controlled by settings in the **Override** property page for the Site Connector, Dynamic RAS Connector, and X.400 Connector. These settings determine how many times and at what interval the MTA sends a message through the connector.

When a message is sent to a connector or gateway for a foreign system, such as the Microsoft Mail Connector or Internet Mail Service, the MTA considers the message delivered when it reaches the connector. Rerouting does not occur, even if the foreign system connector cannot deliver the message.

A message routed to a connector with an activation schedule of *never active* or *remote initiated* is not rerouted unless the activation schedule is changed while the message is waiting to be delivered.

Virtual Rerouting

Virtual rerouting is necessary to prevent loop detection due to circular routes. The MTA performs a virtual reroute from the lowest-cost connector to the currently selected connector when the following occurs:

- A non-optimal route is chosen (that is, a route that does not have the lowest cost) because the lowest-cost connectors are down.
- The message has not yet been rerouted in the MTA.

When non-optimal routes are chosen, it is possible, and sometimes desirable, for the message to travel circular routes before reaching the final destination.

A message destined for D will be routed in the following order: A->B->C. However, if the C->D connector is waiting on an Open Retry counter or is unavailable when the message arrives at C, the MTA on C routes the message to the higher-cost alternate route: C->B->A->D, as shown in the following illustration.

```
A<-----Cost 1------->B<-----Cost 1----->C<-----Cost 1----->D
A<-----Cost 10----->D
```

Without the virtual reroute at MTA C, the message would be loop-detected when it re-entered MTA B. In this situation, it is assumed that the incoming connector is filtered out of the initial routing attempt for a message. Otherwise MTA B would route the message directly back to C due to cost considerations.

Distribution List Handling

If the distribution list has a Home-MTA, messages containing a distribution list recipient are first routed to the designated distribution list expansion point or to the local expansion point, if no distribution list expansion point is defined. When all recipients have been routed, either locally or to a remote connector, the original message is *fanned out* — that is, multiple copies are created, one for each destination. Each message has its responsibility attribute set for all recipients who have been routed to that destination.

If the message is routed locally, a distribution list-expansion message copy whose recipients are the distribution list members is first fanned out. Then the distribution list expansion copy is passed back through the routing process. The process is repeated recursively for each nested level of the distribution list. The MTA verifies that an infinite loop is not generated by distribution list expansion.

An MTA can be configured to not expand replicated remote-site distribution lists.

▶ **To configure an MTA to not expand replicated remote site distribution lists**

1. In the Administrator program, double-click the server's MTA object, and then click the **General** tab.

2. Clear the **Expand Remote Distribution Lists Locally** check box.

3. Click **OK**.

Protocol Conversion

If the message database encoding format (MDBEF) content type is used, only one address can be included for a message originator or recipient. Although the address can be the distinguished name address or the O/R address, it is usually the distinguished name address. For this reason, distinguished name access for the originator and all recipients is required during conversion. That way, the O/R addresses required by P2 can be obtained. The decision to convert from MDBEF to P2 can be delayed only until the final replicated Exchange site (where the MTA can always obtain access to the objects) is referenced by distinguished names in the message. The decision to convert must be made as soon as possible, to ensure that all information required for the conversion is available.

If only a few recipients for a given destination allow MDBEF messages, the message copy for a particular destination is split into two copies. However, this is an atypical situation because conversion on the sending MTA is usually determined on the basis of message and destination MTA or connector properties rather than on recipient properties.

The main conversion decision process is based on the type of message content and the destination (either the local MTA or the recipient, or remote MTA or connector). However, even if the content of a message is in MDBEF and the chosen connector allows MDBEF content, an individual *recipient* might not support MDBEF content.

Per-recipient checking is completed during routing to verify whether a particular recipient can support MDBEF. If a recipient is an Exchange recipient, it is assumed to support MDBEF. A recipient is assumed to be an Exchange recipient if it supports MDBEF and if:

- The remote MTA is an Exchange MTA (Site Connector or Dynamic RAS Connector).

- A distinguished name for the recipient is known.

- The recipient is a custom recipient or one-off, and the proxy address matches the connector's Connected Sites routing proxy.

If a recipient is not known to support MDBEF, the message is converted by the conversion decision routine during fan-out. However, the following exceptions override the per-recipient MDBEF determined during routing:

- Inbound conversion always assumes that all recipients support MDBEF.
- Gateways and Internet Mail Service always allow MDBEF.

Result Processing

Exchange receives and processes result information indicating the following:

- Delivery succeeds or fails.
- Transfer-out succeeds or fails.
- Distribution list expansion succeeds.
- Routing attempt fails.

If a message cannot be sent through its chosen connector, that is, the *transfer-out* fails, the message is rerouted. If delivery fails, an attempt is made to reassign the message, that is, *alternate recipient handling* occurs.

If the message is not rerouted or reassigned, checks are made to determine whether a report is required for the recipients. The report is sent only after all responsible recipients have been delivered or transferred successfully, or if the MTA is unable to deliver a subset of recipients for some reason. The one exception is that a report is sent immediately for any completely invalid recipients that cannot be routed at all.

Rerouting and Retries

If an attempt to send a message through the chosen connector fails, the MTA tries to reroute the message. However, there are exceptions:

- If the message is sent to a gateway, no rerouting occurs and the message is considered by the MTA to have been processed to completion.
- If a message is routed to a *never active* or *remote initiated* connector, no rerouting occurs because association is started (unless the activation schedule is changed later).

During rerouting, only the O/R address of the first responsible recipient is used to reroute the message. This solution is a compromise because some messages could end up traveling a longer path than if they had been rerouted individually, but this method reduces processing time. There are no loop-detect issues because the rerouting action resets the X.400 loop-detect algorithms.

Every connector has a *retry count* and a *retry interval* that determine how many times and at what intervals the MTA tries to send a message through each of the connectors. The Site Connector and the Dynamic RAS Connector default to a 10-minute retry interval and a maximum of 144 retries. On each fan-out message copy, the MTA stores a retry count for each connector and target MTA that has been tried.

When a message is routed to an inaccessible connector, the retry count for that connector is incremented on the message, and the message is rerouted immediately using the routing and selection process outlined earlier. After all connectors have been tried and the maximum retry count has been reached, the message is marked as an NDR.

If the open connection fails for any connector, the connector starts an Open Retry timer to retry the open connection independently of the message.

After a message has been rerouted successfully, the external and internal trace information for the message is updated to indicate that the message has been rerouted.

You can prevent rerouting to the lowest-cost connector using the MTA **General** property page. To do this, clear the **Only use least cost routes** check box.

Recipient Reassignment

Exchange does not expose some X.400 alternate-recipient functions, although the Exchange MTA supports all of these functions when it receives messages with the flags set. The recipient reassignment functions are:

- Recipient-assigned alternate recipient. The recipient redirects the message to someone else. This function, which can be disabled by setting the "Recipient_Reassignment_Prohibited" flag in the message, is supported in Exchange.

- Management domain (MD)-defined alternate recipient or dead-letter recipient. This can be disallowed by setting the "Alternate_Recipient_Allowed" flag appropriately in the message. This is not supported in the Exchange Administrator program.

- Originator-requested alternate recipient. The originator requests that an alternate recipient is used if the message would otherwise return an NDR. This feature is not supported in Microsoft Outlook or the Exchange information store.

The redirect-and-deliver function is specific to Exchange. If this flag is set, a copy of the message is delivered to the recipient *and* to the specified alternate recipient. To maintain X.400 conformance, a delivery receipt is sent only for the copy delivered to the alternate recipient.

Report Handling

Reports can also be received from remote systems. The routing process for reports is the same as for messages and probes, regardless of the report's origin, except when the report is destined for a distribution list.

Exchange generates the following reports:

- Routing
- Result processing
- Recovery

When the report destination is a distribution list, the MTA backtracks through Originator_ and DL_Expansion_History to find the originator of the message. Each O/R name found by this recursive process in turn becomes the next report destination and is passed back through the routing process. If the previous entry in this list was a distribution list, the process is repeated until the actual originator is found.

Loop Detection

Loop detection in Exchange uses standard X.400 internal and external trace information. It also uses Exchange-specific information contained in the per-domain bilateral information of a message or the additional information of a report. This information is used to support multinational enterprises without undue configuration complexity and to avoid triggering X.400 loop detection.

External trace information documents the actions taken on a message, probe, or report by each MD through which the message passes. Each MD the message enters indicates whether the message was relayed or rerouted, plus any other actions (such as redirection or distribution list expansion) performed by that MD. If the message enters the same MD twice without rerouting, redirection, or distribution list expansion, the message loop is detected and it generates an NDR.

Internal trace information is maintained for messages that are routed *within* an MD. Each MTA the message enters indicates whether the message was relayed or rerouted, plus any other actions (such as redirection or DL expansion) performed by that MTA. If the message enters the same MTA twice without a reroute, redirection, or distribution list expansion, the message loop is detected and an NDR is generated. Note that the internal trace information is removed from a message when it is transferred out of an MD.

An X.400 MD is uniquely defined by the c, a, and p components of the O/R address space. These fields are collectively termed the MD's *global domain identifier* (GDI). Because Exchange uniquely identifies sites by using the c, a, p, and o components of the O/R address space, it is possible for a message to traverse a site that has the same c, a, and p values as a different site traversed earlier. To prevent loop detection in this situation, each Exchange site adds Microsoft Exchange-specific per-domain bilateral information to messages and additional information to reports, including the site distinguished name for the site being traversed. If Exchange or the MTA detects a loop in the external trace information, it searches the current site distinguished name for in the Microsoft Exchange-specific information. If the current site distinguished name is not found, it is not a real loop, and therefore X.400 loop detection is suppressed.

PART 11

Security

People who send and receive e-mail rely on their messaging systems to provide reliable and secure service. The following types of attacks can compromise the security of e-mail systems:

- Theft of or tampering with data. By "sniffing" packets or intercepting messages in transit on the network, an attacker can gain access to data or even modify it.

- An attacker can forge messages to make them appear as if they came from someone else as a means of distributing false information or tricking users into sending them sensitive data.

E-mail systems are also susceptible to the following kinds of attacks if they are connected to the Internet:

- Denial of service. Because processing messages requires disk and CPU resources on your server and bandwidth on your Internet connection, an attacker can tie up your system or network by flooding it with mail.

- Trojan horses and viruses. Unsuspecting users can run programs they receive in messages that can infect the system, delete files, or cause other damage.

Microsoft Exchange Server provides a variety of features that you can use to ensure the security of your users' mail and your system. You can protect messages using advanced security (encryption and digital signatures). You can protect communication between clients and servers by configuring encrypted remote procedure calls (RPCs). You can also protect your system from intrusion from the Internet by configuring your server's hardware and software.

Tools

The following security tools are provided with the *Microsoft BackOffice 4.5 Resource Kit*:

- Change Password Tool
- Password Expiration Warning Application
- Bulk Advanced Security Tool

Using Advanced Security to Secure Messages

If your organization has installed the Key Management component on a Key Management server (KM server), you can use advanced security. Advanced security allows users who need to send and receive confidential messages to digitally sign and encrypt them. This security measure provides a higher degree of protection than built-in features such as message sensitivity, which marks messages as personal, private, or confidential. Advanced security actually prevents unauthorized persons from tampering with messages.

Advanced security uses the following industry standard cryptography methods to provide security:

- Digital signatures, which ensure that messages aren't modified during transit. They also prevent forgeries by allowing users to place the equivalent of their signatures on messages. The recipient can then be certain that the message originated from the sender.
- Data encryption, which provides confidentiality by ensuring that only the intended recipients can read a message.

Administrators who work in organizations that use advanced security to protect highly sensitive information should understand how advanced security works so they can be confident that Exchange provides the level of protection their systems require.

How Advanced Security Works

Both digital signatures and encryption are based on encryption technology. Encryption scrambles (encrypts) a message so it can't be read until it is unscrambled (decrypted) by the intended recipient. This process of encrypting and decrypting messages is called *cryptography*.

Microsoft Outlook can scramble a message or convert a scrambled message back to its plaintext format by applying a mathematical formula, called an algorithm, to the message. The algorithm is used with a key, which is a random string of bits used to lock and unlock (encrypt and decrypt) the message. Only the user who has the correct key can encrypt and decrypt the message.

Outlook advanced security is a hybrid encryption system. It takes advantage of two different encryption technologies: public key cryptography and secret key cryptography (sometimes called symmetric key cryptography). Outlook uses complementary elements of these technologies to digitally sign and encrypt messages. For example, Outlook takes advantage of the strengths of public key cryptography to securely distribute keys. However, it relies on secret key cryptography to encrypt the content of messages because this technology is best suited to bulk data encryption.

Public Key Cryptography

Public key cryptography is based on two halves of the same key that are "mirror images" of each other. The two halves of the key are called a *key pair*. One or the other key in the key pair is required to encrypt and decrypt a message. Microsoft Exchange Server uses two key pairs that can be assigned to a user. One key pair is used to digitally sign messages, and the other is used to encrypt messages.

A key pair consists of a public key and a private key. The public key is publicly known and stored in the directory so everyone has access to it. The private key is known only to the owner of the Key and is stored on the user's hard drive. Outlook stores this information in the user's Registry. The Microsoft Exchange Client stores this information in the user's security (.epf) file. By making one key publicly available and keeping the other key secret, public key cryptography simplifies the distribution of keys without compromising their security. For example, a message encrypted with a recipient's public key can be decrypted only with the recipient's private key.

Public key cryptography is computationally slow. Therefore, it is not as effective as secret key cryptography for encrypting large amounts of data. Because of this, Microsoft Exchange Server uses public key cryptography primarily for digital signatures and for the secure exchange of secret keys between users.

To prevent unauthorized persons from tampering with keys after they have been created, Exchange uses *certificates* to establish a trust of keys. A certificate is a user's public key that has been digitally signed by a trusted authority called a Certification Authority (CA). The KM server is a type of CA. Because the KM server uses its private key to sign certificates, a certificate's signature can be verified using the copy of the KM server's public signing key that resides in every user's security file.

In Microsoft Exchange Server, encryption and signing operations use different certificates. Signing certificates are sent with every signed message. This ensures that the recipient can verify a sender's digital signature even when the recipient is offline. In contrast, encryption certificates are available in the global address list so everyone has access to them. Users can make encryption certificates available when they are offline by downloading a copy of the offline Address Book with full details.

Exchange uses a certificate format that complies with the public X.509 standards.

Secret Key Cryptography

Unlike public key cryptography, which uses key pairs, secret key cryptography encrypts and decrypts messages using an algorithm with a single key. A *secret key* is a key known to both the sender and the recipient. It is similar to a password used to log on to a server. Both you and the server must know the same password for you to have access to that server.

Because the secret key must be distributed to both the sender and the recipient in a way that it remains a secret, key distribution is more difficult with secret key cryptography than with public key cryptography. However, secret key cryptography is very fast, making it ideal for encrypting and decrypting large amounts of data. For this reason, Microsoft Exchange Server relies on it to encrypt the contents of messages, including attachments.

Clients use several different types of secret key encryption algorithms to comply with United States export laws, including the Data Encryption Standard (DES) and the Carlisle Adams and Stafford Tavares of Northern Telecom Research (CAST) encryption algorithms. For information about selecting the encryption type best suited for your organization, see "Selecting an Encryption Type" later in this chapter.

DES is a secret-key algorithm based on a fixed-length, 56-bit key. It was first published by the National Bureau of Standards. DES is a United States Federal information processing standard that is available only with the North American version of Microsoft Exchange Server.

CAST is a secret-key encryption based on a variable-length key. The key is a number that specifies a bit length between 40 and 128. This variable length provides for flexible encryption standards. Because longer keys are more secure than shorter ones, Outlook uses CAST 40 (a 40-bit key) and CAST 64 (a 64-bit key). CAST 64 is available only with the North American version of Outlook.

Key Management Server

Key Management server (KM server) is an optional Exchange component that is installed on a designated organization server. It provides centralized administration, archival of private keys, management of public keys and certificates, and it is used to set up an advanced security system.

The KM server performs a variety of important tasks:

- Generates public and private encryption keys.

- Acts as your CA by creating public signing and encryption X.509 certificates. After the KM server has generated keys and certificates and the user's security file has been created, the KM server doesn't need to be running for a user to send and receive encrypted and signed messages, because your client actually performs all of the security operations on messages.

- Maintains a secure copy of every user's private encryption key in an encrypted database in case the key needs to be retrieved after it has been issued. For example, if a user is terminated or leaves the company, the KM server enables an authorized administrator to recover the user's encrypted messages by recovering the user's private keys. You can also recover keys for users when they lose their security (.epf) file or their registry setting, or if they forget their security file password.

- Maintains and distributes a Certificate Revocation List, which is a list of certificates that the administrator has recovered because the user's keys have been compromised and are no longer secure. It is stored in the directory on every server. A replica of the list is also kept on the client computer so certificates can be checked when the user is working offline. When you decrypt a message or verify its signature, the list is checked to make sure the certificate has not been revoked. If it has, the user is warned that the sender has been revoked from the organization. For more information about certificate revocation, see *Microsoft Exchange Server Concepts and Planning*.

Digital Signatures

A digital signature is similar to a person's handwritten signature; it can be used to authenticate a sender's identity and ensure that a message is not modified during transit. It is a string of bits, called a *message hash* or *checksum*, that is calculated and then added to a signed message. Every message has a unique signature or checksum that is generated by applying a 128-bit Rivest-Shamir-Adelman (RSA) algorithm called Message Digest 5 (MD5) to the message.

Exchange relies on public key cryptography to ensure the authenticity of digital signatures. When the user signs a message using the client, the checksum of the message is encrypted using the sender's private signing key. When the recipient verifies the signature of the message using the client, the sender's public signing key is used to decrypt the checksum and verify the sender's identity. The signature on a message is valid only if the public and private keys correspond to each other.

Exchange determines the integrity of a signed message by comparing the checksum on the message with the new checksum of the message that the recipient's client generates. If the two checksums are identical, the message hasn't been modified since it was signed. However, if even one bit in the message has been changed, the messages will have different checksums and the recipient is notified that someone tampered with the message. Encrypting the checksum using the signer's private key also ensures a signed message that no one can tamper with because the checksum on a message cannot be switched without the signer's private key.

Signing a Message

When a user signs a message, the client generates a checksum of the message and adds it to the message. The checksum (digital signature) is then encrypted using the sender's private signing key. Finally, the original plaintext message, the digital signature, and the sender's signing certificate (which contains the sender's public signing key) are sent to the recipient. The following illustration shows the steps in the message signing process.

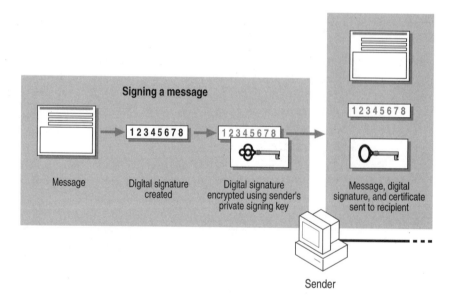

Verifying a Signature on a Message

When a recipient verifies the signature of a message, the client checks the sender's signing certificate against the Certificate Revocation List. If the certificate is on the list, the recipient is warned that the sender's certificate has been revoked. If the sender's certificate is valid, the encrypted checksum (digital signature) is decrypted using the sender's public signing key, which was sent with the message. Finally, the client generates a checksum on the plaintext message so it can be compared with the checksum that was just decrypted. The two checksums should be the same. If they are not, the recipient is warned that the message has been altered since it was originally signed. The following illustration shows the steps in the verification process.

Verifying a signature

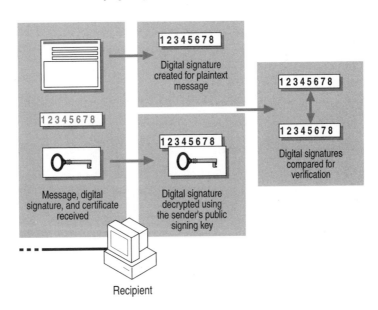

Message Encryption

When a message is encrypted, the client generates a random secret key called a bulk encryption key, which is used to encrypt the message. The recipient's public encryption key is then used to encrypt the bulk encryption key in a lockbox. The lockbox allows the random bulk encryption key to be transmitted securely to the recipients. If an encrypted message is sent to several people, each recipient's public encryption key is used to generate a different lockbox, but the message contents are encrypted only once.

Encrypting a Message

When a sender encrypts a message, the client retrieves a certificate for each message recipient from the global address list. A bulk encryption key is then randomly generated and used to encrypt the contents of the message. Each recipient's public encryption key is then retrieved from the recipient's certificate and used to encrypt the bulk encryption key in a lockbox. Finally, the lockbox and the encrypted message are sent to the recipient. The following illustration shows the steps in the process.

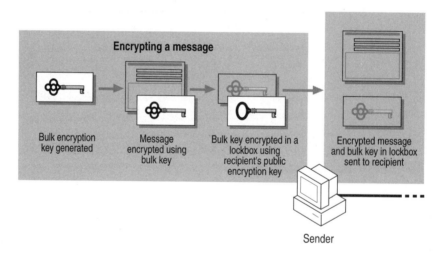

Decrypting a Message

When a recipient decrypts a message, Exchange retrieves the recipient's private encryption key from the recipient's security (.epf) file. The recipient's private encryption key is then used to decrypt the lockbox. Finally, the bulk encryption key contained in the lockbox is used to decrypt the message. The following illustration shows the steps in the process.

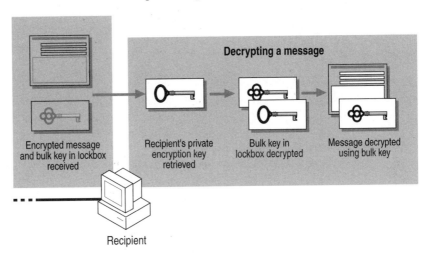

Selecting an Encryption Type

The type of encryption you implement in your organization depends on the level of security your organization requires and whether you are using an international or North American version of Outlook. Organizations that require strong encryption should use either DES or CAST 64.

As you evaluate what type of encryption is appropriate for your organization, keep in mind the following:

- The level of security for each of the different types of encryption
- International considerations for using Exchange
- United States legal considerations for using Exchange
- How your messages are moved from one encryption type to another

Encryption Security

An encrypted message is only as secure as the algorithm that is used to encrypt it. The security of an encryption algorithm is measured by how easy it is to find the weaknesses in the algorithm that can allow someone to decrypt the message without its key. The most secure algorithm is one that can be cracked only by trying every possible key combination, a task that could take many lifetimes depending on the length of the key. The algorithms chosen for Exchange, including DES and CAST, have been studied extensively by cryptography experts and have no known methods of attack other than a brute-force approach of trying every key.

Algorithms that use longer keys are generally more secure than algorithms that use shorter keys because there are more possible key combinations. For example, because 64-bit encryption is approximately 16 million times more secure than 40-bit encryption, it takes 16 million times longer to crack. In Outlook the key for one message doesn't crack the key for another message because every message is encrypted with a unique key.

International Considerations

Because of United States export restrictions that limit the strength of cryptographic systems shipped outside the United States, international versions of Outlook will support only CAST 40 encryption. Currently, DES and CAST 64 are available only in versions of Exchange sold in the United States and Canada. In addition, some countries, such as France, have their own restrictions on the use of cryptography. For example, Outlook cannot use advanced security in France.

International organizations that use Exchange in several countries can mix and match types of encryption. This is possible because Exchange maintains information in the directory about the type of encryption that is supported for every user in the organization. If a message is addressed to multiple recipients using different types of encryption, Outlook automatically attempts to encrypt the message using the type of encryption that all recipients share. For example, if a message is addressed to a recipient using CAST 40 and another recipient using CAST 64, the message is encrypted using CAST 40. If a message is addressed to a recipient who is not using advanced security, Exchange allows the user to either not send the message to that recipient or to send the message in plaintext format.

United States Legal Considerations

Current United States Commerce Department export regulations prohibit the export of software that contains strong encryption outside the United States and Canada. To help administrators in the United States comply with these regulations, the *Microsoft BackOffice 4.5 Resource Kit* includes a form for temporarily exporting encryption products. You can use this form if you are traveling outside the United States with a laptop that uses advanced security with the client. For more information, see the Tools directory on the *Microsoft BackOffice 4.5 Resource Kit* compact disc.

Moving Messages to Another Encryption Type

If users move to a location within your organization that uses a different type of encryption, they can transfer their encrypted messages from one type of encryption to another using the Bulk Advanced Security tool (Sectool.exe). For example, a user transferring from an office in the United States to Britain can use Sectool.exe to convert encrypted mail from CAST 64 to CAST 40.

Follow this procedure when using Sectool.exe.

1. Use Sectool.exe to decrypt your messages.
2. Copy the messages to a personal folder (.pst) file.
3. From your client computer, copy your .pst file to your local disk and add it to your messaging profile.
4. Use Sectool.exe to encrypt the messages again in the .pst file with the new encryption type.
5. (Optional) Copy the messages from the .pst file to your mailbox on the server.

For more information about using the tool, see Help for Microsoft Exchange Server Resource Kit tools, (Exchtool.hlp) which is included on the *Microsoft BackOffice 4.5 Resource Kit* compact disc.

Increasing Exchange Security

In addition to using advanced security to protect messages, you can also increase the security of your Microsoft Exchange Server system by:

- Restricting access to resources by setting permissions for directory objects and public folders. For information about setting permissions, see the "Setting Permissions" section of Part 3, "Deployment."

- Changing permissions for shared directories created during server Setup to minimize the possibility of tampering with Exchange files.

- Configuring your clients to use encrypted RPCs so data sent between clients and servers cannot be altered while it is traveling across the network.

Changing Permissions on Shared Directories Created During Setup

When Microsoft Exchange Server is installed, Setup creates several shared directories so other Exchange Server computers can have access to the files in the directories. By default, Setup sets permissions for these directories that are usually sufficient for most organizations. However, you can change the permissions if those default permissions do not give the files enough protection against attacks by unauthorized users.

Caution Change permissions on these directories only if it is necessary because the changes could damage your Exchange system.

Setup creates the shared directories shown in the following table.

Directory	Description
Add-ins	Contains files that the Exchange Administrator program uses to display information about connectors. This directory is shared as Add-ins.
Address	Contains files for creating e-mail addresses. This directory is shared as Address.
Connect	Contains files for Exchange connectors. This directory is a hidden share that is shared as connect$.
Connect\Msmcon\Maildata	Contains files used for Microsoft Mail. This is a hidden share that is available only if the Microsoft Mail Connector is installed. It is shared as maildat$.
Res	Contains files, such as logs for Event Viewer and Microsoft Windows NT Performance Monitor, used by the local computer and remote computers. This directory is shared as resources.
Tracking.log	Contains files used for message tracking. This directory is shared as tracking.log.

The permissions granted to these directories are shown in the following table.

Permission	Type of access
Everyone	Read (except for Maildata, which has full control)
Service account	Full control
Local administrators	Full control

To restrict access to the shared directories, remove the Everyone permission and grant permissions to specific accounts using File Manager. Use the following guidelines for restricting access on shared directories:

- Only administrators responsible for message tracking should have permissions for the Tracking.log directory because it can contain sensitive information about messages.

- You can give other administrators permissions to the Add-ins, Address, Connect, and Res directories. Only administrators that need to administer the Microsoft Mail Connector should have permissions for Maildata. If you are using the Microsoft Mail External program for message transfer, also give the account for this program permissions for the Maildata directory.

- Do not change permissions for the service account and local administrators because this can have unpredictable results.

Configuring Microsoft Outlook to Use Encrypted RPCs

Microsoft Outlook computers and Microsoft Exchange Server computers communicate using Windows NT Server RPCs. To increase the security of data communication between clients and servers, Exchange enables users to take advantage of the built-in RPC security feature called encrypted RPC. Encrypted RPC uses a 40-bit RSA algorithm called RC4 to encrypt data while it is on the network. If both client and server computers have Service Pack 2 or later of the Windows NT 4.0 North American version installed, the RPC encryption strength is increased to 128-bit. Outlook can be configured to use encrypted RPC so communication between clients and servers is secure and no one can tamper with messages during transit.

Encrypting RPCs is different from encrypting a message using advanced security, it provides protection for data only while it travels from point to point on the network. A message encrypted using advanced security is protected until the recipient decrypts it using the client, regardless of how many hops are used during delivery. Encrypted RPCs provide increased security for messages sent on internal networks, as well as to outside organizations, for example, on the Internet.

▶ **To configure encrypted RPCs**

1. On the **Tools** menu in Microsoft Outlook, click **Services**.

2. In the list of information services, select **Microsoft Exchange Server**, and then click **Properties**.

3. Click the **Advanced** tab.

4. Under **Encrypt information**, select both check boxes to encrypt all client/server communication.

Increasing Security When Connecting to the Internet

Any system that is accessible through the Internet is subject to attempts to infiltrate the operating system's security or to exploit security weaknesses of services running on the system. Administrators should be concerned about not only these kinds of blatant attacks but also inadvertent actions by users. Some of the most serious breaches of security are caused by users whose actions result in the release of sensitive data or cause a flood of mail from the Internet.

If you are using the Internet Mail Service, you should consider how to minimize the security risks when you connect Microsoft Exchange Server to the Internet. You can configure Exchange and Windows NT Server so people in your organization can send and receive Internet mail, but unauthorized users cannot access your system from the Internet. You can also set up other mechanisms such as firewalls that protect against attacks.

Using Firewalls

Firewalls are one of the best ways to protect your system from attack by users on the Internet. You can use a firewall to separate your internal network from the Internet. A firewall restricts inbound and outbound access, and it can analyze all traffic between your network and the Internet. A firewall can range from a simple packet filter to complex bastion hosts that analyze traffic for each application type. A *bastion host* is any computer that must be secure because it is accessible from the Internet and exposed to attack. A firewall can be a single router or computer, or it can be a combination of components such as routers, computers, networks, and software.

There are several types of firewall software and hardware you can use to protect your organization from outside attacks, including:

- Proxy servers
- Dual-homed systems
- Packet filtering
- Firewall software
- Domain Name System (DNS)

Proxy Servers

Some services, such as Web and File Transfer Protocol (FTP), are point-to-point so a client can make a connection directly to a server. Allowing clients inside your network to connect directly to hosts on the Internet is generally unsafe. One solution is to use a proxy server (also called an application-level gateway) to interact with external servers on the client's behalf. The client communicates with the proxy server, which relays approved client requests to servers and relays responses back to the client. External hosts do not connect directly to clients in your network.

Exchange and many other e-mail systems use a store-and-forward design, which uses a proxy mechanism. Clients connect to servers that reside on the local network. Servers then communicate with each other to transfer e-mail messages. If Exchange is configured correctly, separate proxy services are unnecessary.

Dual-Homed Systems

One way to set up a bastion host is to use a dual-homed computer, which has a connection to two networks but does not route packets between them. One connection is to your internal network and allows communication with other servers and clients in your organization. The other connection is to the Internet. You can run Exchange on a dual-homed computer to provide safe e-mail connectivity to the Internet.

Packet Filtering

Implementing a packet filter between the Internet and your network can add a layer of security. You use a packet filter, such as a screening router, to control the ports and Internet Protocol (IP) addresses to which external systems can connect. However, if an intruder is able to get past the router, your network is open to attack.

To minimize this risk, many organizations implement a perimeter network. This is a network that is connected to the Internet through an external screening router and to the internal network through an interior screening router. Computers that are connected to the perimeter network have limited access to both the Internet and the internal network. This can be a convenient architecture if multiple servers require direct Internet access.

This configuration provides three levels of defense. If the external router and a bastion host on the perimeter network are compromised, the attacker does not gain unlimited access to your internal network because the internal router is controlling access.

Firewall Software

There are many commercial firewall products that provide proxy services. Some of these support Simple Mail Transfer Protocol (SMTP) e-mail. There are also free implementations of SMTP proxies, such as smap, which forward messages between internal and external systems. These products are not likely to have security weaknesses because they are typically designed solely for security purposes. Furthermore, they are usually a simple implementation with restricted functionality. However, a disadvantage of firewall software is that different SMTP servers must be managed. If your internal SMTP server is upgraded with new features, the firewall software must also be upgraded.

Because Exchange provides secure Internet access, additional firewall software is unnecessary. However, you can use the Internet Mail Service with firewall software. To do so, configure your Internet Mail Service to forward all mail to the bastion host running the firewall software.

DNS

DNS is a distributed database that translates between host names and IP addresses. It also carries other information about hosts, such as mail exchanger (MX) records that specify what hosts will accept mail for a domain. When a client needs to find out information about another host, such as the IP address for mail.acme.net, it queries its local DNS server for that information. The local DNS server responds if it has the information. If it does not have the information it queries other DNS servers until it either finds the information or runs out of places to check. This forwarding of the query is transparent to the client, which connects only to the local DNS server.

If your system accepts mail directly from other hosts on the Internet, it should be listed in the DNS. A DNS MX record is created that routes all mail to your host that processes incoming mail for your domain. Unless you plan to forward all outbound Internet mail to a relay host (a host outside your organization that has better e-mail connectivity), your server must be able to query DNS to deliver messages. You can configure your Microsoft Exchange Server computer to use DNS services from your Internet service provider (ISP), or you can use your own DNS servers. If you maintain your own DNS servers, they must be registered with your parent domain.

If you are using DNS and do not want DNS queries from the Internet to return information about computers on your internal network, configure DNS so external hosts can query for information about your Internet servers but not about other hosts. To do this, you must set up a pair of DNS servers— an external DNS server that you register with your parent domain and configure with address and MX records for your bastion hosts, and an internal DNS server that is used by clients on your network. Configure the internal DNS server to forward queries it cannot resolve to the external DNS server so clients in your network can resolve Internet host names. Your bastion host also should use the internal server for DNS to resolve both internal and external names. Because the external DNS server does not have complete information for your internal network, and because access to your internal DNS server is not available from the Internet, you can hide most of your computers from external DNS queries by not creating records for them on the external DNS server.

Securing Your Internet Connection

You can take advantage of a variety of features provided with Windows NT Server and Microsoft Exchange Server to prevent attackers from damaging your system over the Internet.

Configuring the Internet Mail Service

You can enhance security when connecting to the Internet by configuring the following options on the Internet Mail Service. For information about how to set these options, see *Microsoft Exchange Server Operations*.

Reject messages by IP address   By default, the Internet Mail Service accepts incoming connections from any IP address. If you want the Internet Mail Service to communicate only with specific SMTP hosts, you can configure it to reject connection attempts from other IP addresses. This makes it more difficult for someone to mount an attack from the Internet against your system.

Set message size limits   You can establish message-size limits for the Internet Mail Service. The default limit applies to both incoming and outgoing mail. If an incoming message from another SMTP host exceeds the specified limit, the Internet Mail Service stops writing data to disk and discards any remaining data. This prevents large messages from filling up the disk on your server, which helps reduce the impact of a denial-of-service attack.

Disable auto-replies to the Internet   The Internet Mail Service can prevent the delivery of automatically generated replies, such as out-of-office replies. When users set up out-of-office replies on their clients, they frequently include a number where they can be reached and also other information. In some cases, this information should not be shared outside the organization. You can configure the Internet Mail Service to disable outbound delivery of automated replies globally or by domain.

Set delivery restrictions You can restrict what users in your organization have permission to send mail through the Internet Mail Service. For example, you can grant Internet mail access to full-time employees. You can grant or deny Internet mail access to users by configuring the Internet Mail Service **Delivery Restrictions** property page in the Exchange Administrator program.

Protecting User Accounts

To ensure that someone cannot gain access to your system by impersonating a user, use passwords that are difficult to guess for user accounts. This is especially important for accounts with administrator permissions. You should also limit the number of accounts that are granted administrator permissions.

Using Windows NT File System

You can use Windows NT file system (NTFS) to restrict access to your files and directories and to limit the amount of damage intruders can do if they gain access to a user account. You can also enable auditing of NTFS files and directories through the File Manager. This produces audit records you can review periodically to ensure that no one has gained unauthorized access to sensitive files.

Using and Configuring Services

You should run only essential services on the server and disable any unnecessary services. The fewer the services that are running, the less likely it is there will be a mistake in the service's configuration that an attacker can exploit.

You should also unbind unnecessary services from network adapters that are connected to the Internet. To do this, double-click the Network icon in Control Panel, and then click the **Bindings** tab. For example, you can use the Server service to copy files from computers in your internal network, but you might not want remote users to have direct access to the Server service from the Internet. To use the Server service on your private network, you can prevent it from binding to any network adapter cards. You can use the Windows NT Server service over the Internet; however, you should understand the security implications and licensing issues of using this configuration.

Transmission Control Protocol/Internet Protocol (TCP/IP) is the only protocol you need to bind to the network adapter card that is connected to the Internet. Make sure routing is disabled so your internal network is isolated from the Internet.

If you decide to bind the Server service to the Internet adapter card, double-check the permissions for your network shares and the permissions for the files in the shared directories.

Connecting to SMTP Hosts with the Internet Mail Service

You can set up a Microsoft Exchange Server with the Internet Mail Service on the bastion host that routes mail between your organization and the SMTP hosts on the Internet. To minimize risk, you can make this a dedicated Internet mail server that does not contain user mailboxes. If an intruder gains access to the bastion host, none of the data stored in users' mailboxes or public folders is at risk because only messages in transit are stored at the bastion host.

If you are using a packet filter, you must configure it to allow TCP connections to and from port 25 on the Exchange Server computer.

Connecting to X.400 MTAs with the X.400 Connector

Request for Comments (RFC) 1006 defines a mechanism for applications defined on the International Standards Organization (ISO) protocol suite to run over TCP/IP. X.400 Message Transfer Agent (MTAs) can use this mechanism to communicate over the Internet. If you are using a packet filter, you must configure it to allow TCP connections to port 102 on the Exchange Server computer. Note that with X.400 authentication, passwords are protected.

Connecting Sites Using the Internet

You can use the Internet Mail Service, the X.400 Connector, or the Site Connector to connect Exchange sites through the Internet. If mail must pass through one or more SMTP hosts to reach its destination, the Internet Mail Service must be used. Note that data is not encrypted when it is sent through these connectors unless messages are encrypted using advanced security.

The Site Connector uses RPCs to communicate between servers. Server-to-server RPC sessions are always encrypted. If you use a packet filter, you must configure it the same as you would when enabling client access over the Internet.

Configuring DNS

If you are using DNS with a packet filtering router, you must configure the router to allow user datagram protocol (UDP) and TCP connections to port 53 on the DNS server.

Enabling Clients to Securely Connect over the Internet

Client computers can connect to mailboxes on Exchange Server computers remotely using TCP/IP over the Internet. By connecting over the Internet, users can read and send mail just as if they were on the same local area network (LAN) as the server. For example, if users from CompanyA need access to mail while visiting CompanyB, they can use CompanyB's Internet connection. Microsoft Outlook does not need to use a modem or Remote Access Service (RAS) to establish a remote connection with Microsoft Exchange Server. However, both the client and the server must support TCP/IP.

You can enable communication over the Internet with the least amount of security risk to your organization by performing these tasks:

- Configure your client to use encrypted RPCs. This ensures that messages transmitted over the Internet between a client and a server are secure and no one can tamper with them. For more information about configuring encrypted RPCs, see "Configuring Microsoft Outlook to Use Encrypted RPCs" earlier in this chapter.

- Specify the client's home server using the server's fully qualified domain name (FQDN). This enables the client to locate the home server.

- If the home server and the user account that is accessing the mailbox are in different domains, enable the client to be authenticated by the home server's domain. This gives the user access to the domain where the home server is located.

- If your organization uses an Internet firewall, configure the firewall to allow RPC communication. If a firewall is not used, RPC communication to the Internet is enabled by default.

Specifying the Home Server

To connect to a Microsoft Exchange Server computer remotely over the Internet, a client must use the server's FQDN. This is because the server name must be in a format that can be resolved over the Internet. Instead of connecting to a server using its computer name (also called a NetBIOS name) as the client on a LAN does, you must specify a name such as *server1.acme.com*. If the server name is not registered in DNS, you can specify the IP address instead.

▶ **To specify the home server name**

1. In Control Panel, double-click the Mail icon, and then click the **Services** tab.

2. Click **Microsoft Exchange Server**, and then click **Properties**.

3. Under **Microsoft Exchange server**, type the name of the server that contains the mailbox you want to use.

4. Click **OK**.

Configuring Authentication by the Home Server's Domain

When users connect to a server using the Internet, they are probably in a different organization that uses a domain other than the one in which their home servers are located. To ensure that the client is authenticated by the server's domain during a remote Internet connection, the user must connect to the home server using a user account that is valid in the home server's domain. To make connecting to the home server easier, the client can be configured to prompt the user for the name and password of the user account in the home server's domain.

▶   **To enable the client to be authenticated by the home server's domain**

1. In Control Panel, double-click the Mail icon, and then click the **Services** tab.

2. Select Microsoft Exchange Server, and then click **Properties**.

3. Click the **Advanced** tab.

4. From **Logon network security,** choose **None**.

5. Click **OK**.

Configuring a Firewall to Allow RPC Communication

For client computers to gain access to Microsoft Exchange Server computers remotely over the Internet, the clients and servers must be able to communicate using RPCs. If you are not using an Internet firewall, RPC communication is enabled by default. This configuration is risky because an attacker can gain access to the server and possibly compromise the security of Exchange resources such as mailboxes and public folders.

If you are using a firewall to increase your system's security, you might have to configure the firewall to allow RPC communication. Some Internet firewalls do not accept TCP/IP port numbers that Exchange uses for RPC communication. To solve this problem, add port 135 to your firewall and configure Exchange to use the same ports as your firewall.

To configure Exchange, set two unique port numbers, one for the information store and one for the directory. The registry value TCP/IP Port controls this setting. This DWORD value is a 16-bit number. This value is set for the port that the firewall will accept.

For the directory, you can modify the port numbers in the following registry location:

**HKEY_LOCAL_MACHINE\SYSTEM\CurrentControlSet\Services\
MSExchangeDS\Parameters\TCP/IP Port**

For the information store, modify the port number in the following registry location:

**HKEY_LOCAL_MACHINE\SYSTEM\CurrentControlSet\Services\
MSExchangeIS\ParametersSystem\TCP/IP Port**

If you are using a packet filter, you must configure it to allow TCP connections to the information store and directory ports in addition to port 135 (for the RPC End-Point Mapper service) on the Exchange Server computer.

▶ **To add TCP/IP port numbers**

1. In the Windows NT registry, select the following key:

   **HKEY_LOCAL_MACHINE\SYSTEM\CurrentControlSet\Services\
   MSExchangeIS\ParametersSystem**

2. From the **Edit** menu, choose **New,** and then choose **DWORD** value.

3. In the **Name** box type **TCP/IP Port**, and then click **Enter**.

4. Double-click **TCP/IP Port**. In the **Value data** box, type the number of the port that the firewall will accept. Set the base to a decimal when entering the value.

Backing Up a Key Management Server

The KM server database contains the private encryption keys for every user in your entire organization. It is recommended that you back up all KM server data files in the Kmsdata subdirectory (for example, Exchsrvr\kmsdata*.*) separately from other data and that you make sure these backup tapes are stored in a more secure manner than your everyday backups. All keys in these files are 128-bit RC2 encrypted, so this database is extremely secure.

PART 12

Public Folders

Public folders are storage areas on public information stores where information can be grouped according to subject or some other criterion for sharing among users. You can store many kinds of information in public folders, from e-mail messages to graphics and sound bites. Public folders also can contain custom forms that serve as a base for creating custom applications such as bulletin boards, discussion forums, or customer tracking. In addition, a public folder can be used as an application, such as a bulletin board service (BBS), customer tracking application, electronic Help desk, or an Internet newsgroup, enabling you to define and organize the type of information you want to display.

Public folders are stored on an Exchange computer in the public information store (Exchsrvr\Mdbdata\Pub.edb). If you have more than one server, you can replicate public folders so that users have access on different servers.

Public folders provide a permanent storage place for information and allow the public folder owners to maintain the information.

You can set up public folders to track customers, store notes from meetings, Microsoft PowerPoint® presentations, links to customers' Web sites, or feedback surveys. You can update information quickly and easily, and then, post it immediately to a public folder where users can access it. You can also restrict user access to a public folder and generate automatic replies to contributors based on the characteristics of information they post.

In addition, users can customize the organization of public folders by using different views. By sorting the specific characteristics of the information, users have direct access to the specific types of information they need without going through a hierarchy of choices. They can also add the public folders they use most frequently to their list of public folder favorites.

Tools

The following public folder tools are provided with the *Microsoft BackOffice 4.5 Resource Kit*:

- Public Folder Administration Tool
- Public Folder Information Tool
- Public Folders Reporting Tool
- Public Folders Tree Info Tool
- Public Folder Verification Tool

Developing a Public Folder Strategy

To develop an effective public folder strategy, you must first understand public folder architecture. It is important to develop a public folder policy for your organization early in the planning process. Policy decisions about the public folder hierarchy and access to public folders influence where public folders are created and how much disk storage, CPU power, and memory you need for adequate performance levels.

When you plan your public folder strategy, consider whether you want all your messages to be located in one or many public folders. This decision is important because it determines whether you need to replicate public folders to other servers.

Single-Copy Public Folders

You can store the contents of a public folder on a single public-folder server. This is the default configuration of a public folder when replication has not been configured.

Replicated Public Folders

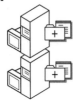

Public folders can be *replicated* to other servers in your organization — that is, an identical copy of a public folder can appear on multiple servers. This is called a *public folder replica*. Replicas contain the same information as the original public folder, but they reside on other Exchange Server computers.

The advantages of this configuration are:

- Automatic load balancing for user requests.
- Availability in a wide area network (WAN). Users at sites with no direct connectivity can still share data.

- Fault tolerance.

The disadvantages of this configuration are:

- Possible public folder conflicts
- Latency issues
- Additional message traffic associated with replication

You can replicate a public folder to a server in the same site as the originating server, or to servers in other sites. Replicating public folders to other servers in your site is useful for balancing the load of users who are using a specific public folder at any given time.

Replicating public folders to servers in remote sites is a good way to distribute the load to the remote site.

For more information on public folder replication, see "Public Folder Replication Strategies" later in this chapter.

Dedicated Public and Private Servers vs. Multipurpose Servers

You can centralize responsibilities among Exchange Server computers by configuring all of them to be either public or private servers. A *dedicated private server* has a private information store (dedicated to private mail storage and user mail), but no public information store. A *dedicated public-folder server* stores and processes requests for information about the public folder, such as its hierarchy and contents. A dedicated public-folder server does not have a private information store.

Having a dedicated public-folder server means that other servers can concentrate their processing efforts on private message storage and user message transfers. Dedicated public-folder servers still participate in directory replication. Consider using a dedicated public-folder server if there is a large amount of data in a public folder system or if frequent and timely access to public folders is critical.

Each Microsoft Outlook client obtains public folder hierarchy information from a public information store. If you have dedicated public servers, those servers respond to the clients for both folder hierarchy information and content data. As a result, it is possible for the servers to become overwhelmed with traffic. In this case, maintaining a public information store on each server enables clients to retrieve the folder hierarchy information from their local server while connecting to the public server for content data. In this way, requests for various types of data can be distributed for best performance.

If you have a large site with more than 20 servers, a dedicated private server can be your best option. In this case, your system benefits from not replicating the public folder hierarchy to every server, especially if public folders are created and deleted frequently.

Configuring separate public and private servers allows you to plan the hardware needs for a particular computer according to its role. In other words, if you know that a public server will be heavily used, you can use a higher-speed processor, more random access memory (RAM), and so on. You can assign different tasks to different servers.

▶ **To assign different responsibilities to public servers and private servers**

1. Move all of the public folders to the public servers using the **Replicas** property page on the public folder, or the **Instances** property page for the target public information store.

2. For each private server, configure the private information store so that the public folder server is the appropriate public server. To do this, use the **General** property page for the private information store server object.

   This step ensures that all top-level public folders that are created in the future are located on the new public servers.

3. Use the Administrator program to remove the private information store from the public servers and the public information store from the private servers. To do this, delete the private information store object from the server container in the Administrator program. Also, move mailboxes off of the public-only servers.

Separating public and private servers also concentrates the flow of public folder traffic. In this way, replication of the public folder hierarchy and contents takes place only between the public servers and does not have an impact on the private servers.

Setting Up Your Public Folders

When you set up public folders, you should understand what types of folders you can create, where the hierarchy and content for the public folders are stored, and how Exchange Server locates public folders when a user accesses them. Review these concepts before you set up your public folders. This will help you create a more efficient public folder system.

When you create a top-level folder, it resides on the public folder server where you created it (for example, on your hierarchy server).

When you create a subfolder, it inherits the replication configuration and replica list of its parent folder. This can be changed later by an administrator so that the parent folder and its subfolders are replicated to different servers.

The advantage of inheriting replication information is that the contents of the subfolders are available in the same locations with the same permissions as the parent folders.

If a top-level folder is not replicated, all of its subfolders are stored on the same public folder server as the top-level folder. If the top-level folder is replicated, its subfolders are stored on all public folder servers that contain a replica.

Creating a Public Folder

You create public folders using Microsoft Outlook. To modify properties of existing folders, use the Administrator program. For information about creating public folders, see Microsoft Outlook Help.

Creating Subfolders

You can create public folders that appear as subfolders. However, to do so you must have been granted permission by the top-level folder owner, also known as the *publishing author*.

▶ **To create a subfolder**

1. In Microsoft Outlook, click the parent folder.

2. From the **File** menu, click **New Folder**.

3. If you are writing a Messaging Application Programming Interface (MAPI) function call, use **CreateFolder()** on the parent folder object.

Public Folder Hierarchy

The public folder hierarchy is the structure that develops when you create multiple public folders using top-level folders and subfolders. The hierarchy appears as a series of folders on the left side of the Outlook window. The public folder hierarchy is replicated to all public information stores within an organization.

Users can choose a public folder from the hierarchy just as they would choose any other folder in their Outlook mail client. The information store on their public folder server supplies the information about the hierarchy structure.

Public Folder Contents

The contents of a public folder include a series of messages with attachments. The public folder contents exist on one or more Exchange Server computers with a public information store, also known as *public folder servers*. Although the hierarchy is stored on all public folder servers, the contents are stored only on some of the public folder servers.

Public Folder Locations

When you create a new public folder, an information store client creates a folder (Folder_Generic) in the public folder store hierarchy. Users who create folders are called *folder owners* and are identified through their personal information store.

After a public folder is created, the information store makes the folder accessible to other information stores. The folder owner can impose restrictions so that certain information store accounts (users) do not have access to the public folder.

All users have a hierarchy server to which they can connect. This hierarchy server determines the hierarchy structure that should be displayed in Outlook. The hierarchy server is set on a per-private-server basis. A server with a private information store provides this setting in the **General** property page.

As mentioned in the preceding section, public folders are *distributed*, that is, not all public folder content resides in every information store. One advantage of this distribution is that the information in all public folders in an organization can be many times the size of the largest information store hard disk. A disadvantage is that additional automatic processing is needed to locate the information store where a particular public folder resides.

Public Folders in the Directory

Each folder that you create has an entry in the directory and appears as a recipient. Public folders are represented in the directory as the Public Folder subclass of Mail Recipient. Each public folder is represented in the directory by an item of the Public Folder object class, as shown in the following illustration.

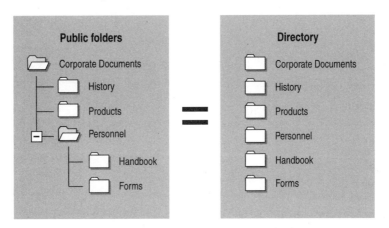

By default, public folders are hidden recipients. To view these hidden folders, use the Administrator program. From the **View** menu, click **Hidden Recipients**.

▶ **To display a hidden folder in the recipient's list**

1. In the Administrator window, double-click a public folder.
2. Click the **Advanced** tab.
3. Clear the **Hide from Address Book** check box.

Because public folders are represented as entries in the directory, you can send messages to them. In addition to mailing items to a public folder, you can post items to a public folder. *Posting* is a method of writing items directly to the information store without mailing them through the message transfer agent (MTA), as you do when you send a message.

MAPI clients with the appropriate permissions can also post messages to a public folder synchronously using the information store application programming interfaces (APIs).

Public folders appear in the Exchange Server Address Book Provider top-level container with other classes of Exchange Server recipients. The Display Name attribute indicates the name of the folder as it appears in the container. The object class is used to indicate to the client (through MAPI) that the recipient is actually a public folder, not another recipient class.

You can create a special container for folder addresses. For example, if you want to group folders about a similar topic, you can create a container. To create a recipient container, select the public information store object and specify that this is where the recipient object is created.

Public Information Store Structure

The public information store is the primary mechanism used by MAPI clients to gain access to public folders. Although public folders may be located in different information stores, the folder hierarchy independently represents all public folders and subfolders, as shown in the following illustration.

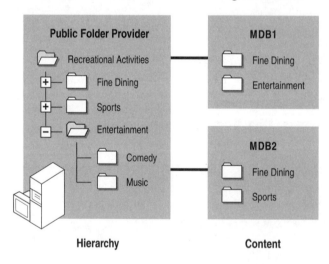

The public folder hierarchy is stored in the information store. The Exchange Server service provider uses an index made up of the public folder objects to list the top-level folders to return to the MAPI client. When a MAPI application is used to view the subfolders of a top-level public folder, the provider connects to an information store that maintains an instance of the folder contents. The provider then goes to that information store for all subsequent contents operations in that folder.

Any changes to the public folder hierarchy are performed by the user's hierarchy server. Content tables and messages are provided by the folder content servers.

Locating Folders by Using Affinities

When you select a public folder to view its contents, the information store must decide where that folder is located. The information store looks for the public folder in the following places in this order:

1. The user's public folder hierarchy server.

2. A *random number* server in the site. If there are multiple replicas in the site, the store provider uses an algorithm that is based on the user's domain name to determine the next location to search. The resulting number is divided by the number of servers that contain the public folder in the site. A connection is then made to the server assigned to that number. Because the number is random, this method distributes connections across all available replicas in the site.

3. An *existing connection* server in the site. If the information store cannot connect to the random number server, then it tries to connect to remaining servers in the site. Connections to servers that already have established remote procedure call (RPC) connections are tried first.

4. Other sites. If no public folder replicas are available in the site but there are replicas in at least one other site, the *affinity number* is used to determine the order in which connections are attempted.

   The affinity number is set in the site's **Public Folder Affinity** property page. This setting allows an administrator to set a cost for each of the other sites in the organization. The cost determines the order in which the information store attempts to connect to sites. The site with the lowest cost is the one to which the information store first tries to connect.

   After the information store finds the site, connections to servers within that site or group of sites are tried in random order. If two sites have the same cost, the servers in those sites are pooled together and tried in random order. The information store does not attempt to connect to a site with no affinity setting.

In the following illustration, a user in Site 1 wants to connect to a public folder. All of the servers shown have a replica of the desired public folder. The numbers in the servers indicate the order in which the connections are attempted.

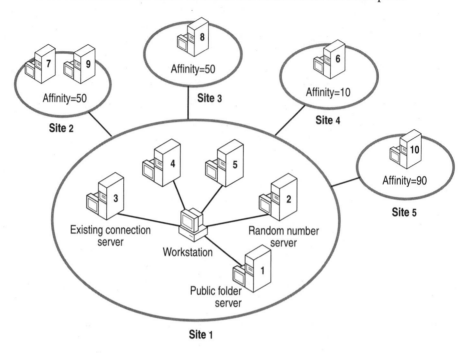

Customizing Public Folders

After you set up your public folders, you can use several features to help manage them. For example, you can obtain information about a folder's properties, designate who has access to a public folder, or create a shortcut or favorite link to a public folder.

Obtaining Information About a Folder

After you create a public folder, you can view information about its characteristics using the Administrator program.

▶ **To obtain information about the type, location, and general description of a public folder**

1. From the Administrator Program, click the folder you want more information about.

2. From the **File** menu, click **Properties**.

3. Click the **General** tab.

▶ **To obtain information about the folder contact, your permission level, and the folder path**

1. From the Administrator Program, click the folder you want more information about.

2. From the **File** menu, click **Properties**.

3. Click the **Summary** tab.

Granting Access Control

You can control access to public folders by using the directory entries represented as mailboxes in the Address Book. Public folder owners can grant access permissions to any mailboxes represented by objects of the **Distribution List**, **Mailbox**, and **Public Folder** classes.

The following access permissions can be maintained for public folders:

Create Items   You can create items in the folder.

Read Items   You can read any items in the folder. This permission is required for a user to open the folder's contents table.

Create subfolder   You can create subfolders in the folder. Users with this permission have Owner permission for the subfolders they create. They can prevent access by other users, including the owners of the parent folder, to those subfolders.

Edit items   You have one of the following permissions:

Option	Description
None	You cannot edit items in the folder.
Own	You can edit only items that you created.
All	You can edit any item in the folder.

Delete items   You have one of the following permissions:

Option	Description
None	You cannot delete items in the folder.
Own	You can delete only items that you created.
All	You can delete any item in the folder.

Folder owner   You are the owner of the folder. Folder owners are granted all permissions. The name of the last owner is never removed from the folder's access control list (ACL).

Folder contact   You receive replication conflict notifications, folder design conflict notifications, and quota notifications.

When you grant permissions to an Address Book entry of the **DistributionList** class, all the sublists of that distribution list are granted the same permissions. Distribution list members that are not represented by an X.500 distinguished name — that is, one-off addresses placed on distribution lists as X.400 originator/recipient (O/R) addresses — are not granted permissions.

A public subfolder inherits the ACL of its parent unless the subfolder owner creates access controls specifically for the subfolder. If a folder has subfolders and you change the permissions for the parent folder, the permissions for the subfolders are not changed automatically. The changed permissions apply only to newly created subfolders.

Access cannot be granted on a per-message basis — that is, you cannot specify different levels of permissions for messages within the same public folder.

Deleting Public Folders

Only folder owners can delete public folders. Deleting a public folder prevents further access to the folder and its replicas and removes the representation of the folder and its subfolders from the directory.

Public folder deletions can be recursive, so if you attempt a nonrecursive deletion of a public folder that contains subfolders, you receive an error message.

Creating Shortcuts

To provide other users with quick and easy access to your public folders, create shortcuts to them. You can save a desktop shortcut file in any of your folders and then drag it into a message or another file to send to another user. For more information, see Microsoft Outlook Help.

Creating a Favorites List

You can create a list of the public folders you use frequently that enables you to go directly to your favorite folders without searching through the entire public folder hierarchy. The list you create will appear at the top of the public folder hierarchy in Outlook.

You can create a link to any favorite public folder or subfolder. Deleting a favorite public folder from this list removes it from the public folder favorite store but does not remove the actual folder from the public information store. For more information about using the favorites list, see Outlook Help.

Public Folder Replication Strategies

Exchange allows you to distribute and synchronize shared information. The process of keeping public folder replicas synchronized is called *public folder replication*. In other words, you can take a public folder and replicate it to different Exchange Server computers. These folders are called *public folder replicas*. Replicas contain the same information as the originating public folder but reside on other Exchange Server computers as well as on the originating server.

Public folder replication ensures that each copy of a public folder contains the same information as the corresponding replicas on other Exchange computers. You can specify replication at regularly scheduled intervals.

To replicate public folders, an Exchange computer sends messages to all other servers on the replica list and updates those replicas. The remote replicas are updated with new messages, attachments, and any other folder contents that have been added, deleted, or modified locally.

The only distinct member of the replica list is the replica on the public folder server with the Home-MDB attribute. The server with the Home-MDB attribute in the public folder directory entry is the delivery location for items mailed to the folder.

For more information about setting a schedule for public folder replication, see *Microsoft Exchange Server Getting Started*.

Public folder replication results in the following benefits:

- Distribution of processing load and subsequent improvement of response times for users viewing information in the folder

- Reduction in the amount of WAN traffic necessary to provide access to information

- Increase in the availability of information for users when their primary server is unavailable

Planning Considerations for Replication

There are several ways to reduce system traffic and increase system efficiency when you replicate public folders.

Maintaining Commonality in Replica Lists One way to increase replication efficiency is to maintain commonality in replica lists when you create folders. This reduces traffic on the system because public folders are replicated more efficiently. Changes are collected for distribution to other servers on the basis of commonality in the replica list.

For example, if you have a set of similar public folders that contain information on department budgets, make sure that all folders have the same replication list. Use the following procedure if you want a subfolder to inherit the replica list from the parent folder:

1. Create a top-level folder.
2. Set the replica list as appropriate.
3. Create subfolders for the top-level folders.

Using Views Instead of New Folders for Similar Content As the number of folders you have on your system increases, so does the time and resources needed to replicate the folder hierarchy. To avoid this situation, create a single folder with different views for displaying information.

For example, instead of creating a folder for each employee in your department, you can create a single folder and designate the name of each employee as a field in that folder. That way, you can sort by employee name when you want to see information about that employee.

Dedicating Servers for Specific Purposes By creating servers that each deal with a specific application, task, or function, you can increase system efficiency. For example, use one server to handle only the BBS folders and another folder to handle only Outlook free and busy information. When you do so, be careful not to overcentralize. This causes every user of a particular application to access the same server. Instead, widely used data, such as Outlook free and busy information, should be distributed to multiple servers.

Configuring Public Folder Hierarchy Replication

Each public folder server contains a replica of the hierarchy of all public folders in the organization. This information is read by Microsoft Outlook users and appears as a series of folders on the left side of the Outlook window.

You cannot configure hierarchy replication the same way as content replication. Hierarchy replication takes place automatically at an interval set in the registry. When a user logs on to a client, the client automatically reads the hierarchy from its public folder server.

When you create a top-level public folder, the folder, its hierarchy, and the folder contents are added to the Pub.edb file on your public folder server. The information is then sent as mail messages delivered by the MTA. After replication, users in the organization who are viewing information in the Pub.edb file for their public folder server see the new public folder in the hierarchy.

As shown in the following illustration, hierarchy changes are replicated to all servers in the organization.

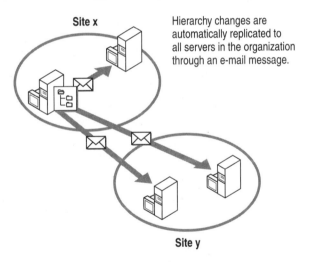

Site x

Hierarchy changes are automatically replicated to all servers in the organization through an e-mail message.

Site y

From then on, when a user searches for information on the new public folder, the public information store on the local public folder server automatically directs the client computer to a public folder server that has the contents.

For more information on configuring hierarchy replication, see *Microsoft Exchange Server Operations.*

Configuring Public Folder Content Replication

You can replicate public folders to different servers in the same site or to servers in other sites. Replicating public folders to other servers is an effective way to balance the load of users viewing a particular public folder at a given time. For example, if you have 100 users and 3 public folder servers in a site and all 100 users are using one specific folder many times a day, this can create an excessive amount of traffic on that server. However, if you create a public folder replica on a second server, the information stores on both servers can balance the load of users.

The information store supports a multimaster replication model for public folders — that is, you can make changes directly to any replica of a public folder or to messages within the folder, and these changes are then reflected in all other replicas. For example, when you modify a message or an attachment in a message in a public folder, the message and its attachments are replicated to all the other public folder instances. Changes are replicated at the document level, which means that if a single document is changed in a folder with hundreds of documents, only the document that is changed is replicated.

Public folder replication is e-mail based. This allows replicated instances of public folders to reside on information stores located on different physical local area networks (LANs) that are connected only by e-mail. The store-and-forward nature of message routing allows for replication message *fan-out*, that is, this minimizes network overhead when the number of replicas is high because of delayed splitting of recipient messages.

Replicating Messages

When more than one instance of a public folder has been configured, the public folder replication agent (PFRA) — a component of the information store — monitors changes, additions, and deletions to the original public folder and other replicated public folders. It is through the PFRA and on the information store that these public folders are configured to have replicas; they are also configured to send change messages to other information stores on which replicated instances reside.

The replicated messages are transported as embedded messages in message database encoding format (MDBEF). Each replicated message includes a change number that identifies it in relationship to existing replication messages.

Tracking Modified Messages

The PFRA maintains the following information about the state of each message in each folder.

- A uniformerly increasing, information store-specific *change number*
- A list of *predecessor change numbers* (all previous change numbers for an information store)

The change number is made up of a unique identifier and a *change counter*, so the change numbers are information-store-specific.

The change counter is assigned a number by the PFRA for each message change that occurs on a server. When a message on an information store is modified, the PFRA for that information store assigns a new change number to the message so that the change counter is greater than the previous one.

By using the predecessor change number list, the PRFA tracks which version of a message is the most current.

Replication of Modified Messages

When you edit a message in a replicated public folder, the PFRA for that information store updates the state information for that message. It then sends a replication message containing the modified message and its attachments to the other information stores that maintain replicas. The list of information stores that maintain these replicas is a property of the folder.

When an information store receives a new replication message, the new message replaces the existing message on the local computer only if the original message modification was made to the same version or a later version of the existing message — that is, if the new message is more current than the existing message.

Which message contains the most recent information is determined by the change number and the predecessor change list. If the change number of the existing message is included in the predecessor change list of the new message, the new message replaces the existing message.

The following illustration shows how replication occurs when there are no conflicts.

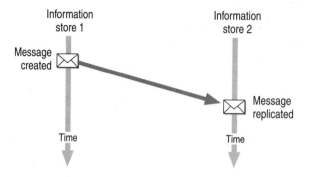

Replication Conflicts

Conflicts occur when a message is modified in two different replicas, where each modification is made before the other can replicate, as shown in the following illustration.

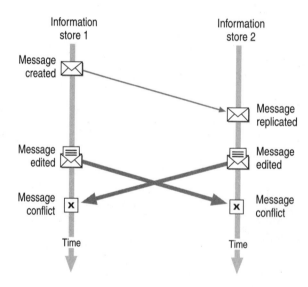

If the change number of the current message is not included in the predecessor list of the new message, the new message is older than the existing message. In this case, a change was made to a message that had not incorporated a previous change from another information store, and a conflict occurred.

When a conflict occurs, the information store alerts the folder contacts of the conflict by attaching the conflicting messages to a *conflict notification*, as shown in the following illustration.

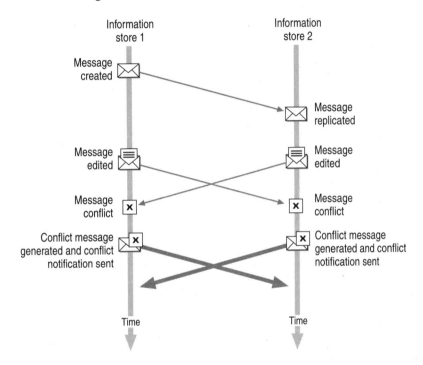

The folder contact can resolve the conflict at any of the instances. As shown in the following illustration, the resolved message replicates to the other folder instances.

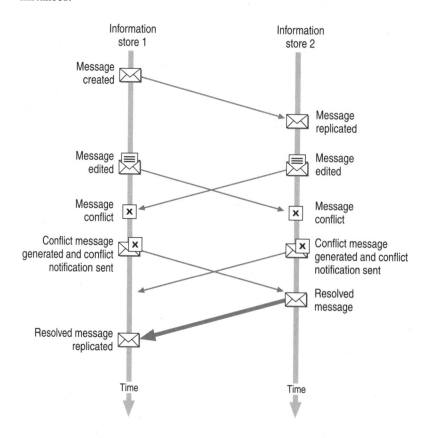

Replication of New and Deleted Messages

When a new message is created in a public folder, the information store assigns a change counter number to the message and then sends a replication message to all other information stores that contain instances of the public folder. Information stores that receive the replication message create the message in their replica of the public folder, using the change number assigned by the information store on which the message was created.

When a message is deleted, the information store from which the message is deleted sends a replication message to all other information stores that contain instances of the public folder. This message indicates that the message has been deleted. Each information store that receives the message deletes the message and maintains a marker, called a *tombstone*, for the deleted message.

Replication Frequency

Because public folder replication is e-mail-based, the amount of time it takes for messages to replicate from one information store to a particular replica depends on the underlying messaging system and topology, as well as on administrator-specified MTA connection parameters.

Scheduling for replication is configured in the Administrator program on a per-folder and per-information-store basis. The **Replication Schedule** property page permits replication scheduling in 15-minute intervals. The same property page exists for the public information store object. If a schedule is set at the folder level, it overrides the schedule set at the information store level.

Backfilling

Although the Exchange Server MTA guarantees a high degree of reliability (particularly in a homogenous environment), it cannot guarantee that replication messages or confirmation notifications will not be lost due to hardware failure or other problems. This is particularly true where public folder replicas are configured to reside in different sites and a foreign system is used for MTA connectivity between the sites. The process by which the information store compensates for lost messages is called *backfilling*.

Backfilling is the process of acquiring information that was lost from an information store as a result of one of the following circumstances:

- A new replica was added to a server and does not have any information replicated to it.
- A message was lost in transit.
- A server was restored from backup.

A server needs to be backfilled when it has not successfully received all the replica messages from other information stores.

When an information store fails to receive complete replica information, it generates a *backfill entry*, which serves as a placeholder to indicate that information is missing. After waiting a specified amount of time to receive the missing folder content packet, the information store issues a *backfill request* to two other servers chosen by a predetermined algorithm. The backfill request indicates what folder content packet is missing and requests that another information store send the information. Any information store can respond to a backfill request, regardless of whether it was the source of the original folder content packet.

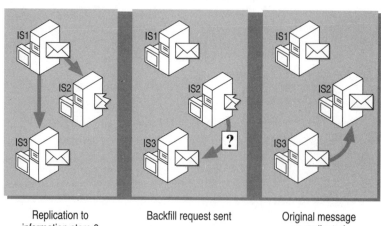

Replication to information store 2 (IS2) incomplete   Backfill request sent   Original message re-replicated

Adding a Replica

To create a replica of an existing public folder, you must have public folder administrator authority. In the Administrator program, either add the new information store to the **Instances** property page of the public folder or add the public folder to the **Replicas** property page of the public information store.

When an information store detects a new replica and determines that it is responsible for that replica, it generates a backfill request for the contents of the folder (the folder content packet).

If an information store receives a folder content packet for a folder that does not exist in the hierarchy or for which it does not currently have a replica, it queues the content packet and waits for the folder hierarchy change. It then processes the content packet. If the hierarchy change does not occur within four hours, the packet expires and will have to be backfilled.

Replication Verification

The Public Folder Replication Verification Tool (Replver.exe) compares public folders on Exchange Server computers and sends periodic status messages if a replica appears to be out-of-date.

For more information, see the Readme file in the Server\Support\Utils directory on the Microsoft Exchange Server version 5.5 compact disc.

Deleting a Directory Replication Connector

Before you delete a directory replication connection between one or more Exchange sites, consider whether to run the DS/IS consistency adjuster, which compares the directory with the information store.

Caution If you delete a directory replication connector between two sites and you plan to reconnect the two sites later, do *not* run the DS/IS consistency adjuster. This could result in a loss of data.

When you disconnect a directory replication connector and then run the DS/IS consistency adjuster tool, you not only prevent replication between the two sites, you also re-establish the home folder between the public folder replicas. Although all public folders that were available before you removed the connector are still available, they cease to be exact replicas of each other. For example, if a user makes a change to a message in a public folder in Site 1 and another user changes the same message in Site 2, their changes do not appear outside the respective sites.

In addition, when the directory replication connector is removed, Exchange Server re-establishes the home folder in the sitewhere the most recent change was made. For example, if there is a public folder in Site 2 and a user edits a message in that public folder before the sites are disconnected, the public folder in Site 2 becomes the home folder. So if the two sites are disconnected and you delete a public folder in Site 1, reconnecting causes the information store to backfill the deleted public folder to the home server (Site 2). The backfill deletes the public folder in Site 2, even if additional changes were made to it while the sites were disconnected.

For more information about the DS/IS consistency adjuster, see *Microsoft Exchange Server Getting Started*.

Folder Permissions

You can set permissions for public folders and mailbox folders by assigning a role to any user name in the global address list. You can define custom roles or use the following default roles:

- Owner
- Publishing Editor
- Editor
- Publishing Author
- Author
- Reviewer
- Contributor
- None

These default roles are associated with specific permissions, as shown in the following table.

Permission	Owner Role	Pub. Editor Role	Editor Role	Pub. Author Role	Author Role	Reviewer Role	Contributor Role	None
Create Items	X	X	X	X	X		X	
Read Items	X	X	X	X	X	X		
Create Subfolders	X	X		X				
Folder Owner	X							
Folder Contact	X							
Folder Visible	X	X	X	X	X	X	X	X
Edit Items	All	All	All	Own	Own	None	None	
Delete Items	All	All	All	Own	Own	None	None	

Every folder has a default user that grants permissions to undefined users. Set the default user to None to give only defined users permission to use a public folder or mailbox folder.

The following table provides descriptions of the permissions associated with user roles.

Permission	Description
Create Items	Grants the user permission to post items in the folder.
Read Items	Grants the user permission to open any item in the folder.
Create Subfolder	Grants the user permission to create subfolders in the folder.
Folder Owner	Grants all permissions in the folder.
Folder Contact	Grants the user Folder Contact permission. Folder Contacts receive automated notifications from the folder, such as replication conflict messages and requests from users for additional permissions or other changes in the folder.
Edit Items	None: Prevents the user from editing any item. Own: Grants the user permission to edit the user's own items. All: Grants the user permission to edit any item.
Delete Items	None: Prevents the user from deleting any item. Own: Grants the user permission to delete the user's own items. All: Grants the user permission to delete any item.

Public Folder Homing

Exchange Server considers all public folder replicas equal; therefore, there is no master copy of the folder. However, a public folder does have a *home*—the server and site where Exchange Server delivers messages and generates conflict notifications.

Public Folder Re-homing

Because public folders create messaging traffic and require maintenance from site administrators, you might want to reevaluate where you have placed a public folder's home and place it on a different server in a different site. User access creates less traffic between two sites than continual replication. Therefore, if a public folder has a replica and its home site is Site A, but most of the folder's users are in Site B using the replica in Site B, it might make more sense to make Site B the public folder's home and remove the replica in Site A. Users in Site A can still have access to the public folder using the public folder hierarchy. And site administrators in Site B also can maintain the folder more accurately and efficiently than those in Site A.

▶ **To re-home a public folder**

1. In the Administrator program, click the public folder you want to re-home.

2. From the **File** menu, click **Properties**.

3. If there is no replica of the public folder on the server that you want to be the new home, you must create one. In the **Replica** tab, create a replica of the public folder on the server in the site where you want to re-home the folder.

4. In the **Advanced** tab, select the name of the new home server from the **Home Server** list.

Limited Administrative Access

In Exchange 5.5, public folders are, by default, attached to their home site and server. With this feature, called *limited administrative access*, a user must have administrative permissions on the public folder's home site in order to perform administrative actions on the folder. For example, public folders with limited administrative access cannot be re-homed by anyone other than the administrator of their home site and server.

If you are creating a public folder hierarchy, new subfolders that you create will inherit the limited administrative access designation from the top-level folder. In a preexisting public folder hierarchy, you can choose to propagate limited administrative access to subfolders.

If limited administrative access is enabled, you must be an administrator on the public folder's home site to perform the following functions:

▪ Placing a replica of a public folder on another site

▪ Changing a public folder's home server and site

You can change a public folder's limited access designation in the General tab of the folder object. Select the **Limit administrative access to home site** box to ensure that access to the public folder and any subfolders is limited. If the box is not selected, the folder does not have limited administrative access.

Note If you have upgraded to Exchange Server 5.5 from an earlier version, the public folder hierarchy will not automatically be set for limited administrative access. You should set limited administrative access in each top-level folder.

When upgrading your mail organization to Microsoft Exchange Server version 5.5 and limiting the administrative access to your public folder hierarchy, you should first ensure that all your public folders are homed in the desired sites.

For the limited administrative access feature to function correctly, you should install Exchange Server 5.5 on all the Exchange Server computers in your organization. Earlier versions may not recognize the limited access designation, and your public folders could be re-homed without your permission.

PART 13

Collaboration

A collaboration application is a program that facilitates groups working together by collecting, organizing, distributing, and tracking information across an organization. When an application that was designed for personal use is placed in a public folder, it becomes a collaboration. An effective collaboration environment streamlines workflow so colleagues can interact efficiently, find and share information, collaborate on documents, and publish information to the company intranet or the Internet.

Collaboration applications are supported by Microsoft BackOffice products including Microsoft Windows NT Server, Microsoft Exchange Server, Microsoft Outlook 97, Microsoft SQL Server, Microsoft Internet Information Services (IIS), Microsoft Internet Explorer, Microsoft Active Server Pages (ASP), and Microsoft Visual InterDev™. These products provide elements of functionality that can be combined as needed.

Examples of collaboration applications in the business environment include workflow and sales automation, document collaboration and publishing, e-mail, scheduling, and discussion groups and newsgroups. All of these are available when you use Exchange as a platform for collaboration applications.

Collaboration applications are either synchronous or asynchronous. Synchronous collaboration is like talking to someone on the telephone, and asynchronous collaboration is like leaving a voice mail message. This chapter describes asynchronous collaboration, which is currently the most widely used method of collaboration.

Microsoft Collaboration Applications Platform

The Microsoft Collaboration Applications Platform consists of Windows NT Server, Microsoft Exchange Server, Outlook 97, SQL Server, IIS, Internet Explorer, Active Server Pages, and Microsoft Visual InterDev.

Windows NT Server Windows NT Server provides the foundation for the Collaboration Applications Platform and the BackOffice products. The BackOffice products are integrated with Windows NT Server to take advantage of its security features, stability, and scalability. All of the BackOffice products require the installation of Windows NT Server.

Microsoft Exchange Server Exchange provides the infrastructure for building collaboration applications. Exchange supports the following Internet protocols:

- Simple Mail Transfer Protocol (SMTP)
- Post Office Protocol version 3 (POP3)
- Internet Message Access Protocol version 4rev1 (IMAP4rev1)
- Lightweight Directory Access Protocol (LDAP)
- Network News Transfer Protocol (NNTP)

It also supports public folders and replication, a central address book, centralized administration, and security.

Microsoft Outlook 97 Microsoft Outlook provides tools for creating programming and nonprogramming collaboration applications. The Desktop Information Manager provided with Microsoft Outlook centralizes all communication, organization, and management of information. Microsoft Outlook supports multiple e-mail providers, scheduling, task management, journals, contacts, and the creation of personal folders for storing and categorizing information.

SQL Server SQL Server is a scalable database management system designed for distributed client/server computing. Its management tools include built-in data replication and open system architecture, which provide a way to deliver collaboration applications for any size organization. SQL Server integrates with Internet applications to provide access to the World Wide Web. SQL Server can be used to store collaboration applications.

Internet Information Services (IIS) IIS simplifies improving communications and delivering Web sites. IIS is the only Web server integrated into Windows NT Server. It is powerful enough to host the world's largest Web sites, yet can be used to easily create an intranet in minutes. You can combine IIS with Microsoft Index Server, Microsoft Internet Explorer, and the Microsoft FrontPage® Web authoring and management tool to make BackOffice a more powerful Internet and intranet tool.

Microsoft Internet Explorer   Microsoft Internet Explorer is the collaboration cross-platform Internet client. The latest release of Internet Explorer supports Dynamic Hypertext Markup Language (DHTML), Microsoft ActiveX®, Java, Hypertext Transfer Protocol (HTTP) version 1.1, and more. Internet Explorer functions as a full messaging client using Microsoft Outlook Web Access, which uses IIS and Active Server Pages.

Active Server Pages   Active Server Pages (ASP) is an open architecture application that does not need to be compiled. This makes it possible for users to combine HTML, scripts, and reusable ActiveX server components to create Web-based collaboration applications. ASP enables server scripting for IIS with native support for both Microsoft Visual Basic® Scripting Edition (VBScript) and Microsoft JScript™.

ASP processes ASP scripts, which typically are files with an .asp extension. When ASP encounters regular HTML text, it does not process it, but passes it through the Active Server computer directly to the browser. When ASP encounters text within server script tags (<% and %>), it processes this script code and generates HTML, which it sends to the browser. Scripts are not stored in a compiled form. They are interpreted when the .asp file is requested from the server.

Visual InterDev   Microsoft Visual InterDev is designed for developers who want to build sophisticated, dynamic Web applications. Using Visual InterDev, teams of developers and nonprogrammers can collaborate on creating Web sites because Visual InterDev integrates fully with FrontPage.

Collaboration Applications

The following sections describe the types of collaboration applications.

Types of Collaboration Applications

In general, collaboration applications are categorized as instant collaborations, discussion group applications, routing and tracking applications, or reference applications.

Instant collaborations Refers to the built-in application modules that are shipped with Microsoft Outlook. These modules can be customized. To become an instant collaboration a module must be placed in an Exchange public folder. The built-in modules are: Calendar, Tasks, Journal, and Contacts.

Discussion group applications Discussion group applications enable users to conduct online discussions. Users do not need to coordinate their schedules to be online simultaneously because they are communicating asynchronously using post forms. Post forms are used to place items in a folder and to post responses to items in a folder. Discussion group applications serve as the foundation for creating threaded conversations in views, so users can view the history of responses to a particular item.

Routing and tracking applications Routing and tracking applications enable the user to record and view information that is constantly updated. Routing and tracking applications determine where the routing process has stalled, a problem that is inherent when passing information to individuals for review. Routing and tracking applications can pass information to individuals in sequence or to a group. They can also track who reviewed the document and whether they approved or made changes.

Reference applications Reference applications enable users to store e-mail messages, and graphic images, Microsoft ActiveX-based documents, World Wide Web addresses, voice mail messages, and Microsoft Office or other documents. These applications can serve as a repository for sales and marketing brochures, employee guidelines, and employee benefits information.

Collaboration Applications Components

Most collaboration applications have the following components in common.

Folders Private and public folders are essential for creating collaboration applications. Private folders are not collaborations, but they do play a role in the design and testing of collaboration applications. Collaboration applications are created, developed, and tested in private folders before they are copied to public folders and made into collaborations. Public folders facilitate online discussion groups and the sharing, recording, tracking, and distribution of information that is constantly updated.

Views Views determine how information is displayed in a collaboration application. When data is collected into a folder application, views are created to display sorted, grouped, or calculated data in an organized presentation for users.

Fields   Fields store information about an object. Objects include tasks, individuals, and appointments. Microsoft Outlook has many fields that can be placed on forms. The fields you create can be simple containers of values or complex formulas based on other fields. Controls, such as the text box control, allow the user to view and edit fields.

Forms   Forms are the graphical interface most often presented to users for composing or reading messages. When you double-click a message, for example, you are looking at a form that you can customize for users.

Databases   Databases provide structured storage for collaboration applications. Open Database Connectivity (ODBC) databases such as Microsoft SQL Server and Microsoft Access, as well as Oracle and others, can store data.

Instant Collaboration

Built-in modules contain predetermined function and design settings, and they require only the services of a public folder to become an instant collaboration. Collaboration applications can be created using one of the built-in modules available in Microsoft Outlook. For example, if you need an application to track individuals or companies, you can use the Contacts module to take advantage of the built-in views and fields.

Creating an application using one of the built-in modules does not require a developer's expertise. The Outlook Forms Designer and Microsoft Visual Basic Scripting Edition (VBScript) are available for more complex applications.

The following paragraphs describe the built-in modules.

Calendar module   When a Calendar module is copied to or created in a public folder, users can share, post, and update schedules for activities such as training classes, sporting events, and company functions. For example, product launch milestones such as trade shows, product ship dates, or press tours can be posted to a Calendar folder for group viewing.

Tasks module   When a Tasks module is copied to or created in a public folder, team members can share a common task list that displays who is responsible for a task and the status of the task. For example, a project manager can create a public Tasks folder that team members can update when tasks are completed or significant progress is made. This provides the product manager with up-to-date information on the status of a project.

Contacts module When a Contacts module is copied to or created in a public folder, users can add to, update, and share a list of contacts. For example, the sales department can share a list of leads, or the entire company can share a list of vendor contacts.

Journal module When a Journal module is copied to or created in a public folder, users can log and track information such as the amount of time an individual spends on a particular task, on a project, or with a specific customer. You can set the Journal to automatically log and store Office documents, contact calls, e-mail, and other communications.

Notes module The Notes module, shared or used privately, is the graphical interface equivalent of self-stick notes. As with the other built-in modules, copying or creating this module in a public folder allows users shared access to it. The color and category can be customized for easy retrieval, and the note can be forwarded as a message.

Building an Instant Collaboration Example

Instant collaborations are applications that are based on built-in modules in Microsoft Outlook. Built-in modules contain predetermined function and design settings, and they require only the services of a public folder to become an instant collaboration.

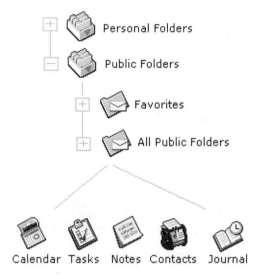

To create an instant collaboration, first create or locate a public folder to contain the module. Then copy a Tasks, Contacts, Calendar, or Journal built-in module into the public folder. After the module is copied or created in a public folder, the combination of the Microsoft Outlook module and Exchange public folder results in a collaboration application.

Collaboration Examples

The following sections give examples of various types of collaborations that are designed to facilitate workflow.

Instant Collaboration Example

The contacts applications example of instant collaboration illustrates one of several built-in applications. Built-in applications have a variety of predefined views and can be integrated easily with the Journal module. Contacts applications offer e-mail and Web integration. For example, users can click on a hyperlink to go to a site on the Internet.

A contacts application provides a group of users with a shared database that stores information about clients, friends, or vendors. To make it a collaboration, users can post it in a public folder.

Discussion Group Applications Examples

The following are examples of discussion group applications.

Product Ideas Application

The product ideas application consists of a Product Idea form for posting ideas in the public folder and a Product Idea Response form for posting responses to those ideas. For example, a company can do a trial release of a product to its employees and use the product ideas application to track feedback, and at the same time create a dialog between the in-house users of the product and the marketing personnel who are going to be selling it.

Job Candidate Application

The job candidate application consists of a Job Candidate form and a Response form. For example, a manager or administrator can submit a Job Candidate item to the Job Candidates public folder. After the candidate is interviewed, each interviewer can complete the Response form and submit hiring recommendations to the Job Candidates folder. The manager or administrator can then review the summary of hiring recommendations. As with all public folders, permissions can be applied to limit access to authorized individuals only.

Routing and Tracking Application Examples

The following are examples of routing and tracking applications.

Purchase Order Application

A purchase order application uses a Microsoft Excel worksheet called the Purchase Request form. To submit a purchase order, the user opens the Purchase Request form in the Purchase Requests folder, completes the worksheet, and then posts the form to the folder. Then, depending on the items requested, amounts, and the person making the request, the application follows a predetermined route for approval. The route and response can be tracked in a secure public folder.

Expense Report Application

An expense report application enables users to submit expense reports by e-mail. The application consists of an Excel worksheet, called the Expense Report form, embedded within a Microsoft Outlook mail item. Users complete this form and then submit their reports by e-mail to the appropriate person. This application can be routed in the same way as the purchase order application is routed, and because this application incorporates an Excel spreadsheet, the built-in routing slip function can be used.

Help Desk Application

The help desk application enables users to submit a request for technical assistance to a help desk group within their organization. In addition, the application allows help desk personnel to assign, organize, track, collaborate on, and resolve help desk requests. This application is typically used by a help desk supervisor, a help desk technician, and the user experiencing the problem.

Reference Application Examples

Reference applications are typically created using e-mail folders that can store a wide range of information, including product specifications, feature proposals, sales reports, software prototypes, employee status reports, Web site addresses, and training materials. The following are examples of reference applications.

Web Sites Reference Folders

Web sites reference folders store Web addresses. These folders can be personal or private, with views that organize sites into categories.

Training Materials Reference Folders

Training materials reference folders can be used to deliver training materials. For example, an entire computer-based training course can be posted in a public folder and made available to the entire company.

Sales Literature Reference Folder

Sales literature reference folders provide a centralized location to store fact sheets and brochures. This makes the materials easy to change or enhance.

Microsoft Outlook Collaboration Applications

The Microsoft Outlook environment for collaboration applications includes a variety of features and tools. For application developers, the Microsoft Outlook application design environment provides advanced design features and tools. Some of these features include the following:

32-bit forms   Because Microsoft Outlook forms are 32-bit and form definitions are usually less than 12 kilobytes, you can display and update forms quickly.

Instant switching between forms and run time   Designers can switch instantly between form design and run time so they can quickly modify and test forms.

Advanced fields and views   Fields of a Microsoft Outlook form or view can include calculated expressions, validation formulas, and number formatting.

Built-in forms modules   Forms support all the features of the built-in Microsoft Outlook forms, including digital signatures and encryption. Using a custom form no longer implies sacrificing standard user interface design and features. Custom forms can be sent from outside the organization. Users can embed form definitions or layouts in a message so they can send them inside or outside their organization to other users who may not have the form definition installed.

Extendable forms   Developers can extend forms with existing ActiveX or OLE controls and with the VBScript language.

Microsoft Outlook Tools for Developing Applications

For folder creation and design, and for customizing forms, the Microsoft Outlook design environment enhances the design features offered previously with Microsoft Exchange Client. Microsoft Outlook provides tools to create and design folders and to customize forms. These tools include Outlook Forms Designer, Microsoft Visual Basic Scripting Edition (VBScript), and the Microsoft Visual Basic Expression Service.

Outlook Forms Designer Outlook Forms Designer is the integrated development environment provided within Microsoft Outlook. It is accessible from within any form in Microsoft Outlook by choosing **Form** from the **Tools** menu. Forms created using the Outlook Forms Designer can be published in folders and saved as .oft files.

Visual Basic Scripting Edition   VBScript is built into Outlook Forms Designer, offering the designer the full capabilities of VBScript, a subset of Visual Basic for Applications. By using the Microsoft Outlook object model and VBScript, designers can add functionality to standard methods such as Open and Close, automatically create items and set properties on them, and add intelligence to forms so fields are automatically completed for the user.

Visual Basic Expression Service Visual Basic Expression Service is built into the Outlook Forms Designer environment, enabling designers to create validated, formula, and combination fields. For example, with Visual Basic Expression Service, the designer can create a formula field for a timecard form that automatically calculates the total number of hours worked in a week.

Collaboration Applications Active Platform

Active Platform is a development environment provided by a Web server. The main components of Active Platform are Active Server and Active Desktop.

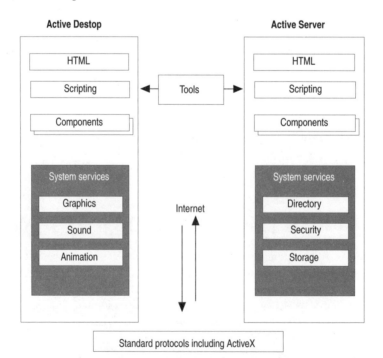

Currently, IIS version 3.0 and later, Peer Web Server, and Personal Web Server all support the Active Platform environment through the installation of ASP.

Active Platform provides an integrated, comprehensive set of client and server development technologies that make it easy to integrate the connectivity of the Internet with the power of the personal computer. The foundation of Active Platform includes HTML scripting and components. Active Platform is also the only development platform that allows developers to choose to target either cross-platform or platform-specific functionality.

Active Server and Active Desktop Common Components

Active Server and Active Desktop have common components that make access across client and server seamless. The following components are common to both Active Server and Active Desktop (also referred to as Active Client).

HTML   Active Platform fully supports HTML 3.2 and will continue to support the latest HTML standards as they are approved by the World Wide Web Consortium (W3C) and standards organizations.

Scripting   ASP offers native support for Visual Basic Scripting Edition (VBScript) and JScript (the implementation of Java Script provided by Microsoft) and supports other scripting languages through ActiveX Scripting plug-ins. ASP also supports ActiveX Scripting, allowing virtually any scripting engine to be used. It allows Web developers to write scripts that are carried out on either the server or the client.

Components   ASP also supports ActiveX components developed in any language, such as C++, Microsoft Visual Basic, Java, COBOL, and others. The resulting applications are compatible with any Web browser running on any operating system. (The server-side scripting processor also allows for multilingual support, defining which language HTML is returned in, based on user preference.)

ActiveX   ActiveX is the set of core technologies that provides a way for networked objects to operate across platforms. Microsoft has provided these technologies along with complete documentation to The Open Group. Any operating system vendor can now port these ActiveX core technologies to its platform for cross-platform compatibility. In addition, under The Open Group's guidance, any vendor can participate in future enhancements of the ActiveX core technologies.

Active Server Component

Active Server is the server-side and script-based programming model that allows developers to easily create server and Web server applications. Active Server is the server component of the Active Platform that is built into IIS version 3.0.

Active Server technologies include the following:

- ASP
- Microsoft Transaction Server
- Microsoft Message Queue Server (MSMQ)

Active Server technologies make the development of Internet and intranet component software faster and easier because they offer a unique language-independent approach that separates business logic from display generation.

Active Server Pages (ASP) An ASP is an HTML page with script embedded in the page. When IIS receives a page with an .asp extension, script within the HTML page is interpreted and presented back to the browser as HTML. Any language can be implemented as the script language, but most commonly the language will be either VBScript or JScript. Script is designated by <SCRIPT> or <%..%> tags.

For more information about ASP, see "Microsoft Collaboration Applications Platform" earlier in this chapter.

Collaboration Data Objects (CDO) Collaboration Data Objects is a technology that provides objects that add messaging functionality to applications. For example, CDO and ASP enable the developer to add script to a Web site to provide support for creating, sending, and receiving e-mail, as well as participation in discussions and other public folder applications.

Note Collaboration Data Objects (CDO) was previously referred to as OLE Messaging and, most recently, as Active Messaging.

Collaboration Data Objects Libraries CDO is available through the two Active Messaging libraries: Collaboration Data Objects Library and Collaboration Data Objects Rendering Library. These libraries expose programmable messaging objects, including folders, messages, recipient addresses, attachments, and other messaging components that can be called from Microsoft Visual Basic, VBScript, JavaScript, JScript, Java, and any application that supports Visual Basic for Applications such as Microsoft Office.

Microsoft Outlook Web Access Microsoft Outlook Web Access for Exchange provides secure access to e-mail, personal calendar, group scheduling, and collaboration applications on Exchange using only a Web browser.

Microsoft Transaction Server   Microsoft Transaction Server is designed to simplify the development of the middle tier of multi-tier applications by providing much of the infrastructure needed to carry out the business logic. Microsoft Transaction Server insulates developers from issues such as connectivity, security, directory, process and thread management, and database connection management. The infrastructure provided by Microsoft Transaction Server supports robust, production-class, business-critical Internet, intranet, or internal local area network (LAN) applications.

Microsoft Message Queue Server (MSMQ)   MSMQ accomplishes communication between applications over a network by using transaction messages. For example, if an Exchange computer needs to communicate with an unavailable remote Exchange computer, the messages destined for the remote server will be stored in a queue and forwarded when the remote server is back online. This functionality provides the reliability required by applications that are critical to an organization's operation.

Using the Active Directory Services Interface

With the Active Directory Services Interfaces (ADSI), you can use high-level tools such as Microsoft Visual Basic, Java, C, or Microsoft Visual C++® to create directory-enabled applications. With ADSI, you need not be concerned about underlying differences between various directory implementations or namespaces because, in the provider-based model that ADSI supports, ADSI can serve as the interface to a number of directory services, accessing each one through its own provider.

This means that you can build applications that use a single point of access to multiple directories in the network environment, whether those directories are based on the Lightweight Directory Access Protocol (LDAP), Novell Directory Services (NDS), or the Microsoft Windows NT version 4.0 Security Account Manager (NTDS).

ADSI and LDAP

ADSI, which provides a Component Object Model (COM) interface to directory objects, is built on a provider-based model. While clients use the COM interfaces exposed by ADSI, providers implement the mapping between those COM interfaces and the underlying directory system. An ADSI application that creates or modifies a user in an NDS directory can also be used to create a user in an Exchange 5.5 directory.

In contrast, LDAP is a protocol, specifically an on-the-wire protocol for directory access. LDAP applications are restricted to accessing directories that expose the LDAP protocol. As mentioned previously, LDAP is just one directory-service provider among others (such as NTDS); ADSI is not limited to accessing directory data through LDAP.

Because ADSI is a set of COM objects, it can be used within Microsoft Visual Basic or JavaScript to make Web-based applications directory-enabled. It is simpler to program tasks of this type using ADSI than using the C-based LDAP API.

ADSI and ADO

ADO is used to perform searches within the directory and present the results in a tabular form. On the other hand, ADSI is used to modify entries in the directory.

A typical way to combine ADSI and ADO is first to use ADO to search for one or more objects, iterate through the result set, and then modify the objects of interest with ADSI. Other uses of ADSI and ADO are illustrated in ADSI samples.

ADSI and Microsoft Exchange Server Version 5.5

The directory service of Microsoft Exchange Server version 5.5 supports LDAP version 3, which means you can use ADSI with its LDAP provider to manipulate any object in the Exchange 5.5 directory. This capability, when used with Collaboration Data Objects (CDO), lets administrators and developers efficiently write collaborative applications or administration tools.

This section provides information on writing directory-enabled applications that use ADSI to access the Exchange 5.5 directory service and directory data.

Microsoft Exchange Server Directory Schema

To write ADSI applications that access the Exchange directory, you need an understanding of the Exchange directory schema. The schema defines the available object classes in the directory, relationships between the object classes, attributes of each object class, and specific characteristics of attributes and classes.

You can use the Microsoft Exchange Server Administrator program to view the Exchange directory schema, and to view individual attributes and object classes.

▶ **To view the Exchange directory schema**

1. Start the Administrator program in raw mode by using the **/raw** (or **/r**) switch. If the Administrator program is installed in the default location, you can start it by clicking **Run** on the Windows NT **Start** menu and using the following command:

   c:\exchsrvr\bin\admin.exe /r

2. On the **View** menu of the Administrator program, click **Raw Directory**.

3. In the hierarchy (left) pane, click the Schema object (the Schema object is child of a Site object). The schema's objects are displayed in the right pane.

4. (Optional) To see information about an object's class and the values of its attributes, open the object's property sheet. To do this, double-click the object in the right pane, or click the object in the right pane, and then click **Properties** (or **Raw Properties**) on the **File** menu.

Using Properties for ADSI Support

As described in the directory schema, directory objects contain attributes, and those attributes function according to the values held by their properties. Every attribute contains the following three properties, which are particularly useful in ADSI support: Heuristics, ACL, and Description. The settings of these properties affect the behavior or use of the attribute on which they exist.

For example, if the Heuristics property on the Address-Home attribute of an object is an odd number, you know that its bit 0 has a value of 1. This value means that, when the object is replicated between sites, this Address-Home attribute is not replicated.

Heuristics Property

To determine the meaning of the Heuristics property and its implications for the attribute it applies to, you can examine its bits. They are interpreted as follows:

Bit	Value	Significance
0	0	Replication of attribute between sites
	1	No replication of attribute between sites
1	0	Not accessible by anonymous clients through LDAP
	1	Accessible to both anonymous and authenticated LDAP clients

Bit	Value	Significance
2	0	Not accessible by authenticated clients through LDAP
	1	Accessible to authenticated clients but not to anonymous clients
3	0	Not an operational attribute
	1	An operational attribute
4	0	Not visible through the Administrator program, on the **Attributes** tab of the **DS Site Configuration** object (property page can be used to configure the non-operational attributes of the site)
	1	Visible through the Administrator program, on the **Attributes** tab of the **DS Site Configuration** object

Using the Heuristics Property

By taking note of the Heuristics property, you can determine the visibility of particular attributes. For example, a Heuristics value of 3 (bit 0 = 1 and bit 1 = 1) means that the attribute is visible by anonymous LDAP clients but is not replicated between sites.

A Heuristics value of 11 (bit 3 = 1 and bit 1 = 1 and bit 0 = 1) means that the attribute is an operational attribute; it is visible to authenticated LDAP clients and is not replicated between sites.

Note If both bit 1 = 1 and bit 2 = 1, the attribute is accessible to authenticated clients but not to anonymous clients.

Operational attributes (attributes with a Heuristics bit 3 set) are not visible through ADSI (though they are visible through ADO), even though it is possible to set their values through ADSI. To obtain the value of an operational attribute, use an ADO query as described in the example under ADSI Samples.

Caution Changing bit 0 of the Heuristics property could cause directory replication to stop. You should not change this bit of the Heuristics property of an attribute.

ACL Property

The ACL property of an attribute determines what permissions a user needs to modify the attribute. The ACL property value definitions are:

Property value	Significance
0	Only the Exchange directory service can modify the attribute.
1	Users with at least the **Modify Admin Attributes** right can modify the attribute.
2	Users with at least the **Modify User Attributes** right can modify the attribute.
3	Users with at least the **Modify Permissions** right can modify the attribute.

Description Property

The Description property determines the name of the attribute or class as used by the LDAP protocol. In fact, in the schema documentation (see About the Directory Schema, Directory Schema Contents, and Obtaining Attribute Information), the Description property is referred to as "LDAPName."

If you are using the Administrator program to view the attributes in the schema, you see the Description property displayed under the name "Description."

For example, the schema documentation for the Address-Home attribute shows that this attribute's LDAPName is homePostalAddress. If you use the Administrator program (in raw mode) to view the tab for the Address-Home attribute, you see the value homePostalAddress by clicking **Description** in the **Object attributes** box.

Caution   Changing the LDAPName of an attribute can cause interoperability problems. However, reading the value of the LDAPName can be useful for an application that, for example, uses LDAP to present a directory-style compendium of information. In this case, it must know the LDAPNames of attributes to be able to read them and respond to queries for user data.

Object Classes Used for ADSI Support

The following four object classes are used frequently when working with ADSI. To see a table explaining more about each class and its attributes, click the class name.

- Mail-Recipient (person) Object Class
- Mailbox (organizationalPerson) Object Class
- Custom-Recipient (custom-recipient) Object Class
- Distribution-List (groupOfNames) Object Class

The columns in the tables in the following topics should be interpreted as follows:

Attribute	Description
LDAPName	Name of the attribute as used by LDAP; matches the "Description" of the attribute in the Exchange schema (see "Description Property" later in this chapter).
Exchange name	Name of the attribute in the Exchange directory schema
Mandatory	Whether the attribute must be present on the object
Heuristics	Heuristics of the attribute as described in Heuristics Property
ACL	Access category of the attribute as described in ACL Property
Syntax	Syntax of the attribute. Values for Syntax can include the following:
	Boolean: Value of TRUE or FALSE
	Integer: Any integer value
	String(Unicode): A Unicode string
	String(Numeric): A numeric string
	String(Octet): A binary string (according to LDAP, binary attributes supported using the string encoding of their binary representation)
	Object(DS-DN): A distinguished name (DN) in rfc1779 format; for example: cn=jsmith,ou=redmond,o=microsoft,c=us
Comment	A comment on the attribute

Mail-Recipient (person) Object Class

The Mail-Recipient object class is exposed through LDAP as the "person" object class. This class is inherited by all object classes to which mail can be sent, such as mailbox, custom-recipient, distribution-list, and public-folder.

This object class is *abstract*, defined only so that other object classes in the directory can inherit its attributes. You cannot create an instance of this object class; rather, you can create instances of the classes that inherit from it.

Mail-Recipient (person) Attributes

The following table describes many of the commonly used attributes present on the person object class.

LDAPName	Microsoft Exchange name	Man-datory	Heur-istics	ACL	Syntax	Comment
rdn	Common-Name	Y	2	1	String (Teletex)	Common name (RDN of this object)
cn	Display-Name	N	2	1	String (Unicode)	String displayed by the address book
language	Language-ISO639	N	3	2	String (Unicode)	ISO639 language
LabeledURI	LabeledURI	N	5	2	String (Unicode)	Uniform Resource Locator (URL) specifying default HTML Web page
Voice-Mail-Recorded-Name	Voice-Mail-Recorded-Name	N	13	2	String (Octet)	Voice mail user's spoken name
Voice-Mail-Password	Voice-Mail-Password	N	13	2	String (Unicode)	DTMF digits representing user account security code
Voice-Mail-Greetings	Voice-Mail-Greetings	N	13	2	String (Unicode)	Voice mail user's recorded greeting(s)
Voice-Mail-User-ID	Voice-Mail-User-ID	N	13	2	String (Unicode)	DTMF digits representing a user account (for example, a phone extension)
MAPI-Recipient	MAPI-Recipient	N	18	1	Boolean	Indicates to a gateway whether it is a messaging application programming interface (MAPI) recipient (True=yes, False=no)
mail, rfc822-Mailbox, OtherMailbox, textEncoded-ORAddress	Proxy Addresses	N	18	1	String (Teletex)	List of foreign mail system addresses for this recipient; exposed as follows: Primary SMTP address: mail (rfc822Mailbox) Primary X.400 address: textEncodedORAddress; Other addresses: otherMailbox
name	Display-Name-Printable	N	18	1	String (Printable)	Printable string version of the Display-Name

(continued)

LDAPName	Microsoft Exchange name	Man-datory	Heur-istics	ACL	Syntax	Comment
uid	Mail-nickname	N	18	1	String (Unicode)	Mail Nickname
info	Comment	N	18	2	String (Unicode)	This recipient's comment in the Microsoft Exchange Server Address Book
url	WWW-Home-Page	N	18	2	String (Unicode)	WWW home page associated with this entry
userCertificate	X509-Cert	N	18	2	String (Octet)	X.509 v3 certificate(s) of the user
Extension-Attribute-9	Extension-Attribute-9	N	20	1	String (Unicode)	General extension attribute for customer use
Extension-Attribute-1	Extension-Attribute-1	N	20	1	String (Unicode)	General extension attribute for customer use
Extension-Attribute-10	Extension-Attribute-10	N	20	1	String (Unicode)	General extension attribute for customer use
Extension-Attribute-2	Extension-Attribute-2	N	20	1	String (Unicode)	General extension attribute for customer use
Extension-Attribute-3	Extension-Attribute-3	N	20	1	String (Unicode)	General extension attribute for customer use
Extension-Attribute-4	Extension-Attribute-4	N	20	1	String (Unicode)	General extension attribute for customer use
Extension-Attribute-5	Extension-Attribute-5	N	20	1	String (Unicode)	General extension attribute for customer use
Extension-Attribute-6	Extension-Attribute-6	N	20	1	String (Unicode)	General extension attribute for customer use
Extension-Attribute-7	Extension-Attribute-7	N	20	1	String (Unicode)	General extension attribute for customer use
Extension-Attribute-8	Extension-Attribute-8	N	20	1	String (Unicode)	General extension attribute for customer use
Extension-Attribute-15	Extension-Attribute-15	N	21	1	String (Unicode)	General extension attribute for customer use
Extension-Attribute-11	Extension-Attribute-11	N	21	1	String (Unicode)	General extension attribute for customer use
Extension-Attribute-12	Extension-Attribute-12	N	21	1	String (Unicode)	General extension attribute for customer use
Extension-Attribute-14	Extension-Attribute-14	N	21	1	String (Unicode)	General extension attribute for customer use
Extension-Attribute-13	Extension-Attribute-13	N	21	1	String (Unicode)	General extension attribute for customer use

Mailbox (organizationalPerson) Object Class

The Mailbox object class is exposed through LDAP as the "organizationalPerson" object class. This class represents an object that contains mail storage in the Microsoft Exchange Server system. One critical attribute on a Mailbox object is Assoc-NT-Account, which contains the security identifier (SID) of the Windows NT account that has access to the mailbox.

Mailbox (organizationalPerson) Attributes

The following table describes many of the commonly used attributes present on the organizationalPerson object class.

LDAPName	Microsoft Exchange name	Man- datory	Heur- istics	ACL	Syntax	Comment
mailPreference Option	Delivery- Mechanism	Y	4	1	Integer	Mechanism by which this mailbox receives mail (should be set to zero)
personalTitle	Personal- Title	N	3	2	String- (Unicode)	Personal title (such as Mr. or Mrs.)
Assoc-NT- Account	Assoc-NT- Account	N	12	1	String- (Octet)	Primary Windows NT account associated with this mailbox
street	Street- Address	N	12	1	String- (Unicode)	Physical street address
generation- Qualifier	Generation- Qualifier	N	13	1	String- (Unicode)	Generation qualifier, such as Sr., Jr., IV
houseIdentifier	House- Identifier	N	13	1	String- (Unicode)	Building within a location
Company	Company	N	18	1	String- (Unicode)	Company of the mailbox owner
department	Department	N	18	1	String- (Unicode)	"Department" of this recipient
givenName	Given- Name	N	18	1	String- (Unicode)	First name (given name) of the mailbox owner
international- ISDNNumber	Internationa l-ISDN- Number	N	18	1	String- (Numeric)	ISDN number associated with the mailbox
manager	Manager	N	18	1	Object(DS -DN)	"Manager" of this recipient
physicalDeliv- eryOfficeName	Office	N	18	1	String- (Unicode)	(for example, "1/1061")

(continued)

LDAPName	Microsoft Exchange name	Man-datory	Heur-istics	ACL	Syntax	Comment
sn	Last Name	N	18	1	String-(Unicode)	Last name (surname) of the mailbox owner
st	State-Or-Province-Name	N	18	1	String-(Unicode)	State or province in which the user is located
teletexTerminalIdentifier	Teletex-Terminal-Identifier	N	18	1	String-(Octet)	
title	Title	N	18	1	String-(Unicode)	Business title of the mailbox owner
x121Address	X121-Address	N	18	1	String-(Numeric)	
	Telephone-Office2	N	18	2	String-(Unicode)	Office phone number (2) of the mailbox owner
co	Text-Country	N	18	2	String-(Unicode)	Country in which the user is located
facsimileTele-phoneNumber	Telephone-Fax	N	18	2	String-(Unicode)	Fax phone number of the mailbox owner
homephone	Home phone number	N	18	2	String-(Unicode)	Home phone number of the mailbox owner
initials	Initials	N	18	2	String-(Unicode)	User's initials
l	City	N	18	2	String-(Unicode)	Location/city of the user
mobile	Mobile number	N	18	2	String-(Unicode)	Cellular phone number of the mailbox owner
pager	Pager number	N	18	2	String-(Unicode)	Pager phone number of the mailbox owner
postalAddress	Address	N	18	2	String-(Unicode)	Street address of the mailbox owner
postalCode	Postal code	N	18	2	String-(Unicode)	Postal/zip code
secretary	Assistant	N	18	2	String-(Unicode)	Mailbox assistant display name

(continued)

LDAPName	Microsoft Exchange name	Mandatory	Heuristics	ACL	Syntax	Comment
telephone-Number	Phone number	N	18	2	String-(Unicode)	Office phone number (1) of the mailbox owner
telexNumber	Telex-Number	N	18	2	String-(Octet)	
employee-Number	Employee-Number	N	21	1	String-(Unicode)	Employee number
employeeType	Employee-Type	N	21	1	String-(Unicode)	Type of employee
homeFax	Telephone-Home-Fax	N	21	2	String-(Unicode)	Home fax number
homePostal-Address	Address-Home	N	21	2	String-(Unicode)	Home address
personalMobile	Telephone-Personal-Mobile	N	21	2	String-(Unicode)	Personal mobile number
personalPager	Telephone-Personal-Pager	N	21	2	String-(Unicode)	Personal pager number

Custom-Recipient (custom-recipient) Object Class

The Custom-Recipient object class is exposed through LDAP as the "custom-recipient" object class.

Custom-Recipient (custom-recipient) Attributes

This object class contains all the attributes of the organizationalPerson object class with the exception of mailPreferenceOption.

This class also contains an additional mandatory attribute with the following properties.

LDAPName	Microsoft Exchange name	Mandatory	Heuristics	ACL	Syntax	Comment
Target Address	E-Mail Address	Y	18	1	String-(Unicode)	Actual address of the recipient in the format: <address Type>:<value> (for example, SMTP:jsmith@org.com)

Distribution-List (groupOfNames) Object Class

The Distribution-List object class is exposed through LDAP as the "groupOfNames" object class.

Distribution-List (groupOfNames) Attributes

The following table describes many of the commonly used attributes present on the groupOfNames object class.

LDAPName	Microsoft Exchange name	Man- datory	Heur- istics	ACL	Syntax	Comment
Company	Company	N	18	1	String- (Unicode)	Used mainly for address-book view grouping
department	Department	N	18	1	String- (Unicode)	Used mainly for address-book view grouping
PhysicalDeliv- eryOfficeName	office	N	18	1	String- (Unicode)	Used mainly for address-book view grouping
st	State-Or- Province- Name	N	18	1	String- (Unicode)	Used mainly for address-book view grouping
title	Title	N	18	1	String- (Unicode)	Used mainly for address-book view grouping
co	Text-Country	N	18	2	String- (Unicode)	Used mainly for address-book view grouping
l	City	N	18	2	String- (Unicode)	Used mainly for address-book view grouping
Hide-DL- Membership	Hide-DL- Membership	N	20	1	Boolean	Indicates if the membership should be hidden from the client (default is FALSE)
owner	Owner	N	20	1	Object (DS-DN)	Distinguished name (DN) of the mailbox that "owns" this distribution list
member	Members	N	20	2	Object (OR-Name)	List of DNs that are members of the distribution list

Retrieving Incremental Changes through ADSI

Certain applications, such as a directory synchronization service, need to retrieve incremental changes from the Exchange directory. This is done through the use of the following operational attributes, which exist on every object in the Exchange directory.

Attribute	Description
USN-Changed	Integer incremented by the Exchange directory every time a modification is made to an object (deletions treated as any other modification to the object)
USN-Created	Integer that represents when an object was created in the Exchange directory
When-Changed	UTC time when the object was changed
When-Created	UTC time when the object was created

By keeping track of the USN-Changed/USN-Created or When-Changed/When-Created attribute pairs, an application can identify changes that have occurred in the Exchange directory since the last time it polled for changes. For more information on using these attributes to track changes, see "Selecting Objects to Export and BatchExport."

By default, these attributes are available to authenticated users but not to anonymous users.

Retrieving Deleted Objects through ADSI

Just as important as retrieving incremental changes from the Exchange directory is the ability to retrieve deleted objects. You can do this by binding using clear text authentication with ",cn=admin" appended to the user's DN (for example, dc=domain,cn=jsmith,cn = admin). For information about clear text authentication, see the online Help for the Administrator program.

After a client is authenticated by the Exchange directory with ",cn=admin" in the user's DN, it can query for an operational attribute called "is-deleted." This is a Boolean attribute that indicates whether the object has been deleted.

A deleted object is referred to as a tombstone. Tombstones exist for a period of time indicated by the Tombstone lifetime parameter on the **DS Site Configuration** tab in the Administrator program. By default, the Tombstone lifetime is set to 30 days. If your application must remove deletions from the Microsoft Exchange Server directory, make sure that it runs within the Tombstone lifetime period.

Limitations of ADSI

This release (version 2.0) of ADSI cannot manipulate Windows NT version 4.0 Access Control Lists (ACLs), which contain security information about the permissions users have for objects. This release also cannot get the Windows NT security identifier (SID), the binary representation of a user's account name, and thus ADSI cannot set the bits necessary to create users' rights.

This means that developers cannot create a functional **Mailbox** object with ADSI alone, because a **Mailbox** object requires the Windows NT account SID in the Assoc-NT-Account attribute as well as the correct security rights on the **Mailbox** object in the NT-Security-Descriptor attribute. The capability to manipulate ACLs is expected in a future release of ADSI.

For More Information

You can visit the following Web sites for more information:

- For Internet drafts, including the LDAPv3-protocol
  ftp://ds.internic.net/internet-drafts

- For ADSI and Windows NT version 5.0 Active Directory
  http://www.microsoft.com/ntserver/

- For information on Microsoft Exchange Server 5.5
  http://www.microsoft.com/exchange/

- For a complete collection of Microsoft technology for developers
  http://www.microsoft.com/msdn/

ADSI and ADO Samples

The following ADSI samples demonstrate authentication against the Exchange directory, searching for objects using ADO, and manipulation of objects using ADSI.

Distribution List Manager

This sample creates a distribution list and populates it with the users found with an ADO query as follows:

- Determines the domain address extension by looking at the mail property of the Microsoft Private MDB object.

- Uses the **OpenDSObject** method to access directory objects, passing the user's logon domain, name, and password as parameters.

- Builds SMTP, MSMAIL, CCMAIL, and X.400 addresses.

- Creates the distribution list.

- Converts data into string values (using the CStr function) to properly format the data for ADSI.
- Creates a multi-valued property.
- Locates a mailbox in the Exchange directory whose City property matches the search criteria.

Distribution List Manager Sample Code

```
'The following code creates a distribution list and populates it with
' the users found using an ADO query:

Option Explicit
Dim strDisplayName      ' DL's Display name
Dim strAliasName        ' DL's Alias name
Dim strDirectoryName    ' DL's Directory name
Dim strUserName         ' User's logon name and domain
Dim strPassword         ' User's domain password
Dim strServer           ' Microsoft Exchange server name
Dim strOrganization     ' Microsoft Exchange Organization
Dim strSite             ' Microsoft Exchange Site
Dim strRecipientsPath   ' ADsPath to the Recipients Container
Dim strMSPrivMDBPath    ' ADsPath to the MS Private MDB
Dim objRecipients       ' Recipients Container object
Dim objMSPrivMDB        ' MS Private MDB object
Dim objNewDL            ' new distribution list object
Dim strMail             ' mail address of the MS Private MDB object
Dim intPos              ' numeric position of the '@' in an SMTP address
Dim strSMTPExt          ' SMTP domain type (ie.com, org, etc...)
Dim strSMTPAddr         ' new DL's SMTP address
Dim aOtherMailbox(1)    ' other addresses created (ie. MSMail, CCMail)
Dim strx400Addr         ' new DL's X400 address
Dim objMyIADs           ' ADSI object
' used by the PutEx method to set a muti-valued property
Const ADS_PROPERTY_UPDATE = 2
strDisplayName = "BellevueDL"
strAliasName = "BellevueDL"
strDirectoryName = "BellevueDL"
strUserName = "dc=redmond, cn=v-sparke"
strPassword = "password"
strServer = "sparker1"
strOrganization = "16"
strSite = "3081"
Set objMyIADs = GetObject("LDAP:")


' The following code determines the domain address extension by
' looking at the mail property of the Microsoft Private MDB object
' (seen as Private Information Store in the Microsoft Exchange Server
administrator program).
```

```
strMSPrivMDBPath = "LDAP://" + strServer + "/cn=Microsoft Private
MDB,cn=" + strServer + ",cn=Servers ,cn=Configuration,ou=" + strSite +
",o=" + strOrganization


' The following application uses the OpenDSObject method to access
' directory objects. The user's logon domain, name, and password are
' passed as parameters. The value of 0 in the first statement means
' that the ADSI LDAP provider will do a simple bind:

Set objMSPrivMDB = objMyIADs.OpenDSObject(strMSPrivMDBPath, strUserName,
strPassword, 0)
objMSPrivMDB.GetInfo
strMail = objMSPrivMDB.Get("mail")
intPos = InStr(strMail, "@")
strSMTPExt = Mid(strMail, intPos, Len(strMail))


' The following code builds SMTP, MSMAIL, CCMAIL, and X.400 addresses.
' The country identifier 'US' is hardcoded into the X.400 address. You
' can parse the textEncodedORaddress property of the Microsoft Private
' MDB object to determine the correct X.400 addressing scheme:

strSMTPAddr = replace(strAliasName, " ", "") + strSMTPExt
aOtherMailbox(0) = CStr("MS$" + strOrganization + "/" + strSite + "/" +
strAliasName)
aOtherMailbox(1) = CStr("CCMAIL$" + strAliasName + " at " + strSite)
strx400Addr = "c=US;a= ;p=" + strOrganization + ";o=" + strSite + ";s="
+ strAliasName + ";"
strRecipientsPath = "LDAP://" + strServer + "/cn=Recipients,ou=" +
strSite + ",o=" + strOrganization
Set objRecipients = objMyIADs.OpenDSObject(strRecipientsPath,
strUserName, strPassword, 0)


' The following code creates the distribution list:
' Set objNewDL = objRecipients.Create("groupOfNames", "cn=" +
' strDirectoryName)


' In VBScript, it is necessary to convert data into string values
' (using the CStr function) to properly format the data for ADSI:

objNewDL.Put "cn", CStr(strDisplayName)
objNewDL.Put "uid", CStr(strAliasName)
objNewDL.Put "distinguishedName", CStr("cn=" + strAliasName +
",cn=Recipients,ou=" + strSite + ",o=" + strOrganization)
objNewDL.Put "mail", CStr(strSMTPAddr)


' The following code creates a multi-valued property. In VBScript, you
' have to de-reference the array by using parentheses:
```

```
objNewDL.PutEx ADS_PROPERTY_UPDATE, "otherMailbox", (aOtherMailbox)
objNewDL.Put "Report-To-Originator", True
objNewDL.Put "Report-to-Owner", False
objNewDL.Put "Replication-Sensitivity", CInt(20)
objNewDL.Put "rfc822Mailbox", CStr(strSMTPAddr)
objNewDL.Put "textEncodedORaddress", CStr(strx400Addr)
objNewDL.SetInfo
Response.Write "DL Created Successfully!<BR><BR>"

' The following code locates a mailbox in the Microsoft Exchange
' directory whose City property matches the search criteria. The ADSI
' LDAP name for the City property is 'l.'

Dim objADOconn              ' ADO connection object
Dim strADOQueryString      ' ADO query string
Dim objRS                  ' recordset object
Dim strCriteria            ' value used to search the directory tree
strCriteria = "Bellevue"
Set objADOconn = CreateObject("ADODB.Connection")
objADOconn.Provider = "ADSDSOobject"
objADOconn.Open "ADs Provider"
strADOQueryString = "<LDAP://" + strServer +
">;(&(objectClass=organizationalPerson)(l=" + strCriteria +
"));cn,adspath;subtree"
Set objRS = objADOconn.Execute(strADOQueryString)
If Not objRS.EOF Then
  While Not objRS.EOF
    objNewDL.Add objRS.Fields(1).Value
    Response.Write objRS.Fields(0) + " added :)<BR>"
    objRS.MoveNext
  Wend
Else
  Response.Write "No mailboxes were added to the DL : <BR>"
End If
objRS.Close
```

Phone List

This sample contains sections of code that perform the following tasks:

- Modify the Phone Number property of a mailbox.

- Cause the browser to display a user identification dialog box.

- Modify the property of an object that contains a string value. If the property does not exist on the object, an error is generated.

Phone List Sample Code

```
' This code modifies the Phone number property of a mailbox. By
' default, all users have access to modify this property on their own
' mailbox.
' This following code will cause the browser to display a user
identification
' dialog. The IIS server's password authentication must be set to
' Allow Anonymous and Basic (Clear Text) only. This way, the browser
' will be able to use the correct security context when using the
' GetObject method.

Dim strAT ' Authorization Type information
strAT = Request.ServerVariables("AUTH_TYPE")
If InStr(1, "_BasicNTLM", strAT, 1) < 2 Then
  Response.Buffer = True
  Response.Status = ("401 Unauthorized")
  Response.End
End If
Dim strMailboxPath          ' ADsPath to the user's mailbox
Dim strServer               ' name of the Microsoft Exchange 5.5 server
Dim intPosPrefix            ' numeric index used used to build ADsPath to
                            ' schema object
Dim intPosSuffix            ' numeric index used used to build ADsPath to
                            ' schema object
Dim strPrefix               ' prefix string used to build ADsPath to
                            ' schema object
Dim strSuffix               ' suffix string used to build ADsPath to
                            ' schema object
Dim strPathToSchemaObject ' ADsPath to the schema object
Dim objMailbox              ' mailbox object
Dim strNewPoneNumber        ' value of the new phone number
Function isUserEditable(strSchemaObjectPath)
  Dim objSchemaObject       ' schema object
  Dim intValue              ' value of the 'Access-Category' property
  Set objSchemaObject = GetObject(strSchemaObjectPath)
  intValue = objSchemaObject.Get("Access-Category")
  If intValue = 2 Then      ' user may modify the mailbox property
    isUserEditable = True
  Else                      ' the value was 0, 1, or 3
    isUserEditable = False
  End If
End Function

' The following procedure modifies the property of an object that
' contains a string value. To set a property to the empty string,
' you must remove it from the object:
```

```
Sub ModifyProperty(strNewValue, strADsProperty)
  On Error Resume Next
  If Len(strNewValue) <> 0 Then
    objMailbox.Put strADsProperty, CStr(strNewValue)
  Else  ' The new value is empty
    objIADs.Get (strADsProperty)

' If the property doesn't exist on the object, an error will be
' generated:

    If Err.Number = 0 Then
' the property exists on the object and must be removed
      objMailbox.PutEx ADS_PROPERTY_CLEAR, strADsProperty, CStr(" ")
    End If
    Err.Clear
  End If
End Sub
Const ADS_PROPERTY_CLEAR = 1

' used by the PutEx method to clear a property from an object
strMailboxPath = "LDAP://SPARKER1/cn=SParker,cn=Recipients,ou=3081,o=16"
strServer = "sparker1"
strNewPoneNumber = "(425) 882-8080 x 13882"
intPosPrefix = InStr(strMailboxPath, "/cn")
intPosSuffix = InStr(strMailboxPath, "ou")
strPrefix = Mid(strMailboxPath, 1, intPosPrefix - 1) + "/cn="
strSuffix = ",cn=Microsoft DMD," + Mid(strMailboxPath, intPosSuffix,
Len(strMailboxPath))
strPathToSchemaObject = strPrefix + "Telephone-Office1" + strSuffix
If isUserEditable(strPathToSchemaObject) Then
  Set objMailbox = GetObject(strMailboxPath)
  ModifyProperty strNewPhoneNumber, "telephoneNumber"
  objMailbox.SetInfo  ' save the object information
  Response.Write "Phone number modified successfully : <BR>"
Else
  Response.Write "You don't have permissions to modify your phone
..'number : <BR>"
End If
%>
```

PART 14

Microsoft Exchange Connector for Lotus cc:Mail

Microsoft Exchange Server provides built-in connectivity to foreign messaging systems including X.400, Simple Mail Transfer Protocol (SMTP), Microsoft Mail, and Lotus cc:Mail. The Microsoft Exchange Connector for Lotus cc:Mail provides messaging connectivity and directory synchronization between Exchange and cc:Mail messaging systems. This facilitates migration from cc:Mail messaging systems to Exchange and provides for seamless coexistence between the two environments.

For more information, the Connector for cc:Mail, refer to *Microsoft About Exchange Server Operations*.

Performance Criteria

The following items are performance criteria that indicate when the Connector for cc:Mail is operating at its peak.

- Delivery time should be similar to or better than end-to-end delivery time within the native messaging environment.

- Directory entries should be maintained in the native messaging system format. Users of cc:Mail should see users of Exchange in the directory as if they also used cc:Mail.

Using the Microsoft Windows NT Performance Monitor

Microsoft Windows NT Performance Monitor allows system administrators to see how well a server is handling its load. Data is written to log files and to the screen, and monitoring can take place from a remote Microsoft Windows NT Server computer. You can configure alerts to run a program automatically, so that when a specified threshold is reached.

Viewing Percent Processor Time Connector for cc:Mail

1. In Performance Monitor, expand **Add Counter**.

2. Select the **Process** object. In the **Counter** list, verify that **% processor time** is selected. Select **CCMC** in the **Instance** list.

This will show the percentage of elapsed time that all of the threads of the CCMC process used to carry out their instructions.

Adding the MSExchange CCMC Object

In the **Add to Chart** dialog box, select the **MSExchange CCMC** object. The following counters can be set for this object.

Name	Explanation
DirSynch to cc:Mail	Number of directory updates sent to cc:Mail since the last directory synchronization (dirsync) started
DirSynch to Exchange	Number of directory updates sent to Exchange since the last dirsync started
Exchange MTS-IN	Messages awaiting delivery in the Exchange IN queue
Exchange MTS-OUT	Messages awaiting delivery in the Exchange OUT queue.
Messages sent to cc:Mail	Number of messages sent to cc:Mail
Messages sent to cc:Mail/hr	Number of messages sent to cc:Mail per hour
Messages sent to Exchange	Number of messages sent to Exchange
Messages sent to Exchange/hr	Number of messages sent to Exchange per hour
NDRs to cc:Mail	Number of non-delivery reports (NDRs) sent to cc:Mail
NDRs to Exchange	Number of NDRs sent to Exchange

Recommended Configuration

The following section describes recommendations for configuring and implementing the Connector for cc:Mail.

Configure directory synchronization The directory synchronization component of the Connector for cc:Mail allows Exchange and cc:Mail directories to be synchronized, which greatly reduces the directory administration burden. When directory synchronization is configured, cc:Mail addresses appear in the Exchange global address list and appear as custom recipients. Exchange addresses are exported into the cc:Mail messaging system and appear as if they were native cc:Mail addresses. In the cc:Mail system, Exchange sites appear as if they were cc:Mail post offices.

Although automatic directory exchange (ADE) is not supported, the Connector for cc:Mail exports Exchange addresses using the cc:Mail **Prop** option. If the post office directly attached to cc:Mail is configured to propagate addresses through cc:Mail ADE, the Exchange addresses are repaginated throughout the cc:Mail environment based on the ADE configuration within cc:Mail.

Locate cc:Mail addresses in a separate Recipients container When configuring directory synchronization, a Recipients container must be selected to designate the location for importing cc:Mail directory entries. For ease of management, configure a separate container in which to import cc:Mail users. Note that cc:Mail users will be displayed in the Microsoft Exchange global address list regardless of which container they are imported into.

Install cc:Mail address generator in nonconnector sites Each directory entry in Exchange receives proxy addresses by default, including Microsoft Mail, SMTP, and X.400 addresses. The Connector for cc:Mail automatically installs a cc:Mail e-mail address generator in the site in which it resides. The cc:Mail address generator creates a CCMAIL address type (username at site proxy) for every recipient in the site. These are the addresses that are sent to the cc:Mail environment during directory synchronization. The cc:Mail e-mail address generator must be installed on every Exchange site that communicates with cc:Mail. A separate mode for cc:Mail e-mail address generator setup is used for Exchange sites that do not have the Connector for cc:Mail installed. Note that Microsoft Exchange Server version 4.0 sites must have at least one Microsoft Exchange Server version 5.0 to have cc:Mail proxy addresses generated for users in that site.

Standardize Microsoft Exchange directory proxy address format When using the Connector for cc:Mail, you can customize Exchange address formats to export Exchange addresses into the cc:Mail environment. Be sure to configure the address export format so it is consistent with the existing cc:Mail environment standards to minimize impact on cc:Mail users during coexistence and migration. The cc:Mail proxy addresses can be customized by using the **Site Addressing** property page in the Exchange Administrator program.

Enable message tracking The Connector for cc:Mail supports the message-tracking feature, allowing administrators to track messages that have been submitted to the Connector for cc:Mail for delivery. This is useful in troubleshooting.

Use multiple connectors for load balancing and redundancy   In many cases, a single Microsoft Exchange Server and Connector for cc:Mail can be used to connect Exchange and cc:Mail messaging systems. For redundancy and load balancing, multiple Connectors for cc:Mail and cc:Mail hub post offices can be configured. However, multiple Connectors for cc:Mail cannot be installed on the same Exchange server. Within Exchange, equal costs and address space can be used to configure load balancing for Exchange mail destined to the cc:Mail messaging environment. Mail flowing to the Exchange environment from cc:Mail can be balanced by strategically defining the route to the Exchange sites from within the cc:Mail directory. For example, three cc:Mail hub post offices can each be configured for a direct connection to an Exchange site by defining the site as a directly attached post office ("P") in the cc:Mail directory. Then three cc:Mail connectors can be configured, one connecting to each of the cc:Mail hub post offices.

Optimize Microsoft Exchange Server for connector configuration   It is important that Microsoft Exchange Server computers, on which Connectors for cc:Mail (or any other connector) reside are tuned properly. Use the Exchange Performance Optimizer and select **Connector/Directory Import** to ensure proper system tuning to support the Connector for cc:Mail. In fact, prior to a large directory synchronization or import process, it is recommended that the Exchange Server computer running the Connector for cc:Mail is tuned as a Connector/Directory Import computer only. This will increase the directory import performance several times. Be sure to tune the computer back to the desired production settings after the import using the Performance Optimizer.

Avoid setting directory synchronization schedule to always   When configuring the directory synchronization schedule, a setting of **Always** can often cause unnecessary processing to take place on the Exchange Server computer. This setting means that the directory synchronization process will occur every 15 minutes. The Connector for cc:Mail uses the cc:Mail import.exe and export.exe programs. When directory synchronization occurs, the entire cc:Mail directory is exported from the cc:Mail post office and then parsed. If synchronization is required, a button is available on the Connector for cc:Mail **Import** property page to request a directory synchronization cycle immediately. If you are viewing the schedule page by the hour and select a given hour, directory synchronization will occur four times during that hour. When scheduling is based on selected times, it is best to view the page in 15-minute intervals.

Avoid using the same name for a Microsoft Exchange Server site as existing cc:Mail post offices For message routing to work from cc:Mail to Microsoft Exchange, the Exchange Server site name (by default) must be defined in each cc:Mail post office directory in the cc:Mail environment. If a cc:Mail post office exists with the same name as the Exchange site, then you must use the **Site Addressing** property page in the Exchange Administrator program to change the name of the default proxy addresses for Exchange users. Then, define the Exchange site using this customized proxy name. By default, proxy addresses are generated by using User at SITE.

PART 15

Setting Up a Successful Messaging Operations System

This chapter discusses guidelines for establishing a messaging operations group within an organization, including functions, staff, and utilities for achieving successful messaging operations. These guidelines are based on Microsoft's internal messaging system, which is perhaps one of the more complex and most heavily used in the world. By understanding best practices used by this complex system, you will be better equipped to set up efficient messaging operations of your own.

Messaging Operations

This section discusses basic guidelines for efficient messaging operations, including the following:

- Departmental staff
- Monitoring
- Metrics

Departmental Staff

A typical messaging services department begins at the director level. The number and type of staff that report to the director varies widely according to the size of the organization's messaging system and the number of users. The following example discusses an organization that consists of 45,000 users.

- The organization uses a single messaging platform, Microsoft Exchange Server.

- A typical department supporting an organization of this size has a director of messaging operations. Reporting to this director are a manager of messaging operations and a manager of messaging system engineering. Reporting to the manager of messaging operations are a number of messaging operations technicians, and possibly a supervisor of network accounts.

- The messaging operations group should handle the day-to-day maintenance of the Microsoft Exchange Server messaging system. These tasks include monitoring, troubleshooting, and logging problems and procedures with the system. In some organizations, the network accounts management is in the network infrastructure department. The infrastructure department usually handles Microsoft Windows NT account management. In these cases, it is important that the message services and infrastructure departments work together to determine such issues as how Microsoft Exchange Server mailboxes are created.

- The messaging system engineering group should handle the more complex problems in the system escalation from messaging operations. The engineering team should also have adequate staff to handle the evaluation, measurement, and planning of future technologies. The engineering team should also concern themselves with performance measurement and enhancement.

For Microsoft's 45,000-user messaging system, monitored continuously (24 hours a day, 7 days a week), the messaging services department would most likely be staffed as in the following illustration.

Director (1)			
Manager, Messaging Operations (1)		**Manager, Messaging System Engineering (1)**	
Sr. Operations Analyst (2)	Operations Analyst (3)	Sr. Operations Engineer (2)	Operations Engineer (2)
Assoc. Operations Analyst (0-1)	Technicians (17)	Assoc. Operations Engineer (0-1)	

Note that the key to a successful messaging services department is attracting and keeping good people at the Operations Analyst, Senior Operations Analyst, Operations Engineer, and Senior Operations Engineer positions. It's important to have people at those job levels who know your company's network, business, and political infrastructure. A high rate of turnover or attrition in these positions means you must spend more time training new staff and less time improving your messaging system.

The following are job descriptions of positions in the messaging operations department.

Director Provides messaging technology vision based on inputs of technology capabilities and business need. Coordinates activities of messaging operations and messaging system engineering. Represents all aspects of the organization's messaging system to internal and external sources.

Manager, Messaging Operations Ensures that the messaging system is functioning at peak performance and that, in case the system is not functioning at peak performance, the messaging operations team knows before anyone else is affected. Makes sure that all messaging operations technicians and operations analysts have the tools they need. Represents messaging operations to users.

Manager, Messaging System Engineering Drives the team towards constant analysis and design with the goal of improving the messaging system's performance. Makes sure that his or her team has the necessary tools and training. Takes on the responsibility of escalation from operations.

Associate Operations Analyst Installs, configures, and documents new production servers in the messaging environment. Performs basic troubleshooting of messaging system problems.

Operations Analyst Installs, configures, and documents new production servers in the messaging environment. Performs all troubleshooting of messaging system problems. Ensures that problems are properly documented in the daily log.

Senior Operations Analyst Assists with mentoring new Operations Analysts, performs duties of the Operations Analyst when required. Escalates issues not resolved by Operations Analyst and Technicians. Ensures that the daily log remains a useful record of system troubleshooting information.

Associate Operations Engineer Takes input from operations and performs basic analysis and design. Brings ideas and recommendations to other members of the engineering team for discussion.

Operations Engineer Takes input from operations and performs detailed analysis and design. Handles initial escalations from operations. Troubleshoots and follows-up on all escalations received from operations. Evaluates features of released product for usability in the messaging system.

Senior Operations Engineer Evaluates released and unreleased messaging systems. Provides detailed test plans for features to be implemented. Attempts to minimize all impact of next generation releases of messaging products. Handles extreme escalations and interfaces with Microsoft Technical Support, if necessary.

Messaging Operations Technician Handles day-to-day monitoring and reporting on the messaging system. Ensures that events are properly recorded in the daily log. Ensures that all events that transpired during his or her shift have been duly recorded and reported to appropriate personnel. Also handles escalation requests from standard PC Help desk department.

Monitoring

The following section discusses basic guidelines for monitoring your messaging system.

When to Watch

Most messaging operations for a global organization must be watched 24 hours a day, 7 days a week. National organizations may be able to scale back the number of shifts or provide skeleton shifts for off-hours monitoring. Some large, global companies may also choose a "follow the sun" approach to support and monitoring.

Location From Which to Watch

This question deals with the best location for a messaging services control center. Does the company distribute the control center function to geographic regions where language could be a barrier? Or does the company completely centralize the control center function and deal with the issues of cross-geographic differences? This question will differ from organization to organization and must be answered based on company culture and political climate.

How to Watch

There are a variety of methods for monitoring your system, including utilities available with Microsoft Exchange Server and Windows NT Server that can be used to build a monitoring system. Many third-party tools are also available that allow you to monitor messaging systems.

For large organizations, it is recommended that you set up a number of Windows NT Server computers. On these computers, configure several different Windows NT Performance Monitor instances, which are configured to display statistics for each of the objects and counters recommended for monitoring in "Microsoft Exchange Server Administration Procedures" later in this chapter. It is a good idea to use a large monitor with these computers because running many instances of Performance Monitor can quickly consume screen space. You don't need a powerful computer to do this job. You can configure a basic Windows NT Server computer for these tasks, which includes a single, high-speed processor, 64 to 128 MB of RAM, 2 to 4 GB of disk space (sometimes used for temporary storage of log traces).

The monitoring area described doesn't need to be large; it can be less than 225 square feet. Typically, there are two messaging operations technicians at this monitoring station. One of these technicians is responsible for dispatching in the event that a server console must be visited. The Performance Monitor instances should be configured with alerts at predefined thresholds such that the on-duty technicians are audibly and visually alerted when a threshold is surpassed. Do not rely on a warning system that is triggered simply by a person watching a set of screens.

What to Watch

Messaging operations involves making sure that messaging system users get their messages delivered within the stated service levels. Typically, the most critical area of monitoring is in the queue lengths on the message transfer agent (MTA) process computers. If there are problems in the system, they usually manifest in lengthy message queues. What you watch varies by the functions performed by the Microsoft Exchange Server computer in question. Typically, in a large organization, Microsoft Exchange Server computers take on specialized roles, such as the following:

- User mailbox server
- Public folder server
- Messaging hub
- Internet mail server

Acceptable Thresholds

Thresholds are those values for object counters monitored by Performance Monitor. Acceptable, as a definition, will vary by company. Normal system usage should be documented to establish a baseline prior to setting threshold values.

Who Watches

Staffing a messaging system monitoring area can be difficult. You need people who are motivated to learn more, but who are at the same time happy to perform routine tasks such as checking current system status. Look for individuals who have the ability to learn quickly, are flexible to shift work (for 24x7 monitoring), have the willingness to follow established procedures, have the ability to find improved methods of procedures, and have good communication skills. They should also have technical expertise with Windows NT Server, Microsoft Exchange Server architecture, and client applications.

Metrics

The following sections discuss guidelines for measuring performance.

What to Measure

Items to consider for measurement should be chosen for their contribution to development of trend data and performance tuning. Trend data becomes valuable for capacity planning. You should consider the following when planning your system:

- Number of mailboxes
- Number of distribution lists
- Number of messages delivered per time period by destination area (such as the Internet)
- Storage size by mailbox by department
- Top *n* senders
- Top *n* recipients
- Gateway and bridgehead traffic

How Often to Measure

While you can get as exact as you want to in metrics, be sure to not overburden your messaging system with systems that measure its performance.

Acceptable Service Levels

When setting acceptable service levels, you must first understand the infrastructure that supports the messaging system. Service levels in a company that has an ATM network everywhere will exceed those of companies that have many dial-up links.

The following is a typical service level statement: "Messages sent from one Exchange user to another Exchange user within our company's network will be delivered in *x* minutes or less."

Service level statements are important primarily for setting expectations in other areas of a company outside messaging operations. If a user sends a message, then that user should wait the *x* minutes stated in the service level for the message to be delivered to its destination prior to assuming there is a problem in the messaging system.

It is good practice to be conservative in stating service levels for messaging in a large organization. Allow your department at least to react to a problem in the system within the stated service level times. For example, assume your company's network consists of high bandwidth links that are rarely utilized above 35 percent. In this environment, Exchange systems can be designed and implemented to deliver messages almost instantaneously anywhere. Even with this type of performance, you should not issue a service level statement that states, "…messages will be delivered in less than 30 seconds." This timeframe does not allow you time to identify and react, in any way, to a problem. A better service level statement would be, "…messages will be delivered in 10 minutes or less." Messaging, for all its importance in today's organizations, rarely needs to be faster than that. Also, this amount of time allows your monitoring and systems staff to become aware of a problem and begin reacting to that problem. Don't set your service level time lower than the time it takes to see that there is a problem, notify someone, and let someone begin to resolve the problem.

Microsoft Exchange Server Administration Procedures

This section expands on the guidelines presented in the previous sections.

Monitoring

By monitoring Exchange, you can reduce the amount of manual checking that occurs. This section provides basic procedures for daily operations.

Monitoring is the daily task of ensuring that all critical Exchange services are running properly. The procedure is to check the performance of Exchange and established monitors on a regular basis and resolve any problems. When a problem cannot be resolved, it should be escalated to the next defined support level.

The messaging operations technician monitoring the system is responsible for handling the phones and logging entries into the messaging operations daily log system. If it is necessary to troubleshoot a computer, the technician on duty is responsible for dispatching another technician to handle the incident.

Frequency of Monitoring

Critical servers (mailbox, gateway, and bridgehead) should be checked every 10 to15 minutes. Other, less critical servers can be checked every 30 to 45 minutes.

Reporting Incidents

It is imperative that all incidents are documented. It is this documentation that builds and grows into a knowledge base of your organization's messaging system. With a well-documented knowledge base, messaging operations troubleshooting is often reduced to a simple query of your log system.

The on-duty technicians should keep written records of any interaction with the servers. The log should contain any pertinent details, messages, and observations.

Each day, the daily log report should be mailed to various messaging operations staff and management.

Methods of Monitoring

The following tables define Performance Monitor settings for each type of Microsoft Exchange Server computer in the organization.

Use the following configuration for a standard mailbox server. Configure the following chart settings: Update Interval is 120 seconds, Vertical Max is 100, and Chart Type is Histogram.

Object	Counter	Scale	Instance
MSExchangeMTA	Work Queue Length	1.0	N/A
Processor	%Processor Time	1.0	0 (,1,2,3 if multiprocessor)
Process	%Processor Time	1.0	MAD
Process	%Processor Time	1.0	DSAMAIN
Process	%Processor Time	1.0	STORE
Process	%Processor Time	1.0	EMSMTA

Use the following configuration for a server running the Internet Mail Service. Configure the following chart settings: Update Interval is 120 seconds, Vertical Max is 300, and Chart Type is Histogram.

Object	Counter	Scale	Instance
MSExchangeMTA	Work Queue Length	1.0	N/A
Processor	%Processor Time	1.0	0 (,1,2,3 if multiprocessor)
Process	%Processor Time	1.0	MAD
Process	%Processor Time	1.0	DSAMAIN
Process	%Processor Time	1.0	STORE
Process	%Processor Time	1.0	EMSMTA

(continued)

Object	Counter	Scale	Instance
Process	%Processor Time	1.0	MSEXCIMC
MSExchangeIMC	Queued Inbound	1.0	MSExchangeIMC
MSExchangeIMC	Queued Outbound	1.0	MSExchangeIMC
MSExchangeIMC	Queued MTS-IN	1.0	MSExchangeIMC
MSExchangeIMC	Queued MTS-OUT	1.0	MSExchangeIMC
MSExchangeMTA Connections	Queue Length	1.0	Internet Mail Service Server

Use the following configuration for a bridgehead server. Configure the following chart settings: Update Interval is 120 seconds, Vertical Max is 100, and Chart Type is Histogram.

Object	Counter	Scale	Instance
MSExchangeMTA	Work Queue Length	1.0	N/A

Expected Server Behavior

The following guidelines for Performance Monitor counters are taken from large, complex organization messaging system with more than 45,000 messaging system users. Note that these results can vary by a wide margin in different environments. Variables such as network infrastructure, messaging system user profiles (such as light, medium, or heavy users), and topology affects the outcome of the following counters.

MSExchangeMTA, Work Queue Length   The level should increase and decrease. An acceptable range would be 0–50. When messages are stuck in the queue, the counter will remain level, or only increase for extended periods of time. Watch for *artificial floors* on the MTA queue. Used here, artificial floor means the work queue length remains at or above a non-zero, positive integer. This could mean that there are corrupt or stuck messages in the queues, or it could simply mean your queues house a number of messages that have been sent with the deferred delivery option in Exchange clients.

MSExchangeMTA, Messages Delivered per Minute   This counter measures the rate of the number of messages being delivered by the MTA to the information store. Normal load is 10–40 messages per minute. If this number is constantly under 5 per minute when there are pending items in the MTA queue, then it is likely the server is under severe load or there is a problem with one of the processes. If this number is extraordinarily high (greater than 200 per minute) for an extended amount of time, then it is likely that there is a stuck message in the MTA queue.

Microsoft Exchange Server services processes This is the object: Process, Counter: % Processor time, Instances: DSAMAIN, EMSMTA, MAD, and STORE. No object should be at 0 percent or at 100 percent all of the time. An object always at 0 percent indicates a dead process. Check Service Control Manager to verify that the service is running. An object always at 100 percent usually indicates that something is out of order. Check other services and the Windows NT Event Viewer to identify the problem.

Paging File, % Usage Verify that the usage is in a reasonable range, generally 15–35 percent. When the level of usage exceeds 60 percent, there is usually something wrong. If the usage constantly exceeds 90 percent, then the situation needs to be treated as a problem. There is either a problem with one of the processes, the server needs to have a RAM upgrade, or the paging file was incorrectly allocated during setup.

LogicalDisk, Free Megabytes, Instance: E This is the amount of free space on the transaction log drive. Monitor this object to ensure that the drive does not fill up with .log files. Normally, the .log files are removed whenever an online backup is performed. If the .log files are not being removed, verify that the backups are being done correctly and completed successfully.

MSExchangeIS, Active Connection Count This measures the number of logons to the information store service. This number should be greater than zero. If the server has active mailboxes and there are zero connections, then a problem exists. Use a test account to see if there is a problem making a connection to the server.

MSExhangeDS, Pending Replications Shows the number of replication objects yet to be processed.

MSExchangeDS, Remaining Replication Updates Measures the number of objects being processed by the directory service. This number usually starts at 100 and decreases to 0 within 1 to 3 minutes.

Troubleshooting

The following are guidelines for troubleshooting.

Customer Notifications

Before taking any action that can cause a long-term interruption in service, attempt to inform the customers that there is a problem being worked on. Notification consists of an update to the daily log system and any other status applications in place.

If the affected server is in a state that messages can be sent to the mailboxes, use an announcements-type mailbox or the server's test mailbox to send the message. Essentially, you want a mailbox named something like "Messaging operations." This gives users a good reason to read the message.

Performance Monitor Counter Configurations

The Performance Monitor counter configurations described earlier should be used under normal operating conditions. However, when monitors detect an anomaly in the messaging system, it is necessary to focus the monitoring for the problem server(s), using the Performance Monitor configurations described in the following tables. Run these instances of Performance Monitor on any server where you suspect a problem. The added detail is meant to make troubleshooting easier and should not be run constantly due to the increase in system load. These secondary monitors are intended to chart items that change over time until the problem has been resolved.

The following is a Performance Monitor configuration for detailed, secondary monitoring for all server types. Configure chart settings as follows: Update Interval is 5 seconds, Vertical Max is 100, and Chart Type is Graph.

Object	Counter	Scale	Instance
Processor	%Processor Time	1.0	0 (,1,2,3 if multiprocessor)
Process	%Processor Time	1.0	MAD
Process	%Processor Time	1.0	DSAMAIN
Process	%Processor Time	1.0	STORE
Process	%Processor Time	1.0	EMSMTA
MSExchangeMTA	Work Queue Length	1.0	N/A
MSExchangeIS Private	Messages Delivered/Minute	1.0	N/A
MSExchangeIS Private	Messages Sent/Minute	1.0	N/A
MSExchangeDS	Pending Replication Synchronizations	1.0	N/A
MSExchangeDS	Remaining Replication Updates	1.0	N/A
MSExchangeMTA	Messages/Second	10	N/A

Servers with the Internet Mail Service installed will have these additional counters configured. Configure chart settings as follows: Update Interval is 5 seconds, Vertical Max is 100, and Chart Type is Graph.

Object	Counter	Scale	Instance
Process	%Processor Time	1.0	MSEXCIMC
MSExchangeIMC	Queued Inbound	1.0	MSExchangeIMC
MSExchangeIMC	Queued Outbound	1.0	MSExchangeIMC
MSExchangeIMC	Queued MTS-IN	1.0	MSExchangeIMC
MSExchangeIMC	Queued MTS-OUT	1.0	MSExchangeIMC
MSExchangeMTA Connections	Queue Length	1.0	Internet Mail Service Server

Exchange Services

Although Exchange services are set to start up automatically when the server is rebooted, you may need to start up services manually.

Service Start Order

The following is the startup order for Microsoft Exchange Server services.

1. System attendant
2. Directory
3. Information store
4. MTA
5. Microsoft Exchange Event Service
6. Internet Mail Service
7. Key Management server (KM server)

Service Dependencies

Because there are dependencies between services, starting a dependent service starts the needed service(s). For example, if the information store is requested to start before the system attendant and the directory, the Windows NT service manager will start the system attendant and the directory.

The following are the Exchange dependencies.

Service	Depends on
Directory	System attendant
Information Store	Directory System attendant
Microsoft Exchange Scripting Agent	Directory Information store
MTA	Directory System attendant
Internet Mail Service	Directory Information store MTA

Application Event Log

Each service logs an event to the application event when startup is finished.

Service	Event source	Event number
System attendant	MSExchangeSA	1000
Directory	MSExchangeDS	1000
MTA	MSExchangeMTA	9298
Information store	MSExchangeIS Public	1001
	MSExchangeIS Private	1001
Internet Mail Service	MSExchangeIMC	1000
Key Management server	MSExchangeKMS	1001

Starting and Stopping Exchange Services

In the event that a server needs to be shut down and restarted, it is important that the system is stopped as cleanly as possible. Remember that mail may not be accessible while a problem is being resolved.

The following table provides useful information for each of the Microsoft Exchange Server services.

Name	Command prompt	Location
System attendant	MSExchangeSA	Exchsrvr\Bin\Mad.exe
Directory	MSExchangeDS	Exchsrvr\Bin\Dsamain.exe
Information store	MSExchangeIS	Exchsrvr\Bin\Store.exe
MTA	MSExchangeMTA	Exchsrvr\Bin\Emsmta.exe

(continued)

Name	Command prompt	Location
Internet Mail Service	MSExchangeIMC	Exchsrvr\Connect\Msexcimc \Bin\Msexcimc.exe
Microsoft Exchange Event Service	MSExchangeES	Exchsrvr\Bin\Events.exe
Key Management server	MSExchangeKMS	Security\Bin\Kmserver.exe
KeyToken	KeyToken	Keytoken\Keytoken.exe

Built-in Recovery

The directory, information store, and MTA all have built-in startup recovery methods. These methods are automatically invoked if the service did not stop cleanly.

The directory and information store both go through database recovery (also called JET). This is the technique of replaying the last transactions against the database if the database is out of synchronization with the transaction logs. It normally takes 3 to 5 minutes to replay a 5 MB log file. Not all of the transaction logs will be replayed. Only the transactions that haven't been flushed to the database are replayed.

If the MTA service did not stop cleanly, it will perform a MTACheck at startup. This check scans and makes repairs to the MTA database files. The MTA database files are the Db*.dat files in Exchsrvr\Mtadata.

The application event log shows when one of the components goes into recovery mode.

Component	Event Log
JET Recovery	EDB #18 - JET recovery started.
	EDB #71 - logged for each file replayed by the recovery.
MTACheck	MSExchangeMTA / Field Engineering #2119 - MTACheck start
	MSExchangeMTA / Field Engineering #2206 - Once for each internal MTA queue checked. The MTA queues are: XAPIWRKQ OOFINFOQ REFDATQ MTAWORKQ

Component	Event Log
	MSExchangeMTA / Field Engineering #2207 - MTACheck completed

The MTACheck will save the process results in the file Exchsrvr\Mtadata\Mtachek.Out\Mtacheck.log.

It may take a few minutes to a few hours to run MTACheck, depending on the number of files in the MTADATA directory.

If desired, the MTACheck can be run manually. However, it cannot be run remotely. It must be run from a console command prompt. The syntax for MTACheck is:

Exchsrvr\Bin\Mtacheck /V /F *Logfilename.***Log**

Where *Logfilename* is the name of the file you want to create.

Special Components

Some sites in a Microsoft Exchange Server environment have the KM server component installed. Although the service is set to automatic, it is necessary to verify the service has started. For security purposes, the KM server requires that the password diskette be inserted in the disk drive for KM server to start properly.

Stopping Microsoft Exchange Server Services

Before a server is rebooted, it is recommended that you stop Exchange services before rebooting. This will help ensure a clean stop of Exchange databases.

If the system is in a controllable state, manually stop each of the services before shutting down and restarting the server. Stopping the services individually greatly improves the chances of the server restarting successfully. This also makes it easier to determine where a problem originated if a service cannot be controlled. You can quickly stop services by creating a command file, for example, stopExchange.cmd, that contains the necessary NET STOP *service name* commands to completely stop all Exchange services. For example, to stop the four core Exchange services, use the following lines in a .cmd or .bat file (not case-sensitive).

```
Net stop MSExchangeMTA
Net stop MSExchangeIS
Net stop MSExchangeDS
Net stop MSExchangeSA
```

If a service has been running for a long time, it may take a long time to stop. This is especially true of the information store and directory, which need to flush transactions to the database and close threads when the services are stopped. For example, a directory on a new server may take 10 to 15 minutes to stop.

Use Performance Monitor to verify that the service being stopped is still attempting to stop. If the process time for the service drops and stays at zero, it is likely that the service is in an uncontrollable state.

Service Start Failures

If a service will not start, then there is a problem with it that you need to resolve. First, determine which service is not starting. You can troubleshoot the problem using the following utilities.

Net Start Shows the active services, all completely started processes, and any process attempting to start.

Control Panel Services Shows the active services, and only completely started processes.

Always check the application event log for errors. Any service failure should log at least one event. The event will provide a starting point for troubleshooting.

Validated Permissions

Each of the Exchange services require network connectivity to start. The account being used to start the service is validated for each service startup.

Information Store and Directory

If the information store or directory is the problem, check to see if they are in a state of recovery. A normal recovery can take from 5 to 50 minutes, depending on the number of log files. Check the Event Viewer to verify that recovery is taking place.

System Attendant

If the system attendant will not start then there is something fundamentally wrong with the Microsoft Exchange Server computer. Check the Event Viewer to make sure the network and related services are not causing problems. The network-related services must be running before the system attendant will start.

MTA

Most of the problems that cause the MTA to fail to start are related to the contents of a message. If the MTA will not start, try stopping the information store prior to starting the MTA. If the MTA then starts, start the information store and monitor the server. Always check the Event Viewer to get additional information. If there is a problem with one of the files in the MTA database, an entry will be made in the application event log. It may be necessary to remove a file from the database if it is causing problems.

If the MTA does not communicate with MTAs on other servers, wait at least 10 minutes. The MTA is designed to reset the association and retry the connection after 10 minutes. Stopping and starting an adjacent MTA can cause the process to "wake up" and recognize that the restarted server is available.

If the MTA service starts but messages remain in the work queue, use Performance Monitor or the Exchange Administrator program to determine the destination. This will provide the information needed to continue the troubleshooting process.

Internet Mail Service

If the Internet Mail Service fails to start, check the hosts file. The Internet Mail Service server must know each target server. The hosts file is Winnt\System32\Config\Etc\Hosts. If you are using DNS for your Internet Mail Service name resolution, then use a command prompt and the NSLOOKUP TCP/IP utility to determine if you are having DNS problems. More documentation of the **NSLOOKUP** command can be found by typing **NSLOOKUP**, waiting for the > NSLOOKUP prompt, and then typing **help**.

Last Resort

Be sure to attempt to start the service multiple times before assuming failure. Sometimes it helps to wait a few minutes before starting a service. This is especially true if a service depends on another service. Check to make sure that the prerequisite service is fully started.

Restarting the server can do wonders. Sometimes the computer is simply in a state where a restart is required. Programs and subsystems may require cleaning up that only a restart will fix.

If all else fails, run the service as an application. While it is not a perfect solution, it is an acceptable short-term workaround. An advantage of running the service as an application is that the error reporting is usually more detailed. The service should be run as an application only until the service start problem can be solved.

Service Stop Failures

If a service is in an uncontrollable state, the process will have to be terminated before the service can be brought online.

If a service stop is aborted, it leaves the service in an unknown state. Use SRVINFO and the application event log to verify the state of a service.

To force a process to terminate, use Kill.exe or Pview.exe. Both of these work only at the console. However, because Kill.exe is a character-based application, it can be used in an RPROMPT session.

Terminating Services Using Kill.exe

Before terminating a service using Kill.exe, check Performance Monitor and the Event Viewer for additional information. If the service shows some activity for the service being stopped, it may just be a matter of time before the service stops. If Performance Monitor shows zero activity for a period of time (for example, 10 minutes), the service is most likely uncontrollable.

By having the uncontrollable process stopped, it may be possible to cleanly stop the other services.

If the KILL utility is used against the information store or directory, database recovery will occur when the service is started. Monitor the Event Viewer and Performance Monitor when such a situation occurs.

Terminating the MTA will force the service to run an MTACheck at the next time the service is started.

When using the KILL utility, it's easiest to specify the service by using its executable file name. It is also possible to terminate the process using Kill.exe based on the process ID. The process ID is assigned by Windows NT Server and is not a fixed identifier. Tlist.exe shows each process and its process ID. The following table shows services and their process names.

Service name	Process name
System attendant	MAD.EXE
Directory	DSAMAIN.EXE
Information store	STORE.EXE
MTA	EMSMTA.EXE
Internet Mail Service	MSEXCIMC.EXE
Key Manager	KMSERVER.EXE

Verifying Active Processes

Use Tlist.exe to verify the process has been successfully terminated. If the process is still active, try Kill.exe a few more times. Always give the server a few minutes to terminate a process.

Tlist.exe is a character-based application and can be used in an RPROMPT session. Tlist.exe is available with the *Microsoft Windows NT Server Resource Kit*.

The following is sample TLIST output:

```
c:\winnt\system32>tlist
0 System Process
  2 System
 30 smss.exe
 44 csrss.exe
 36 winlogon.exe     Winlogon generic control dialog
 50 services.exe
 53 lsass.exe
 77 spoolss.exe
113 benser.exe
120 beserver.exe
137 LOCATOR.EXE
148 RpcSs.exe
151 AtSvc.Exe
157 snmp.exe
164 SYSDOWN.EXE
176 CPQMGMT.EXE
180 MAD.EXE
186 NetIQmc.exe
127 dsamain.exe
278 store.exe
286 emsmta.exe
363 metrics.exe
540 logon.scr        Screen Saver
501 rprompt.exe
499 remote.exe
333 cmd.exe
313 TLIST.EXE
```

There will be occasions where the process cannot be stopped. If this is the case, the server needs to be restarted.

Location of Utilities

Kill.exe, Tlist.exe, and Pview.exe are available with the *Microsoft Windows NT Server Resource Kit.*

Testing and Monitoring

If a server is having problems that require the services to be cycled, continue to monitor the server after it is online. The problem can reoccur many times. This happens most often with MTA and information store problems.

If you are unable to determine whether the server is functioning normally, log on using the server's test account and send some test messages. Verify with the target recipient that the test messages have been received.

Sending messages between the test mailboxes using delivery receipts is a useful way of verifying server-to-server communications.

Exchange Maintenance

The following sections discuss daily maintenance guidelines.

Restoring Exchange

In the event of a major catastrophe, you may need to restore Exchange databases from tape backup. There are two scenarios when the information store and directory must be restored:

- If Windows NT Server stops responding and has to be entirely rebuilt.
- If the information store or directory becomes corrupt beyond repair or recovery.

Restoring individual mailboxes on a Microsoft Exchange Server computer can be a long and arduous process that requires extra hardware and time. Therefore, it is imperative that you establish a process for restoring individual mailboxes. Without a process, mailbox restores can be overwhelming.

Microsoft Outlook provides several options to guard against the accidental deletion of messages. Users can protect themselves from simple mistakes by using the Deleted Items folder and either emptying it manually or emptying it only when the user closes the client.

With Exchange 5.5, users and administrators can also take advantage of a feature called Deleted Items Retention. This feature allows administrators to configure their public and private information stores to retain deleted items for a specified number of days before they are permanently deleted. Using Microsoft Outlook version 8.03 (or 8.0, 8.01, or 8.02 with the proper client extension installed), users can retrieve items deleted over the past number of days as configured by administrators. This feature alone can serve as the basis for a restoration policy, such as, "We'll retain deleted items for 3 days, after which they will be purged from the system." You can make exceptions for the occasional vice president or CIO/CEO whose mail is accidentally deleted.

Other successful organization messaging services departments require that departments requesting individual mailbox restorations must pay a standard fee. These charges range from $100 to $250 per mailbox restored.

Developing a Messaging Operations Toolkit

One of the common threads running through all successful messaging operations departments is the ongoing development of a messaging operations toolkit.

In beginning your toolkit development, follow some simple guidelines:

- Find out if the tools you need are available with Exchange.

- If the product does not supply the needed tool functionality, look to resource kit or third-party solutions. Many times, resource kit utilities together with third-party utilities can be used to build a comprehensive toolkit.

- If the first two guidelines do not apply, you must begin developing the tool yourself.

Daily Log

As part of your messaging operations toolkit, you should have a method by which your operations staff can report events and procedure outcomes. The daily log becomes a knowledge repository about your organization messaging system. As events occur and procedures are applied to those events, the daily log system becomes a knowledge base that less experienced users can query when troubleshooting.

The daily log should have the following characteristics:

- It should be easily accessible from any desktop system.
- It should have adequate storage capacity for growth.
- You should be able to generate reports of daily log activity.
- It should be easily searchable using text strings as search criteria.

Solutions in use at successful organization messaging operations centers include Web-based entry and searching systems, and Microsoft Exchange Server electronic form-based implementations. In either case, the most important part of the system is the backend database and its design and maintenance. If you don't index the database properly or keep its record count manageable, you will find no shortage of complaints when messaging operations staff use it for troubleshooting purposes.

Web-based implementations have an advantage over other implementations because there are little or no client configuration changes that need be addressed. You can provide users with a URL and the Web server handles presentation of the data. Other implementations, especially those based on electronic forms, require logging on to the computer and creating a messaging profile for accessing the appropriate public folder or forms library on the Microsoft Exchange Server computer. These steps are sometimes enough to discourage use of any daily log system. Ease of use and access are important for successful daily log systems. The daily log system should be as easy to use as a notebook and pen for recording events. This ease of use will better ensure frequent and correct usage of the daily log system.

Checking the Log

The daily log system is a useful repository of your messaging system's performance. In addition to performance data, the daily log can be used to establish problem resolution times and audit trails for verification of service level agreements.

Checking the daily log should be the responsibility of all messaging operations technicians, particularly at the beginning of shifts. This way the oncoming shift is aware of the events of the preceding shift. Methods for checking the daily log vary, but common ones are reports generated by an automated process, and a simple, Web-based query interface to the daily log database.

Report Distribution

A log report that shows all log entries for a given day should be distributed daily to messaging operations management and engineering. Event and procedure severity levels indicated should elicit the appropriate response within these groups. Messaging system engineering can assist with those issues that require escalation out of the messaging operations regular staff.

The most effective report distribution media is e-mail. However, if your messaging system is not working, then you can't receive the daily log report that is supposed to notify upper-level messaging operations personnel of problems. If your messaging system is not working for lengthy periods of time, then upper-level staff should already know about it. The daily log report is not needed in such an event. The daily log report is a monitoring method for regular operations.

Incident Reporting

The details of each server incident should be recorded in the daily log system. Each incident should include the date and time, operator's user ID, and a brief, but accurate description of the incident. If any error messages were encountered, be sure to include them in the details section.

It is best if incidents are reported as they happen. However, this is not always possible if there are numerous problems occurring at the same time. At a minimum, all messaging operations operators need to record dates and times of incidents and record them in the daily log when time permits, but no later than the end of their shift.

The following is a sample report entry:

```
[public]
Severity B
joeuser
Location
14 Mar 1997
14:25:33
MSG-33 Message Transfer Agent (MTA) service stopped unexpectedly.
Running MTACHECK. ETA to normal service is 14:45:00. Users should be OK
to log in and send mail. Delivery times to other destination servers may
be negatively impacted.
```

The sample daily log entry is succinct, yet informative. The messaging operations technician has documented a relatively severe ('A' being the highest) event by describing what happened, what is being done to rectify the event, an estimate time (ETA) for normal service, and how the problem will most likely manifest itself as to users.

Descriptions of Useful Utilities

Any successful message services department will have developed a number of utilities for making operations easier. Typically, products do not satisfy the needs of a great number of differing environments straight from the manufacturer. Subsequently, technology implementers build supplemental tools and utilities for making products much more effective. Below are some descriptions of tools and utilities that can be developed. Some of these utilities are provided with Exchange.

Mailboxes

In most Exchange implementations, the mailbox object is both the most numerous and most critical. It is therefore imperative to be able to address needs and problems with mailboxes quickly and efficiently. The Administrator program covers the majority of issues you will encounter with mailboxes. The following tools are recommended in cases where the Administrator program does not provide the necessary functionality.

In large, multisite organizations, when a user moves across site boundaries, it is not a simple matter to move that user's mailbox directory information and mailbox contents. Procedures should be defined that efficiently move user information and mailbox content data to the destination. This requires the user to store mailbox contents in personal folder files (.pst files) prior to the move and restore the contents from the personal folders after the move. After the user has stored the mailbox contents in personal folders, export the user data to a file using the Export command in the Administrator program, remove the mailbox from the local site, and change the file that was exported to reflect the new site location. If necessary, you can then import the mailbox into the new site. After completion, the user must move any mailbox contents back to the new home server. There are some utilities in this resource kit that can help automate much of the process.

Distribution Lists

The following tools are useful for maintaining distribution lists (DLs).

Forms- or Web-based Distribution List Update Utility In many large organizations, the number of distribution lists often rivals that of the number of mailboxes. It is imperative that the messaging services department provide leadership in this area. There should be an easy to use, low administrator intervention method for modifying and creating distribution lists.

Distribution List Membership Display Utility A command-prompt utility gives you a quick way to view the membership of a distribution list so you don't have to use the Administrator program.

Standard Distribution List Build Utility Many organizations maintain generic distribution lists such as Everyone, Accounting – All, and Corporate Campus. It can be useful to have a tool that builds distribution lists based on user attributes, such as location or building name. This tool would keep your generic distribution lists in a state of high integrity. This is important when blanket messages are sent out by executives. To be successful in this automatic DL build arena, you must ensure that your directory contains the most accurate information for your users. Otherwise, you may have users on lists to which they do not and should not belong.

Distribution List Update Utility A good distribution list update tool will offload a significant amount of your messaging system support burden.

Public Folders

The following tools are useful for maintaining public folders.

Public Folder Ownership Fix Utility In many large organizations, the ownership and responsibility for public folders is delegated to the public folder requestor. An entry in the Address Book shows who owns the public folder. In addition to the person who requested that the public folder be created, you should consider adding a second owner of the public folder – a global, public folder administrator distribution list. By adding the global, public folder administrator distribution list as an owner of a public folder, you can track the status messages on the public folder. Because the person who owns the public folder has sufficient permissions to remove the distribution list from the public folder owners, it is recommended that you develop a tool to reset this ownership and add the distribution list to those public folders from which it has been removed.

Public Folder Reporting Utility Tracking public folder usage is important for numerous reasons, for example, capacity planning and successful load leveling across servers. The following are important areas to monitor:

- Search for all public folders owned by a given user or having other attributes, such as what forms are in the folder library.

- Report of public information store database growth over a time period.

- Replication volume, by folder and time period.

- Folder owner report/query tool.

- Disk space used by public folder or hierarchy.

- Report of access to public folders by user. This is useful for determining when to replicate a public folder to a remote location to conserve wide area network (WAN) bandwidth.

- Report, by folder, of number of new postings, and breakdown of post type. For example, normal, attachments, and forms.

- Report, by server, of number of new folders created.

- Report, by folder/tree of folders, of number of messages and total K used.

- Report, by folder, of number of accesses per time period.

- Report/query of last access date and time. For example, all folders not accessed in the last month.

- Report/query of the last date and time a folder had items posted in it. Searchable as above.

- Security auditing tool. For example, find all folders that have forwarding rules installed. Messages could be sent to the Internet that you don't want to be distributed outside of your organization.

APPENDIX A

Creating an .Ini File for Microsoft Exchange Server Batch Setup

This appendix describes the format for creating an .ini file that you can run with Microsoft Exchange Server Setup in batch mode (**Setup /q**). Using an .ini file is equivalent to selecting options in dialog boxes during setup; however, the .ini file provides additional options. For more information about batch Setup, see Part 1, "Planning."

.Ini File Format

Each section of the .ini file is shown with the setting, a description of the setting, and the value. These settings are not case-sensitive.

[Product ID]

This section specifies the product identifier (ID) for this copy of Microsoft Exchange Server, which is required information. If the product ID information is not included, batch setup fails unless this copy of Exchange was received under the Microsoft Select Agreement.

Entry	Description	Value
pid=	Product ID number used by OEMs	XXXXOEMXXXXXX
cdkey=	The product ID number	Number in XXX-XXXXXXX format

[Paths]

This section contains entries that specify the location where optional components are installed. All entries are optional.

Entry	Description	Value
ServerDest=	Location where the server component is installed if it is selected	Server name
AdminDest=	Location where the Administrator program is installed if it is selected	Path

[Components]

This section contains entries that specify which components are to be installed. All entries are optional.

Entry	Description	Value
Services=	Whether to install services for the system attendant, the directory, the information store, and the message transfer agent (MTA)	True or false
Administrator=	Whether to install the Administrator program	True or false
MSMailConnector=	Whether to install the Microsoft Mail Connector	True or false
CC:Mail=	Whether to install the cc:Mail connector	True or false
Internet=	Whether to install the Internet Mail Service	True or false
X400=	Whether to install the X.400 Connector	True or false
Active Server Components=	Whether to install Microsoft Outlook Web Access	True or false
NNTP=	Whether to install NNTP	True or false
KMServer=	Whether to install KM server	True or false
Sample Applications=	Whether to install the sample applications that clients can use	True or false
Books Online=	Whether to install online documentation	True or false
Event Service=	Whether to install the Microsoft Exchange Scripting Agent	True or false

[Site]

This section contains entries that specify the names of directory objects in the site, such as the site and server names.

Entry	Description	Value
ExistingServerName=	Name of the server in the existing site	Server name
SiteName=	Name of the new site if ExistingServerName is not provided	Site name
SiteProxyName=	Proxy name of the new site that is used to determine the site addresses for connectors	Site proxy name
InternetSiteName=	Internet site name if Internet Mail Service is being installed	Internet site name

[Organization]

This section contains entries that specify the names of directory objects in the organization.

Entry	Description	Value
OrganizationName=	Organization name if a new site is being created	Organization name
OrganizationProxyName=	Organization proxy name that is used to determine the site addresses for connector if a new site is being created	Organization proxy name

[ServiceAccount]

This section contains entries that specify the service account name and password.

Entry	Description	Value
AccountName=	Service account name (required if a new site is being created)	Service account name
AccountPassword=	Service account password (required)	Service account password

[Licensing]

This section contains entries that specify licensing information.

Entry	Description	Value
PerSeat=	Whether to set up licensing on a per-seat basis	True or false

[SitePermissions]

This section contains entries that specify the user account(s) that are to have Administrator permission in the site.

Entry	Description	Value
Account1=	Account that is to be granted site Administrator permission. Up to four accounts can be specified. These accounts are in addition to the service account specified in the [ServiceAccount] section.	User account (for example, Namerica\mariab)
Account2=		
Account3=		
Account4=		

[X.400]

This section configures X.400 support and is optional. For more information about these entries, see your X.400 documentation.

Entry	Description	Value
Organization=	X.400 attribute for organization	X.400 O
OrgUnit1=	X.400 attribute for organizational unit	X.400 OU1
OrgUnit2=	X.400 attribute for organizational unit	X.400 OU2
OrgUnit3=	X.400 attribute for organizational unit	X.400 OU3
OrgUnit4=	X.400 attribute for organizational unit	X.400 OU4
PrivManDomName=	X.400 attribute for the private management domain (PRMD)	X.400 PRMD
AdminManDomName=	X.400 attribute for the administrative management domain (ADMD)	X.400 ADMD
Country=	X.400 attribute for country	X.400C

APPENDIX B

System Management Checklist

You should check the following items on your Microsoft Exchange Server computer regularly. The list is divided into daily, weekly, monthly, and periodic maintenance tasks.

For more information, see *Microsoft Exchange Server Maintenance and Troubleshooting* and *Microsoft Exchange Server Concepts and Planning*.

Daily Maintenance Tasks

- Examine Microsoft Windows NT Performance Monitor counters.
- Monitor services and links.
- Back up your data.
- Purge unneeded transaction log files. Monitor the Edb*.log files in the Dsadata and Mdbdata directories to check for build up of transaction log files.

> **Warning** Do not manually delete the Edb*.log files. To remove these files, perform a full or an incremental backup or turn on circular logging.

- Check available disk space.
- Check the Alerter service.

Weekly Maintenance Tasks

- Check event logs for errors and warnings.
- Check for message tracking log file buildup.
- Verify that public folders are being replicated.

Monthly Maintenance Tasks

- Validate information store backups by restoring them to an alternate server that is not part of your organization.

Periodic Maintenance Tasks

- Run information store maintenance. Check the **IS Maintenance** property page for the server object in the directory to ensure that maintenance routines run during off-peak hours and at least once per day.

- Defragment the server offline. Take the server offline and use the defragmentation utility (Eseutil.exe) to defragment the directory and information store.

- Check mailbox and public folder use as follows:

  - Check the **Logons** property pages in the private and public information stores.

  - Check the **Mailbox Resources** and **Public Folder Resources** property pages to see how individual users and public folders are using storage space.

- Check storage limits. Monitor storage limit settings on mailboxes and public folders. You might need to adjust these limits periodically for specific users or public folders.

A P P E N D I X   C

Performance Monitor Chart Views

Microsoft Exchange Server provides several Microsoft Windows NT Performance Monitor chart views with pre-selected counters that you can use to troubleshoot performance problems. You usually have to use more than one chart view at a time to isolate a performance problem. The following chart views are available in the Exchange program group.

Performance Monitor chart	Description
Microsoft Exchange Server Health	Tracks the server's memory use in pages per second and also the amount of processor time used for each server core component
Microsoft Exchange Server Load	Tracks the amount of load on the server from client requests and replication operations
Microsoft Exchange Server History	Tracks statistics such as the number of messages the server processes and the pages per second that have been generated since the server was started
Microsoft Exchange Server Users	Tracks the number of users who are accessing the server's information store
Microsoft Exchange Server Queues	Tracks the amount of time the server requires to respond to client requests and tracks the speed of replication operations

Performance Monitor chart	Description
Microsoft Exchange Server IMC Traffic	Tracks the amount of traffic that the server's Internet Mail Service processes
Microsoft Exchange Server IMC Statistics	Tracks the number of inbound and outbound messages that the server's Internet Mail Service processes
Microsoft Exchange Server IMC Queues	Tracks the number of inbound and outbound messages that the server's Internet Mail Service sends to the Internet or to Exchange

Note If you haven't done so already, start the disk performance counters by typing **diskperf -y** at the command prompt. Then, add the LogicalDisk: Disk Bytes/sec and LogicalDisk: % Disk Time counters to the Microsoft Exchange Server Health chart view. These counters indicate the amount of data that is transferred to or from the disk during write or read operations. For more information about adding counters to charts, see your Microsoft Windows NT Server documentation.

Server Health Chart View

The following counters are available in the Microsoft Exchange Server Health chart view.

Counter	Object	Instance	Description
% Total Processor Time	System	—	The amount of time that the processor is busy
% Processor Time	Process	Directory	The amount of time that a processor is busy servicing directory requests
% Processor Time	Process	MTA	The amount of time that a processor is busy servicing message transfer agent (MTA) requests
% Processor Time	Process	Information store	The amount of time that a processor is busy servicing information store requests
% Processor Time	Process	System attendant	The amount of time that a processor is busy servicing system attendant requests
Pages/sec	Memory	—	The number of memory pages that are read from or written to the system's pagefile on disk

Server Load Chart View

The following counters are available in the Microsoft Exchange Server Load chart view.

Counter	Object	Description
Message Recipients Delivered/min	Private information store	The rate at which messages are delivered to mailboxes
Messages Submitted/min	Private information store	The rate at which users send messages
Message Recipients Delivered/min	Public information store	The rate at which messages are delivered to public folders
Message Submitted/min	Public information store	The rate at which users send messages to public folders
Adjacent MTA Associations	MTA	The number of connections this MTA has to other MTAs
RPC Packets/sec	Information store	The rate at which remote procedure call (RPC) packets are processed
AB Browses/sec	Directory	The rate at which users browse the Address Book
AB Reads/sec	Directory	The rate at which users perform read operations on the Address Book
ExDS Reads/sec	Directory	The rate at which Extended Directory Service clients (the information store, MTA, system attendant, and Administrator program) perform read operations on the directory
Replication Updates/sec	Directory	The rate of directory replication activity on this server

Server History Chart View

The following counters are available in the Microsoft Exchange Server History chart view.

Counter	Object	Description
Total Message Recipients Delivered	Private information store	The total number of recipients who have received a message since the server was started
Total Messages Delivered	Private information store	The total number of messages delivered to recipients since the server was started
Total Messages Sent	Private information store	The total number of messages the MTA has sent to store providers since the server was started
Total Messages Submitted	Private information store	The total number of messages that users have sent since the server was started

(continued)

Counter	Object	Description
Total Message Recipients Delivered	Public information store	The total number of recipients who have received a message since the server was started
Total Messages Sent	Public information store	The total number of messages the MTA sent to information services since the server was started
User Count	Information store	The total number of users who are connected to the information store
Work Queue Length	MTA	The total number of messages the MTA has not yet processed
Pages/sec	Memory	The total number of memory pages that are read from or written to the system's pagefile on disk

Server Users Chart View

The following counters are available in the Microsoft Exchange Server Users chart view.

Counter	Object	Description
User Count	Information store	The number of users who are connected to the information store

Server Queues Chart View

The following counters are available in the Microsoft Exchange Server Queues chart view.

Counter	Object	Description
Work Queue Length	MTA	The number of messages that the MTA has not yet processed
Send Queue Size	Private information store and public information store	The number of sent messages that are waiting for final delivery
Receive Queue Size	Private information store and public information store	The number of received messages that are waiting for final delivery

Server IMC Traffic Chart View

The following counters are available in the Microsoft Exchange Server IMC Traffic chart view.

Note Internet Mail Service must be running to use these counters.

Counter	Object	Description
Messages Entering MTS-IN	Internet Mail Service	The number of messages received from the Internet that are waiting for final delivery to Microsoft Exchange Server
Messages Entering MTS-OUT	Internet Mail Service	The number of messages being sent to the Internet that are waiting to be converted to Internet mail format
Messages Leaving MTS-OUT	Internet Mail Service	The number of messages that are waiting for final delivery to the Internet
Connections Inbound	Internet Mail Service	The number of current Simple Mail Transport Protocol (SMTP) connections to Internet Mail Service that other SMTP hosts have established
Connections Outbound	Internet Mail Service	The number of current SMTP connections that Internet Mail Service has established to other SMTP hosts

Server IMC Statistics Chart View

The following counters are available in the Microsoft Exchange Server IMC Statistics chart view.

Note Internet Mail Service must be running to use these counters.

Counter	Object	Description
Inbound Messages Total	Internet Mail Service	The total number of Internet messages Internet Mail Service receives
Outbound Messages Total	Internet Mail Service	The total number of messages Internet Mail Service sends

Server IMC Queues Chart View

The following counters are available in the Microsoft Exchange Server IMC Queues chart view.

Note Internet Mail Service must be running to use these counters.

Counter	Object	Description
Queued Inbound	Internet Mail Service	The number of messages received from the Internet that are waiting to be converted for Exchange
Queued MTS-IN	Internet Mail Service	The number of messages received from the Internet that are waiting for final delivery to Exchange
Queued MTS-OUT	Internet Mail Service	The number of messages that are waiting to be converted to Internet mail format
Queued Outbound	Internet Mail Service	The number of messages that are waiting to be delivered to the Internet

A P P E N D I X   D

Microsoft Exchange Client

Microsoft Exchange Client is available with version 4.0 only. The client included with Microsoft Exchange Server 5.5 and later is Microsoft Outlook.

This appendix provides information about the Microsoft Exchange Client that may not be available elsewhere.

Client Setup

You can install the Microsoft Exchange Client locally (from a client installation point or floppy disks) or from a network share.

New Client Installation

Most Microsoft Exchange Client files are stored in several compressed cabinet (.cab) files until they are installed. When Setup is run, the cabinet files are uncompressed and the files are copied to the client's disk or a network server. Knowing where the Microsoft Exchange Client files are stored when they are installed can be useful information if you need to troubleshoot a problem. For example, if the Microsoft Exchange Client will not start and it is running from a network server, the server containing the Microsoft Exchange Client files might be down. The location of the files depends on the following:

- Whether the Microsoft Exchange Client is run from the local disk or from a network share.

- Whether the operating system for the client computer is run from the local disk or from a network share.

Microsoft Exchange Client installs configuration files, application files, and Messaging Application Programming Interface (MAPI) files. Configuration files (including .ini files, spelling DLLs that Microsoft Exchange Client and other applications share, and information about forms) are copied to and run from the Windows directory or the user's home directory on the local disk or another location on a network server where user files are stored. The following table shows where application files and MAPI files are copied to or run from depending on the Microsoft Exchange Client computer's configuration.

	Application Files		MAPI System Files	
	Copies to Exchange directory	Runs from network share	Copied to local Windows System directory	Runs from Windows System directory on operating system network share
Local operating system and client	X		X	
Local operating system and shared client		X	X	
Shared operating system and local client	X			X
Shared operating system and client		X		X

Local Installation

Setup uses the following process when installing the Microsoft Exchange Client to the local disk from a client installation point or floppy disks. If you encounter problems during setup, you can use this information to help you troubleshoot. The operating system is running locally.

1. Reads the Setup.lst file in the client installation point to determine what files must be copied to the local disk. The Setup.lst file also instructs Setup to create a temporary, hidden directory for these files on the local disk that is called ~Mssetup.t\~Tmpjnk.t. The cabinet (.cab) files are uncompressed as they are copied to the temporary directory.

2. Reads the Exchng.stf file that was copied to the temporary directory and gathers the user's installation information. This file contains information such as the name of the user's organization and whether the installation is local or shared. By default, Setup obtains the user's name and organization from the registry or, depending on the operating system, the Win.ini file.

3. Copies files to the local disk as described in the preceding section, "New Client Installation."

4. Writes the Exchng.stf file to the Exchange directory. Edits the registry or Win.ini file to indicate the location of the Exchng.stf file. Deletes the temporary directory.

5. If a Default.prf file exists in the client installation point, Setup copies the file to the Windows directory and runs the automatic profile generator (Newprof.exe) to create a default profile. If a default profile does not exist, Microsoft Exchange Client runs the Profile Wizard the first time the client is run.

Shared Installation

To set up a network share and install Microsoft Exchange Client, you must first create the share by running Setup with the **/a** option. Then you or the user can run Setup to install Microsoft Exchange Client from the network share. If you encounter problems during Setup, you can use the following information to help you isolate the cause of the problem.

How a Network Share Is Created

Setup /a creates a network share depending on whether the operating system on the computer setting up the share is running from a network share or from a local disk.

-   If the operating system is local, Setup copies all files from the client installation point to the new network share. Cabinet (.cab) files are uncompressed as they are copied to the new location.

-   If the operating system is shared, Setup copies all application files to the new network share. Cabinet (.cab) files are uncompressed as they are copied to the new location. Setup also installs MAPI system files to the Windows System directory on the operating system share.

How Microsoft Exchange Client Is Installed from a Network Share

After you have created the network share, you can install Microsoft Exchange Client to run from the network share. The setup process to install from a network share is similar to installing to a local disk, with the following differences:

-   Files required for setup are not copied to a temporary directory as they are during a local installation.

-   Files are copied to directories on either the local disk or the network. For more information, see "New Client Installation" earlier in this appendix.

Client Maintenance Installation

After you have installed Microsoft Exchange Client, you can run Setup again to add or remove components as needed. For example, you can remove online Help for the Microsoft Exchange Client or add Microsoft Schedule+.

Setup relies on the Exchng.stf file to perform maintenance installations, which include the **Add/Remove**, **Remove All**, and **Reinstall** options. Setup reads the Exchng.stf file to determine what components are already installed. Then Setup writes information to the file, identifying which components should be added or removed. If a component is removed, Setup removes all references to it from the system.

Customizing Your Client Installation

You can customize Microsoft Exchange Client in the following ways:

- Use the Setup Editor to modify default Setup options.
- Configure default messaging profiles using the automatic profile generator (Newprof.exe).
- Run Setup unattended from the command line or by using Microsoft System Management Server (SMS).
- Change the remote procedure call (RPC) binding order to improve client performance.

Using the Setup Editor

If you want to set up Microsoft Exchange Client on many computers in your organization and use the same configuration on all clients, you can customize Setup options. When you run Setup, Microsoft Exchange Client is installed with the settings you specify.

You can use the Setup Editor to change default Setup options by editing the Exchng.stf file located in the client installation point. You can specify options such as how users will be notified of new mail, the RPC protocols binding order, and which information services are installed on the client. You can also use the Setup Editor to specify default profile settings that can be used with the automatic profile generator (Newprof.exe) during setup. These settings are stored in a Default.prf file created by the Setup Editor.

Caution Use the Setup Editor to edit the Exchng.stf file. Editing the file manually can have unpredictable results because the file has a unique way of tracking whether components have been installed.

Configuring Default Messaging Profiles

Microsoft Exchange Server provides a tool called the automatic profile generator (Newprof.exe) that can be used as an alternative to the Profile Wizard. If you use Newprof.exe, users do not need to create their own profiles using the Profile Wizard after Microsoft Exchange Client has been installed. It creates a default messaging profile with settings that you have specified. This process is transparent to the user.

Newprof.exe can be run during Setup or from the command line. It uses a .prf file to determine the settings for the new profile. If there is no default profile in the user's home directory and a .prf file is present, Newprof.exe creates a profile based on the information that you specified in the .prf file.

You can run Newprof.exe with a .prf file from the command line with a variety of distribution mechanisms such as SMS, logon scripts, and e-mail. If you use it with logon scripts, Newprof.exe can be used to create default profiles for *roving users* when they log on to a new computer. Roving users are users who log on to Microsoft Exchange Client from different computers in an organization.

Automatically Creating Profiles for Roving Users

Many users need access to their e-mail from different Microsoft Exchange Client computers. For example, a roving user can have offices in two different locations. You can make it easier for a roving user to log on to a new Microsoft Exchange Client computer by using the automatic profile generator to create a default profile. If you preconfigure a default profile, roving users do not need to create a profile using the Profile Wizard every time they log on to a new client computer because the automatic profile generator creates one if needed.

To create profiles for roving users automatically, you can create a .prf file with the user's logon name and home server defined. You can also configure the logon script to verify that a profile does not exist for that user on the computer. If the computer doesn't already have a profile defined for the user, the logon script calls Newprof.exe. Newprof.exe uses the .prf file in the user's home directory to create a new profile.

Using Newprof.exe with a .Prf File

You can use the Setup Editor or any text editor to specify settings in the .prf file. The .prf file can be in the client installation point or the user's home directory. If Setup is used to run Newprof.exe, the file must be named Default.prf or it will be ignored. To use a different name, you can run Newprof.exe from the command line as follows:

Newprof.exe -p *filepath*

where *filepath* is the path and file name of the .prf file.

You can use the sample Template.prf file provided with Microsoft Exchange Client to create a customized .prf file.

Creating a .Prf File

Some of the most common entries in a .prf file are described in the following table. For a list of entries in a .prf file and their formats, see the sample Template.prf file.

Entry	Description	Value
MailboxName=	The name of the Microsoft Exchange Server mailbox	The user's name
HomeServer=	The name of the Microsoft Exchange Server computer where the user's mailbox is located	The server name
OfflineFolderPath=	The location of the offline (.ost) folder file	The path and file name
PathToPersonalAddressBook=	The path to the personal address book (.pab)	The path and file name
EmptyWastebasket=	Whether to empty the Deleted Items folder when quitting	True or false
GenReadReceipt=	Whether to generate a read receipt	True or false
GenDeliveryReceipt=	Whether to generate a delivery receipt	True or false
SaveSentMail=	Whether to save sent messages	True or false

If the default profile's user name is not specified in the .prf file, Newprof.exe obtains the user's name from the registry or the Win.ini file. If this information is not available, the system prompts for a name when the user logs on to the client.

Running Setup Unattended

There are two options that you can use to install Microsoft Exchange Client quickly on several computers. You can distribute Microsoft Exchange Client by running Setup from the command line or by using SMS.

Running Setup from the Command Line

There are several command-line parameters that you can use to perform an unattended batch mode installation. Running Setup from the command line is useful if you need to install Microsoft Exchange Client quickly and do not want to be prompted to enter additional information. The following parameters can be used for batch setup. These parameters are case-sensitive.

Command-line parameter	Description
Setup /Q	Installs Microsoft Exchange Client using the Typical option. This cannot be used with MS-DOS® or when installing a shared installation of the client.
/N "*name*"	The user's name (not case-sensitive).
/O "*organization*"	The organization name (not case-sensitive).

For example, typing the following at the command line installs Microsoft Exchange Client for a user named Bill Lee without prompting for additional information.

Setup /Q /N "Bill Lee"

You can use the following command-line parameters to perform unattended maintenance installations. Like batch mode Setup, these parameters are useful if you need to reinstall, remove, or restore Microsoft Exchange Client quickly and do not want to be prompted to enter additional information. These parameters are case-sensitive and cannot be used together.

Command-line parameter	Description
Setup /R	Reinstalls Microsoft Exchange Client.
Setup /U	Removes all Microsoft Exchange Client components.
Setup /Y	Restores the Microsoft Exchange Client default settings.

Using SMS to Distribute Microsoft Exchange Client

If you use SMS to install applications on clients in your network, you can also use SMS to distribute Microsoft Exchange Client software. SMS makes it easier to install Microsoft Exchange Client on many computers without user input. SMS packages (.pdf files) for installing Microsoft Exchange Client are provided with the Microsoft Exchange Client software. SMS packages are provided for computers running the following operating systems:

- Microsoft Windows 95
- Microsoft Windows NT Server

- Microsoft Windows NT Workstation
- Microsoft Windows version 3.1
- Microsoft Windows for Workgroups

For information about installing .pdf files, see your SMS documentation.

Changing the RPC Protocol Binding Order

When Microsoft Exchange Client is installed, it sets the default RPC protocol binding order. This setting determines the protocol sequence that Microsoft Exchange Client uses to communicate with Microsoft Exchange Server. You can change the RPC binding order before or after the client is installed.

Performance can be improved by changing the RPC binding order if the client uses multiple protocols or if the single protocol your client uses is not the first listed in the RPC binding order. If the protocol used is last in the sequence, Microsoft Exchange Client attempts to bind over the protocols listed before it when connecting to the server.

The protocols are represented in the binding order, using the following entries. The string ncacn refers to Network Computing Architecture Connection.

Protocol name	RPC protocol string
Local RPC	ncalrpc
Transmission Control Protocol/Internet Protocol (TCP/IP)	ncacn_ip_tcp
Sequenced Packet Exchange (SPX)	ncacn_spx
Named pipes	ncacn_np
NetBIOS	netbios
VINES IP	ncacn_vns_spp

For example, the following entry attempts to establish connections over SPX, TCP/IP, and NetBIOS in that order.

```
RPC_Binding_Order=ncacn_spx,ncacn_ip_tcp,netbios
```

Clients Running Windows 95, Windows NT Server, and Windows NT Workstation

By default, Microsoft Exchange Client uses the following RPC binding order for Microsoft Windows 95, Windows NT Server, and Windows NT Workstation when attempting to connect to a server:

1. Transmission Control Protocol/Internet Protocol (TCP/IP)
2. SPX

3. Named pipes

4. NetBIOS

5. VINES IP (Windows NT Server and Windows NT Workstation only)

You can change the RPC binding order for clients running Windows 95, Windows NT Workstation, and Windows NT Server before or after you have installed Microsoft Exchange Client.

Before installation   In Setup Editor, select the **Binding Order** property page.

After installation   Use the Registry Editor to modify the binding order in HKEY_LOCAL_MACHINE\Microsoft\Exchange\Exchange Provider. For example, the following entry attempts to establish SPX, TCP/IP, and NetBIOS connections in the order indicated.

```
RPC_Binding_Order=ncacn_spx,ncacn_ip_tcp,netbios
```

Clients Running Windows and Windows for Workgroups

By default, Microsoft Exchange Client uses the following RPC binding order for Windows for Workgroups when attempting to connect to a server:

1. Named pipes

2. SPX

3. TCP/IP

4. NetBIOS

5. VINES IP

You can change the RPC binding order for clients running Windows and Windows for Workgroups before or after you have installed Microsoft Exchange Client.

Before installation   In Setup Editor, click the **Binding Order** property page.

After installation   In the Exchng.ini file in the Windows directory, edit the [Exchange Provider] section. For example, the following entry in the Exchng.ini file attempts to establish SPX, TCP/IP, and NetBIOS connections in the order indicated.

```
[Exchange Provider]
RPC_Binding_Order=ncacn_spx,ncacn_ip_tcp,netbios
```

Clients Running MS-DOS

By default, Microsoft Exchange Client uses the following RPC binding order for MS-DOS when attempting to connect to a server:

1. Local RPC
2. Named pipes
3. SPX
4. TCP/IP
5. NetBIOS

You can change the RPC binding order for clients running MS-DOS after you have installed MS-DOS. To change the order, edit the RPC_BINDING_ORDER line in the Mlsetup.ini file. This file is installed automatically on the client or on a network share. For example, the following entry in the Mlsetup.ini file attempts to establish local RPC, named pipes, TCP/IP, and NetBIOS connections in the order indicated.

```
RPC_Binding_Order=ncalrpc,ncacn_np,ncacn_ip_tcp,netbios
```

Uncompressing Installation Files for the Microsoft Exchange Client

Installation files for client setup are stored on the Microsoft Exchange Client compact disc in multiple cabinet files. A cabinet (.cab) file includes many files that are stored as a single file. To view or access a file in a cabinet file, you can uncompress the cabinet file by using a command-line tool called Extract.exe. For example, if you want to use Newprof.exe, you can uncompress it from the Exchng3.cab file.

To uncompress a file in a cabinet file and place it in the current directory, type the following at the command prompt:

Extract *cabinetfile* **/e** *filename*

where *cabinetfile* is the name of the cabinet file and *filename* is the name of the file you want to uncompress.

For more information about using Extract.exe, type **Extract /?** at the command prompt.

Roving Users

Individuals who use the Microsoft Exchange Client on more than one computer are called roving users. The profile generator can be used to create profiles and set up roving users.

Using the Profile Generator

The profile generator simplifies the process of creating Microsoft Exchange Client profiles for roving users. When you create profiles for each type of operating system, users can use any computer with any operating system and still have access to their mailbox by double-clicking the Microsoft Exchange Client icon. Users do not need to re-create their profiles.

You can use the profile generator from the command line or with the Profgen.ini file. If you do not specify command-line options, the profile generator looks for a file called Profgen.ini and reads options from that file.

Windows Version 3.*x* and Windows for Workgroups

To support roving users who are using computers running Microsoft Windows 3.*x* and Microsoft Windows for Workgroups, Microsoft Exchange Clients should be running from a network share. During Setup, Messaging Application Programming Interface (MAPI) profiles are stored in the user's home directory or another location on a network file server.

You can assign logon scripts to users and make it easier for them to use the Microsoft Exchange Client on other computers in your organization. Logon scripts can connect users to their home directory when they log on to Microsoft Windows and Windows for Workgroups. After a user is connected to the home directory and the Microsoft Exchange Client is started, the user's default profile is used.

When Microsoft Exchange Client is installed locally, it supports roving users. However, roving users must edit the Win.ini file.

▶   **To edit the Win.ini file**

1. Open the Win.ini file using a text editor.

2. Add the following line to the [MAPI] section.

   ```
   ProfileDirectory16=<path to messaging profile>
   ```

   where *path to messaging profile* is the location of the user's messaging profile on the network.

3. Restart the computer.

▶ **To use the profile generator with Windows 3.x or Windows for Workgroups computers**

1. Copy Profgen.exe to the Exchange directory.

2. Copy Profgen.ini to the Windows directory.

3. In the Profgen.ini file, edit the PathToExeFile and PathToPRFFile to point to the automatic profile generator (Newprof.exe) and .prf files respectively. Normally, these entries should be as follows.

   ```
   PathToExeFile=c:\exchange\newprof.exe
   PathToPRFFile=h:\Win16.prf
   ```

   where h:\ is the user's home directory on the server.

4. Edit the Load= line in the Win.ini file as follows.

   ```
   Load=c:\exchange\profgen.exe
   ```

5. In the Win.ini file, ensure the following line is present in the [MAPI] section.

   ```
   ProfileDirectory16=home_directory:
   ```

   where *home_directory* is the user's home directory on the server.

Windows NT Workstation and Windows 95

To support roving users who are using computers running Windows NT Workstation or Microsoft Windows 95, you must store a user's MAPI profiles on the domain controller in a user's home domain. Storing the profiles in the user's home domain allows users to access their profiles from any computer in your organization. If roving users intend to use computers in other domains, you must permit the roving users to log on to multiple domains, and those domains must trust the user's home domain.

In addition, for Windows NT Workstation, ensure your roving users have user rights on the Windows NT Workstation computers they intend to use in your organization. If your roving users do not have user rights, they will be unable to log on.

To set up a roving user for Windows NT Workstation and Windows 95, you must do the following:

- Create a new user profile for the roving user.

- Specify the path to the roving user's profile.

- If the user is using computers from more than one domain, permit the roving user to log on to a different trusted domain.

▶ **To create a user profile for a Windows NT or Windows 95 roving user**

Before creating the profile, log on to your domain's primary domain controller and the Microsoft Windows NT Server computer as domain administrator. Ensure the **Domain** box displays the domain you want the account for the roving user to belong to.

1. In the Administrative Tools program group, click **User Profile Editor**.

2. On the **File** menu, click **New**.

3. In the dialog box that opens, click the button next to the **Permitted to use profile** box.

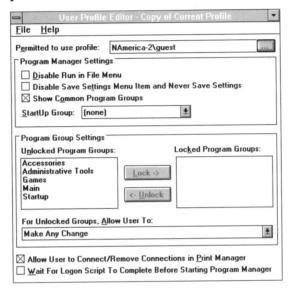

1. In the **Names** box, select the user account that should have permission to use this profile. If the user is not in this list, type the user name in the **Add Name** box, and then click **Add**.

1. Click **OK**.

2. On the **File** menu, click **Save As File**.

3. In the **Save File As Type** box, click **Per-User Profile**.

4. In the **Directories** box, choose the path for the profile.

   You should store the profile in a shared user directory for security reasons. The profile also can be stored in a shared public directory.

5. In the **File Name** box, type a profile name, click **OK**, and then close the **User Profile Editor** dialog box.

Before Windows NT roving users use Microsoft Exchange Server for the first time, you must verify that their copy of Microsoft Exchange Server points to the network directory where the user profile is located. If it does not, change the working directory.

▶ **To change the working directory for the Microsoft Exchange Client on Windows NT**

1. In the Microsoft Exchange program group of the Microsoft Exchange Client computer, click **Microsoft Exchange**.

2. On the **File** menu, click **Properties**.

3. In the **Working Directory** box, type the path of the directory where the roving user's profile is located.

▶ **To specify the path to a Windows NT or Windows 95 roving user's profile**

1. In the Administrative Tools program group, click **User Manager for Domains**.

2. Double-click the appropriate user account to open the **New User** dialog box.

3. Click **Profile**.

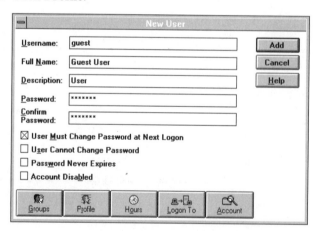

4. The **User Environment Profile** dialog box is displayed. In the **User Profile Path** box, type the path to the profile (.usr) file you created earlier.

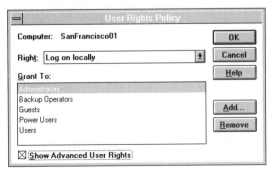

5. In the **Home Directory** box, select **Connect To**, and type the drive letter and path to the home server where the roving user's profile is located.

Before Windows 95 roving users use Exchange for the first time, you must enable multiple users to customize preferences and desktop settings.

Note Windows 95 profiles can be stored on any type of server, including a Novell NetWare server.

▶ **To permit a Windows NT or Windows 95 roving user to log on to a different domain**

1. In the Administrative Tools program group, click **User Manager for Domains**.

2. On the **Policies** menu, click **User Rights**.

3. In the **Right** box, select **Log on locally**.

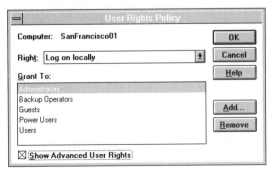

4. Select the **Show Advanced User Rights** box, and then click **Add**.

5. In the **List Names From** box in the **Add Users and Groups** dialog box, select the domain to which you want to add the roving user account.

6. In the **Names** box, select the user account for the roving user, click **Add**, and then click **OK**.

7. In the **User Rights Policy** dialog box, click **OK**, and then close the **User Manager for Domains** dialog box.

▶ **To enable multiple users of a Microsoft Exchange Client computer to personalize their settings on Windows 95**

1. In the Microsoft Exchange Client computer Control Panel, double-click **Passwords**.

2. Click the **User Profiles** tab.

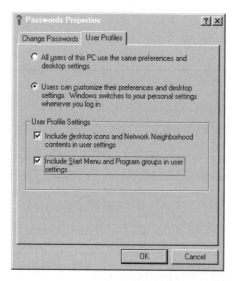

3. Select **Users can customize their preferences and desktop settings**.

▶ **To use the profile generator with Windows NT Workstation**

- Add the following line to the Windows NT Workstation domain logon script.

```
\\Server Name\Share Name\PROFGEN.EXE  C:\EXCHANGE\NEWPROF.EXE -P
H:\Winnt.prf
```

where H:\ is the user's home directory.

The automatic profile generator (Newprof.exe) must be located in the Exchange directory. The profile generator (Profgen.exe) can be located on the local computer or the server.

▶ **To use the profile generator with Windows 95**

1. Copy Profgen.exe to the Exchange directory.

2. Copy Profgen.ini to the Windows directory.

3. In the Profgen.ini file, edit the PathToExeFile and PathToPRFFile entries to point to the automatic profile generator (Newprof.exe) and .prf files, respectively. Normally, these entries should be as follows.

```
PathToExeFile=c:\exchange\newprof.exe
PathToPRFFile=h:\Win95.prf
```

where h:\ is the user's home directory on the server.

4. In the Win.ini file, edit the Load= line as follows.

```
Load=c:\exchange\profgen.exe
```

MS-DOS

To support a roving user on MS-DOS®, you must store the profile in the user's home directory on a file server, and the Microsoft Exchange Client .exe file must be on a network share. When users run workstation setup from the network share, they must specify the home directory where they want to store their profile.

Assign logon scripts to users to make it easier for them to use the Microsoft Exchange Client on other computers in your organization. Logon scripts can automatically connect users to their home directory and the network share when they log on to MS-DOS. When a user is connected to the home directory and the Microsoft Exchange Client is started, the user's default profile is used.

▶ **To modify the logon scripts to connect users to their home directory**

• Modify logon scripts to include the following lines.

```
set EXCHANGE=<home directory path>
set RPC_BINDING_ORDER=ncalrpc,ncacn_np,ncacn_spx,ncacn_ip_tcp,netbios
```

Note If the user's logon script has been modified to set the home directory and the remote procedure call (RPC) binding order, the user should not modify the Autoexec.bat file during Setup. Otherwise, the information in the logon script and the Autoexec.bat file can conflict.

Using the Command Line

Using the profile generator from the command line allows you to customize the options each time you run it. Use the following syntax:

```
Profgen <path>\Newprof.exe -P <path>\Default.prf [-S] [-X] [-L] [-U]
```

The following table is a list of the command-line options.

Option	Description
<path>\Newprof.exe	Specifies the full path to Newprof.exe.
-P <path>\Default.prf	Specifies the full path to the .prf file.
-S	Runs Newprof.exe with the -S option.
-X	Runs Newprof.exe with the -X option.
-L	Creates a log file named C:\Profgen.log.
-U	Updates the MailboxName= entry in the .prf file specified with the -P option, even if it already contains a value. By default, if the entry contains a value, it is not updated.

Note The -S and -X options are added to the command line for Newprof.exe only if they are specified on the Profgen.exe command line or in the Profgen.ini file.

Using the Profgen.ini File

The settings in the Profgen.ini file can be in the [NEWPROF] or [PROFGEN] sections. The following example is an entry in the [NEWPROF] section.

```
[NEWPROF]
; Provide the path to the NEWPROF.EXE executable
; e.g. c:\exchange\newprof.exe
PathToExeFile=c:\exchange\win95\newprof.exe
```

The following table describes the settings used in the Profgen.ini file.

Section and setting	Description
[NEWPROF]	
PathToExeFile=	The path to the Newprof.exe file. For example, PathToExeFile=c:\exchange\win95\newprof.exe.
PathToPRFFile=	The path to the .prf file used to create the profile. For example, c:\exchange\default.prf.
	If this entry is blank, the program looks for the file Default.prf in the Windows directory. If a file is specified, but does not exist, the program quits and no profile is created.
DisplayUI=	Set to 1 if you want the profile generator user interface to be displayed. This setting is translated into the -S command-line option for Newprof.exe.

(continued)

Section and setting	Description
AutoExecute=	Set to 1 to run Newprof.exe with the -X command-line option.
[PROFGEN]	
Logging=	Set to 1 to create a log file called Profgen.log in C:.
UpdateMailboxName=	Set to 0 to replace the value of the MailboxName= entry in the .prf file with the current Windows NT logon ID.
	The MailboxName= entry in the .prf file must contain a value.

Setting Up Users Accessing Microsoft Exchange Client from Multiple Windows Operating Systems

You can set up Microsoft Exchange Client users so they can move to any computer and access their mailbox, regardless of the Windows operating system.

Note Roving users using Microsoft Exchange Client for MS-DOS have access to their mailboxes only from the MS-DOS client.

▶ **To set up a roving user for all operating systems**

1. Set up each operating system to allow roving users. See the procedures later in this section.

2. Assign Windows NT domain logon scripts for each domain user.

3. Using Windows NT Server User Manager for Domains or a logon script, create a home directory for each user.

4. Copy three profile (.prf) files into each user's home directory, one for each platform. See the procedures later in this section. The profile is created the first time the user logs on to a computer with that operating system. The user should save the profile in the home directory and the profile will be available the next time the user logs on to any computer with the same operating system.

5. Follow the steps for each operating system that will be used. For more information, see "Using the Profile Generator" earlier in this appendix.

▶ **To set up the operating system to allow roving users**

• Set up each operating system as follows.

Windows NT Use User Manager for Domains to create a user profile for each user.

Windows 95 Enable user profiles for Windows 95. In Control Panel, double-click **Passwords**, and then click **User Profiles**.

Windows 3.*x* and Windows for Workgroups Add the **ProfileDirectory16**=<*home directory*> line to the [MAPI] section of the Win.ini file.

▶ **To create profile files**

1. Run the Microsoft Exchange Server Setup Editor at the client installation point for each operating system. Running the Setup Editor creates a Default.prf profile file in the client installation directory.

2. On the **File** menu, click **Set User Options**, and then click the **Home Server** tab. Ensure the **Home Server** box is selected.

3. Copy Default.prf to Win95.prf, Winnt.prf, and Win16.prf. These profile files can be identical and must contain all of the information that is to be added to the user profile, except the MailboxName. This is entered by the profile generator (Profgen.exe).

Windows NT Mandatory User Profiles

If you have mandatory user profiles, no changes to the Windows NT user profile are saved. Each time the user logs on, the default Windows NT profile overwrites the local Windows NT profile; therefore, the Microsoft Exchange Client profiles created during one Windows NT logon session are not available the next time the user logs on.

Use the profile generator to automatically re-create the user's profile each time the user logs on to the Windows NT domain. The profile generator automatically renames the .prf file, so you use the Windows NT logon script to copy the .prf file.

▶ **To set up roving users with mandatory user profiles**

1. Modify the Windows NT logon script to copy a .prf file into the user's home directory by adding the following line:

   ```
   Copy \\<ServerName>\<Share>\Default.prf  H:\
   ```

   where H:\ is the user's home directory.

2. Complete the steps in the "Using the Profile Generator" section earlier in this appendix.

Preventing Roving Users from Creating Local .Pst Files

For a roving user's mail to be accessible from each computer, the user must use only the server-based information store. If the user moves mail to a local .pst file (personal folders in Microsoft Exchange Client), it is not available from other computers.

You can prevent users from creating personal folders by installing Microsoft Exchange Client without the personal folders service. Without this service, users cannot add personal folders to their profile.

▶ **To install Microsoft Exchange Client without personal folders**

Note This works only if Microsoft Exchange Client has never been installed on the computer.

---

1. Run the Microsoft Exchange Setup Editor at a client installation share point.
2. On the **File** menu, click **Select Client Installation Point**.
3. Click the **Services** tab.
4. In the **To be installed on the client** box, select the **Personal Folders** service, and then click **Remove**.
5. Click **OK**, and then quit the program.
6. Run Microsoft Exchange Client Setup from the modified installation share point. The installed client will not have the personal folders service available.

If Microsoft Exchange Client was previously installed on the computer with personal folders, personal folders are available even if you remove the client by selecting **Remove All** in Setup or if you reinstall with different services. The only way to remove the service is to edit the Mapisvf.inf file manually.

▶ **To remove personal folders from a Microsoft Exchange Client that has already been installed**

1. Open the Mapisvf.inf file using a text editor.
2. Remove the following line from the [Services] section.

```
MSPST MS=Personal Folders
```

Remote Users

Microsoft Exchange Client remote users can establish network connections to personal and public folders on Microsoft Exchange Server computers by using a modem, a telephone line, and remote access software. Users who need access to the client from a remote location using a portable computer have several options for installing the Microsoft Exchange Client. They can install from:

- A client installation point.
- A Microsoft Exchange Server compact disc.
- Floppy disks.

▶ **To copy Microsoft Exchange Client to floppy disks for remote users to install**

1. Format several floppy disks. Label and number them sequentially.
2. From the Microsoft Exchange Client compact disc, go to the subdirectory for the client operating system where you are installing Microsoft Exchange Client.

3. Copy all files except the .cab files to Disk 1. Also copy Exchng1.cab to Disk 1.

4. Copy Exchng2.cab to Disk 2, Exchng3.cab to Disk 3, and so on until you have copied all of the files to the disks.

Installing and Configuring ShivaRemote on a Microsoft Exchange Client

Microsoft Exchange Server includes ShivaRemote, a tool for accessing the server remotely, for users running Windows version 3.*x*, Windows for Workgroups, and MS-DOS. For information about installing ShivaRemote for other operating systems, see the Config.hlp file located in the directory where ShivaRemote is installed.

Note ShivaRemote does not support the Microsoft IPX/SPX protocol; however, it does support the Novell IPX protocol. For more information, see the Config.hlp file in the Shiva subdirectory.

▶ **To install ShivaRemote for users on Windows 3.*x* and Windows for Workgroups**

1. Copy ShivaRemote files to the Exchange\Shiva directory on a local disk.

2. In the Microsoft Exchange program group, choose **ShivaRemote Setup**.

▶ **To install ShivaRemote for users on MS-DOS**

- During Microsoft Exchange Client Setup for MS-DOS, select the option to install ShivaRemote files to the Exchange\Shiva directory on a local disk.

Configuring a RAS Server for ShivaRemote Clients

A Microsoft Exchange Client user running ShivaRemote can connect directly to a server running Shiva LanRover or Windows NT Remote Access Service (RAS). If a Windows 3.*x* or Windows for Workgroups user is using ShivaRemote to connect to a Windows NT RAS server computer, Microsoft Exchange Client must be configured as follows:

- Users must have logon accounts with RAS enabled on the Windows NT Server

- The Windows NT Server computer must have RAS installed and be configured to accept encrypted authentication.

▶ **To configure a Windows NT RAS Server computer to accept encrypted authentication for Microsoft Exchange Clients using ShivaRemote**

1. Ensure RAS is installed on the Microsoft Exchange Server computer.

2. In Control Panel, double-click **Networks**.

3. In the Installed Network Software box, select Remote Access Service, and then click Configure.

4. In the **Remote Access Setup** dialog box, click **Network**.

5. In the **Network Configuration** dialog box, select **Require Encrypted Authentication**, and then click **OK**.

6. Close all open dialog boxes.

7. Restart Windows NT Server.

Scheduling Resources

You can use Microsoft Schedule+ to automatically schedule resources used in meetings, such as conference rooms and audio visual equipment. First set up a mailbox account for the resource, called a *resource account*, and then configure the resource account to accept meeting requests automatically. Users can then check the availability of resources through Schedule+ and automatically book resources by adding them to the **Resource** box in the **Select Attendees** dialog box.

▶ **To set up a resource account to book meeting requests automatically**

1. Create an account and profile for the resource.

2. Log on to Microsoft Schedule+ version 7.0 as the resource account you have created.

3. In the **Welcome to Schedule+ 7.0** dialog box, select **I Do Not Want a Schedule File on this Machine**.

4. On the **Tools** menu, click **Options**, and then click the **General** tab. Select the following options:

   ▪ **This Account is for a Resource**

   ▪ **Automatically Accept Meeting Requests**

   ▪ **Automatically Remove Canceled Meetings**

5. On the **Tools** menu, click **Options**.

6. Select **Synchronize** and click to clear the **Work Primarily from Local File** box.

7. On the **Tools** menu, click **Set Access Permissions**.

8. Click the **Users** tab, and then set the following options:

   ▪ Set the **User Role** in the **Permissions Details for Default** box to **Create** or higher.

   ▪ Click **Add**, and then select all users that should have access to the resource. Click **OK**.

9. Log off Schedule+.

▶ **To invite the resource to attend a meeting**

1. Log on to Schedule+ as a user (not a resource account).

2. On the **Insert** menu, click **Appointments** to display the **New Appointment** dialog box.

3. Click the **General** tab, and then type a description of the appointment.

4. Click the **Attendees** tab, and then select required and optional attendees (other than the resource).

5. Select the resource by typing the resource account name in the **Resources** box.

Note Automatically booking resources is enabled only when the resource account is entered in the **Resource** box of the **Meeting Attendees** dialog box. It is disabled if the resource is placed in the **Required** or **Optional** boxes.

Setting Permissions for Clients

Users frequently need to have access to other users' mailboxes, schedules, and public folders. For example, a manager can give an assistant permission to send e-mail on his or her behalf. Users can also grant other users access to their mailboxes and schedules.

Setting Up a Delegate User on a Mailbox

You can assign another user to act as a delegate for a user's mailbox or Schedule+. A delegate can perform various activities depending on the permissions the mailbox owner grants to the delegate.

▶ **To grant a user Delegate permission for a mailbox**

1. Log on to the Microsoft Exchange Client as the mailbox owner.

2. In the folder list, select the mailbox or a mailbox folder.

3. On the **File** menu, click **Properties**, and then click the **Permissions** tab.

4. To add a name to the **Name/Role** list, click **Add**.

5. Under **Type Name Or Select From List**, type or select the name, click **Add**, and then click **OK**.

6. In the **Name/Role** list, select the name of the user you want to grant permission to.

7. Under **Permissions**, select a predefined role in the **Roles** box or select the individual permissions.

   You must grant a minimum of **Read Items** (**Reviewer** role) permission to allow another user to open the mailbox.

8. Click **OK**.

▶   **To open another user's mailbox as a delegate**

1. On the **Tools** menu in the Microsoft Exchange Client, click **Services**.

2. In **The Following Information Services Are Set Up In This Profile** box, click **Microsoft Exchange Server**, and then click **Properties**.

3. Click the **Advanced** tab, and then click **Add**.

4. In the **Add Mailbox** box, type the name of the additional mailbox you have permission to access.

5. Click **OK** until all open dialog boxes are closed.

Note   When a delegate opens the mailbox, the delegate can open only the folders for which the user has granted permission.

Setting Up a Mailbox to Send on Behalf of Another Mailbox

Send On Behalf Of permission enables a user to send messages with the user's name after "Sent On Behalf Of" and the delegate's name after "From." This permission can be set up using either Microsoft Exchange Client or the Microsoft Exchange Server Administrator program. You can use the Administrator program to grant Send On Behalf Of permission if the mailbox owner is not available.

▶   **To grant Send On Behalf Of permission using Microsoft Exchange Client**

1. On the **Tools** menu in the Microsoft Exchange Client, click **Options**, and then click the **Exchange Server** tab.

2. Click **Add**.

3. Under **Type Name or Select from List**, type or select the user's name.

4. Click **Add**, and then click **OK**.

▶   **To grant Send On Behalf Of permission using the Administrator program**

1. In the Administrator window, choose **Recipients**, and then select the name of the recipient you want to configure.

2. On the **File** menu, click **Properties**, and then click the **Delivery Options** tab.

3. Under **Give Send On Behalf Of permissions to**, click **Modify**.

4. In the Address Book, select the recipient, and then click **Add**.

Setting Up a Mailbox to Send As Another Mailbox

If a user has Send As permission on a mailbox, that user can send a message with the return address of the mailbox so it appears that the message was sent by the mailbox owner. Send As permission can be granted to user accounts only with the Administrator program.

Note Send As permission overrides Send On Behalf Of permission. For example, if a user has both Send As and Send On Behalf Of permissions for another user, any message sent in the other user's name has that user's name as the return address.

▶ **To grant Send As permission**

1. In the Administrator window, choose **Recipients**, and then select the name of the recipient you want to configure.

2. On the **File** menu, click **Properties**, and then click the **Permissions** tab.

   If the **Permissions** tab is not available, click **Options** on the **Tools** menu, click the **Permissions** tab, and then click the **Show Permissions page for all objects** and **Display rights for roles on Permissions page** check boxes.

3. Select the user account to which you are granting permissions, or click **Add** to add another account.

4. Under **Roles**, select **Send As**, and then click **OK**.

Setting Permissions on a Schedule

By default, all users have access to the free and busy times for other users; however, a user must have permission to open another user's appointment book or to view details of another user's busy times. A user can grant permissions for access to his or her appointments, contacts, events, or tasks to another user. However, a user does not have access to Schedule+ items marked Private unless the user is an owner or delegate owner on the item.

▶ **To set up access to a user's schedule**

1. On the **Tools** menu in Schedule+, click **Set Access Permissions**.

2. Click **Add**, double-click the delegate, and then click **OK**.

3. In the **User role** box, select a role, and then click **OK**.

▶ **To view another user's schedule**

1. On the **File** menu in Schedule+, click **Open**, and then click **Other's Appointment Book**.

2. Select a user name, and then click **OK**.

Setting Permissions on Public Folders

This section describes how to set up a public folder owner or contact and how to set permissions on public folders.

Setting Up a Public Folder Owner or Contact

The owner and contact of a public folder have special permissions on the public folder. A public folder owner can design public folders and grant other users permissions. A public folder contact receives notification when there are public folder conflicts or the contents of a public folder exceed the storage limit. Only a public folder owner or an administrator using the Microsoft Exchange Server Administrator program can make someone a public folder owner or contact.

▶ **To set up a public folder owner or contact**

1. In Microsoft Exchange Client, select the public folder.

2. On the **File** menu, click **Properties**, and then click the **Permissions** tab.

3. Click **Add**, double-click the name of the user to which you are granting permissions, and then click **OK**.

4. Select the name of the user you added.

5. In the **Roles** box, click **Folder Owner** or **Folder Contact**, and then click **OK**.

Granting Permissions on Public Folders

You can use the Administrator program to grant users permissions for public folders or enable them to create top-level folders. If you are the owner of a public folder, you can also use Microsoft Exchange Client to grant other users permissions to create subfolders.

▶ **To grant permissions for public folders using the Administrator program**

1. In the Administrator window, choose **Public Folders**, and select the public folder you want to configure.

2. On the **File** menu, click **Properties**, and then click the **General** tab.

3. Click **Client Permissions**.

4. Click **Add**, double-click the user to which you are granting permissions, and then click **OK**.

5. Click the user you added.

6. Select **Folder owner** or **Folder contact**, and then click **OK**.

▶ **To grant permissions to create top-level folders using the Administrator program**

1. In the Administrator window, select **Configuration**, double-click **Information Store Site Configuration**, and then click the **Top Level Folder Creation** tab.

2. Click **Modify** to change the list of users who can create top-level folders.

3. Double-click the user to which you are granting permissions, and then click **OK**.

4. Click **OK**.

▶ **To grant permissions to create subfolders using Microsoft Exchange Client**

1. In Microsoft Exchange Client, select the public folder.

2. On the **File** menu, click **Properties**, and then click the **Permissions** tab.

3. Click **Add**, double-click the user you are granting permissions to, and then click **OK**.

Troubleshooting

The following sections provide suggestions for troubleshooting problems you might be having with the Microsoft Exchange Client and Schedule+.

Microsoft Exchange Client Setup

If you have problems installing Microsoft Exchange Client, ensure the following are true:

- The user and server names are correct.
- The directory is running on the Microsoft Exchange Server computer to which Microsoft Exchange Client is connecting.
- If Windows for Workgroups is installed, the patch available on the Microsoft Windows NT version 3.51 compact disc is installed.

Microsoft Exchange Client and Schedule+

This section contains troubleshooting information and tips for Microsoft Exchange Client and Schedule+.

Messages Remain in the Outbox

The following are reasons messages remain in the Outbox for more than a few seconds:

- The message is incorrectly addressed.
- The information service used to send this message is unavailable.

- Microsoft Exchange Server is unavailable.
- The user is working offline.

Unread Message Count Is Incorrect

If the unread message count on a personal folder file (.pst) or an offline folder file (.ost) is incorrect, you can run the Scanpst tool included with the *Microsoft BackOffice 4.5 Resource Kit* compact disc. You should run this tool if the user's unread message count is off by one or more messages.

Offline Synchronization Stops Responding

When using an offline folder file (.ost), Microsoft Exchange Client can stop responding during startup if offline synchronization isn't completed successfully. You can disable offline synchronization by editing the user's messaging profile as described in the following steps:

▶ **To disable offline synchronization**

1. On the **Tools** menu, click **Services**.
2. Under **The following information services are set up in this profile**, select **Microsoft Exchange Server**.
3. Click **Properties**.
4. Click the **Advanced** tab, and then click **Offline Folder File Settings**.
5. Choose **Disable Offline Use**.

Note If the problem persists, you might also have to rename the .ost file.

Resource Won't Automatically Book Meeting Requests

If a resource such as a conference room does not automatically book meeting requests, the resource may have been put in the **Required** or **Optional** boxes instead of the **Resource** box. Entering resources in any address box other than the **Resource** box disables this feature in Schedule+.

Note Automatically booking appointments does not work when meeting requests are sent between Microsoft Mail for PC Networks post offices and Microsoft Exchange Server.

To ensure that resources can be booked automatically:

- Inform users to put conference rooms in the **Resource** list box when requesting meetings.

- Place the resource account in the **Resource** box of the **Select Attendees** dialog box so the resource is included in the **Bcc** box of the Meeting Request form and displayed in the **Where** box of the meeting request message. Schedule+ searches only for users listed in the **Bcc** box to automatically book appointments.

Password Can't Be Changed When Using Novell VLM Client Software

When you try to change the password on a Microsoft Exchange Client computer that is running Novell VLM client software, the following error can occur.

```
The NT Domain password could not be changed. A required action  was not
successful due to an unspecified error.
```

To solve the problem, try the following troubleshooting suggestions.

- Install Gateway Services for NetWare on the primary domain controller where the user accounts are located.

- Ensure the Novell client is running the latest Novell connectivity files.

- Ensure the remote procedure call (RPC) service is configured to start automatically. This can be changed by choosing **Services** in the Control Panel.

- Ensure the registry on the primary domain controller has the following entries:

```
HKEY_LOCAL_MACHINE\SYSTEM\CurrentControlSet\Control\LSA
```

If the primary domain controller has NWLINK installed, add the following entry to the registry:

```
NetWareClientSupport:REG_DWORD:0x1
```

If the primary domain controller has TCP/IP installed, add the following entry to the registry:

```
TcpipClientSupport:REG_DWORD:0x1
```

- Ensure the primary domain controller is running the same version of Windows NT Server as the Microsoft Exchange Server, including all service packs.

A P P E N D I X   E

Microsoft Exchange Forms Designer

Exchange provides an application design environment, including Collaboration Data Objects (CDO) and the Microsoft Exchange Server Forms Designer, that is ideal for rapidly changing business requirements. These tools enable all users, from novices to skilled programmers, to create custom applications to improve efficiency and communication. They provide a scalable design environment that makes it easy to modify those applications quickly and in a cost effective manner. They also offer reliable, versatile options for connecting to the Internet and X.400 systems to distribute those applications to users virtually anywhere.

In this appendix, you will learn how to develop custom Exchange solutions to make business communications easier. The Microsoft Exchange Server Forms Designer and sample applications are provided with the *Microsoft BackOffice 4.5 Resource Kit* compact disc in the Samples\Efd directory. For more information on CDO, see Part 12, "Collaboration."

The following topics are discussed:

- The scope of applications that can be developed

- The role each component plays in providing these solutions

- The capabilities of each component (demonstrated in customer scenarios)

Applications range from those that can be created by novice users who are modifying existing sample applications, to complex groupware applications that are developed with high-end development tools such as the Microsoft Visual Basic programming system and the Microsoft Visual C++ development system.

Using Forms Designer with Public Folders

You can use custom forms to create surveys, classified ads, or order forms that you want to manage by working with public folders. Use Microsoft Exchange Forms Designer to create forms and applications, and then use Visual C++ to extend the functionality of these forms and applications. The Forms Designer also contains sample applications that you can adopt as is or modify to suit your purposes.

For more information, visit the Application Farm Web site at:

- http://www.microsoft.com/technet/boes/bo/mailexch/exch/tools/appfarm/appfarm1.htm

When you store forms, there are two locations from which to choose:

- Public folders
- Organization forms library

Public folders allow many users to view and store information and are useful when you have many people adding information or posting forms.

The organization forms library is more restrictive because only an administrator can install the forms. However, you can change this to allow all users full ownership permissions for the organization forms library.

The Microsoft Exchange Server Infrastructure

Exchange provides application development capabilities within an easy-to-administer infrastructure for messaging and replicated databases. This infrastructure includes the following components:

- **Exchange** — Includes client and server software, including the directory service, information store, message transfer agent (MTA), and system attendant.

- **Microsoft Exchange Client** — Includes clients for the MS-DOS®, Microsoft Windows® 3.1, Microsoft Windows NT Workstation, and Microsoft Windows 95 operating systems. These clients enable users to find the important information, structure it in a meaningful way, and build common information-sharing solutions without relying on the information services department.

- **Microsoft Outlook Client** — Includes clients for the Windows NT Workstation and Windows 95 operating systems. The Outlook client is a desktop management system that integrates messaging, scheduling, contact, and task and file management into one environment.

- **Microsoft Schedule+** — Makes it easy to organize meetings, resources, tasks, and contact information. It provides a programmatic interface for integrating these capabilities into custom solutions.

- **Microsoft Exchange Forms Designer** — A Microsoft Windows-based forms-design capability that enables users to develop forms-based applications for Windows without programming. It also generates Visual Basic source code for additional customization.

- **Exchange sample applications** — Provide examples and source code for three categories of applications:

    - Applications designed with the tools available in Exchange

    - Customized Visual Basic-based applications integrated with Exchange

    - Server applications that run as a service of Microsoft Windows NT Server and can be integrated with Exchange

- **The MAPI subsystem** — An open, widely used set of messaging application programming interfaces known as Messaging Application Programming Interface (MAPI) on which Exchange is built. MAPI enables developers to use tools such as OLE Messaging (an OLE Automation interface to MAPI) and OLE Scheduling (an OLE Automation interface to Schedule+).

Understanding the MAPI Subsystem

The following diagram shows the MAPI subsystem infrastructure. Either messaging client applications communicate with service providers through the MAPI subsystem, or the MAPI subsystem initiates contact and the services communicate directly. Through broad publication of messaging APIs and their robust messaging and workgroup functionality, MAPI has become a widely used standard throughout the industry for messaging and groupware clients and providers.

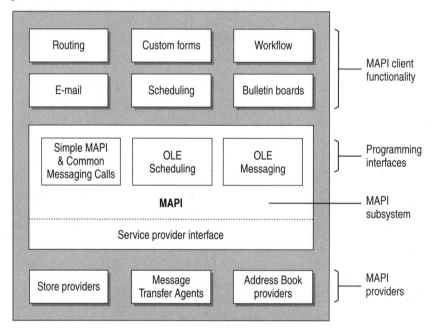

As the preceding diagram shows, MAPI-compliant clients span a variety of messaging- and workgroup-based applications; they support either 16-bit applications running on Microsoft Windows 3.*x*, or 16-bit or 32-bit MAPI applications running on Windows NT Server or Windows 95. Each of these types of applications has access to the service provider functionality required without having a specific interface for each provider. This is analogous to applications that use the Microsoft Windows printing subsystem without requiring drivers for every available printer.

Not shown in the preceding diagram, but frequently employed, are third-party programming interfaces that can be built upon MAPI. Because MAPI is an open and well-defined interface, a proprietary third-party API can be implemented on top of MAPI without having to revise the MAPI subsystem itself. You can also implement your own MAPI solutions to meet your particular needs without incurring the development costs that would otherwise accrue with other messaging infrastructures.

Messaging applications that require messaging services have access to them through any of five MAPI subsystem interfaces:

- Simple MAPI (sMAPI)
- Common Messaging Calls (CMC)
- OLE Messaging/Active Messaging
- OLE Scheduling
- MAPI itself

Client requests for messaging services are processed by the MAPI subsystem—either as function interface calls (for sMAPI or CMC) or as manipulations of MAPI objects (for OLE Messaging or MAPI itself)—and are passed on to the appropriate MAPI-compliant service provider. The MAPI service providers then perform the requested actions for the client and pass the action back through the MAPI subsystem to the MAPI client.

Each MAPI subsystem interface provides specific functionality as follows:

- **sMAPI** — Contains 12 Windows-based function calls that enable messaging-aware applications to perform basic messaging tasks such as sending e-mail and resolving conflicts in e-mail names. It provides the programming interface primarily used by Microsoft Mail Server.

- **CMC** — Provides functionality similar to that available in sMAPI but also supports cross-platform configurations.

- **OLE Messaging** — An OLE Automation server that presents a large subset of MAPI functionality to the developer. OLE messaging empowers developers using Visual Basic or Visual Basic for Applications to tap into the messaging and workgroup functionality inherent in MAPI. It also permits users to maximize their software investment, by integrating applications created with Visual Basic for Applications and desktop software into custom Exchange solutions.

- **OLE Scheduling** — An OLE Automation server that provides developers who use Visual Basic or Visual Basic for Applications with an interface for gaining access to the information stored in Microsoft Schedule+ version 7.0.

- **MAPI** — A Component Object Model (COM) interface that enables MAPI objects such as messages, forms, and folders to be manipulated. It was designed to be used by complex messaging and groupware applications. For this reason, MAPI is used by developers who want the full range of MAPI functionality in their applications and the higher performance of writing directly to an API.

Integrating Schedule+ Applications

In addition to the MAPI interfaces, Schedule+, a key component available with Microsoft Exchange Client, includes an OLE Automation interface known as OLE Scheduling. Developers using Visual Basic and Visual Basic for Applications can readily integrate Schedule+ into their applications.

For example, you can use the telephony application programming interface (TAPI) and Schedule+ to create an application that sends Schedule+ meeting reminders, including a text message, to a user's pager. Or, using Microsoft Project, tasks can be scheduled in both Microsoft Project and Schedule+.

Tight integration between Microsoft Office for Windows 95 and Schedule+ enables you to quickly build applications that integrate that suite of applications by using Visual Basic for Applications through the OLE Scheduling interface. For example, you can create an application that enables new contact information entered into Schedule+ by a company's sales staff to be copied to Microsoft Excel for reporting and analysis, and reports to be generated in Microsoft Word based on information in Schedule+.

Building a Range of Solutions on a Single Platform

Most organizations need a wide range of business applications to improve processes and respond to competitive opportunities. In many organizations, this results in a heterogeneous collection of operating systems, e-mail systems, security platforms, and user directories, along with the corresponding overhead of supporting those systems, training users on a variety of interfaces, and hiring a development staff versed in a wide array of technologies.

By providing an extensible messaging platform to which users have access and can use to build messaging and groupware, Exchange eliminates the need for duplicating the security systems, user directories, client interfaces, systems management interfaces, and development technologies that often accompany process-automation solutions. Exchange doesn't require its own security system; it uses the security system that is part of the operating system.

Because Exchange is built on MAPI, custom-application developers and third-party software developers can write to a powerful, widely accepted programming interface to provide customers with a wide selection of groupware applications. By bringing these components under the control of a single messaging-based platform, organizations can focus their resources on creating customized applications, rather than on managing the complexities of multiple and often incompatible systems for each type of messaging or workgroup application.

Factors to Consider When Automating Business Processes

Most organizations recognize the importance of automating business processes. But most organizations must also answer a number of fundamental questions before they can determine what processes should be automated and how to automate them:

- What kind of applications do my users need?

- What are the associated development costs?

- What if I want to add custom functionality to those applications?

Building Common Groupware Applications

Building applications on a messaging server goes well beyond sending rich-text notes with attachments. Exchange includes built-in groupware for routing, discussion, reference, and tracking applications. It also supports highly customized groupware applications and can even be integrated into customized desktop or Microsoft BackOffice server applications. The following sections illustrate typical groupware applications supported natively by Exchange.

Routing Applications

Exchange enables end users to easily create person-to-person routing forms. For example, a sales manager can design a form to gather weekly sales data from salespeople. Any salesperson, whether connected to the network or mobile, can fill out the pre-addressed form (shown in the following illustration) and send it back to the sales manager.

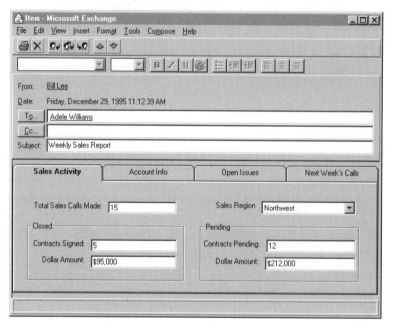

Discussion Applications

Exchange also supports *discussion*, or *bulletin board* applications using the form shown below. These applications enable users to discuss topics with their co-workers through public folders, rather than carrying out conversations over e-mail and wading through their Inboxes to find relevant e-mail threads.

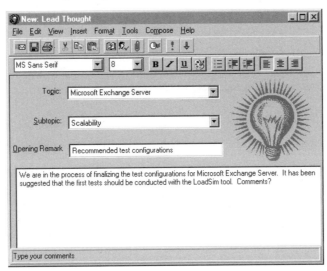

Reference Applications

Most organizations need a central repository where users can find information. Exchange *replicated public folders* provide a useful infrastructure for this type of application. Employee handbooks, product information, monthly reports, and sales data are all examples of useful information that can be published in public folders.

You can also make Internet newsgroups easily accessible to public folder users by developing applications for the Microsoft Exchange Internet Mail Service and the Microsoft Exchange Internet News Service.

Tracking Applications

In most organizations, sales people need access to information sources before they make account calls. They might need to call other sales people to determine who last contacted the customer or they might need to review sales orders and find out whether the customer has orders outstanding. Many organizations provide this functionality through third-party products. Exchange tracking applications eliminate this complexity and bring tracking functionality under the same user interface as other groupware applications.

For example, by creating a customer-tracking public folder, a salesperson can find information on the last contact with the customer, new customer contacts, and the company profile in a single location.

Microsoft Exchange Client enables sales people to customize the way they display data, to view the information in the same interface as other Exchange applications, and to use custom forms designed with Forms Designer to organize and report the information. The following figure shows how a customized view can enable users to view account data by company.

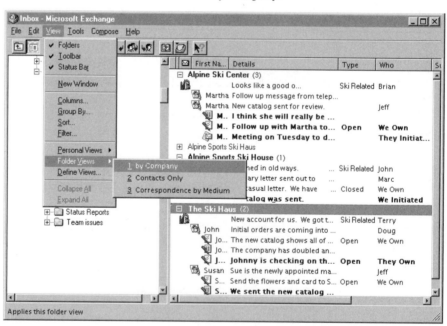

Cutting Development Costs

Competitive pressures dictate that organizations must find ways to reduce the time it takes to complete processes and access information. As a result, organizations are constantly building custom workgroup solutions. Organization-wide workgroup solutions are typically built by professional software developers who are part of the Information Services department. At the department level, solutions are often developed by technical "power users" who have learned how to write programs.

Both of these development resources are expensive, and so are the solutions they provide. Because custom solutions are in high demand, Information Services departments are overwhelmed with requests for new software systems and enhancements to existing solutions. As a result, solutions often take a long time to be delivered and are difficult to modify when business conditions change, as they inevitably do.

Creating Simple Applications Without Programming

Programming often is a major obstacle to developing custom solutions. Although programming is required for more complex applications, it hinders users who are willing to build simpler systems but lack programming skills.

If users can build their own solutions without writing programs, Information Services departments have more time to focus their resources on building organization-wide systems. Users at the departmental and group levels do not have to wait as long to get what they need. At the same time, programmers benefit from a development environment that can support advanced and highly specialized solutions designed to solve more demanding problems.

Developing Scalable Applications

Exchange includes a scalable set of tools that enables almost anyone, even users who have never programmed, to develop custom groupware applications. It also enables professional programmers to build advanced business software systems. The following sections contain information about key Exchange features that enable end users and programmers to create custom solutions.

The rapid application design and delivery process made possible by Exchange enables those who have the best understanding of the functionality needed for specific applications to respond quickly to their organization's requirements. As a result, an organization can dramatically reduce the costs of adapting and rolling out those applications.

Rapid Application Development Without Programming

The Exchange application design environment enables users to build complete groupware applications, such as customer-tracking systems or electronic discussion forums, without programming. Assuming they have the appropriate permissions, users can copy an existing application (including forms, views, permissions, and rules) and modify it as needed with the functionality available in Microsoft Exchange Client. They can easily modify existing forms or create new ones with Forms Designer, which requires no programming knowledge.

Central Application Management

After users complete an application, they usually hand it off to an administrator for further testing or for distribution to others within the organization. The Exchange replication engine manages the distribution of the application or any new forms that were revised or created for existing applications. You can also replicate these applications from one Exchange site to another over the Internet using the Internet Mail Service.

Both of these capabilities translate into reduced cycles for creating, modifying, and distributing groupware applications. This means that end users can build applications that are valuable to them without having to wait for a response from Information Services. The Information Services department can further customize these applications because forms created or modified with Forms Designer are extensible with the Visual Basic programming system. With the Exchange replication engine, revisions and new applications can be deployed inexpensively as well.

Application Extensibility

As mentioned earlier, Forms Designer permits end users to create forms for public folder and routing applications without programming. It also enables software developers to further customize an application by generating Visual Basic source code for the form developed. For example, Forms Designer can generate the source code required to send a form through e-mail or to post a form in a folder. To customize forms even further, advanced programmers can use the Professional Edition of Visual Basic.

Other workgroup application design tools either require a high degree of programming skill or become outdated whenever an application requires additional functionality. Exchange bridges the gap between end-user application design and more powerful programming languages.

Sample Applications

The following sample applications that are included on the *Microsoft BackOffice 4.5 Resource Kit* compact disc demonstrate the range of customization that can be supported.

Chess Game Sample Application

The chess game sample application shown in the figure below is a custom application written in Visual Basic. The application displays moves that have been made in a game between two Exchange users.

The right side of the chess board displays the moves that have been made so far. If you click one of the earlier moves, the chess pieces rearrange themselves to the positions they occupied at that earlier point in the game.

This application demonstrates how *any* application can be created to view information in an Exchange public folder or browse information in the public folder. The application also can act as the interface through which data is moved in and out of Exchange, independent of the Microsoft Exchange Client.

Survey Sample Application

The survey sample application is another example of the level of customization that can be incorporated into Exchange groupware applications. It is a reusable survey design tool that enables end users to create surveys, either from scratch or by using another survey as a starting point. The sample application was developed using Visual Basic. The following figure shows a survey in the process of being designed.

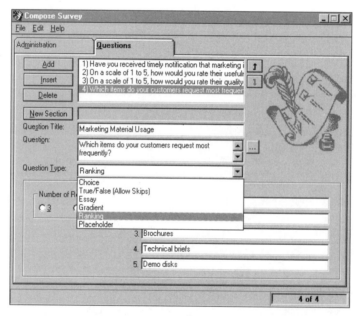

The survey sample application illustrates how you can integrate Microsoft Office and Exchange applications. For example, a summary of the information collected through the Survey application can be output to Microsoft Word. You can then copy the data into a Microsoft Excel spreadsheet for further analysis or into a Microsoft Word document that can be printed. Because Visual Basic and Microsoft Office applications use the same engine to build custom solutions, you can take advantage of the strengths of each application and programming interface.

If you want to build a customized application that is closely tied to Exchange, you can use *Messaging Application Programming Interface (MAPI) Programmer's Reference* to integrate your applications with Exchange or to build a custom gateway. You can tailor the Microsoft Exchange Client interface to meet your specific needs, add functionality to the administrative module, or give you access to virtually any part of the Exchange infrastructure.

Exchange provides a broad and readily defined infrastructure, including support for connectivity to the Internet and X.400 systems, as well as a powerful development kit upon which to build the custom applications you need.

Two Case Studies

The best way to learn about the application design capabilities in Exchange is to see how organizations can apply them. The following scenarios illustrate how two fictitious companies use these capabilities.

Fabrikam, Inc.: Using the Core Functionality in Microsoft Exchange Server

Fabrikam, Inc. is a multinational company with branch sites throughout the world. It has been running a host-based system as its primary internal e-mail system, although some branches have implemented local area network (LAN)-based e-mail in response to user requests.

A re-engineering effort has made it apparent to upper management that to reduce administrative, support, training, and custom-development costs, the company eventually needs standardize on a single e-mail system. E-mail is considered mission-critical because it is relied on heavily by internal users to transfer information.

In addition, users of the company's LAN-based messaging systems frequently send rich-text objects, such as documents and spreadsheets, and they are frustrated with the current messaging environment because it does not enable them to share that information with other branches of the company. Although users have many good ideas for automating processes by using the messaging infrastructure, the Information Services department often lacks the ability to implement them because of the heterogeneous messaging environments, the difficulty in programming applications on their existing messaging system, and a lack of resources.

Recommendations

The re-engineering effort has produced several key recommendations, including the following:

- **Taking advantage of the messaging infrastructure for groupware applications.** The best way to meet cost and functionality objectives is to build groupware applications on a messaging system capable of serving as a mission-critical infrastructure.

- **Using distributed information effectively.** The company believes it is important to have an information infrastructure that enables it to expand the capabilities of LAN-based messaging systems. This can be accomplished by making the information available where users need it and can interact with it.

- **Empowering end users.** An organization's messaging system needs to empower end users, making it easy for them to find the information they need and to create applications that enable them to solve business problems.

After conducting a comprehensive review of a variety of products, Fabrikam, Inc. chose Exchange as its messaging and workgroup platform. In addition to offering strong messaging, connectivity, and administrative capabilities, Exchange was selected because it includes built-in groupware and supports building additional groupware applications on top of its messaging system, which can handle the mission-critical demands placed upon it.

Leveraging the Messaging Infrastructure for Groupware Applications

Exchange provides the functionality that is required for the following types of groupware applications used by Fabrikam, Inc.:

- **Person-to-person routing applications.** Although the company's host-based messaging systems don't support this capability, users of the company's LAN-based system want to use e-mail for routing documents, spreadsheets, and other types of files. This capability and the frequent need to include other structured information with an attachment (such as forwarding a budget forecast spreadsheet to a vice president who might then expose information from the spreadsheet as a viewable field in a form), make the creation and routing of point-to-point forms an important capability.

- **Bulletin board applications.** A bulletin board can eliminate the usual difficulties associated with storing information in a file system and can automate and provide ready access to that information. Users no longer have to remember a multitude of network paths or passwords to find information. A variety of object types can be stored, including e-mail messages, documents, spreadsheets, slide presentations, and even voice-mail files. The user has a much broader set of options for viewing and finding files that contain OLE custom properties because the properties can be made visible in the client view.

- **Discussion area (public folder) applications.** Discussion areas enable users to participate in discussions in easily identifiable locations, rather than through e-mail, as is currently done at Fabrikam, Inc. It also eliminates the problem of trying to keep track of e-mail threads in end users' Inboxes.

- **Tracking applications.** In a workgroup-tracking application, users can combine the capabilities of bulletin boards and threaded conversations to create applications that help a group of people collaborate and share information. For instance, a customer-tracking application can enable sales staff to gather the latest information on a potential customer. After a call on the customer, the sales person can post information about the call and about outstanding customer issues, correspondence, and so on. This capability enables the sales personnel, who are typically connected only intermittently, to have the latest information. It also enables groups of people who are not necessarily in close physical contact to share information.

Using Distribution Information

Exchange support for multimaster data replication provides Fabrikam, Inc. the benefits of a *distributed information infrastructure*. This structure enables users to share ideas and work as a team to reach decisions, even if they are thousands of miles and many time zones apart. Fabrikam, Inc. plans to use this capability to create public folders that contain process discussion plans, which enables each functional unit to participate in discussions on the plans, including how they might be improved. In this way, the company benefits from the involvement of the people who best understand how to re-engineer a process.

Another benefit of replicated information is the minimal administrative overhead that is required to keep multiple versions up-to-date. This overhead has been a problem in the company's current system because much of the information the company wanted to distribute worldwide first had to be copied manually to local office servers. This meant working with links that might or might not be functioning, that disconnect in the middle of transmissions, and that cause a variety of other administrative problems.

Enabling End Users to Accomplish More

Users at Fabrikam, Inc. can make decisions more easily because they have immediate access to the information they need. This functionality is provided by Microsoft Exchange Client and Exchange working together. The server moves the information throughout the organization; the client provides the ability to search through data to find the necessary information. The ability of the Microsoft Exchange Client to group, sort, and filter information creates intelligent agents for handling tasks, support for group scheduling, and the ability for users to develop custom forms and build custom applications without programming. All of these capabilities make it easier for users to communicate.

Fabrikam, Inc. users will also be able to create applications quickly and easily. For example, a user may find a public folder application and want to make a similar application with only a few changes (such as copying the customer-tracking application, including its forms, rules, and permissions).

The purpose of each public folder is similar—to provide a centrally accessible location where information on outside organizations can be kept and to enable users of the folder to enter information as it is gathered. To accomplish these tasks, Fabrikam, Inc. intends to use Forms Designer and will install Forms Designer on most of the company's desktops that are running Microsoft Exchange Client. However, the administrator retains the sole ability to distribute applications created by users to the rest of the company, usually after the application has been completely tested.

Results

Exchange provides an e-mail infrastructure that is capable of handling Fabrikam, Inc. employees scattered across the globe but centrally managed from a single desktop. By providing built-in groupware applications, Exchange provides users with the ability to work together more efficiently without incurring the additional infrastructure, end-user training, or administrative costs that a separate infrastructure requires. Finally, users have quick and easy access to the information they need and can build applications that they feel are most valuable.

Trey Research: Taking Full Advantage of the Microsoft Exchange Server Programmable Interface

Trey Research is a diversified global financial investment company whose organizations provide personal banking, investment counseling and sales, and financial market and economic analysis for internal and external customers. Like Fabrikam, Inc., this company has chosen to standardize its messaging system on Exchange for a variety of reasons. Key to its decision is the native X.400 and Internet connectivity in Exchange. This capability is not only an internal standard, it enables the company to share information with its many international customers and information suppliers.

Another key advantage of Exchange is its ability to build custom applications that integrate the company's desktop application suite with Exchange. Management at Trey Research plans to take advantage of the built-in customization ability of Exchange to provide users with quick access to the information they need and the ability to use their desktop tools to analyze and format the information.

These capabilities are to be provided through customized applications, which enable users to use Exchange public folders as repositories for status reports or news feeds that are downloaded and then output that data to Microsoft Office applications for spreadsheet analysis, graphing, and charting. After data analysis has been completed, new statistical information is to be placed in an Exchange public folder that is accessible only to executives for review and comment. By using the replication facility in Exchange as a distributed information transport and using Internet Mail Service to connect Exchange sites, Trey Research will ensure that important information is distributed automatically to its offices worldwide.

Trey Research also plans to use Schedule+ for project scheduling by linking data maintained in public folders, Microsoft Project, and Schedule+. Exchange can also enable the company to take advantage of its investment in Visual Basic training for its corporate developers.

In short, Trey Research plans to take advantage of the same capabilities that Fabrikam, Inc. found useful, including the following additional application design benefits of Exchange:

- **Scalable tools for application design** — Many of the solutions Trey Research evaluated as possible workgroup and e-mail infrastructures could only support a limited amount of functionality, or they required highly skilled and expensive development resources to implement. Now Trey Research has the tools they need to build applications quickly and enable their internal development staff to customize applications without worrying about exceeding the functionality available through the tools.

- **Native support for Internet standards** — Trey Research can develop applications that gather relevant information from the Internet and distribute it to its other Exchange sites worldwide over an Internet backbone.

- **Integration with the Microsoft Office applications suite** — Trey Research wants to make the most of its investment in Microsoft Office by integrating its groupware and e-mail with desktop applications and by adopting a common programmable interface for the two. As a result, users can work with a familiar interface, even with custom applications. In addition, the company's development staff have a common tool set and programming interface available in Microsoft Office applications—Visual Basic and the scripting language of Visual Basic for Applications—to integrate desktop applications into workgroup solutions.

Support for Scalable Application Design

If an application created by an end user becomes popular and can be rolled out to the rest of the company, Trey Research wants its more experienced development teams to be able to further customize the application. This means that the company needs a solution that can meet the dual—and often conflicting—goals of enabling users to design applications and forms and enabling the development staff to make these applications more robust, to integrate them with existing applications, and to add additional functionality. Exchange was the only workgroup and messaging product evaluated by Trey Research that could provide a scalable application design environment.

After an application is rolled out, users inevitably find ways to improve it, and the competitive environment might require additional customization. Because forms can be customized with Visual Basic, the desired functionality can be added to Exchange workgroup solutions that use forms. Because Visual Basic is a powerful programming language capable of calling any Windows-based API, there is virtually no limit to the functionality that can be added.

Integrating with Desktop Software

Trey Research chose Microsoft Office largely because of the powerful programmability provided by Visual Basic for Applications and the various OLE Automation interfaces available in each Microsoft Office application. Exchange provides an OLE Automation server for MAPI that can be accessed from Microsoft Office applications and Visual Basic. This integrates the company's applications with Exchange and enables the company to take advantage of its existing investment, to build applications quickly, and to add, customize, or change applications rapidly.

Microsoft Office applications can also be integrated into workgroup solutions offered by Exchange. Microsoft Office documents and spreadsheets, for example, can be stored in the Exchange information store, as well as shared between the Microsoft Office applications and Exchange.

Trey Research plans to use Microsoft Excel as a reporting mechanism for public folder applications. It is to be used by sales managers to compile periodic contact and sales data automatically. For example, a sales representative can enter information about new customers, outstanding customer issues, and sales closed. A sales manager can use the analysis and charting capabilities of Microsoft Excel to evaluate trends, track the business, and automate the compiling, publication, and distribution of a report by using Microsoft Word and Exchange.

Results

By investing in a common technology, Trey Research provides key benefits for its users and developers. Sales managers, for example, are familiar with Microsoft Excel as a data analysis tool. By integrating Exchange applications into Microsoft Excel for additional analysis and data manipulation, Trey Research's managers do not have to learn a new tool or interface to conduct their analysis.

APPENDIX F

Technical Papers

An excellent source of information about Microsoft Exchange is the technical papers available on Microsoft Web sites. Technical papers provide detailed information about a specific subject related to Exchange.

You can download free technical papers from the following Web sites:

http://www.microsoft.com/exchange/guide/papers/cdo2.asp?A=2&B=6

http://support.microsoft.com/support/exchange/content/whitepapers/
    whitepapers.asp

Additional technical papers are available by subscribing to Microsoft TechNet (http://www.microsoft.com/technet/default.htm) and the Microsoft Developer Network (http://msdn.microsoft.com/developer/default.htm).

For your convenience, the BackOffice 4.5 Resource Kit compact disc includes the following technical papers. However, new technical papers are added frequently, and existing papers are updated, so check the Web sites for the latest updates. The technical papers are located in the **\whatever\tech** directory.

Technical Paper	File Name	Description
Active Directory Services Interface in the Microsoft Exchange 5.5 Environment		How to create directory-enabled applications without worrying about the different directory implementations or namespaces
Active Messaging Now Collaboration Data Objects		Where to get information about CDO
Automating and Extending Microsoft Outlook™	Automate.doc	How to program Outlook, add Microsoft Visual Basic® Scripting Edition (VBScript) to built-in Outlook forms, and manipulate data within forms

(continued)

Technical Paper	File Name	Description
Best Practices for Exchange Database Management		How Exchange maintains database consistency and helps users understand how the system works, so they can make informed policy decisions regarding the maintenance of their Exchange databases
Building Exchange and Outlook Solutions	Solution.doc	How to use the features of the Microsoft Exchange application design environment to develop collaborative solutions that streamline business processes and enhance communication
Common Microsoft Exchange Server Directory and Information Store Problems		Information to help you troubleshoot common Directory and information store problems
Connecting Exchange Server to the Internet		The minimal steps to configure SMTP, POP3, HTTP, and NNTP support
Connector Notes for Lotus Notes	Notes.doc	An introduction to the Connector for Lotus Notes
Directory Integration with the Windows NT 5.0 Active Directory		The benefits of migrating to the Active Directory and the simplicity with which migration is achieved
Directory Synchronization Troubleshooter		How to solving known problems with DirSync between Exchange Server and Microsoft Mail for PC Networks
Disaster and Recovery Planning	Disaster.doc	A disaster-recovery strategy to protect your investment in Exchange Server and to help meet user expectations of 24/7 service and minimal system downtime
Dynamic RAS Connector	Dras.doc	Configuration instructions and troubleshooting suggestions for implementing the DRAS Connector using TCP/IP
Exchange Chat Services		The IRCX protocol and how it relates to Exchange Chat Services

Technical Paper	File Name	Description
Exchange Server 5.5 Upgrade Procedures		Upgrade paths from older versions of Exchange Server to Exchange Server 5.5
Import/Export Troubleshooter		Solving known problems with importing and exporting Directory information
Introduction to Collaboration Data Objects	Cdointro.doc	CDO 1.2 is a scripting-object library that developers can use to design collaborative applications on both the client and server
Microsoft Exchange Internet Protocols		Exchange Server Internet protocols and basic guidelines for troubleshooting them
Microsoft Exchange Macintosh client version 5.0 and Microsoft Schedule+ 7.5		How to obtain and install the Microsoft Exchange Macintosh client version 5.0 and Microsoft Schedule+ 7.5
Microsoft Exchange Naming Standards		How to plan an effective naming strategy for Exchange
Microsoft Outlook Web Access		Troubleshooting known issues with the OWA components
Microsoft's Commitment to the Internet Mail Standard Environment		Exchange Server and Outlook compliance with standard Internet protocols
MTA Troubleshooter	Mtashoot.doc	Diagnostic configuration and troubleshooting for the Microsoft Exchange Message Transfer Agent (MTA)
SMTP Market Bulletin		Preventing an SMTP denial of service attack for Exchange Server 5.0
TNEF/MIME Market Bulletin		Potential for server crash resolved in Exchange 5.0 Service Pack 2
Understanding the Microsoft Exchange Performance Optimizer		What the Performance Optimizer does, how to run it, and when to run it
Windows NT Clusters	Clusters.doc	Cluster architecture and implementation to enable multiple server nodes to run their best

Glossary

A

Address Book Displays recipient names (mailboxes, distribution lists, custom recipients, and public folders) in the directory. The Address Book can contain one or more address lists. See also global address list.

address list A collection of recipients (mailboxes, distribution lists, custom recipients, and public folders) in the Address Book, organized by their Recipients containers. *See also* global address list.

address space Address information that identifies a message and its route.

Administrator program A graphical user interface that enables administrators to manage and configure Exchange objects, such as organizations, sites, and servers.

advanced security Provides administrators and users with the ability to protect and verify messages.

alias Typically a shortened version of the mailbox owner's name, used to address messages.

anonymous public folder A public folder that anonymous users can access.

anonymous user A nonvalidated user who is not recognized by Exchange, and who can only access published folders and address lists.

authentication Validation of a user's Windows NT Server logon information. *See also* trust relationship.

B

backbone The network connection between local area network (LAN) segments.

bridgehead server An Exchange computer that acts as the endpoint of a connection between two sites and is responsible for routing messages through that connection.

browser Software that interprets Hypertext Markup Language (HTML) files posted on the World Wide Web, formats them into Web pages, and displays them to the user.

C

certificate Information used for digital signatures and encryption that binds the user's public key to the mailbox.

client/server architecture The structural basis of Exchange. The client sends requests to a server, and the server carries out the instructions.

connector An Exchange component that routes messages between Exchange sites and other messaging systems. For example, the Internet Mail Service enables Microsoft Outlook users to exchange messages with other users on the Internet.

container In the Exchange Administrator program, an object that contains other objects. For example, the Recipients container is composed of recipient objects.

control message A command used by USENET host computers to create and remove newsgroups or cancel messages that have already been posted.

cross certification Enables organizations to establish trust with other organizations so that users can verify the digital signature of messages sent by users in other cross-certified organizations.

custom recipient A recipient in a foreign system whose address is in the Address Book.

D

delegate A person with permission to manage mail for another user, send mail for another user, or do both.

delivery receipt (DR) A notice confirming that a message was delivered to its intended recipient.

digital signature An advanced security feature that enables users to verify the source of messages and to verify that the contents have not been modified during transit.

directory Stores all information about an organization's resources and users, such as sites, recipients, and servers. Other components use the directory to address and route messages.

directory export The process of exporting user account information from the directory.

directory import The process of importing user account information into the directory.

directory hierarchy In the Administrator program, the hierarchical structure of objects in the directory.

directory object A record such as a server, mailbox, or distribution list in the directory. Every object has properties that can be defined.

directory replication The process of updating the directories of all servers within and between sites.

directory replication bridgehead server
An Exchange computer that acts as the endpoint of a directory replication connection between its site and a remote site, and requests directory updates from the remote site.

directory synchronization The process of synchronizing an Exchange directory with directories from Microsoft Mail for PC networks and Microsoft Mail for AppleTalk Networks (also known as Quarterdeck Mail).

direct postoffice A postoffice connected through a local area network (LAN), an asychronous connection, or an X.25 connection.

distribution list A group of recipients addressed as a single recipient. Administrators can create distribution lists that are available in the Address Book. Users can create distribution lists and add them to their personal address books.

domain A group of servers running Windows NT Server. A domain can also include other types of servers and clients.

domain controller The Windows NT Server computer that maintains the security database for a domain and authenticates domain logons. Windows NT domains can have one primary domain controller (PDC) and one or more backup domain controllers (BDCs).

domain name system (DNS) A collection of distributed databases (domain name servers) that maintain the correlation between domain name addresses and numerical Internet protocol (IP) addresses.

Dynamic RAS Connector An Exchange component that routes messages between sites on the same local area network (LAN) using the Windows NT Remote Access Service (RAS).

E

e-mail addresses The addresses by which recipients (mailboxes, distribution lists, custom recipients, and public folders) are known to foreign systems.

encryption An advanced security feature that provides confidentiality by allowing users to conceal data. Data is encrypted as it resides on disk and travels over a network.

F

fault tolerance The ability of a system to respond to an event such as a power failure so that information is not lost and operations continue without interruption.

firewall A combination of hardware and software that provides a security system, usually to prevent unauthorized access from the Internet to an internal network or intranet.

foreign system A messaging system other than Exchange.

form A structure for posting and viewing information. An example is a Send form, such as a purchase requisition.

G

gateway Delivers messages from Exchange to foreign systems.

global address list Contains mailboxes, custom recipients, distribution lists, and public folders in an organization.

H

home server The Exchange computer that contains a user's mailbox.

Hypertext Markup Language (HTML)
A system of marking up, or tagging, a document so that it can be published on the World Wide Web. Documents prepared in HTML contain reference graphics and formatting tags. You use a Web browser (such as Microsoft Internet Explorer) to view these documents.

Hypertext Transfer Protocol (HTTP)
The set of conventions that World Wide Web servers use to send Hypertext Markup Language (HTML) pages over the Internet for display by a Web browser. This protocol enables a user to use a client program to enter a Uniform Resource Locator (URL) or to click a hyperlink to retrieve text, graphics, sound, and other digital information from a Web server.

I

inbound host The host computer that provides a newsfeed.

Internet Message Access Protocol, Version 4rev1 (IMAP4rev1) Enables clients to access and manipulate messages stored within their private and public folders on an Exchange computer.

information service A tool that enables Exchange and foreign systems to exchange mail.

information store An Exchange core component that stores users' mailboxes and folders. *See also* public information store, private information store.

Internet The collection of networks and gateways that use Transport Control Protocol/Internet Protocol (TCP/IP) to handle data transfer and message conversion from the sending network to the receiving network.

Internet e-mail address Consists of a user name and a domain name, with the two separated by an at (@) sign, such as username@company.com.

Internet Mail Service An Exchange component that enables users to exchange messages with Internet users. It can also be used to connect sites over any Simple Mail Transfer Protocol (SMTP) backbone.

Internet News Service Enables Microsoft Outlook users and users of third-party Network News Transfer Protocol (NNTP) applications to participate in USENET newsgroup discussions.

intranet A network within an organization that uses Internet technologies such as the Hypertext Transfer Protocol (HTTP) or File Transfer Protocol (FTP). Access to an intranet is available only to certain people, such as users within an organization.

K

key Digitally signs and encrypts data for security-enabled users.

Key Management server (KM server)
An Exchange computer installed with advanced security information.

L

Lightweight Directory Access Protocol (LDAP)
Enables LDAP clients to access directory information from an Exchange directory.

local delivery message A message sent between recipients that share the same home server.

M

mailbox The delivery location for incoming messages.

message transfer agent (MTA) An Exchange core component that routes messages to other Exchange MTAs, information stores, connectors, and third-party gateways.

Messaging Application Programming Interface (MAPI) A standard interface that Exchange and Microsoft Outlook components use to communicate with one another.

messaging profile A group of settings that provide Exchange with information about a client's configuration.

Microsoft Mail Connector An Exchange component that provides connectivity to Microsoft Mail for PC Networks gateways and Microsoft Mail for AppleTalk Networks (also known as Quarterdeck Mail) gateways.

Microsoft Outlook Web Access Interact with the ActiveX Server function built into Microsoft Internet Information Server. These components create Hypertext Markup Language (HTML) for a Web-based e-mail client on an Exchange computer.

Microsoft Schedule+ Free/Busy Connector
Enables users to share free and busy information with one another.

multiple password policy Enables administrators to configure the Key Management (KM) server to require multiple passwords to perform certain tasks.

Multipurpose Internet Mail Extensions (MIME)
A standard that enables binary data to be published and read on the Internet. The header of a file with binary data contains the MIME type of the data; this informs client programs (such as Web browsers and mail packages) that they connect process the data as straight text.

N

Network News Transfer Protocol (NNTP)
An application protocol used in TCP/IP networks. Enables clients to read and post information to USENET newsgroups.

newsfeed The flow of items from one USENET site to another.

newsgroup An Internet discussion group that focuses on a particular category of interest.

non-delivery report (NDR) A notice that a message was not delivered to the recipient.

non-read notification (NRN) A notice that a message was deleted before it was read.

O

object A record, such as a site, server, connector, mailbox, or distribution list in the Exchange directory.

offline address books Contain the recipient objects found in any Recipients container in the directory.

organization A collection of Exchange computers grouped into sites.

outbound host The host computer that receives a newsfeed.

P

permission Authorization to access an object or perform an action.

Post Office Protocol version 3 (POP3)
Enables users with POP3 clients to retrieve mail from their Exchange Inbox.

private information store The part of the information store that maintains information in users' mailboxes.

profile *See* messaging profile, user profile.

protocol The part of an Internet address before the colon (such as http, ftp, and news) that specifies the access scheme for the address. Examples of protocols within an Internet address are: http://www.someones.homepage/default.html and news:alt.hypertext

public folder A folder stored in the public information store; includes information such as messages, spreadsheets, graphics, and voice mail.

public folder affinity Enables users in one site to open public folders on servers in other sites.

public folder replication The process of updating identical copies of a public folder on multiple Exchange computers.

public information store The part of the information store that maintains information in public folders.

R

read receipt (RR) A notice that a message was read by its intended recipient.

recipient In the directory, an object that can receive messages and information. Recipients are mailboxes, distribution lists, custom recipients, and public folders.

remote procedure call (RPC) Standard protocol for client/server communication; a routine that transfers functions and data between client and server processes.

replication *See* directory replication, public folder replication.

revocation Warns users when they receive signed messages from users whose advanced security has been revoked.

role A group of permissions.

routing The process of transferring and delivering messages.

routing table Contains information that the MTA needs to route messages.

S

security context An aspect of Windows NT Server that controls the type of access a user, process, or service has to system services.

service account A Windows NT user account that is used to run Exchange services.

signing An advanced security feature that verifies the sender's identity and verifies that the message hasn't been modified during transit.

Simple Mail Transfer Protocol (SMTP)
A protocol used by the Internet Mail Service to transfer messages between an Exchange site and an SMTP messaging system, such as the Internet.

site One or more Exchange computers (usually in the same geographical location) that share the same directory information.

Site Connector An Exchange component that enables users in sites on the same local area network (LAN) to exchange messages.

system attendant A core maintenance service included with Exchange.

T

target server An Exchange computer that acts as the end point of a connection between two sites.

temporary key A random character string given to users to enable advanced security.

transaction log file A file that provides fault tolerance in the event that data needs to be restored to the information store or directory databases.

trust relationship The relationship between two domains that enables a user in one domain to access resources in another domain.

U

Uniform Resource Locator (URL)
An address of an object, document, or page or other destination. A URL expresses the protocol (such as Hypertext Transfer Protocol [HTTP]) to be accessed and where the destination is located. A URL may also specify an Internet e-mail address.

USENET The collection of host computers and networks that exchange news articles organized by subject.

USENET site One or more host computers that run the Network News Transfer Protocol (NNTP). A USENET site is different than an Exchange site.

user account Contains information such as the user name, password, group membership, and permissions.

user profile A group of settings that provides the operating system with information about a client's configuration.

W

World Wide Web The World Wide Web is a system for exploring the Internet by using hyperlinks. When you use a Web browser, the Web appears as a collection of text, pictures, sounds, and digital movies.

X

X.400 Connector An Exchange component integrated with the MTA that can be configured to connect sites within Exchange, or to route messages to foreign X.400 systems.

X.400 Recommendations Defines the standard interfaces of an electronic messaging system. These recommendations specify the structure of a message handling system, message structure and components, and the method used to transfer messages.

X.400 transport stack Networking software required to support X.400 server-to-server message transport.

Index

P

T

U

Microsoft Press offers *comprehensive* learning solutions to help new users, power users, and professionals get the most from *Microsoft technology.*

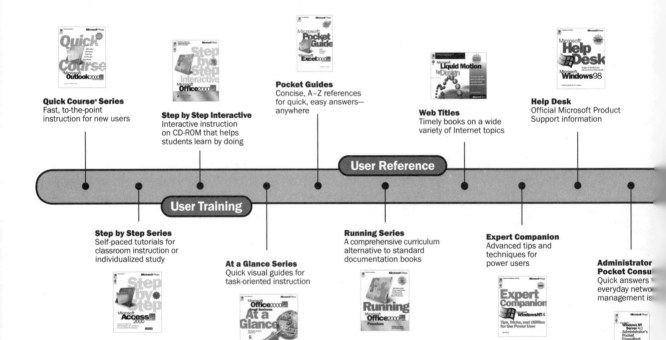

Quick Course® Series
Fast, to-the-point instruction for new users

Step by Step Interactive
Interactive instruction on CD-ROM that helps students learn by doing

Pocket Guides
Concise, A–Z references for quick, easy answers—anywhere

Web Titles
Timely books on a wide variety of Internet topics

Help Desk
Official Microsoft Product Support information

User Reference

User Training

Step by Step Series
Self-paced tutorials for classroom instruction or individualized study

At a Glance Series
Quick visual guides for task-oriented instruction

Running Series
A comprehensive curriculum alternative to standard documentation books

Expert Companion
Advanced tips and techniques for power users

Administrator Pocket Consu
Quick answers everyday netwo management is

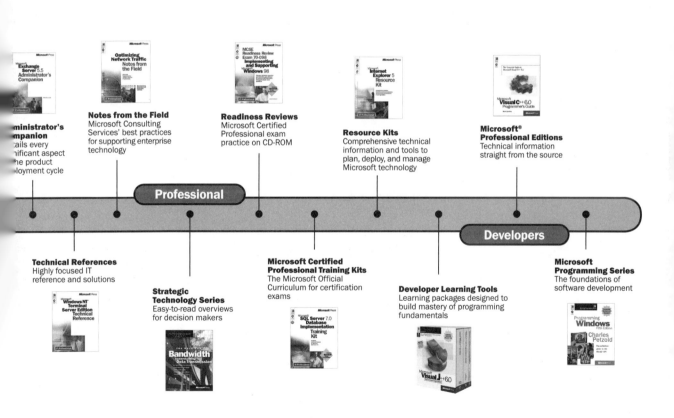

http://mspress.microsoft.com/reslink/

ResourceLink—your online IT library!

Access the full line of Microsoft Press® Resource Kits for the Windows® and BackOffice® families, along with MCSE Training Kits and other IT-specific resources at mspress.microsoft.com/reslink/. Microsoft Press ResourceLink is the essential online information service for IT professionals. Get the latest technical updates, support alerts, insider tips, and downloadable utilities—direct from Microsoft. If you evaluate, deploy, or support Microsoft® technologies and products, the information you need to optimize their performance—and your own—is online and ready for work at ResourceLink.

For a complimentary 30-day trial CD packed with Microsoft Press
IT products, order through our Web site: mspress.microsoft.com/reslink/

mspress.microsoft.com

The *intelligent* way
to practice for the
MCP exam.

If you took the Microsoft, Certified Professional (MCP) exam today, would you pass? With the READINESS REVIEW MCP exam simulation on CD-ROM, you get a low-risk, low-cost way to find out! Use this electronic assessment tool to take randomly generated, 60-question practice tests covering actual MCP objectives. Test and retest with different question sets each time, then consult the companion study guide to review all featured exam items and identify areas for further study. READINESS REVIEW—it's the smart way to prep!